RENEWALS 4..

D0743297

Chorus and Community

WITHDRAWN
UTSA LIBRARIES

Chorus and Community

Edited by

KAREN AHLQUIST

UNIVERSITY OF ILLINOIS PRESS

Urbana and Chicago

Library
'University of Texas'
at San Antonio

©2006 by the Board of Trustees of the University of Illinois
All rights reserved
Manufactured in the United States of America
1 2 3 4 5 C P 5 4 3 2 1
∞ This book is printed on acid-free paper.

Library of Congress Cataloging-in-Publication Data
Chorus and community / edited by Karen Ahlquist.
p.   cm.
Includes bibliographical references (p.   ) and index.
ISBN-13: 978-0–252-03037-6 (cloth : alk. paper)
ISBN-10: 0-252-03037-0 (cloth : alk. paper)
ISBN-13: 978-0-252-07284-0 (pbk. : alk. paper)
ISBN-10: 0-252-07284-7 (pbk. : alk. paper)
1. Choral music—Social aspects. I. Ahlquist, Karen, 1948–
ML1500.C59   2006
782.509—dc22   2005031427

Contents

Acknowledgments

As editor, I owe my first thanks to the authors in this volume, who wrote, cut, waited, and at the end dealt with the book's many details with precision and patience. My most humble thanks to them all. As in the case of any collection, however, the overall responsibility for the book's content and quality lies with the editor.

I am grateful to many people who helped the book in many ways. Gage Averill, Philip Brett, Friedhelm Brusniak, Margo Chaney, Beverley Diamond, Jacqueline DjeDje, J. Michele Edwards, Jesse Johnston, Kip Lornell, Judith McCulloh, Amy Moore, and Nico Schüler helped search for authors and/or appropriate bibliography. Marc Benamou brought the work of Bernard Lortat-Jacob to my attention, acted as an intermediary with the author, and translated his essay. J. Michele Edwards, Roy Guenther, Bruno Nettl, Catherine Pickar, and Duncan Vinson read and commented on all or part of the text. Robert Baker, Marva Carter, and Eileen Guenther facilitated performances for the CD. The George Washington University Singers, Matthew Mehaffey, conductor; the West Singers of Cherry Hill, N.J., High School West, Christine Bass, conductor; and the Jewish People's Philharmonic Chorus, Binyumen Schaechter, conductor, recorded CD performances. The Heritage Signature Chorale, Stanley Thurston, conductor, and Dana Anderson, executive director, changed a concert program on short notice to include Hall Johnson's "Elijah Rock" for the recording. Alice Mikolajewski and the members of Dobrovol'tsy recorded the Soviet workers' music. Robert Baker, Rebecca Ocampo, and Alice Mikolajewski helped with vocal preparation; Robin Armstrong provided the Russian text underlay; and Maya Rozenblat and Ludmila Guslistova coached the diction. Steven Hilmy recorded four CD tracks and mastered a compact disk of diverse musical and technological origin. Ann Meier Baker, executive director of Chorus America, offered information, ideas, and sources. Douglas Boyce, Khalil Ghannam, and Daniel Oliver solved technology problems. Bernice Ahlquist, Robin Armstrong, Marc Benamou, Lewis Holmes, Madelyn Holmes, Amy Nelson, and Catherine Pickar offered ideas and encouragement, listening sometimes at length to the tale of the "chorus book" as it unfolded. A grant from the University Facilitating Fund of the George Washington University gave me time over a summer to assemble the collection. Judy McCulloh of the University of Illinois Press helped guide the book from the beginning with enthusiasm tempered by pragmatism and a mountain of patience.

Finally, I thank the many conductors, singers, and instrumentalists with whom I worked for more than forty years of shared music making, organizing, travel, learning, and fun. Although I no longer conduct, my experience as a "choral person" has influenced my life as a music scholar and this book in particular, including the notion of chorus and community itself. In this regard I thank especially my first musical mentor, Tamara Brooks. Her intellectually challenging and emotionally powerful rehearsals led to performances I will never forget, helping me understand the importance of choruses and their music, the need for a book such this one, and the inspiration behind it.

Introduction

Nearly everyone knows someone—the local elementary school and the church down the street count—who sings in a chorus. The essays in this collection play on that fact. Drawing on choral singing in cultures of markedly different character worldwide, they consider an activity seemingly as natural as breathing and as easily taken for granted. Based on historical and contemporary sources, they use the chorus's dual nature—as music and as people—to explore a musical instrument, a vehicle for a verbal text, and a social, economic, religious, and/or political organization. In so doing, they show how the chorus communicates a variety of messages to serve a variety of human needs.

Choruses in today's world are of many types; merely listing them can be daunting. A 1999 directory for the San Francisco Bay Area includes more than 500 choruses in twenty-nine categories: academic, barbershop, chamber, children's, Christmas, church/sacred, contemporary music, corporate, early music, ethnic/folk, festival, gay-lesbian, Gilbert and Sullivan, gospel, healing arts, holiday, jazz, men's, *Messiah*, musical theater, opera, popular, professional/semi-professional, rock, senior, shape note, sing along, specialty, and women's.[1] Ruth Finnegan finds some of these same types among the "hidden musicians" whose pursuits she explores in her book of the same name. In an English community of around 100,000, she documents about 100 choruses, each with its constituency, traditions, and contribution to local musical life.[2]

Finnegan's use of the term *hidden* is apt. As Dave Russell and Stephen Banfield explain for Great Britain, the amateur societies, including choruses, that formed the backbone of music making in the nineteenth century have since lost ground to instrumental and mass-mediated repertoire that serves as popular musical expression in contemporary life.[3] Yet despite the chorus's seemingly subcultural position, its musical appeal and symbolic value remain: Depending on the music and the setting, choral performance can assert artistic and educational achievement, aesthetic merit, and social, national, religious, or ethnic identity. Moreover (and not to be neglected), it often entertains performers and audience alike.

This volume focuses on the chorus historically in the Western world since the decline of aristocratic patronage and at the present time worldwide. Although choral singing dates from antiquity, today's most common choral model developed from eighteenth-century notions of individuality and freedom of association. The burgeoning choral tradition of the nineteenth century allowed Western art music to be handed down not only by professionals, as had been done in the opera house and the church, but by ordinary amateurs—thousands of them—as well. The continued popularity of such works as Handel's *Messiah* and Beethoven's Ninth Symphony speaks to the movement's success. Yet it is not the only story. Nor is the chorus's appearance around the world merely a matter of imitating Western approaches and styles. On the contrary, some of the essays in this book show just how far the model can be stretched and varied to accommodate locally determined purposes and cultural norms.

Regardless of the chorus's current reach, however, its study began in the nineteenth century with the German male chorus movement. Eager to document a development seen as politically and socially momentous, writer-participants chronicled the growth of individual choruses, festivals, and regional organizations [*Bunden*]. Eventually, in Otto Elben's volume *Der volksthümliche deutsche Männergesang* [*Popular German Male Singing*] (1855), they had a choral history that antedated not only the German national choral federation, but even Germany itself. Other volumes followed, as did histories of the Orphéon (the French equivalent) and the English choral festival tradition.[4]

Western music-history writing has not consistently followed up on these beginnings. Especially for Europe, general histories have emphasized composers and compositions, rather than music making and organization, as historical determinants. Ethnomusicologists, folklorists, and scholars of American music, among others, on the other hand, have presented "music" more broadly. Accepting non-composers as historical actors, studying "composerless" musical expression and grassroots practices, and relying on sound-based rather than written models of transmission have opened up space for work on the chorus commensurate with its ubiquity and appeal. From this point of view, one finds studies on the chorus and choral singing in many traditions, among them British, continental European, African, and American. The authors of these studies include musicologists, ethnomusicologists, historians, anthropologists, and scholars in women's studies, religion, cultural studies, and area studies. Authors without scholarly credentials have also contributed valuable research.[5]

Moreover, the chorus as a topic encourages work in which the themes and ideas come from the sources best suited to the material at hand. For example, a church choir may sing in a formal high service or in informal worship with music in a current popular style. Traditionally, the former would be studied historically by a musicologist focused on the repertoire and its composers, while the latter would be subjected to fieldwork. However, some elements of both scholarly traditions may be appropriate for either event performed by either group. This mixed approach is found in the essays here, sometimes exposing the reader to the role of the scholar as a learner and to the process of learning itself.

Although the label "chorus" has been attached to a wide variety of musical groups, the choruses in this book do have characteristics in common. All of them have a more or less fixed membership. They all rehearse and perform, distinguishing between preparation and a culminating musical event given for listeners. They all have a chosen repertoire. They all have acknowledged musical leaders. With one exception, their members are not soloists; sounds are produced by an aggregate of voices, either in sections or by the chorus as a whole.[6] However, the choruses do not necessarily read from musical scores or sing "classical" music. And few of these community-based groups earn income for their members as individuals.

The word "community" is more complex than "chorus." Thus the first essay in the collection includes a disquisition on community that extends this introduction. Gregory Barz defines a community as "a group of people that gathers for a reason: whether to remember and recall, to share, or to create new experiences." As he shows in his study of Tanzanian *kwayas* [choirs], a choral community exists as a group of individual members and in relation to such entities as other *kwayas,* a church, various ethnic groups, and (in this case) the city of Dar es Salaam. This multiple embeddedness creates an all-encompassing role for the choir, including not only music making, but also fostering an idealized social system to help replace traditional mores being undermined by modernization. "Communities are never simple gatherings of people," Barz writes. "They are gatherings of people involved in social action, in processes that allow performance to function in the definition of self/selves within society/-ies."

Defining selves within societies also concerns Melinda Russell. She casts a wide-angle lens on choral communities and traditions in a small city to demonstrate the variety and importance of choral singing in the "blue-collar" Midwest. By discussing attitudes toward the locally predominant show choir tradition, she also explores relationships among history, organizational purposes, aesthetics, and musical styles and genres. Like Barz, Russell emphasizes the permeability of community borders. Just as Barz notes how the Kwaya ya Upendo overlaps with other *kwayas* in the same church, Russell shows how choral singers take on different musical and social identities by singing with more than one group.

Community borders are not always for crossing, however, as musical performance can in fact bolster them. This kind of reinforcement took place among the German-speaking Mennonites in early-twentieth-century Russia, a vulnerable community at a time of upheaval in the majority population. As Wesley Berg explains, under disciplined and inspired leadership the Mennonites turned congregational hymn singing into formal choral performance, thereby creating an artistic goal and unifying force for the isolated German villages across the expanse of Russian territory.

Like the Mennonites, many of the groups chronicled here recognize the power of the chorus as an artistic tool. So do individuals. The link between the individual singer and the collective musical instrument is the subject of Bernard Lortat-Jacob's essay. He begins at the center of the choral art and its aesthetics—with the human voice. The members of the Sardinian brotherhood he has studied compete for the honor of performing in one of several quartets on Holy Monday before Easter. In Lortat-Jacob's words, the chosen singers "give an acoustic form to shared experiences" by offering each other trust, concentration, and love to such a degree that they sing exactly as well as they get along—no better and no worse. This vocal, social, and emotional interaction creates an ensemble with a unique personality, itself the essence of the performance.

Besides building from the inside out, of course, choruses also build from the top down, for they have long been highly dependent on their leadership. Control from above has its limits, however, and legitimacy of leadership cannot always be taken for granted. In the next two essays, aesthetic conflict undermines imposed "reform" when singers reject music chosen for ideological reasons. Charles McGuire traces the growth of the Tonic Sol-fa sightsinging movement in nineteenth-century Britain through the efforts of John Curwen, a Protestant minister eager to offer singing as an alternative to vice. Curwen's method taught thousands of people to read music, but the singers by and large preferred Handel, Mendelssohn, and eventually Elgar—the larger, artistically more ambitious works of the Western canon—to the temperance hymns and moralizing cantatas composed for them. In a similar vein, cultural reformers in the early Soviet Union understood the chorus's potential as an instrument of the Revolution. But as Amy Nelson shows, how it could be so was not clear. Even as cadres of reformers (some self-appointed) competed to promote their own political and musical agendas, most of their approaches were in fact rejected by choral singers in workers' clubs at the grass roots.

Both the British Tonic Sol-fa and the Soviet aesthetics were addressed to choruses expected to represent the community at large or the general interest. Other choruses make no such claim. On the contrary, minorities in a given society have used choral singing to maintain cultural or religious traditions and present them to their own communities and to the majority.[7] Since the earliest days of the European choral movement, choruses have traveled, and when they do, they may be taken as tokens of an "other" that brings complexities in the home society to the fore. As Helen Metzelaar shows, such was the case with the African American Fisk Jubilee Singers, who reached the European continent for the first time in the Netherlands in 1877. The singers reminded Dutch audiences of their nation's participation in the slave trade, abandoned within living memory. They also brought out divisions among the Christian sects who debated the merits of religious music performed for a secular public.

Generations after the Jubilee Singers, other American examples of minority self-presentation have been equally explicit. Coming out of the New Negro movement of the 1920s, the Hall Johnson Choir gave concerts, made recordings, and appeared in plays and eventually in film. Marva Carter argues that Johnson aimed to create a musical voice for the New Negro—educated, proud, and demanding of rights—but also sought an authentic expression of the African and African American heritage. Johnson adapted styles learned in his southern youth to the role of the choir in mainstream performances. But as Carter shows, he was also willing to be misunderstood in order to mold the chorus's image to his own interpretation of the tradition. Similarly, scholar-participant Marion Jacobson explains how the Jewish People's Philharmonic Chorus of New York City has made adaptation an ongoing project. Originally part of the proletarian arts movement of the 1930s and 1940s, in recent years the chorus has had to rebuild itself from the inside out, redefining its politically oriented labor music, formerly the center of its repertoire, as part of a new musical practice in service of a new Jewish identity based on culture rather than politics.

As Jacobson's essay suggests, social or political messages may be important to a chorus's work. Two essays present choruses whose politics determine everything from repertoire to structure to venues, even as their performances provide the musical spoonfuls of sugar to help the political medicine go down. The chorus of the International Ladies Garment Workers Union of northeastern Pennsylvania, founded in the 1940s, began as an educational tool for newly unionized employees, but eventually sang for Democratic candidates and officeholders including Harry S. Truman and John F. Kennedy. In so doing, the chorus presented, in Kenneth Wolensky's words, "clear messages to express the union's views regarding economic, political, and social justice," thereby advocating and documenting "the transformation of the women workers from powerlessness to activism."

The political message of the Lesbian and Gay Chorus of Washington has much in common with that of the garment workers. Moreover, it is carefully played out in a consensus-based model of organization that stands in sharp contrast to the legislated inequality in, for example, some of Karen Ahlquist's nineteenth-century German mixed choruses. As Jill Strachan shows, the chorus also uses a variety of music, chosen by theme and performed in formal and informal settings, to promote a message of commonality between its lesbian and gay members and the community at large.

The model of organizational self-creation fostered in the union and lesbian-gay choruses can also be found in the Western art tradition. Retrospectively, however, the building process may be hard to see in the completed structure. In the nineteenth century, for example, German mixed choruses experimented widely to define their role within a flourishing urban musical life and establish organizational relationships among their members. At a time when legal and ideological traditions emphasized contrasting roles for women and men, women's performance was nevertheless recognized in these groups as essential to their goals of visibility, musical achievement, promotion of the Western tradition, and society building through artistic participation. As organization members, however, the female singers lost ground over the course of the century. Karen Ahlquist suggests that the women's diminished role may have been designed to help enhance the status of these amateur choral groups in a professionalizing musical culture.

The breach between amateur and professional models of music making comes to the fore in the final essay. The ideal of the music professional, for whom a high performance standard is the goal and remuneration an important reward, is rarely fully achieved by concert choruses. Nevertheless, the standard is integral to assumptions about Western music and, as has been argued, has become increasingly important as the number of professional choruses has risen.[8] Using surveys and interviews, Rosalynd Smith expands on the theme of professional-amateur tensions found elsewhere in this book, exploring their effect on the members of a major symphony chorus in Australia. Rising to a professionally based standard of performance, yet sometimes treated like musical non-entities, the singers articulate their insistence on a level of respect commensurate with their efforts, accomplishments, and above all, their dedicated, unremunerated service. Smith's essay examines a set of assumptions uncommon among the choruses depicted in this book: the formal, professionally oriented view of music making that minimizes the model of the chorus-as-community. Singers ejected from the Australian chorus questioned the assumption that exclusion necessarily made a superior ensemble. Ironically perhaps, they thereby invoked the idea of the community chorus—*not* the professional ethos—as an essential source of the respect to which they felt entitled.

*   *   *

Of course, the essays in a single book—especially a first-ever collection on a topic—cannot fully convey an understanding of the chorus's multiple roles in historical or contemporary musical life. Rather, taken together, they can show how varied approaches to the theme can inspire new questions, answers, and alternative ideas of what is important and what is marginal. The essays offer a range of stances toward their objects of study, from those of historians to participant-authors such as Barz, Jacobson, and Strachan. They also offer a range of rhetorical styles. Included among them is the celebratory; as *Keywords* author Raymond Williams notes, the word *community* "seems never to be used unfavorably, and never to be given any positive opposing or distinguishing term."[9] More analytical or critical styles are also found, however. As the sounds of the individual choruses vary widely, so do the individual voices and perspectives of the writers about them.

The world of the chorus-as-community also furthers a more inclusive music history, that is, a broader outlook on continuity and change over time. Ethnomusicologist Kay Shelemay recommends ethnography as practice for historical work, "bringing into focus transmission processes and musical meanings as situated among real people in real time, . . . [to] enhance the historical musicologist's appreciation of the workings of a fully contextual-ized music culture."[10] Indeed, the human relationships at the center of choral life can flesh out the composer-work-reception model common in today's historical studies. Yet as any conductor whose chorus has balked at a new piece will attest, even on this model, choral music's first line of reception is not the audience in a public performance but the singers themselves.

Such an approach to music study opens a way into questions of history—ones that begin with "how?" "why?" and "to what effect?"—regardless of where in the cultural texture the answers may be found. From this angle and for some traditions, one can imagine institutions such as the chorus moving closer to the center of an inquiry. For Western art music in particular, one can also imagine scholarship on the chorus as advocacy for live performance in the face of continued challenges from the mass media.

That said, what remains to study? To start, the territory is vast: The com-prehensive Internet site ChoralNet includes 1,900 web pages from all conti-nents, each ensemble with a history and an individual place in local social and musical life. Beyond them are choruses not affiliated with the International Federation for Choral Music (which runs the Web site) or other umbrella groups.[11] Sometimes the standards many of these organizations promote inspire changes in local traditions. Continued efforts to create and support professional concert choruses in Western countries speak to conflicts between community-based models and an interest in professionally oriented respect and compensation.[12] For example, the Handel and Haydn Society of Boston, founded as a chorus in 1815, now calls itself "this country's premier period instrument orchestra and professional chorus." One notes the order of the ensembles as the old society reinvents itself in a new mode.[13]

As this book makes clear, however, choruses can muddy the waters on the subject of art. The activist groups discussed here—the union, Jewish, and gay-lesbian choruses—may be understood as "left" of the status quo; other groups have furthered more conservative, even radical, agendas.[14] How, in fact, have choruses been used politically? Why? Why have groups with politi-cal agendas often chosen choruses as public bearers of their messages? How have they shaped their organization, activities, and music to fit their mission to the broader community? And why—as in the Mozart and Verdi Requiem performances on the first anniversary of the September 11, 2001, terrorist attacks—are choruses and their music often used as statements of Western human values at a fundamental level?

A second area of inquiry concerns gender.[15] Gender roles have shaped cho-ral life in the West from the beginning. One thinks in particular of the male choir tradition in European Christianity exemplified today by groups such as the Vienna Boys' Choir and the St. Thomas Choir of Leipzig. In recent years, independent boys', girls', and mixed children's choruses have proliferated in the United States, arguably in response to the decline in public school funding for music.[16] The girls' groups have become a larger piece of the single-sex choral pie. In the 1990s, for example, the San Francisco Girls Chorus and the Northwest Girlchoir made impressive recordings of sometimes challenging music, the Washington National Cathedral added a girls' choir, which alternates singing services with the choir of men and boys, and the Girls Choir of Harlem appeared on the front page of the *New York Times*.[17] But by and large the major venues still more often host all-male ensembles (youth and/or adult) than equivalent all-female groups. Male groups record more often as well. Exploring the implications of opportunities and visibility, especially for youth, would enhance an understanding of gendered meanings in an activity the sexes have in common and encourage thoughtful re-evaluation of some aspects of choral tradition.

Indeed, as so many of these essays show, links between aesthetic and other kinds of meaning in choral performance can be strong. Points for study in this regard include the choice of new music, new uses or meanings for old repertoire, performance practice and ritual, and choral sound. Particularly important (some would argue centrally important) is the effect of a sound James Smith and Percy Young call "a monolithic ideal in terms of choral organization and sonority." Pursued during the first sixty years or so of the twentieth century and linked with prominent American conductors including F. Melius Christiansen, John Finley Williamson, Fred Waring, Roger Wagner, and Robert Shaw, this combination of beauty, blend, and control can be understood and heard as an end in itself.[18] Walter Turnbull, conductor of the Boys Choir of Harlem, calls it European and notes that for his organization, sound "was the subject of debate from the very beginning."[19] By contrast, the livelier, less polished, and more individual sounds of, for example, an American gospel choir, the Tapiola Choir of Finland, or, for that matter, some of the choruses on the CD for this book serve communicative ends independent of the *bel canto* ideal.[20] Performance practice can be resonant in more ways than one. Relationships among alternative sound ideals, repertoire, arrangement styles, and intent contribute to the effect of a choral performance in ways that offer potential for interpretation.

Finally, at least two more topics offer opportunities for further study. One is the role of the individual professional musician in shaping choral life and activity. Throughout the twentieth century, conductors created their own careers by founding choruses that could realize their approach to the instrument, often (in the United States at least) naming the ensembles after themselves. Robert Shaw is a prominent example. So is Hall Johnson, whose vision is treated in this volume. Founding a chorus is a relatively cheap way to make ensemble music; as the essays here show, the capital required is more human than monetary. The relationship of the conductor to the singers can vary from a personality cult to one of collegial self-effacement, the latter a rarer but growing phenomenon today. Further study of the psychology and the politics of this bond would enhance our grasp of the choral instrument in human terms.

Some traditions also benefit from the work of living composers. Understanding who composes for chorus, what they compose, and why would yield insight into the chorus's musical role in this century. In practical terms it could also help bridge a persistent gap between a historical approach to programming and current musical styles.

Second, as Helen Metzelaar's essay on the Fisk Jubilee Singers demonstrates, there is much to be learned from exploring the perspective of the listener. As she shows, the specific identity a chorus displays can force audience members to face unanticipated questions about their own society. Unlike genres usually presented in formal, aesthetically oriented settings (opera and the symphony come to mind), choral music can be used in many ways to support many kinds of events. For the chorus is a flexible instrument. It can switch-hit, so to speak, reaching beyond the formal audience of the Western tradition to listeners from a vast array of cultural positions. And, of course, its music is disseminated technologically to a potentially enormous audience worldwide, opening it up to *Billboard* charts, Grammy Awards, marketing, and other forms of exposure and reinterpretation.[21]

These constellations of topics, among others, forge links between musical scholarship and social understanding, reminding us that values labeled "social" and "artistic" can be deeply intertwined, and that what may look like an undifferentiated mass of humanity is in fact a community of individuals who see their participation as essential to the success of the whole. While the essays found here are scholarly, not journalistic, they reach out of the ivory tower in hopes of being read by singers, other musicians, listeners, and perhaps even the occasional community leader, policy maker, or potential musical philanthropist. Above all, however, I hope choral people who read this book will see (or hear) something of themselves in it, even if from another era or continent. For it may best show that a chorus is not just one thing, but an adaptable idea of community that places serious attention to matters artistic at the center of its world.

Notes

1. Helene Whitson and Valerie Howard, *The San Francisco Bay Area Chorus Directory*, 4th ed. (Berkeley: San Francisco Bay Area Choral Archive, 1999), 663–93. Prominent chorus types not listed here include the military chorus, the currently popular "a cappella" group, and the European radio choir. For another inventory of chorus types in a region, see Friedhelm Brusniak, *Das grosse Buch des Fränkischen Sängerbundes*, 2 vols. (Munich: Schwingenstein, 1991) on the choruses in Franconia, northern Bavaria.

2. Ruth Finnegan, *The Hidden Musicians: Music-Making in an English Town* (Cambridge: Cambridge University Press, 1989), 38–40.

3. Dave Russell, "Amateur Musicians," 145–50, and Stephen Banfield, "Vocal Music," 402–3, in *Music in Britain: The Twentieth Century*, ed. Stephen Banfield, The Blackwell History of Music in Britain, vol. 6 (Oxford: Blackwell, 1995).

4. Otto Elben, *Der volksthümliche deutsche Männergesang* (2nd ed., 1887), reprint ed. Friedhelm Brusniak and Franz Krautwurst (Wolfenbüttel: Möseler, 1991). On Germany, see also the bibliography in Friedhelm Brusniak, "Chor und Chormusik," *Die Musik in Geschichte und Gegenwart*, 2nd ed. (Kassel: Bärenreiter, 1995), *Sachteil* vol. 2, cols. 766–824. Early scholarship on the Orphéon includes Henri Maréchal and Gabriel Parès, *Monographie universelle de L'orphéon* (Paris: Delagrave, [1910]); and Henri Radigueur, "L'orphéon," *Encyclopédie de la Musique*, ed. Albert Lavignac and Lionel de la Laurencie (Paris: Delagrave, 1931), pt. 2, v. 6, 3715–47. On English festivals, see Charles Burney, *An Account of the Musical Performances in Westminster Abbey and the Pantheon . . . in Commemoration of Handel* (London, 1785; New York: Da Capo, 1979); Robin Humphrey Legge and W. E. Hansell, *Annals of the Norfolk and Norwich Triennial Musical Festivals, 1824–1893* (London: Jarrold, 1896); Fredrick Robert Spark and Joseph Bennett, *History of the Leeds Musical Festivals 1858–1889* (Leeds: F. R. Spark, 1892); and Charles Lee Williams, Harry Godwin Chance, and T. Hannam-Clark, *Annals of the Three Choirs of Gloucester, Hereford and Worcester. Continuation of History of Progress from 1895 to 1930 . . .* (Gloucester: Minchin and Gibbs, 1931).

5. Studies focused entirely or in large part on choruses include Gage Averill, *Four Parts, No Waiting: A Social History of American Barbershop Harmony* (New York: Oxford University Press, 2003); Horace Boyer, *How Sweet the Sound: The Golden Age of Gospel* (Washington: Elliott and Clark, 1995); Donna Buchanan, "Metaphors of Power, Metaphors of Truth: The Politics of Music Professionalism in Bulgarian Folk Orchestras," *Ethnomusicology* 39, no. 3 (fall 1995): 381–416; Alan Clark Buechner, *Yankee Singing Schools and the Golden Age of Choral Music in New England, 1760–1800* (1960; Boston: Boston University Scholarly Publications, 2003); Jacqueline Cogdell DjeDje, "The California Black Gospel Tradition: A Confluence of Musical Styles and Cultures," in *California Soul: Music of African Americans in the West*, ed. Jacqueline DjeDje and Eddie S. Meadows (Berkeley: University of California Press, 1998), 124–75; Conrad Donakowski, *A Muse for the Masses: Ritual and Music in an*

Age of Democratic Revolution, 1770–1870 (Chicago: University of Chicago Press, 1977); Veit Erlmann, *African Stars: Studies in Black South African Performance* (Chicago: University of Chicago Press, 1991); Erlmann, *The Early Social History of Zulu Migrant Workers' Choral Music in South Africa* (Berlin: Das Arabische Buch, 1990); Erlmann, *Nightsong: Performance, Power, and Practice in South Africa* (Chicago: University of Chicago Press, 1996); Jane Fulcher, "The Orphéon Societies: 'Music for the Workers' in Second-Empire France," *International Review of the Aesthetics and Sociology of Music* 10, no. 1 (1979): 47–56; Mark Gresham, *Choral Conversations: Selected Interviews from Chorus! Magazine* (San Carlos, Calif.: Thomas House, 1997); Philippe Gumplowicz, *Les travaux d'Orphée: 150 ans de vie musicale amateur en France. Harmonies-Chorales-Fanfares* (N.p.: Aubier, 1987); Michael Hicks, *Mormonism and Music: A History* (Urbana: University of Illinois Press, 1989); Max Kaplan, ed., *Barbershopping: Musical and Social Harmony* (Rutherford, N. J.: Fairleigh Dickinson University Press, 1993); Joza Karas, *Music in Terezin 1941–1945* (New York: Beaufort Books, 1985); William Lynwood Montell, *Singing the Glory Down: Amateur Gospel Music in South Central Kentucky, 1900–1990* (Lexington: University Press of Kentucky, 1991); Michael Musgrave, *The Musical Life of the Crystal Palace* (Cambridge: Cambridge University Press, 1995); William Osborne, *American Singing Societies and their Partsongs: Ten Prominent American Composers of the Genre (1860–1940) and the Seminal Singing Societies that Performed the Repertory* (Lawton, Okla.: American Choral Directors Association, 1994); Erkki Pohjola with Matti Tuomisto, *Tapiola Sound,* trans. William Moore (Ft. Lauderdale, Fla.: Walton, 1993); Linda Pohly, "Welsh Choral Music in America in the Nineteenth Century" (Ph.D. dissertation, Ohio State University, 1989); Brian Pritchard, "The Musical Festival and the Choral Society in England in the Eighteenth and Nineteenth Centuries: A Social History" (Ph.D. dissertation, University of Birmingham, 1968); Bernice Johnson Reagon, *If You Don't Go, Don't Hinder Me: The African American Sacred Song Tradition* (Lincoln: University of Nebraska Press, 2001); Robert Reid, "Russian Sacred Choral Music and Its Assimilation into and Impact on the American A Cappella Choir Movement" (D.M.A. treatise, University of Texas, Austin, 1983); Lennert Reimers and Bo Wallner, eds., *Choral Music Perspectives Dedicated to Eric Ericson* (Stockholm: Royal Swedish Academy of Music, 1993); Gayle Sherwood, "'Buds the Infant Mind": Charles Ives' *The Celestial Country* and American Protestant Choral Traditions," *Nineteenth-Century Music* 23, no. 2 (fall 1999): 163–89; Guntis Smidchens, "A Baltic Music: The Folklore Movement in Lithuania, Latvia, and Estonia, 1968–1991" (Ph.D. dissertation, Indiana University, 1996); Amy Stillman, "*Himene Tahiti:* Ethnoscientific and Ethnohistorical Perspectives on Choral Singing and Protestant Hymnody in the Society Islands, French Polynesia" (Ph.D. dissertation, Harvard University, 1991); Dwight Thomas, "A Study of Meaning in Three White Gospel Music Traditions of Central Pennsylvania" (Ph.D. dissertation, University of Michigan, 1995); Laurence Duncan Vinson III, "An Ethnomusicological Study of the Chorus of Westerly, an Amateur/volunteer Chorus in Rhode Island" (Ph.D. dissertation, Brown University, 2004); Larry Ward, "Filled with the Spirit: The Musical

Life of an Apostolic Pentecostal Church in Champaign-Urbana, Illinois" (Ph.D. dissertation, University of Illinois, 1997); William Weber, *The Rise of Musical Classics in Eighteenth-Century England* (Oxford: Clarendon Press, 1992); Gareth Williams, *Valleys of Song: Music and Society in Wales 1840–1914* (Cardiff: University of Wales Press, 1998); Anne Bagnall Yardley, "Choirs in the Methodist Episcopal Church, 1800–1860," *American Music* 17, no. 1 (spring 1999): 39–64. David P. DeVenney's *Source Readings in American Choral Music: Composers' Writings, Interviews and Reviews* (Missoula, Mont.: College Music Society, 1995) considers the chorus from the points of view of various composers. On the nineteenth-century United States, N. Lee Orr and W. Dan Hardin's *Choral Music in Nineteenth-Century America: A Guide to the Sources* (Lanham, Md.: Scarecrow Press, 1999) is indispensable. See also the individual essay notes in this volume.

6. The performances of the Sardinian brotherhood in Bernard Lortat-Jacob's essay are solo quartets selected from the membership.

7. On choral communities and minority identity, see Theodore Albrecht, "German Singing Societies in Texas" (Ph.D. dissertation, University of North Texas, 1975); Mellonnee Burnim, "The Black Gospel Music Tradition: Symbol of Ethnicity" (Ph.D. dissertation, Indiana University, 1980); Joao De Carvalho, "Choral Musics in Maputo: Urban Adaptation, Nation-Building and the Performance of Identity" (Ph.D. dissertation, Columbia University, 1997); Mary Sue Morrow, "Somewhere between Beer and Wagner: The Cultural and Musical Impact of German *Männerchöre* in New York and New Orleans," in *Music and Culture in America, 1861–1918*, ed. Michael Saffle (New York: Garland, 1998), 79–109; Paula Savaglio, "Polka Bands and Choral Groups: The Musical Self-Representation of Polish-Americans in Detroit," *Ethnomusicology* 40, no. 1 (winter 1996): 35–47; Suzanne G. Snyder, "The Indianapolis *Männerchor*: Contributions to a New Musicality in Midwestern Life," *Music and Culture in America*, 111–40; Wei Hua Zhang, "The Musical Activities of the Chinese American Communities in the San Francisco Bay Area: A Social and Cultural Study" (Ph.D. dissertation, University of California, Berkeley, 1994).

8. Phillip Jeffery Morrow, "The Influence of the Robert Shaw Chorale, the Roger Wagner Chorale and the Gregg Smith Singers on the Professional Chorus in the United States" (D.M.A. dissertation, Southern Baptist Theological Seminary, 1993), 26–28, 166–70, and chapter 3, passim. On amateur vs. professional, see Finnegan, *Hidden Musicians*, 12–18, 278–79, and the Jacobson and Russell essays in this book.

9. Raymond Williams, *Keywords: A Vocabulary of Culture and Society*, rev. ed. (New York: Oxford University Press, 1983), 76.

10. Kay Kaufman Shelemay, "Toward an Ethnomusicology of the Early Music Movement: Thoughts on Bridging Disciplines and Musical Worlds," *Ethnomusicology* 45, no. 1 (winter 2001): 1–29, here 5–6.

11. On the IFCM up to 1992 see Sheila Prichard, "International Federation for Choral Music: Background, Beginnings and First Decade, 1982–1992" (D.M.A. dissertation, Boston University, 1995). Other noted choral umbrella organizations include

the American Choral Directors Association, the American Choral Foundation, and the Gay and Lesbian Association of Choruses (GALA Choruses). The IFCM is on the ChoralNet website (www.choralnet.org), which also offers links to affiliate organizations in Europe, the Americas, Australia, South Africa, and Japan.

12. This conflict may be seen in the membership in Chorus America, a service organization that formerly represented professional choirs but which now offers professional services to a broader range of member organizations and advocacy on behalf of the choral art.

13. Handel and Haydn Society website (www.handelandhaydn.org [2002]).

14. Gage Averill, in "Bell Tones and Ringing Chords: Sense and Sensation in Barbershop Harmony," *The World of Music* 41, no. 1 (1999): 37–51, argues that American barbershop chorus harmony symbolizes an idealized past of "old fashioned values" and fraternity. At a more extreme level, see Michael Meyer, *The Politics of Music in the Third Reich* (New York: Peter Lang, 1991), 115–19, on the integration of the male chorus federation, the *Deutsche Sängerbund,* into the Reich Music Chamber in Nazi Germany.

15. On women and gender issues in choral music, see Christine Ammer, *Unsung: A History of Women in American Music,* 2nd ed. (Portland: Amadeus Press, 2001), 268–73; Sophie Drinker, *Brahms and His Women's Choruses* (Merion, Pa.: the author, 1952); Annette Friedrich, *Beiträge zur Geschichte des weltlichen Frauenchores im 19. Jahrhundert in Deutschland* (Regensburg: Bosse, 1961); Liz Garnett, "Separate but Equal? Sexual Politics in the Barbershop," *Women & Music* 3 (1999): 28–42; Kurt Gudewill and Helen Geyer, "Frauenchor," *Die Musik in Geschichte und Gegenwart,* 2nd ed., *Sachteil* vol. 3, cols. 843–49; Catherine Roma, "Women's Choral Communities: Singing for Our Lives," *Hotwire,* January 1992: 36–39, 52; Naomi Stephan, "Is it Just(,) You Girls? A Plea for Women's Choral Music," *Journal of the International Alliance for Women in Music* 11, no. 2 (2005): 1–9.

16. Ann Meier Baker, executive director of Chorus America, June 28, 2001, personal communication.

17. Northwest Girlchoir and Friends, Rebecca J. Rottsolk, artistic director, *Echo in My Soul* (Arsis 121, 1999); San Francisco Girls Chorus, Sharon J. Paul, conductor, *I never saw another butterfly: Songs of the Twentieth Century* (SFGC 9601, 1996); Randy Kennedy, "A Girls' Choir Finally Sings in Spotlight," *New York Times,* November 24, 1997: A1.

18. James G. Smith and Percy M. Young, "Chorus," *New Grove Dictionary of Music and Musicians,* 2nd ed. (London: Macmillan, 2001), vol. 5, 783–84. This sound may be exaggerated by chromatic writing in close textures at slow tempi. For examples, hear the Roy Ringwald arrangements on the CD accompanying Virginia Waring, *Fred Waring and the Pennsylvanians* (Urbana: University of Illinois Press, 1997), especially nos. 12, 20, and 26, and some of the a cappella performances on *Voice of Music: How Can I Keep from Singing?* (Walsingham CD 8027, 1996, especially no. 5). *Voice of Music* was recorded in 1996 at the Fourth World Symposium on Choral Music in Sydney.

19. Walter Turnbull with Howard Manly, *Lift Every Voice: Expecting the Most and Getting the Best from All of God's Children* (New York: Hyperion, 1995), 106–7.

20. Tapiola Choir, Erkki Pohjola, conductor, *Water Under Snow Is Weary* (Finlandia CD 1576-59921-2, 1988); *The Tapiola Choir Christmas Album* (Finlandia CD 566092, 1993).

21. Donna Buchanan, "Bulgaria's Magical *Mystère* Tour: Postmodernism, World Music Marketing, and Political Change in Eastern Europe," *Ethnomusicology* 41, no. 1 (winter 1997): 131–57.

PART 1

A Communal Art

1

"We Are from Different Ethnic Groups, but We Live Here as One Family": The Musical Performance of Community in a Tanzanian *Kwaya*

GREGORY BARZ

It is 5:00 P.M. Kwaya ya Upendo gathers around the palm-shaded benches in the parking lot of the Azania Front Lutheran Cathedral in downtown Dar es Salaam. The women of the East African *kwaya* [choir][1] sit on circular stone benches, holding folded *kangas*[2] in their laps while the men stand off to the side passing greetings, joking with each other, and slapping each other's hands. Due to the extreme heat, the smell of rotting fish comes up from the Indian Ocean harbor front and remains thick in the heavy air. The previous evening the *kwaya* learned that one of Mama Ruth Luyobya's sisters had passed away, and we quickly decided that we should visit Ruth's family to participate in the *maombelezo* [lamentations] rather than hold our regular Friday evening rehearsal. Along with twelve of the younger members of the *kwaya* I pile into the back of Fredson Mbala's pickup while others cram into miscellaneous cars.

The sun begins to set as we leave the parking lot, and the temperature quickly drops. We drive through downtown Dar es Salaam in silence. Mbala blasts a *kanda* [audiocassette tape] of a local *kwaya* from the cab of the truck for us, and for most of the trip those of us in the back listen in silence. As we approach the Save region where the family of the deceased is gathering, Gideon Mdegella begins humming the call for an improvisatory, call-and-response *pambio* [sung chorus, for example, CD no. 1].[3] The *kwaya* members in the back of the truck slowly join in the *pambio*'s response. I look over at Mdegella and he is smiling. The *pambio* is closely associated with Mama

Ruth—she frequently sings the calls. We begin winding through the dirt paths of Save, and the singing becomes more animated: "I depend, I depend / Oh, in all things, I depend / I hope, I hope / [That] all things are well, I hope / Oh, in every situation, I hope" ("Nategemea" [I Depend]).

We are unable to park near the family home as there are already too many cars and trucks blocking the narrow pathway. We proceed to the house on foot as Mdegella initiates a clapping pattern. The women of the *kwaya* finish wrapping themselves in their *kangas*. Mama Mgana and Mama Sizya run over to Mama Mona and readjust her *kanga*, poking fun at her for inadvertently wrapping it upside down. The men of Ruth's family, home region, and *kabila* [ethnic group] come out to greet us and welcome us into the family compound. A large plastic tarpaulin has been set up on one side of the house as an awning to shield family, neighbors, and friends who will remain at the house to sleep during the period of mourning from any possible rain.

After removing our shoes the *kwaya* forms a line and moves around the area, first greeting the men seated in the outside area. I am unable to understand the language used in people's conversation and look over questioningly at Mdegella, who tells me that most people are speaking KiHaya (the language of the Haya people of the Bukoba region), and that it is customary at a ritual gathering of the *kabila* to speak the home language. The women of the *kwaya* curtsy as they shake hands, with the left hand wrapped underneath the right arm as if supporting it. Mdegella begins the call for "Nategemea" again as we enter the house where the women, more than forty in all, are seated on the floor with their legs straight out in front of them. Most of the women of the immediate family have shaved their heads out of respect for the deceased. We bend over and greet as many women as we can: "Pole, pole sana" ["I pity you, I pity you greatly"]. Meanwhile, the men set up chairs outside under the tarpaulin so that the *kwaya* can sit, visit, pray, and sing. Several women bring cases of beer over to us, but Mama Mgana rushes up to them, takes the crates away, and returns with a case of soda pop.[4] Several members of the *sauti ya nne* section (basses) audibly grumble when they see Mama Mgana disappearing with the cases of beer.

After we finish our sodas, Mama Ruth's husband stands up and formally welcomes Kwaya ya Upendo. He thanks us for coming and for singing. He then asks Obama, the *kwaya*'s *mwenyekiti* [chairperson], to introduce the *kwaya*, read from the Bible, and address the group at large. The women come outside to join the singing and praying. Obama reads a few passages from the Bible and then offers some commentary. He highlights how important it is for the *kwaya* to mourn and grieve with their sister, Mama Ruth. He then presents the *rambirambi*, a bereavement offering of condolence, in this case an envelope with shillings inside, to Ruth's husband as a token gesture from the *kwaya* to help pay for funeral-related expenses. Obama sits, and Mdegella stands up and leads a simple *wimbo* [song] usually sung by the *kwaya* during times of bereavement and sadness: "Be quiet and listen / Put the word of the Lord in your heart / God is with us, waiting for us / He welcomes us so that He may teach us / Be quiet, this is a holy place / The word of grace is being preached / It is the message of life from the Lord / He welcomes us so that He may inform us" ("Kaa Kimya Usikilize" [Keep Quiet and Listen], CD no. 2). The *wimbo* has the desired calming effect, and as we sing Mama Ruth emerges from the house, moving over to where Mama Mgana is sitting with the *sauti ya pili* [alto section]. Mama Mgana sees her approaching and shuffles people around to make room for Mama Ruth next to her. The sounds of the *kwaya* fill the family compound and pour out into the darkness of the Save neighborhood. Children gather at the fence to listen to the *kwaya*, and as Mama Ruth begins singing, Mama Mgana comforts her, wrapping her own *kanga* around Ruth's shaven head.

After a few hours of singing, drinking more soda, and visiting, the *kwaya* prepares to leave. We form another line after retrieving our shoes, shaking hands again with the men to say goodbye. Mdegella begins another *pambio*, and we "extend the pole" [*kutoa pole*] again. As we leave, Mdegella turns to me and says, "If we were in the village we would have sung all night and slept there for several days."[5]

*　*　*

In this essay on the musical performance of community in an East African *kwaya*, I focus specifically on Kwaya ya Upendo as a unique, interdependent social system. Focusing on the musical performance of *kwaya* as an expression of community moves me beyond understanding and representing the phenomenon of *kwaya* solely as a musical genre; *kwayas* are distinct sociocultural structures, or systems "compelled" into "engagement and union," as folklorist Henry Glassie suggests.[6] While I have found it important to understand and represent the musical sounds, structures, and repertoires of traditional and indigenous *kwaya* music elsewhere,[7] I also now find it important to address a different question: Why do members of Tanzanian *kwayas* gather on a regular basis to sing, pray, mourn, play sports, seek counsel and advice, learn about their spirituality, and look for potential spouses? The answers to these questions illustrate some of the many ways that a *kwaya* functions as a microcosm of an idealized social system. Perhaps most important is the function of a *kwaya* as a critical means for meeting the needs not only of a greater community but as a community in and of itself. In her ethnography of Kpelle, ethnomusicologist Ruth Stone makes a similar observation: "Music performance represents a cultural microcosm. . . . It is an occasion for the confirmation or restructuring of relationships within a separate but related sphere of interaction."[8]

Throughout this essay I present urban *kwaya* communities in Dar es Salaam as distinct formations of disparate peoples gathering for the purpose of meeting communally determined needs. And I suggest that community formation occurs as a result of the various processes of communal social consciousness that take place within a *kwaya*. The growing urban migration in Tanzania stimulates the rich cultural practices, religious values, and musical conventions of varied rural traditions within the membership of *kwayas* in cities such as Dar es Salaam. In this section I illustrate the features of this social identity within Kwaya ya Upendo and other *kwayas* with specific ethnographic examples.

My experiences as a *mwanakwaya*—as a member of a *kwaya*—lead me to hypothesize that any attempts to separate the so-called "Christian" element from the so-called "traditional African religion" and "Islamic" elements of *kwaya* performance are misguided, since all often coexist at a deep level within *kwaya* community formation. *Kwayas* exist as interdependent communities, and as Dele Jegede suggests, creating borders between what is distinctly "Christian" and what is more "traditional" is not easy and certainly never "crisp and beautiful": "A map of religions in Africa which graphically compartmentalizes the three religious streams [traditional African religions, Islam, and Christianity] may look crisp and beautiful. But it does not adequately demonstrate that the predominance of either Christianity or Islam in one region does not imply the demise of African systems of thought in that region. On the contrary, the acceptance of these two dominant religions is not unrelated to the extent that both have been grafted onto indigenous systems of thought, becoming so intertwined in the process that, in the view of many Africans, professing one religion and believing in another is not inconsistent."[9] In my experience, it is not possible to define the boundaries within *kwaya* performance between what is Christian and what is not Christian. Such a definition would lead to superficial analyses that would ignore the interdependence of multiple traditions in contemporary urban *kwaya* performance. For example, I opened this chapter with the experience of Kwaya ya Upendo participating in the highly prescribed *ombelezo* [grieving] ritual. My ethnography was punctuated with strong images: women wearing *kangas,* men sitting separately from women, the *kwaya* choosing not to drink alcohol, the expectation of remaining for a defined period of time at the home of the bereaved, women sitting on the floor with outstretched legs, shaking hands with one hand supporting the other, among others. It would be all too easy to attach labels to these images—"this is Islamic, this is Christian, and this is a feature of traditional African religions"—but ultimately it is a much more rich and complex matter. And while the practice of "naming of parts" is frequent in scholarship on post-colonial Africa, I have come to question whether it may be problematic if not misleading.

Kwayas are unique communities within the greater church communities they serve. As the late Mzee Clement Maganga, one of my field colleagues, suggests in the excerpt from an interview below, *kwayas* serve particular needs of a community, needs that are particular to the *kwaya* as a subculture.

> Gregory Barz: So, the music makes the group unique because, are there other groups in churches that do the same things that don't sing?
> Clement Maganga: Not any that I know of, no. Let me see. No. For other groups that don't sing, but they are church groups. I think their main activity would normally be prayers, or even visiting people or visiting the sick and helping them out, lending them support and such, but I don't think they engage in some sort of income earning because at least they know at least from the parish if there are people to be helped, then the parish normally would be of greater assistance than themselves. So in many cases they just offer the service.

As communities, *kwayas* often function as social indemnity groups, as Mzee Maganga suggests above, and as such they are sources of financial security for many disparate and displaced urban Tanzanians who live far from the resources of their village-based community or "clan." However, there is seldom a problem with the mixing of tribal identities in urban *kwaya* communities that might occur in village *kwayas*. According to Gideon Mdegella, teacher of Kwaya ya Upendo, during the post-independence period, Tanzania fortunately did not suffer from the "tribal" divisions experienced by other developing African nations. As one *mwanakwaya* of the Kwaya ya Usharika at the Kinondoni Lutheran Church in Dar es Salaam once told me: "*We are from different makabila* (ethnic groups), *but we live here as one family.*"

For Mdegella, the intertribal mixing occurring in urban *kwayas* reflects the everyday life of the urban Dar es Salaam environment itself. In January

1994, eight weeks before the plane carrying the presidents of Rwanda and Burundi was tragically shot down as it left Tanzania, Mdegella and I discussed the "tribal" factor as it relates to both urban and rural *kwayas:*

> Gregory Barz: Now, in Iringa [Mdegella's home area], a *kwaya* would be, would it be all Wahehe? Or would it be mixed?
> Gideon Mdegella: No, you cannot find that phenomenon [mixed *kwayas*] in the villages. Only in towns. No.
> GB: So in Iringa a *kwaya* would be mixed?
> GM: In Iringa it's a mixture of Chagga, Wahehe, Wanyakyusa, even Americans!
> GB: So it's no problem here in Dar es Salaam with everyone mixing together?
> GM: There has never been that problem because Nyerere[10] did a lot in cutting down these tribalistic attitudes. Yes. He did a lot. We now feel more Tanzanian. I feel more of a Tanzanian than an Mhehe. Yeah.

Since independence, the very concept of "Tanzanianness" has been reinvented and reaffirmed on multiple levels. Although originally from a small village, Mdegella today feels, as he states above, more Tanzanian than Mhehe [of the Wahehe *kabila*]. A village *kwaya* would, of course, still presumably be mono-*kabila* or represent the cultural mix of the area, and presumably would also reflect the communally held traditions and beliefs of those peoples. According to many of my field colleagues, however, the mixing of multiple *makabila* in urban *kwayas* has not created a problem, due in part to Mwalimu Nyerere's attempts to diminish the distinctions between *makabila* identities in independent Tanzania. I should note, however, that younger field colleagues suggested that the degree of unity among various *makabila* was not as great as I was often told.

Despite the efforts (or perhaps because of them) in the direction of ethnic cohesion among the multiple *makabila* typically represented in urban *kwayas,* distinct musical styles associated with individual *makabila* continue to be represented. Within the multiethnic relationships that form within urban *kwayas,* a "Tanzanian" *kwaya* music, a universally accepted approach to compositional styles, has not emerged, and perhaps cannot emerge. Mzee Maganga's response to this issue is typical of the answers I received when I posed this query to field colleagues:

> Gregory Barz: Is there really such a thing as "Tanzanian *kwaya* music" and if so, what is "Tanzanian" about it?

Clement Maganga: Well, if one were to generalize about the whole country, I think it's not easy to have such an entity.

GB: As "Tanzanian *kwaya* music"?

CM: No, it's not easy. What one can have is, you may have within a particular denomination, say the Catholic Church. Then you have church music which is "African" in the sense that the rhythm and even the composition reflects its "Africanness." But of course it would vary depending on the composer. If the composer has, say, *Kinyamwezi* as his first language, then you can hear aspects of Kinyamwezi surfacing from his music. And if another composer happens to be of Ngoni origin like the great Father [Stephen] Mbunga, you can hear the Ngoni music at least being portrayed within the music. So it's not easy to talk of Tanzania as one unitary entity of music. No, it's not easy. But we Tanzanians, we can always know that this music, a certain composer comes from *this* place and that one comes from *that* place. Although it's the same country you can always locate from where that music normally originates.

GB: OK, so a Tanzanian, if I could take it one step further, a Tanzanian would always know whether he or she is singing music *muziki wa kienyeji* (traditional music) or *muziki wa ulaya* (music of Europe)?

CM: Yeah, that one, *muziki wa kienyeji,* yeah, quite obvious. Yes. Sometimes the demarcation becomes difficult because those composers are also influenced by the school of music where they got the art so you might find that they might bring in some Tanzanian art within it but then it may be anyway, how shall I put, saturated with European, you know, aspects. So you must find it sometimes difficult, but normally it's easy to demarcate in some cases.

Maganga's comments support the belief held by many that the basic characteristics of Tanzanian *kwaya* music—whether harmonic, melodic, or rhythmic features—retain their individual, ethnic-based nature. Music, therefore, complements the social processes of community formation in contemporary urban *kwayas.*

*   *   *

In the context of my field research, a "community" can be defined as a group of people that gathers for a *reason:* whether to remember and recall, to share, or to create new experiences. Communities are often fluid social structures that allow people of similar or dissimilar backgrounds to cooperate on shared objectives. A community gathers to re-enact ceremonies, stories, rituals, and memories through performance, and it typically functions as a direct connection between one's cultural past and present. In this way community is not a static object; rather it is a process by which people come together for a particular cause or purpose. In speaking of the people of Ballymenone in Ireland, Henry Glassie describes their community as "a matter of constant negotiation, always shifting, sometimes radically."[11] Communities may, in fact, as Glassie suggests, often be more *factious* than we might normally recognize them to be.

Just what are the boundaries, then, of community? And where does one officially cross the borders of community? As a field researcher, I often ask myself if I am, in fact, creating the "community" of Kwaya ya Upendo in order to elaborate on what is contained within it (and produce a dissertation, papers, and articles based on my reflections and analyses!). I also question the extent to which I assume homogeneity within *kwaya* communities where it does not exist. What do I have at stake by doing so? What is my unarticu lated agenda? Have "they," Kwaya ya Upendo, formed themselves—after all, what's in a name? Is the act of labeling yourself, such as a *kwaya* naming themselves Kwaya ya Upendo, a self-conscious/self-reflective way of indicating community to themselves as well as to a greater, "unnamed" group? Smaller than "collective"—*kabila,* religious affiliation, neighborhood, village, etc.—a community may have many reasons to form.

A Tanzanian urban *kwaya* functions as a metacommunity within the greater structure of the church community. *Kwayas* assemble to form community, gathering to sing the praises of God, enact and expand their Christian values, and support and encourage the evangelizing efforts of the church community as a whole. Urbanization, the migration of people from remote villages and towns throughout Tanzania to larger cities such as Dar es Salaam, has compelled many *kwayas* to function as base communities, that is, *kabila*-like home communities away from a distant regional home. On the other hand, an equally valid argument could be made that the contemporary urban *kwaya* communities may, in fact, act more like *chamas* [clans] than "tribes." In prescribed ways, a *kwaya* models the ideals of the church community while simultaneously reflecting those values back to that community during the performance of weekly liturgies. However, I posit that a *mwanakwaya* would most likely provide a simpler, less academic answer to my opening question—it is God who makes the creative create. And I am comfortable with this response, because if we assume that God gives people the capacity and ability to create, then the need to "create" (through music) a core Christian community is logical and understandable.

The elastic and malleable concept of "culture" is the typical material used to construct academic boundaries around peoples and their musics in contemporary ethnomusicological and ethnographic thought. The concept of "community," however, while central to many contemporary and historical ethnographic studies, is seldom treated sufficiently. When reference to the concept of community does appear, it is usually in prefaces and introductory materials, and many of these allusions to community lead readers to believe that communities are well-bounded, well-determined entities.

Several ethnomusicologists bring to their analyses of community a unique view; they focus on the expressive process of being human *in* and *as* community. Distinctive musical repertoires often serve as distinctive musical badges for a particular community, and musical performance is a significant tool to bind communities together. Several important works pay attention to community, and they inform my own research and understanding of the musical borders, boundaries, and badges of "communities." In *"The Land Where Two Streams Flow,"* Philip Bohlman focuses specifically on community in the larger sense of the term, community as part of the process of nation formation. His hypotheses concern the (re-)formation and development of Jewish communities in Israel, and they challenge us to consider that communities themselves may be forced to consider the values of that community. In his concluding section, "A Sense of Community, a Sense of Nation," Bohlman teases out the difficult layers that exist for contemporary German-Jewish communities in Israel. It is within the performance of music that Bohlman locates the defining characteristics of community formation. As Bohlman suggests, music "has the ability to organize the German-speaking community as a group and to distinguish that group from the rest of Israeli society."[12] In Bohlman's view, musical performance functions as a highly politicized site for the exchange of knowledge and for the projection of a community's definition to both self and other. Similarly, in *Powerhouse for God,* Jeff Titon borrows a term from Dell Hymes to refer to the language of religious practice as a system of communicative events, *"established by* such a system."[13] In my own field research I found this to be true; *kwaya* communities both form and are formed by the social system in which they participate. There is another dimension to this structure, however. If communities are in fact "systems" of communicative events, then they may only exist in relation to the reformation, reaffirmation, and continuous expectation of that system. Communities, therefore, are active participants and organizers of their own action and existence.

Jeff Titon and Mark Slobin extend this view by suggesting that a community not only "carries the traditions and norms of performance," but in so doing perpetuates those "prescribed rules" mentioned earlier.[14] Titon and Slobin propose a music-culture model that places community directly within the level of performance: "Musical affect, performances, and communities change over time and space; they have a history, and that history reflects changes in the rules governing music as well as the effect of music on human relationships."[15] And history can (and often does) exist in many levels in a community's collective memory.

For ethnomusicologist John Miller Chernoff, community serves a specific function; it is a site for the ongoing musical performance of tradition, and within this site music defines community and community defines music: "Most people in Africa do not conceive of music apart from its community setting and cultural context."[16] Chernoff attempts to understand the aesthetics of music within the framework of community, and in his experience in West Africa, music and community are interdependent. Chernoff also suggests that the primary aesthetic concern of performance is the creation of a framework within which the "realization of community" can take place, meaning that performance facilitates the very definition of what it means to be a community, not only the (re-)creation of community but, perhaps more important, the realization of community.[17] Chernoff's greatest contribution to the issue of musical performance and community is, perhaps, the suggestion that meaning is continuously emergent "through time."[18] In his article "When Music Makes History," ethnomusicologist Anthony Seeger presents a similar argument, namely that communities "create their past(s), their present(s), and their vision(s) of the future partly through musical performances."[19] "In each repetition lies the possibility for reaffirmation, reinterpretation, representation, repression, rebellion, or some combination of these."[20] Ruth Stone also focuses on the process of musical community formation in *Let the Inside Be Sweet* by elaborating on the "event" as process, a distinctly musical process. For Stone, performance is a heightened form of cultural manipulation, a "thick performance" separable from everyday life.[21] Concerning the separation of "performance" from "everyday life," sociologist Paul Connerton suggests that through "commemorative ceremonies" a smaller community may purposefully join a larger community. Through (re-)enactment or (re-)engagement, the original community is approached (which itself used the commemorative ceremony to create community). Connerton locates commemorative events throughout Christian liturgy and ritual: "But indeed there is no prayer and no act of devotion which does not refer back, whether directly or indirectly, to the historical Christ; the historical narrative reaches the minutest particulars. The fact of the crucifixion is symbolized in each sign of the cross: itself a condensed commemoration, a narrative made flesh, an evocation of the central historical fact and the central religious belief of Christianity."[22]

Ethnomusicologists and other ethnographic-based scholars (in anthropology, folklore, and sociology) experience and represent the musical performance of community on different levels. In the few examples given above, the expression of community is mostly interpreted as a performance that develops, maintains, and (re-)asserts human relationships. In this light, communities are never simple gatherings of people. They are gatherings of people involved in social action, in processes that allow performance to function in the definition of self(selves) within society(-ies). This definition of community is central to my engagement of Tanzanian *kwayas.*

Kwayas exist in multiple worlds and espouse multiple worldviews. Thus, labeling a *kwaya* as a singular "community" is not a simple matter. In the section that follows I trace the growth of my awareness during my field research of the everyday functioning of Tanzanian *kwayas* as communities on multiple levels: (1) *kwaya* as *kikundi* or "group," to (2) urban *kwayas* as extended or dislocated *makabila* or ethnic family units, and finally to (3) a *kwaya* as a specific *jumuiya* or "community."

Kikundi (Group)—In my earliest interviews with *walimu* and *viongozi* of urban Tanzanian *kwayas,* I was curious to discern why individuals would dedicate such a large amount of time and energy—sometimes up to five or six evenings each week—to participate in the collective communities of church *kwayas.* For example, for most *wanakwaya* of Kwaya ya Upendo, participation involves some degree of hardship. Demands include regularly commuting to and from the city center, in many cases arranging for child care, contributing to the *kwaya* financially, attending late evening rehearsals and early Sunday morning services—thus a significant loss of personal time, energy, and resources. I was eager to determine just what needs were met within the *kwaya* network that would counterbalance the personal demands placed on *wanakwaya* through their participation.

I soon found that my line of thinking and the very introduction of the question were problematic. I realized that the way I was posing the question in KiSwahili, "What is a *kwaya*?" was not teasing out the verbal description I thought would develop for me a distinct view of a *kwaya*. I assumed this to be a benign question, but in retrospect I should not have been surprised at the answers I received. Invariably, the answer I received was: "*Kwaya ni kikundi cha wanaoimba*" [literally, "a *kwaya* is a group of some people who sing"] or "*kwaya ni kikundi fulani cha watu fulani cha uimbaji*" ["a *kwaya* is a certain type of group of people who sing"]. As I later learned through my ongoing participation in Kwaya ya Upendo, a *kwaya* is not a "what." As the excerpt given below illustrates, once I asked the initial "what" question, I was usually given responses that referred to a *kwaya* as "*kikundi*" [a/the group] for the rest of the interview. "The chairperson is responsible for leading *the group,* to prepare meetings, to meet with the counselors, and discuss matters pertaining to *the group,* in collaboration with the secretary. So, you will find that I am the spokesperson for *the group* and the leader of *the group.*" Once I initiated the "what" question in this particular interview, the respondent, Nd. Machange, reflected back to me a definition of his *kwaya* as *kikundi,* a group, for the duration of the interview. After transcribing and translating several such interviews in which the conceptualization of *kwaya* as *kikundi* predominated, I began to recognize that in fact *I* was responsible for this characterization due to the way I posed the question.

Family or *Kabila* [Ethnic Groups]—After consultation with several field colleagues, I redirected my questions and approached several different ways of understanding the phenomenon of *kwaya*. I decided to take a step in a different direction and address the issue more directly during a series of interviews with two leaders of the *kwaya ya vijana* of the Msasani Lutheran Church. In the extended passage that follows, the concepts of the urban *kwaya* as an indemnity group and as an urban community away from the home village are introduced:

> Gregory Barz: Is a *kwaya ya vijana* (youth *kwaya*) like a family?
> Leader 1: I can say that a *kwaya ya vijana* is like a family.
> Leader 2: Because we cooperate. That is, there are people here in town who have no parents. When such a person has a problem, such as being sick, or his/her relative dies, or has a wedding, the *kwaya ya vijana* participates. When he/she has received information about a death we sing to comfort, we contribute money as our condolence, or when he/she marries we contribute to the preparations of the wedding by providing money. When he/she is ill we sometimes give her/him money and things like fruit to help, so we can say it is like a family.
> Leader 1: It is true. You know when people come from upcountry regions—a person comes from Mbeya, Arusha, Mwanza—I don't know where he/she is coming from, here he/she has no relative or friends, so he/she finds him-/herself joining the Umoja wa Vijana (Youth Association), which becomes a part of his/her family. So in many cases, probably some of her/his needs, though not all, she/he gets from the *vijana,* and together she/he is counseled on how to live or how to be helped, we are helping each other as a family.

Leader 2: Sometimes one comes here without any job.

Leader 1: Sometimes she/he is helped to be employed. There are some who are helped here to be employed. When a person hears an advertisement for a job opportunity somewhere she/he rushes to the *vijana* to inform them. Hey guys, for those who are jobless, there are job opportunities somewhere. If she/he likes and has the qualifications she/he goes to work there. So, I can say it is like a family.

GB: *Vijana* learn a lot of things concerning the spirit and they learn together.

Leader 2: Yaa, yes together.

As I sat in the second story loft overlooking the sanctuary of the Msasani Lutheran Church with these two youths, who were the same age as I was, I began to catch glimpses of not just "what" a *kwaya* is, but "how" a *kwaya* functions and participates in the everyday life of its members. I began to view *kwaya* as process. Through the open-brick walls I could hear the women of one *kwaya* singing and clapping a *pambio*. The *kwaya ya vijana* was gathered in the sanctuary below us for their weekly Bible study session. As Kileo and Rupia continued to explain to me their understanding of *kwaya*, I realigned my thinking to incorporate *kwaya* as a specific type of community that typically acts as a family. Outlined below are several ways in which a *kwaya* acts as an extension of the *kabila* [ethnic group] or family unit as mentioned in the excerpt above:

- Acts as surrogate parents/family for displaced urban *kwaya* members
- Participates in death rituals of families of *kwaya* members
- Finances funeral and bereavement processes for families
- Participates in wedding preparations and ceremonies
- Helps to finance weddings
- Supplies money and/or food when illness occurs
- Provides counseling on urban living skills
- Provides counseling on support services available to *kwaya* members
- Provides job placement assistance and ongoing support

Many field colleagues confirmed for me that *wanakwaya* of urban *kwayas* interact in their daily lives much in the same way as the extended family—the *kabila*—does in the village. Nevertheless, I felt uncomfortable attaching the label of "family" to a *kwaya*. It limited my understanding of the varied experiences of community in *kwayas*. Even if in many ways a *kwaya acts* like a family, it is in just as many ways *not* a family. Again, it was *I* who interjected the term "family" into these conversations (as illustrated in the excerpt quoted above); it had yet to emerge on its own.

Jumuiya [Community]—One afternoon I sat on a large rock with John Mgandu, head of the music subdepartment at the University of Dar es Salaam, taking off our shoes and socks and rolling up our pants as we prepared to cross by foot the waterway linking Mlimani to Msewe, outlying communities of Dar es Salaam. Mgandu is a respected leader in the communities of Tanzanian music and a highly regarded composer of *kwaya* music. I frequently went to him when I needed to seek advice or talk through an issue that had arisen in my field research. When I shared my concern about gaining an understanding of the *kwaya* phenomenon in a *kwaya*'s own terms, he got a very serious look on his face. "Barz, *singing in a kwaya is part and parcel of everyday life—kwaya ni kama jumuiya* (a *kwaya* is like a community)," he told me. When he deliberately code switched from English into KiSwahili, I know he was communicating something important, something that could not be expressed in English. Why did he not say that *kwaya is* a community? Why did he refer to *kwaya* as being *like* a community? When I asked him about his use of the term *jumuiya*,[23] Mgandu said he was encouraging me to understand and appreciate *kwaya* as a phenomenon that was totally integrated into the lives of its members.

The following evening I arranged to meet informally with the leaders of the Kwaya ya Usharika na Vijana of the Kinondoni Lutheran Church, and I was curious to follow up on the notion of *kwaya* as *jumuiya*. I came early to hear the *kwaya* sing, and after the rehearsal concluded in the yard behind the church, a small group of us crammed into the front parlor of the *mwinjilisti*'s [evangelist's] small house within the church compound. In the course of the interview, I interjected a question that intentionally referred to the *kwaya* as both family and *jumuiya*:

> Gregory Barz: Is a *kwaya* like a *jumuiya* (community) . . . or like one family?
> Mwanakwaya: This *kwaya* is like a *jumuiya*. Everybody comes and joins the *kwaya* coming from his/her own area of the country. Our *kwaya* consists of people from different ethnic groups, for example from the south, east, north, and west. Therefore, here we are people of different *makabila* (ethnic groups), so long as he/she is a Christian who has received Holy Communion. So, *this kwaya is not a family kwaya.*
> GB: Anyone else?
> Mwanakwaya: Although we come from different *makabila we live here as if from one family.*
> GB: Is this the same with Kwaya Kuu?
> Mwanakwaya: Even they come from different places. They are also a *jumuiya* (community) anybody is able to join.

During this conversation, I had not anticipated that the concepts of "*jumuiya*" and "family" would become conflated. The first *mwanakwaya* stated strongly that the *kwaya* is *not* like a family but like a *jumuiya*, only to be quickly contradicted by a colleague who claimed that *kwayas* do, in fact, function as families. "Family" as a marker of designation was quickly losing its distinctive qualities for me. With the meaning of "family" directly collapsing onto "*jumuiya*," I began to wonder if the difference was purely academic.[24]

As communicated to me, in its ability to function as *jumuiya*, the urban *kwaya* embraces multiple *makabila*. As the Kinondoni *mwanakwaya* in the conversation quoted above repeated twice, "We are from different *makabila*." It was important and significant enough for this to be stated several times during the conversation. This issue of multiple ethnicities is an important one for urban *kwayas*. While technically a "non-issue" in the contemporary Tanzanian political landscape since colonial independence, it is nevertheless something that *kwayas* feel they need to talk about.

As the atrocities of Rwanda and Burundi took place during my field research, I asked James Obama, chairman of Kwaya ya Upendo, if the same thing could happen in Tanzania. Without pausing he quickly glanced over at the *kwaya*, pointing out for me different members, enumerating their home *kabila*: "This could never happen here. Look around you at this *kwaya!* We sing together as one people here in Dar es Salaam."[25]

The overwhelming acceptance of multiethnicity in urban *kwayas* is the subject of a *wimbo* [song] composed by Washington Mutayoba and recorded and frequently performed by the Kijitonyama Kwaya ya Usharika, "Twendeni kwa Yesu" ["Let's Go to Jesus," CD no. 3]. In the *wimbo*'s text, the *kwaya* sings in multiple regional or ethnic languages. When I interviewed one of the teachers of the Kijitonyama *kwaya*, Joachim Kisasa, I asked specifically about the text for "Twendeni kwa Yesu." I had heard the *wimbo* many times before meeting the Kijitonyama *kwaya;* it is the title track on the most popular of the five recorded audiocassette tapes produced by the *kwaya*. Kisasa told me that the languages sung in the *wimbo*—Kichagga, Kipare, Kimeru, Kimasai, Kisambaa, Kinyaturu, Kinyiramba, Kigogo, Kizaramo, Kihehe, Kinyakyusa, and Kihaya—represent the ethnicities of the members of the *kwaya* at the time the *wimbo* was composed. In his words, the *wimbo* was composed to express the inclusiveness and diversity of the Kijitonyama *kwaya*, and in the process of learning the *wimbo*, individual members helped direct the pronunciation of their native languages. "Twendeni kwa Yesu," therefore, functions as an important tool in the formation of *jumuiya* for the Kijitonyama *kwaya*.

The diverse ethnic or "tribal" composition of urban *kwaya* communities reflects the multi-*kabila* urban environment, unlike the traditional Tanzanian extended family that has traditionally been mono-*kabila*.[26] While *kwayas* may in fact model the structure(s) of extended family, they perhaps model the formation of *jumuiya* more closely. As I quoted Gideon Mdegella earlier, the plurality of ethnic identities has seldom been an issue for urban *kwayas* in the post-independence, one-party socialist system in Tanzania. I suggest, however, that the rapid movement toward multipartyism might change this. There were predictions that in order for any new party to succeed against the ruling C.C.M. party (Chama cha Mapinduzi, party of the revolution) in the 1995 elections, for example, that the new parties would have to be formed along ethnic, "tribal" lines.

⁂ ⁂ ⁂

I opened this essay with a narrative account of a particular event in my dissertation field research, my participation and observation, singing and interacting in the everyday life of Kwaya ya Upendo, my field research "*jumuiya.*" Understanding the unique meaning of community that is shared, practiced, and performed by Kwaya ya Upendo was central to my field research. I was fortunate to have many experiences with other important Tanzanian *kwayas*—through interviews, judging *kwaya* competitions, participating in *kwaya* retreats, and attending services. I now ground my observations on the performance of community in my experiences of singing and worshiping with a particular *kwaya,* Kwaya ya Upendo.

When I initially approached Gideon Mdegella about singing and undertaking field research with Kwaya ya Upendo, he invited me to come downtown and observe a rehearsal at the Azania Front Lutheran Cathedral. The *kwaya* had recently finished filming a video they intended to present to the president of then West Germany (von Waizsacker) as a token of remembrance of his recent visit to Dar es Salaam, during which he came to Azania Front to hear Kwaya ya Upendo sing. The *kwaya* offered to sing several selections included on this video for me. One of the *nyimbo za kwaya* [*kwaya* songs], "Neema Imefunuliwa" ["Grace Has Been Opened to Us"], struck me as an important self-reflective moment for the *kwaya:*

> Grace has been revealed to us
> Grace has been revealed to us
> Grace has been revealed to us at Azania, has been bestowed on us
> Which He has brought for his servants

Today we remember the blessings of God
His servants devoted to building His church here at Azania Front
We thank God's grace, it has been opened to us
People are devoted to building this house.

This *wimbo* clearly defines Kwaya ya Upendo as a community existing within the greater structure of Azania Front. In the *wimbo*, Mdegella, the composer, reflects on the church community and their beliefs, history, and collective worldview(s). The *wimbo* refers to "Azania," the physical and spiritual home for both the *kwaya* and the *usharika* [congregation/community].[27] In subsequent verses, a list of pastors and evangelists—both German and African—is outlined, tracing a lineage back to the founding of the church in the 1890s. This interaction with history (pre-colonial, colonial, and post-colonial) is critical for the ongoing formation of musical communities at Azania Front.

Figure 1.1 Kwaya ya Upendo performing the benediction for early morning services on the steps of the Azania Front Lutheran Cathedral, Dar es Salaam. Gideon Mdegella, the *kwaya's mwalimu*, moves into position in front of the *kwaya*. Time release photo by Boyd Christenson.

The formation of community for Kwaya ya Upendo is an ongoing process—communities continually form and re-form, always already in process. While the Cathedral and several of the outlying colonial and mission buildings of Azania Front have existed for more than a hundred years, the indigenous Tanzanian element has not always been present. Azania Front began as a colonial mission station for expatriate German Lutherans living in the Dar es Salaam area. Only later was the community culturally redefined and repatriated to the native, indigenous population of Dar es Salaam.[28]

Each Sunday morning "temporary communities"[29] form at Azania Front, facilitated in large part by the service *kwayas*. The simple repetition of known, expected, and anticipated acts guides the prescribed Lutheran liturgy, the coming together of disparate peoples. Participation in the community is identified by repetition—sitting and standing, singing and reading, following along with others in the service book, taking part in the *sadaka* [offering or collection] processional, partaking in *Chakula cha Bwana* [the Lord's Supper], kneeling at the appropriate times, etc. The formation and performance of community at this level are highly participatory and in constant flux.

Like the larger community at Azania Front, the Kwaya ya Upendo community is not static. The *kwaya* continually reinterprets itself in reaction to and in relationship with other communities. It reaches out to the larger Azania Front community by projecting advice and counseling regarding social behavior through its songs. Yet the building of community is dependent on various levels of participation for ongoing spiritual formation. When I initially began field research with Kwaya ya Upendo, I experienced the *kwaya* on a very basic and what I later came to realize as a superficial level; during that early stage, I perceived the *kwaya* to be an independent, self-sufficient community.

There are many options available for someone seeking membership in a *kwaya* community. Kwayas are typically categorized in terms of age, gender, time of Sunday service, time of weekly rehearsals, musical repertoire, non-singing activities, and specific social needs of the individual participants. Below is a list of the various and diverse *kwaya* community types found in Lutheran churches in the Dar es Salaam area:

Kwaya ya Akina Mama	Kwaya of the Women's Group
Kwaya ya Bible Study	Bible Study Kwaya
Kwaya ya Fellowship	Fellowship Kwaya
Kwaya ya Kati na Usharika	Kwaya of the Congregation and those in between Youth and Adult

Figure 1.2 The bell tower of the Azania Front Lutheran Cathedral looms large on Dar es Salaam's downtown waterfront. Photo by Gregory Barz.

Kwaya Kuu	Main Kwaya
Kwaya ya Usharika	Kwaya of the Congregation
Kwaya ya Usharika na Vijana	Kwaya of the Congregation and Youth
Kwaya ya Vijana	Youth Kwaya
Kwaya ya Watoto	Children's Kwaya
Kwaya ya Wazee	Kwaya of Elders
Kwaya ya Wainjilisti	Kwaya of Evangelists or:
Kwaya ya Uinjilisti	Evangelical Kwaya

Congregations often support multiple *kwayas* with memberships varying in composition and purpose. There are, however, most often two main *kwayas* that function within a typical congregation—*kwaya ya vijana* and *kwaya kuu* (or *kwaya ya usharika*). These two *kwayas* participate either in the same service or in separate services. At Kinondoni Lutheran Church, for example, the *kwaya kuu* leads the 7:00 A.M. service and the *kwaya ya usharika na vijana* leads the 9:30 A.M. service.

Why is there a distinction between the two *kwayas* when the term *vijana* generally is used to refer to anyone up to the age of forty, married or single? Age is not always a clear determinant of an individual's choice of *kwaya* community, *vijana* or *kuu/usharika*. There are major differences, however, between the types of community formed by a *kwaya ya vijana* and a *kwaya ya usharika* [adult congregational *kwayas*]. Musical repertoire, social activities, and frequency of gatherings are only a few of the factors that go into an individual's choice of *kwaya* community. In an interview with Hosea Mwambapa, an important *mwenyekiti* of a local *kwaya ya vijana*, I asked why people join a *kwaya ya usharika na vijana* as opposed to joining a *kwaya ya usharika* or *kwaya kuu*. Mwambapa responded that there were many reasons, primarily the number of activities and events. Some join the *kwaya* to participate in competitions, while others are merely attracted to the singing in the church service. Mwambapa conceded that age was also a defining factor; those under forty naturally gravitate toward a *kwaya ya vijana*, while those over forty lean toward a *kwaya kuu*. Yet even age seems an ambiguous factor in choosing a *kwaya* community. Nd. Philemon Rupia, *mwalimu* of the Msasani *kwaya ya vijana*, told me in passing that he would continue to sing with the *kwaya ya vijana* even after he turned forty in a few years. In the Kwaya ya Upendo, there is a wide range of ages—from young Elioth Mujumba, still working to pass his secondary school examinations, to Mama Sanga, the oldest member of the *kwaya*, a range in ages from approximately twenty to sixty years. Yet there are significant reasons for younger people choosing to join a *kwaya ya vijana* community over a *kwaya kuu/usharika* [main or congregational], foremost of which is the use of modern musical instruments—electric guitars and keyboards—according to Nd. Isaac Kileo. According to Kileo, other *kwayas* use only "note songs," that is, they sing without using instruments. Other activities also attract. Kileo pointed to the activities involving drama, poetry, and especially sports such as volleyball and netball.

The *kwaya ya vijana* is a site not only for the expression of what it means to be a Tanzanian youth, but also for the transmission of cultural knowledge—learning, training, and understanding of cultural values, religious traditions, and spiritual growth. The community generated by a *kwaya ya vijana* is quite distinct from other *kwaya* communities. Most adult *kwayas* meet three or four times each week for rehearsal, with attendance optional at organized Bible studies. Singing in a *kwaya ya vijana,* however, involves much more group activity, contact time, and commitment, as outlined by the assistant chairperson of the *kwaya ya vijana* at the Kinondoni Lutheran Church: "*Kwaya* practice takes place every Monday, Wednesday, Saturday, and Sunday. Sports and drama practices take place every Tuesday and Thursday. Bible study takes place every Saturday before starting singing practices. So Bible studies begin at 4:00 P.M. to 5:00 P.M. and from 5:00 P.M. to 6:00 P.M. there is singing practice." According to Kinondoni's assistant chairperson, this *kwaya* community gathers in the church compound a minimum of six days each week. The *kwaya ya vijana* at the Msasani Lutheran Church has a similar schedule. Unlike Kinondoni, however, they gather as a community every day of the week. I offer below a detailed, typical schedule for both the *kwaya ya vijana* of Msasani and of Kinondoni.

Being a *mwanakwaya* in a *kwaya ya vijana* community involves more than an interest in singing. *Kwaya ya vijana* is a place to seek out and maintain

Table 1.1. Weekly Schedules of Two Lutheran Kwayas in Dar es Salaam

	Msasani	Kinondoni
	Kwaya ya Vijana	*Kwaya ya Usharika na Vijana*
Monday	*Kwaya* practice	*Kwaya* practice
Tuesday	Sports (netball, soccer)	Participation as *kwaya* for fellowship, Bible study, or drama practice
Wednesday	*Kwaya* practice	*Kwaya* practice
Thursday	Sports (netball, soccer)	Fellowship/Bible study or drama practice
Friday	*Kwaya* practice	
Saturday	*Kwaya* practice	Games, sports
Sunday	Weekly service	Weekly service

friendships, a forum for learning and exploring Christian values, for studying the Bible, for learning cultural and historical traditions, for participating in popular music, and, perhaps most important, for meeting potential
spouses. During a series of interviews with *viongozi* of several *kwaya ya
vijana,* I began to suspect that the urban *kwayas* were serving a particular
function that would normally have been the responsibility of the extended
family system—matchmaking—as demonstrated in the response to my question of whether *wanakwaya* at a particular *kwaya ya vijana* have wives or
husbands:

> Leader 1: [laughter] We have a few [he looks down and smiles]. We have a
> few women—four or five. Then we have men, four or five. One of them
> is married and has a wife—they sing together in the *kwaya ya vijana.*
> Gregory Barz: Haal Yes. [laughs] Did you meet your wife in the church?
> Leader 1: We sing together. Fortunately I came here in 1986. I began singing
> and my wife was also singing here, so we fell in love and married, and
> continued to sing.
> GB: So a *kwaya* is not only for singing.
> Leader 1: Yes. It helps in life also.
> GB: Did the other married members meet in the *kwaya* also?
> Leader 1: There are others. Dr. Mrema and his wife also sing with the
> *kwaya ya vijana.* And they met in the *kwaya ya vijana.* We have Mjema.
> He met his wife in the *kwaya.* We have no more. Others sing, but their
> wives do not.

As this leader suggests above, singing in a *kwaya ya vijana* "helps in life also."
One evening after attending a rehearsal of the *kwaya ya vijana* at the Ubungo
Lutheran Church, I had a conversation with the *kwaya*'s teacher, Ndugu Ami-
nieli Mkichwe, perhaps the most respected *mwalimu wa kwaya* [teacher of a
kwaya] in Dar es Salaam.[30] Mkichwe and I became good friends during my
field research, and I came to trust his insight greatly. Midway through our
conversation I noticed that most of the youth from the *kwaya* were still in
the church; they had remained after the *kwaya* rehearsal in spite of the late
hour and the long rehearsal. I asked Mkichwe whether there was another
function going on now. He began to laugh and slapped my hand, assum-
ing I had made a joke. He then told me that youth find their husbands and
wives from within *kwayas,* and he proceeded to count how many couples
had married while he was at Kinondoni Church. I paused and asked him
where he met his own wife. Without missing a beat he responded that it was
within a *kwaya,* of course.

The *kwaya ya vijana* is a unique community among *kwaya* communities. When youths gather in the church a state of *communitas* is entered into. The youths progress through stages of liminality in which they practice prescribed rites of passage and experience different aspects of the life cycle, both "religious" and secular. The *kwaya* is a nurturing place for youths to express their faith, form small Christian communities, musically perform their spirituality, and meet potential spouses.

Community formation in contemporary Lutheran *kwayas* in Dar es Salaam is a significant social act within which varied traditions—both new and old—become fused within performance, forming interdependent stylistic units. *Kwayas* both determine the parameters of their community and social network while simultaneously maneuvering freely within these boundaries to break off and form new and interdependent relationships. In urban Dar es Salaam new interdependent systems of family and community develop to meet the needs of displaced rural migrants within *kwayas,* providing opportunities, particularly in a *kwaya ya vijana,* for meeting potential spouses, locating employment, and maintaining connections to one's home culture. *Kwayas* exist today within a series of such relationships, and as such they are fluid communities that draw on multiple musical and cultural traditions to perform themselves into being on a daily basis.

Notes

An earlier version of this essay appeared in Gregory Barz, *Performing Religion: Negotiating Past and Present in Kwaya Music of Tanzania* (Amsterdam: Rodopi, 2003).

1. Throughout this essay I use KiSwahili titles and designations, such as "*mwenyekiti,*" "*mwanakwaya/wanakwaya,*" "*kwaya,*" and "*mwalimu.*" Although these terms may seem easy enough to translate, the translations often do not have exactly the same meanings in English. For example, a *kwaya*'s *mwalimu* is more than a "choir director," and it would be misleading to translate it as such. A *mwalimu* often composes the musical repertoire for his or her *kwaya,* teaches it to the *kwaya,* maintains the repertoire in memory, and conducts the *kwaya,* in addition to serving as a spiritual guide or mentor. Other terms are equally difficult to translate. Translating *kwaya* as merely "choir" is the most problematic.

2. *Kangas* are brightly colored pieces of printed cotton cloth worn by women as wraps, used as cushions for carrying items on the head, used as slings for toting infants, in addition to other uses. The elaborate *kanga* borders contain messages in KiSwahili or Arabic (a few in English), often cryptic aphorisms or brief parables. It is traditional for women to wrap themselves in *kangas* (top and bottom) when bereaved or when attending funeral rites or memorial services.

3. *Mapambio* (pl. of *pambio*) are the most pan-denominational music in Tanzanian Christian churches. In Mdegella's words, "*Mapambio* are short, locally originated songs, short ones which can easily be sung by everybody in their local melodies."

4. Mama Sizya whispered in Mona's ear, "The *kwaya* does not drink alcoholic beverages at public events. We represent the Christian element!"

5. I later asked Mdegella about the specific requirements, duties, and obligations of a *kwaya* to a bereaved *mwanakwaya*.

> Gideon Mdegella: If some are sick, someone has lost his or her relative, someone is sick . . . Now, it is part and parcel of the *kwaya,* yeah.
>
> Gregory Barz: It's like the *kwaya* chooses to kind of live out its Christian life as a community, kind of serve the spiritual and material need of its community.
>
> GM: It's even more in other *kwayas.* For instance, [in Iringa] if one of the members loses a relative, we simply go and sing once, but in other *kwayas* they have to spend all the three days of mourning there. . . . With the family, yes, as a group we have to spend nights there. Sometimes for the whole week. Yeah.

6. Henry Glassie, *Passing the Time in Ballymenone: Culture and History of an Ulster Community* (Philadelphia: University of Pennsylvania Press, 1982), 583.

7. "Soundscapes of Disaffection and Spirituality in Tanzanian *Kwaya* Music," in *The World of Music* 47/1:5–24 (2005); *Performing Religion: An Ethnography of Post-Mission Kwaya Music in Tanzania (East Africa)* (Amsterdam: Editions Radopi, 2003); "The Performance of Religious and Social Identity: An Ethnography of Post-Mission *Kwaya* Music in Tanzania (East Africa)" (Ph.D. dissertation, Brown University, 1997); "*Kwayas, Kandas,* Kiosks: A Tanzanian Popular Music," in *Ethnomusicology Online* 2 (1997); "Confronting the Field(note) in the Field: Music, Voices, Texts, and Experience in Dialogue," in *Shadows in the Field: New Perspectives for Fieldwork in Ethnomusicology,* ed. Gregory Barz and Timothy Cooley (New York: Oxford University Press, 1997).

8. Ruth Stone, *Let the Inside be Sweet: The Interpretation of Music Event among the Kpelle of Liberia* (Bloomington: Indiana University Press, 1982), 135.

9. Dele Jegede, "Popular Culture in Urban Africa," in *Africa,* ed. Phyllis M. Martin and Patrick O'Meara (Bloomington: Indiana University Press, 1995), 274.

10. Julius Nyerere, first president of independent Tanganyika and later the joint Republic of Tanzania (Tanganyika and Zanzibar).

11. Glassie, *Passing the Time in Ballymenone,* 26.

12. Philip Bohlman, *"The Land Where the Two Streams Flow": Music in the German-Jewish Community in Israel* (Urbana: University of Illinois Press, 1989), 232.

13. Jeff Todd Titon, *Powerhouse for God: Speech, Chant, and Song in an Appalachian Baptist Church* (Austin: University of Texas, 1988), 193.

14. Jeff Todd Titon and Mark Slobin, "The Music-Culture as a World of Music,"

in *Worlds of Music: An Introduction to the Music of the World's Peoples,* 3rd ed. Jeff Titon (New York: Schirmer Books, 1996), 4–5.

15. Ibid., 5.

16. John Miller Chernoff, *African Rhythm and African Sensibility: Aesthetics and Social Action in African Musical Idioms* (Chicago: University of Chicago Press, 1979), 36.

17. Ibid., 149.

18. Ibid., 162.

19. Anthony Seeger, "When Music Makes History," in *Ethnomusicology and Modern Music History,* ed. Stephen Blum and Philip Bohlman (Urbana: University of Illinois Press, 1991), 23.

20. Ibid., 24.

21. Stone, *Let the Inside Be Sweet,* 136.

22. Paul Connerton, *How Societies Remember* (Cambridge: Cambridge University Press, 1989), 47.

23. "*Jumuiya*" and "*Ujamaa,*" Tanzania's brand of socialism, both share the same linguistic root stem, "*jamaa,*" meaning a number of people gathered together to form an organic unit. *Jamaa* has a strong undertone of blood relationship. *Ujamaa* loosely translated means kinship, and as a socialist program it stressed self-reliance and dependence on the family system for support.

24. The concept of "*jumuiya*" is significant since it is also the term used to describe the construction of a post-independence political union of Uganda, Kenya, and Tanzania, the East African Community. See Ruth E. Meena, *Historia Fupi ya Jumuiya ya Afrika Mashariki Tangu 1900–1975* [Short History of the East African Community from 1900–1975] (Dar es Salaam: Longman Tanzania Ltd., 1981); and Fr. Augustine Mringi, *Tujenge Jumuiya Ndogondogo za Kikristu* [We Build a Small Christian Community] (Peramiho, Tanzania: Benedictine Publications Ndanda, 1991). There are distinct economic overtones to the term *jumuiya,* indicating a clear distinction from the more general term, *usharika* [congregation], used to refer to the larger church community.

25. As ethnomusicologist Frank Gunderson communicated to me, however, closer to the borders of Rwanda and Burundi, people felt less secure about the social harmony among the many different *makabila* [ethnic groups], especially as the 1995 elections neared.

26. Growing urbanization is, of course, changing this in contemporary Tanzania. There is a higher rate of mixed marriages—marrying outside one's ethnic group—in urban centers.

27. Even though today "*usharika*" has a religious connotation, it shares the same root with "*ushirika*" [community of interest, intimate, union, partnership, cooperation, or sharing].

28. I am not concerned in this essay with the musical or philosophical expressions of Azania's original community other than for what was "handed down" (materi-

ally and theologically) to the present-day community. The aspect of community I am most interested in is the contemporary, participatory process that continually re-forms and reshapes community at Azania Front.

29. I borrow the term "temporary community" from Richard Schechner, who uses it to describe the changing, ongoing community formation that takes place in theaters (from a 1994 submission to the "Perform-L" e-mail list [Perform-L@ACF-Cluster.NYU.EDU]).

30. Mkichwe is also *mwalimu* for the prestigious Kwaya Kuu at Azania Front Lutheran Cathedral, the main service *kwaya* for the 9:00 A.M. Sunday service.

2

"Putting Decatur on the Map": Choral Music and Community in an Illinois City

MELINDA RUSSELL

Located near the middle of Illinois, the city of Decatur has a population of just under 84,000.[1] Decatur lies roughly an hour each from the comparably sized communities of Bloomington-Normal, Springfield, and Champaign-Urbana, and differs from these other cities in that its economic base has historically been in agri-industrial businesses and heavy manufacturing, while the other three enjoy the stabilizing presence of such forces as state government, state universities, and established corporate headquarters. Though Decatur is home to Millikin University and to Richland Community College, the presence of such corporations as ADM (Archer Daniels Midland), Caterpillar, and Bridgestone/Firestone is better known: Many residents describe Decatur as "blue-collar" in contrast to nearby cities. This essay surveys choral music in Decatur during the early to mid-1990s, drawing selected examples from various facets of choral life. In the 1990s, Decatur's choral music included the numerous church choirs, school choral groups, and barbershop quartets one might expect in any U.S. city, and the city was also home to at least one independent choir and three groups sponsored by the local Park District: the Decatur Park Singers, The Young Park Singers, and the Greater Decatur Chorale. While any one choir or choral tradition would have been worthy of sustained attention, the purpose here is to give a holistic sense of choral music in one community, to see where similarities and differences present themselves, and to understand a bit about how people negotiate aspects of musical production within and between traditions.

In the late 1980s and early 1990s, Decatur saw a serious economic downturn, a decrease in population, and numerous labor problems. From 1980 to 1990, for example, durable-goods manufacturing jobs declined more than 35 percent.[2] In the mid-nineties, three of the city's top ten employers, including two of the remaining locally owned firms, were being struck simultaneously by an estimated 4,000 members of the workforce.[3] Decatur's numerous difficulties did not leave local musical life unscathed, but the city maintained a vibrant cultural life, including the choral activities from which the examples presented here are drawn.

Some of Decatur's musical life may well be typical of many cities in the United States, and other parts may be truly idiosyncratic. There is nothing necessarily "average" about Decatur, and it is not to be understood as a representative microcosm of the United States. Indeed, a consideration of its choral music provokes more comparative questions than it answers. Its usefulness, I think, is not that it provides an average or characteristic site, but rather that it provides a specific one.

Is choral music important in Decatur's musical life? Using a variety of criteria, one may well conclude that choral music has a prominent role in the city, perhaps even unusually prominent. What is not present, though, is a single choral tradition with multiple instances, uniting the entire community. Rather, Decatur has a variety of choral musics, practiced in a variety of ways by diverse groups of people. These choral music traditions vary not only in their sound component, but in their conception, their perceived function, and their underlying rules. This essay explores the civic, independent, church, and school choral groups in Decatur, then briefly explores some issues that transcend those boundaries.

*   *   *

Civic music groups of many sorts have long been staples of American musical life, but they are neither ubiquitous nor evenly distributed. Indeed, a consideration of civic and independent groups might—perhaps more than a consideration of church and school music making—contribute to a highly differentiated picture of American musical life. Because they depend on tax revenue and/or survival in the public marketplace rather than enjoying the support of a church or school system, such groups are evidence of a community's support for certain kinds of musical activity. The endangered status of many American civic orchestras during the 1980s and 1990s provoked explicit discussion about the value and purpose of local performing groups, and while outcomes may be a function of budgetary considerations, they are also unquestionably suggestive of community values. Although Decatur's economic downturn of the 1980s and 1990s left it in far more desperate straits than its neighbors, its civic music groups were not seriously imperiled, while those in wealthier communities faced the threat of extinction.

It may be worthwhile to briefly consider the history of civic and independent choral groups in Decatur. Choral music in the schools and churches of Decatur does not seem to have attracted the attention of the few historians who have written accounts of the city, but some writers have included observations about local civic and independent musical groups. These histories usually begin in the 1850s and include reports of informal glee clubs and a choral society.[4] During this same period, a "Handel Society" was founded and gave concerts locally and in nearby cities, including one in Bloomington in 1897. Later, a "Decatur Oratorio Choir" existed for some years, presenting oratorios annually, with its largest membership and success reportedly from about 1919 to 1923.[5]

The choral society appears to have evolved rather quickly into the Decatur Musical Union, founded in 1861 and directed by George F. Wessels, also mentioned as one of the glee club members. Its object was "to bring together the musical talent of Decatur for educational and charitable purposes," and it is reported to have been for more than twenty years the chief source of revenue for Decatur charities.[6] According to a 1912 memoir by Jane Martin Johns, the Decatur Musical Union met weekly on Tuesdays and gave "about six entertainments a year."[7] Happily, Mrs. Johns also took the trouble to say a bit about the group's repertoire: "There are only a few programs of the entertainments of the Musical Union extant. In addition to the more pretentious oratorios, given in costume, they gave a great many popular concerts. A quartet of their number could always be secured to sing patriotic, war songs and Negro melodies at every social held by the hospital aid society. 'The Battle Hymn of the Republic,' 'Tramp, Tramp, the Boys are Marching,' 'The Red, White, and Blue,' [and] 'Marching Through Georgia,' were supplemented by 'Massa's in the Cold, Cold Ground,' 'Down in the Cornfield,' 'Old Shady' and other popular Negro melodies of the day, and the audience invariably joined in the chorus."[8]

The function of the Decatur Musical Union as a fund-raising tool for those in need is one that has echoes in modern Decatur musical life, as we shall see. Of interest too is the report of the audience's "invariably join[ing] in" on the choruses of songs. This suggests a less rigid separation of audience and performers than is generally the case in modern performing contexts, although there are some important exceptions.

Recalling the Decatur Musical Union in a *Decatur Review* interview in 1905,

Director George Wessels called it "the greatest organization of the kind ever formed. There never was another town that had a Musical Union like the old one in Decatur. They were fine men and girls; they could sing and they did and they had a jolly time. There will never be another like it."[9] Similar praise was bestowed by the paper itself, which described the performances of the Union as "not tiresome and amateurish affairs. People went to hear the singing and then they went the second night."[10]

The Decatur Musical Union appears to have augmented its numbers with additional community members for specific performances, particularly oratorios. It appears, though, to have disbanded, spawning a series of subsequent organizations detailed in a history of Decatur: "Some years after the Musical Union ceased to exist, a new musical club was formed, known as the Decatur Musical Club. It was started about 1885. . . . During the years of this club's activities, much outside musical talent was brought to Decatur. Finally the club ceased activity. Later[,] in 1895, another club, the Decatur Musical Culture club, afterwards the Decatur Musical Club, was organized and flourished for some time. After it went out of existence Decatur had no music club until 1924 when the present day Decatur Music Club was organized."[11]

The Musical Club seems to have moved increasingly toward sponsorship of musical events rather than performance, and the current-day civic and independent choral groups trace their roots only back to the 1970s (their most obvious roots, at least). Still, during the 1990s Decatur had some choral groups that might reasonably be compared with the sorts of organizations profiled above. Among these modern-day choral organizations were those sponsored by the Park District and one independent choral group.

In terms of musical life, the Decatur Park District[12] can reasonably be considered one of the most important sponsoring bodies in town. During the early 1990s, the Decatur Park District sponsored a variety of musical groups, including three choral groups (it has since added a fourth) and a summer musical theater program for children. This sponsorship of music through the Park District reflects the conception of music as a leisure activity and the apparent local consensus that music is worthy of support. The music program is extensive and has grown significantly, sprouting a new group every few years. The three choral groups considered here are the Greater Decatur Chorale, the Decatur Park Singers, and the Young Park Singers.

Founded in the 1970s, the 115–120-member Greater Decatur Chorale has fewer than ten performances a year, with major concerts each January and May. Consisting almost entirely of local residents, it is the only one of the ensembles active year-round and the only ensemble welcoming adults of all ages. The size seems somehow reminiscent of the large, ambitious scale of oratorio societies, but certainly oratorios are not the mainstay of the Chorale's repertoire, which leans heavily toward Broadway musicals and somewhat less to popular songs of the 1940s through 1980s. In a recent interview, the director of the Park Singers explained that the Greater Decatur Chorale performs music "from pop to gospel to show tunes" and said that each show includes one "full-featured showpiece," with acting, costumes, and scenery.[13] He gave excerpts from *Phantom of the Opera* as a recent example. In January and August, local adults audition to join this group. Members are not charged a fee, but they must pay for their costumes, and tickets for the yearly concerts cost about eight or nine dollars each. Competent singing is expected, but the director told me that "frankly," some "less than stellar" singers are included; the Chorale is "a community chorus," he explained, and includes "some church choir people and some people in it for recreation."[14] Here the intended function of the chorus as a unifying body, open to all comers, directly shapes its practices with regard to musicianship. Similarly, its repertoire is broad, varied, popular, and accessible, maximizing the number of people who can perform and enjoy the material.

With sixteen singers and a half-dozen band members, the Decatur Park Singers are the best known and most visible of the Decatur Park District choral groups. Though derided by a few, they are a source of great local pride for many people—their program notes boast that they "have put Decatur on the map with a package that serves our entire community and entertains thousands annually."[15] Decatur Park Singers shows typically have a "theme" with corresponding costumes and musical numbers. To call their image wholesome barely begins to convey the irrepressibly cheerful atmosphere of their energetic performances. Active in the summer, following a rigorous touring schedule that includes local, upstate, and out-of-state appearances, the Park Singers are a sort of "show choir," with their reliance on show tunes, popular song arrangements, and medleys, in a format that includes solos, costumes, and choreography. Unsuspecting audience members are not infrequently pulled onto the stage, and the Park Singers wander into the audience at intervals, shaking hands with local residents. The age range of the Park Singers is limited, with members from their late teens to early twenties.

The Decatur Park Singers began in 1972 as a group of Park District employees organized into a singing group by Jerry Menz, director of recreation. Menz reports that Park District employees were in his office enjoying homemade ice cream when one of them began playing his guitar. "Three of them sang 'Leaving on a Jet Plane,' and I thought if they can sound this good, this is just what I'm looking for."[16] The group of singers originally appeared with the Decatur Municipal Band in 1972, and, as Menz tells it, "one day someone called from the Moweaqua Pow Wow Days and said if I'd bring out singers, they'd pay us. Gadzooks! We started charging a fee, and it just went from there."[17] "From there" includes the substantial regional success of the Decatur Park Singers that followed, including their evolution into a fund-raising tool to support Park District programs. We might compare the history of this group with that of the Decatur Musical Union; both not only paid for their own needs, but were eventually to generate revenue. According to Menz, the Park Singers have raised more than a million dollars, which has been funneled back into Park District programs. The ensemble grew to a high of thirty-two members before "it leveled off to sixteen vocalists and eight instrumentalists in the mid-1980s and eventually became predominantly music, education, and performing arts majors."[18]

The Decatur Park Singers perform extensively (dozens of shows each season) in Illinois and around the Midwest, often to capacity crowds. The performances incorporate "show choir" costuming and choreography into vocal programs that are usually themed, "light," and skillfully rendered. The emphasis is on lively arrangements of up-tempo pop and rock songs, popular and Broadway tunes, country, and patriotic songs (CD no. 4), usually in medley form. In recent years, their director has shifted their repertoire away from Broadway tunes—"Who wants to hear a heavy ballad from *Miss Saigon* when it's 100 degrees in the park?"[19]—and toward (or back toward, recalling the group's beginnings) "cover" versions of popular songs. The director recalled approvingly Jerry Menz's description of the music as "up, fun, bubbly," and "it's got to be K-Tel."[20] Further, he added, "It's got to be so popular it would be on one of those K-Tel records; *we* might think it's even corny, but it's what they want."[21] Sources for programs of the mid-nineties included Gloria Estefan, Huey Lewis, George Gershwin, Clint Black, Wynonna Judd, and Garth Brooks. More recent performances have included hits from the British Invasion and songs by the Backstreet Boys. Increasingly, the Decatur Park Singers have produced and sold recordings of their music and now have a video as well as a fan club. Since 1997, they have sold CDs, which they produce just prior to going on the road. While their audience is regional and the recordings are primarily bought by fans at concerts, a certain degree of professionalism attaches to such packaging. Along the way, the *raison d'être* of the Decatur Park Singers seems to have shifted from "fun" to "performance," or from the enjoyment of the participants to the enjoyment of an audience. Not surprisingly, and as the educational backgrounds of recent members listed in the program notes illustrates, there has also been something of a shift from amateur to professional in terms of membership, activities, and expectations. "People depend on their being there and being good," said their director.[22]

The Park Singers now pack more than fifty performances into the summer, appearing all over Illinois and in adjoining states, at state and county fairs, festivals, concert halls, and other venues. They recruit from several states, advertising with glossy posters in music schools throughout the Midwest. A minority of members are actually local residents, though the figures rise if one counts as residents those members who are Millikin University students, a group comprising at times one-third of the Park Singers. The Decatur Park Singers maintain a strong local presence, however, with nearly half of their summer performances taking place in Decatur, most of those free to the public. These performances are primarily in the local parks and include central local events such as the Fourth of July and the Decatur Celebration, a community festival held in August.

As the Decatur Park Singers have become increasingly professionalized, singing sometimes seems the primary role of the worker and the Park District "day job" the afterthought, rather than the other way around. Park Singers

Figure 2.1 The Decatur Park Singers greet the crowd at Oak Grove Park, Decatur, June 1994. Photo by Melinda Russell.

work a variety of jobs, from doing laundry or setting up for concerts to acting as instructors in some of the many Decatur Park District participatory
and educational activities in dance and music for young people. Two of these
are the B.O.S.S. ("Best of Summer Stock") musical theater program and the
Greater Decatur Youth Band, established just recently.

Program notes for the Decatur Park Singers describe this arrangement as
"a job experience by day and performance experience by night—a winning
combination for all involved,"[23] but there appeared—at least in the early
nineties—to be some tension between goals of recreation and professionalism, as illustrated in this excerpt from an interview with a disgruntled former
Park Singers band member:

> Daniel Freeman: See, the only thing that really keeps you going as a Park
> Singer performer, you don't get paid since you're a volunteer who just
> *happens* to work this other job for the recreation department and that's
> what [you get] paid for. And then we go out on the road and play. So the
> total working day on the timesheet might be four to six hours, but in
> reality it's more like ten to twelve. There's a lot [of gigs] in the Chicago
> area, and there is an overnight stint. There's like a four-day trip out to
> Rockford.
> Melinda Russell: So the fifty dollars?
> DF: You get your salary, and then there's an additional $50 that they save
> for you, which, if you've done everything they ask of you and you're a
> good little Park Singer and you don't break any rules, you don't show up
> to any gigs late, you have your music at every show, and you don't screw
> up too much, then you get this bonus. . . . They kept saying that this
> was a professional organization, and I didn't feel that we were treated as
> professionals at all. If it were a professional organization, we would've
> walked![24]

In more recent years, their director informed me, the day jobs and Park
Singer jobs have "been rolled into a package" of Park District jobs during
the day and Park Singers performances at night. Participants are paid for
the entire arrangement, perhaps in part to avoid the sort of bitter feelings
displayed above. Moreover, he indicated that while in auditioning prospective members, he seeks "the best musicians [he] can find," he "will back off
on that a little for job skills," and is most intent on finding members who
will fulfill the demands of living together and working together, rehearsing
twelve to fifteen hours a day in the three weeks prior to the beginning of the
season. His varied comments describe a complicated balance among musicianship, non-musical skills, personality traits, and general work habits.

The Young Park Singers, established in 1983, are as distinctively in the show choir mold as the Park Singers. With thirty-four singers and dancers, this group of young performers (of high school age) puts on about twenty-five shows each summer, almost always with the Park Singers and accompanied by the Park Singers band. The Young Park Singers Program, for which participants pay, draws from local residents. As with the Park Singers, the image presented by the Young Park Singers is one of homogeneity (in age, race, and costume) and wholesomeness. Both groups tend to dress in red, white, and blue. The costumes are never immodest, the program content never controversial, and the performers are never caught without a smile unless they are looking earnest or lovelorn. The mission statement of the Young Park Singers Program asserts that their "concentration is focused toward presenting the audience with the highest possible vocal quality, while maintaining their entertainment value through intricate staging and choice of literature."[25]

These three choral programs share largely similar repertoire and employ similar stylistic boundaries, including pop but not heavy rock, drawing on gospel music but not on rap. In its more inclusive structure, the Greater Decatur Chorale differs from the other two groups, remaining open to relative amateurs and to adults of all ages and requiring less commitment from participants. All three groups have in common an overwhelmingly white membership and audience, something particularly notable since African Americans constituted 16.7 percent of the local population in the 1990 census.[26]

The support for and growth of these three choral programs bespeaks a prominent place for music in Decatur's civic life, at least in comparison to some of the surrounding cities. Decatur had (and retains) three such groups while surrounding cities, and many major cities, sometimes had or have no such choral groups.

The Park District is by no means the only path to participation in local choral music. Independent and ad hoc groups, though comparatively less significant, also contribute to Decatur's choral music scene. In her illuminating study of music making in Milton Keynes, England (pop. ca. 112,000 at the time of her study), Ruth Finnegan found an extremely dynamic choral tradition and estimated that in addition to church and school choirs, about 100 independent choirs existed, ranging in size from as many as ninety members to as few as twelve.[27] Even lacking a survey of the U.S. choral practice or any comparative study of a U.S. city, it seems difficult to imagine a comparably sized U.S. city with so many independent choirs. A comparison of Milton Keynes with Decatur, at least, would provoke questions as to whether choral music has a more prominent role in U.K. versus U.S.

musical life, or whether some "critical mass" of population is necessary to support choral music, and so on. In Decatur, I found many musicians, but only a few independent choral groups. Although not attempting a complete inventory of independent choral groups, I found only barbershop quartets (and Sweet Adelines, their female counterparts), one independent choir, and occasional ad hoc groups.

The independent choir, Opus 24, was founded in 1991 by local individuals "to establish a new choral group for the city of Decatur and surrounding communities."[28] It has about thirty-two members. As with the Greater Decatur Chorale, with whom it has some members in common, most Opus 24 singers are not professional musicians, although there are some music teachers and professors involved. Members include nurses, teachers, engineers, administrators, and other professionals: Singers' names, vocal parts, and occupations are given in a 1993 program.

The mission of Opus 24 is described in program notes as follows: "to offer an opportunity to sing challenging choral literature that represented a broad historical basis and also incorporated various forms of choral literature."[29] I asked the director to clarify this further and to compare his group with the Decatur Chorale:

> Melinda Rusell: Now you described the Chorale as doing lighter things?
> Milton Scott: Yes, they do a couple of concerts a year, or they do two weekends, yes, they do show tunes and spirituals and medleys and things like that. They don't get into the heavier, traditional choral [material].
> MR: And how would you characterize your repertoire?
> MS: Well, if you look at that, you can probably characterize it as well as I can. It is the more traditional [literature]. I mean, we do Bach, Vaughan Williams, we do Randall Thompson, and we do some fun things too, but it is more of the meat and potatoes.[30]

Like the Decatur Musical Union and the Decatur Park Singers, Opus 24 seems to have been formed first for the enjoyment of its members, and then to have evolved into a formal group for a specific occasion, in this case the hundredth anniversary of a local church. From there its path seems, at least by its director's description, to have been driven by its own success: He estimates that there were perhaps 200 people at that first appearance, and "[at] this last concert that we did we had about 600. We've had to move to bigger places, to higher ground [laughs] each time. We have a very loyal following."[31] The group has also been incorporated as the "Decatur Choral Society," with the aim of eventually establishing other community choral groups "solely for the purpose of educating choral singers and providing opportunities for performance."[32]

The name "Opus 24" (after a favorite composition of the director) and the vocabulary employed—"challenging," "literature," "historical," "heavier," "meat and potatoes"—helps to situate this group in relation to others in the city. Black concert dress and printed programs further articulate the position of this group as representing "legitimate" choral art music, a position analogous to the role of the Millikin-Decatur Symphony in local instrumental music. Unlike the Decatur Park Singers, this group performs indoors, does not employ choreography, and maintains the audience-performer separation traditional in Western art music; listeners have no fear of being pulled on stage and singers do not enter the crowd to shake the hands of audience members in between pieces. In a community often described as "blue-collar," there is some danger of such a group being seen as an exclusive enterprise. The listing of members' occupations in the program, explicitly linking the singers to many of the best-known local institutions—the hospitals, the power company, the schools—may in part be intended prophylactically.

In addition to barbershop and Sweet Adelines groups, Decatur has some groups that form on an ad hoc basis for certain events or times of year. For example, each New Year's Eve a number of Decatur's African American churches (and sometimes some white churches as well) form a joint choir for a gospel concert. Similarly, an aggregate choir is formed for the Decatur Celebration, a street festival held each summer.

Decatur's labor struggles occasionally led to a kind of ad hoc choral music not often found in the United States, though once more common. In June 1994, for example, members of United Paperworkers Local 7837, on strike against A. E. Staley Manufacturing Company (one of the top three local employers), were holding a "Solidarity March and Rally" to mark the one-year anniversary of their being locked out by the company. Near the end of the rally, which moved from the U.A.W. hall to Staley's headquarters, a small group remained and, accompanied by one man on acoustic guitar, sang "Solidarity Forever."[33] As the protesters allegedly tried to break the police line defending the gate, the police sprayed them with pepper gas, large quantities of it wafting into the air. "What about the dope dealers?" one man shouted repeatedly at the police, rubbing his eyes in pain. In addition to the protesters, a union member's children and a local television reporter were gassed, and one person was arrested. Those in pain or exhausted sat down on the street and rubbed or shielded their eyes, and one woman began to sing "We Shall Not be Moved." There was no accompaniment, and she was joined by about a dozen others, including some of the people with their heads in their hands. This use of choral music for protest was, in my experience in Decatur, singular. One wonders whether it was occasioned entirely by the unique labor struggles of the period, or if it represents a genre that will appear elsewhere.

Choral music is included in a wide array of Decatur's musical occasions. In the brief examples above, choral music is used to entertain, to learn, to celebrate, and to protest. Despite this variety of purpose, these groups have in common their strategic use of choral music as uniquely suited to express group solidarity. Choral music is widely seen as a uniting force, joining singers with one another and the choral group to its various audiences. Not everyone agrees, however, on the merits of particular genres of choral expression. Next is an exploration of choral music in the schools, including consideration of a genre whose desirability was a matter of debate in Decatur.

As with its churches, Decatur's schools provide numerous music learning and performance opportunities. Also similarly, school music making is a local instance of a larger phenomenon; we may expect both adherence to national and regional patterns and distinctive local cases. In the public schools, virtually every school offers something from the district menu of glee clubs, choirs, and show choirs (where costumes, scenery, and staging are added) in addition to orchestral and band participation. Participatory singing forms at least part of general music instruction (given in grades K–6, with nine-week segments in grades seven and eight). While instruction tends to focus increasingly on music theory and on reading musical notation, participatory singing is part of every general music program.

In addition to these classroom music offerings, voluntary choral music programs in the schools draw large numbers of participants. All nineteen Decatur elementary schools have glee clubs in fourth, fifth, and sixth grades, meeting once a week. The average district participation rate in elementary schools is 51.2 percent. At the middle school level, participation rates vary enormously. In Decatur's four middle schools, 1994 participation in choral music varied from 9.8 percent at the lowest to 76.7 percent at the highest, with the other two schools at 11.6 percent and 30 percent.

The extraordinary rate of 76.7 percent participation reflects that school's use as an "arts magnet" school. The great drop in participation in "chorus" as compared to the elementary school glee clubs may in part be due to more individual choice in activities, but it is interesting that the choral participation rate is so high at Jefferson Middle School. Some consultants hypothesize that this is due to the stability and favorable reputation of the director. The degree of difference suggests that some localized factors—a "critical mass," a popular director, a history of strong choral participation—influence participation rates. This argument can be made again regarding the 1994 rates of participation in Decatur high schools. The three high schools had choral participation rates of 4.8 percent, 6.1 percent, and 14.9 percent. One notes the decreased popularity, in general, of choral music in the later grades. Still, significant variation is found among the schools. The strength of the most popular choral program (Eisenhower) is, like that at Jefferson, locally attributed to the well-known and well-liked choral director and to the reputation of the established groups.

Elements that may seem insubstantial to the casual observer may also play a role in participation rates; the choral director from Eisenhower High School (who wears numerous "musical hats" in the community) suggests some:

> Milton Scott: Choir, for instance, in the public schools, also band and orchestra, are each a full academic credit a year. Some systems have half a credit, or a quarter credit, or no credit. . . . We have a lot of children involved in music. . . . For instance the national average of students involved in performing groups is maybe 9–10 percent of a school, state average is maybe 12 percent, and at Eisenhower we have 22 percent of the student body . . . because we also have good counseling, and we have zero hour which is an extra period before the day, where the kids can take P.E. or other stuff.
>
> Melinda Russell: So they can adjust their schedules.
>
> MS: That suggests that the school prioritizes this too; makes it possible; well, we've had a real drive to say, "Look, the arts are *not* a frill, they *are* a basic, and this is what needs to be done to, to do that." And we've had pretty good cooperation with that. Funding is still a problem.

In addition to specific aspects such as academic credit or space in the schedule, the director underscores the attitudinal milieu within the school and the school system. Popular choral directors establish popular programs in particular schools, and as a result, participation in choral programs in those schools becomes increasingly popular, acting as "arts magnets" without being so designated.

The literature performed by school choirs is drawn variously from segments of Western classical music, recently composed choir literature, and a variety of subgenres of American traditional and popular song; teachers and administrators often described it as varied or inclusive, as in this quotation from the coordinator of music for the Decatur Public Schools: "Well, as a rule of thumb, I like to see all styles of music be given an opportunity to our students, and Music Educators National Conference supports that. . . . We just can't offer, for example in the choral program, all classical music. I just don't think we can do that, that's not fair, we're not exposing children to things that are out there in the *world* and that's part of our job as educators. Most of our teachers do a well-balanced diet."

At the same time, there is a fairly uniform absence—with some important exceptions—of some styles, such as gospel, jazz, and rock. Again, the coordinator addresses this:

> Marilyn Mertz: Yeah, we don't like, we don't find rock performed in our school groups. . . . Kids have that at home, they have it driving to school, they have it everywhere, they don't need to have it in school, too.
> Melinda Russell: And do you think that you are providing music that they don't have elsewhere?
> MM: Yes. *Good* music. You know, both from classical to light.

The perceived underenrollment of African American students was linked by the coordinator of music for the Decatur Public Schools to other lacunae in the school choral repertoire: "I think maybe that's why, the fact that maybe we don't emphasize more black, African American music, although we do the traditional folk songs and spirituals and that type of thing, and jazz all the time, but, and some gospel, but maybe if we did more of a diet of gospel, maybe we would have more appeal or enrollment from our black students."

While schools provide opportunities for many musicians, it is important to note that many people become singers and musicians without participating in school activities. I found well-known local singers who had participated heavily in church singing but little or not at all in school choral groups, particularly among female singers in predominantly African American churches.

I have argued elsewhere that school music making sometimes has the quality of planned obsolescence, since so few adults continue amateur music making and since opportunities like band and orchestra have relatively few adult analogues available to the amateur.[34] The music coordinator for the Decatur public schools acknowledges the likelihood of the discontinuation of performance, but notes that singing is an important exception: "Helping students become discerning listeners [is] a goal that all music educators should have because not all of our students are going to always perform. They'll be buyers of music, listeners of music, although we'd like to see them all perform, continue performing, probably those people who are involved in churches, probably singing will be more carried through in adult life than playing an instrument."[35]

Of course, church choirs aren't necessarily appropriate venues for everyone who would like to sing in groups. In Decatur, the Greater Decatur Chorale provides an additional opportunity.

During its economic downturn, Decatur found it necessary to cut visual arts programming from the education budget, but music suffered less (temporarily losing, for example, music at the kindergarten level and music theory at the high school level), maintaining its significant place in local curricula. As with the civic groups, this suggests some degree of local consensus about the importance of music in local life. Perhaps the two realms of music making, with a shared aesthetic to some degree, help to reinforce one another. With adult music making prominent in the community, it becomes less difficult to formulate the case for music making in the local schools. Still, any such consensus applies only generally, and while some musical activities or styles are widely appreciated, admiration is not universal. Next is a consideration of a genre whose merits provoked much debate in Decatur.

"Show choirs" seem especially dominant in midwestern parts of the United States and were prominent in Decatur and surrounding areas. This energetic genre combines various aspects of theatrical production—scenery, costumes, dancing—with choral renditions of show tunes and related literature, often in medley form. Though obviously inappropriate for church, they were otherwise extremely widespread. In Decatur, they were an object of contention among musicians, arts professionals, and music educators. While I was interviewing the then-director of the Kirkland Fine Arts Center at Decatur's Millikin University (an important force in local musical culture whose own choral groups could merit a separate essay), he mentioned that show choirs were touted by townspeople during his interview visit, while subtly conveying his own apparent distaste for them:

> Ken Crossley: [When I first visited the town, there were] two things that impressed me. One was the number of churches in the town, and the other thing which was almost a phenomenon to me, was, this show choir business.
> Melinda Russell: Now how did you happen to notice that on a short trip to town, were you in high schools, or—?
> KC: No. . . . People kept talking about the show choirs. There was reference to the show choir here at Millikin University, there was reference to the show choir camp that comes into Millikin each year, which they're here

this week, there was reference made to the Mt. Zion Swingsations, their
national reputation, in fact, Melinda, I must tell you, I thought it was
a little humorous that the people that were asked to host me used the
show choirs as a selling point that they have culture in Decatur: We have
show choirs. And yet it was obvious to me that there was another level of
sophistication, of cultural appreciation, musical sophistication, beyond
show choirs.[36]

A Millikin University faculty member and local musician brought up
the subject during an interview, reflecting a view I'd heard other colleagues
share: "Musicals are not my favorite [pauses] form, and I'm really overdone
with it in Decatur, between Kirkland and the School of Music, there's a lot
of that. . . . And I'm not into it at all, but it does go over. In the School of
Music, you know, we have show choir and, you know, there's just too much
of that for me."

In amplifying his description of the Decatur Park Singers and their transition since the 1980s, their director described them as adhering to "a more
polished show choir image," which included "all sixteen standing there,
singing each number," to which he has added solos in many songs.[37] With
costumes, props, staging, and medleys, though, both the Decatur Park Singers and the Young Park Singers draw heavily from show choir style in their
presentations.

While show choir is a dominant force in Decatur choral music, the domi-
nance does not reflect total agreement about the desirability or merits of the
genre. Arguments about this can most clearly be seen in the case of Decatur's
schools as they negotiate the place of "show choir" within the music curriculum. In addition to curricular choirs, the schools feature numerous "show
choirs." The relegation of show choirs to "uncredited" status within the
schools reflects their position as newcomers in the music curriculum and
the disagreement about their worth. Quotations from two interviews show
divergent views on show choir, revealing where adherents find merit and
detractors find problems. The first interview is with the music coordinator
for the Decatur Public Schools:

> Marilyn Mertz: Well, I think both traditional and show choirs can exist,
> and do exist, side by side . . . and kids who are in the show choir usually
> are required to be in the traditional choirs, which is good, so they get
> a sampling of all kinds of styles of music. And I think the show choir
> idiom can allow kids an expression of themselves in different ways than
> a traditional choir, you know. They can develop all kinds of non-musi-

cal skills, aside from musical skills. And because of the dance element of
that, you can't look at it solely as a singing, . . . so you can't be a purist in
looking at show choir, and try to measure it against the purist values of a
traditional choir.

Melinda Russell: Is that the conflict?

MM: Exactly, they don't want to see it as a medium of expression. . . .
You're building a lot of poise and self-confidence in students . . . more so
than in traditional choir, because each performer has to be an individual, where in choir you're kind of one of fifty, you know? In show choir,
you're as important as the next guy, even more so than in traditional
choir. It's a visual and an aural expression. So I mean, and in the real
world, it's important for students to have poise and self-confidence and,
those are important non-musical qualities. . . . You see kids come out of
those show choirs and stand in front of audiences and give a talk or do
a presentation or apply for jobs, they have a lot more [laughs] pizzazz,
they come across with a lot more convinceability, what do I want to say,
uh, ability to, you know, be poised and confident.[38]

This second assessment is from the same high school choral director
quoted above in the "schools" section: "It appeals to a number of people,
yes. Yes, certainly. Sure, there's a show choir following, in this area. It's actually a corridor, from Wisconsin on down. . . . Wisconsin, Indiana, Iowa, Illinois, that's the show choir thing. My kids at Eisenhower sing [pauses] good
literature. . . . All the kids that are in show choir, with the exception of two,
are in my choirs." He goes on to explain why it's important that students be
in his curricular choir in addition to the extracurricular show choir: "Well,
first of all, the place that they learn vocal technique day after day is in the
curricular choir. What they do on the show choir is pretty fun for them,
and I'm supportive of what the kids do. . . . And I give them, I have a vocal
abuse paper which I hand out to a show, to a choir member if they want it.
. . . It's a very big issue. One weekend, a three-day weekend, the show choir
had thirty-seven hours of rehearsal, before they went to a festival. Um, my
battle also with the show choir idea is that the time spent versus what they
receive educationally is not, it's pretty thin. . . . You will find that, of every
five hours spent for show choir, four of those are spent on staging and choreography. . . . It's been a very big source of strife in my teaching career for
four years."[39]

Show choirs and other innovations that generate disagreement offer
opportunities to find people articulating musical values. The choral director finds show choir potentially abusive to the voice and educationally "thin,"

while conceding that it is "pretty fun" for students. The music coordinator believes show choir allows expression, builds poise and self-confidence, and permits performers to be individuals. The former director of the concert hall finds show choir a bit "humorous," in contrast with what he considers more "sophisticated" music, but his hosts clearly pointed to it with some pride. These stances reflect not just divergent tastes, but divergent views on what a choral group is for.

As in many communities, churches are the source of some of the most important opportunities for choral music making in Decatur. Local churches provide numerous musical occasions, and many also offered musical instruction of various sorts. In 1996, Decatur had one synagogue, five Catholic churches, and 146 Protestant churches.[40]

Sizes of choirs vary throughout the city, with the smallest memberships being fewer than ten and the largest nearing fifty (near or past that point, most congregations divided the choirs into two or more). Age gradations are by far the most popular divisions among churches having more than one choir, and gender divisions thereafter. Some churches report particular problems attracting men to sing, but others had active all-male groups.

Choir rehearsals generally consist of a one- to two-hour rehearsal on a weeknight just after dinnertime; membership in specialty choirs means additional meeting time. Some choir directors are paid, others are volunteers from the congregation, and still others are the ministers themselves. Much variation is found in pedagogical practice as well, with many choirs reading from standard notation and others learning by ear or from some combination.

In 1996, I surveyed a few dozen local churches to gain further understanding of the use of music. There were many differences, of course, along lines of denomination, but there were also areas of congruity. A variety of genres and of descriptive terms are used by music directors in describing their ensembles: "worship," "praise," "spiritual," "choir classics," "folk," "jazz," "southern gospel, "gospel,"and the like, suggesting that repertoire (or at least taxonomy) is not uniform; further research shows more cohesion within particular denominations, subgroups, or even geographic areas. Asked about particular musical styles, many directors distinguished between "traditional" and "contemporary" musical practices, and the majority employed multiple "preferred styles" of music, often stressing (one even using the term) eclecticism. My Decatur church consultants often emphasized the importance of appealing to multiple musical tastes while not compromising the spiritual function of the music. Thus some choir directors were careful to describe music not considered appropriate, for example "rock or synth."

My inquiries about the purpose of music in churches yielded answers that center on its function in worship, where it "helps," "supports," "enhances," and "adds an additional dimension," or alternatively "leads" or "brings" people to God. Some described the purpose of music as contributing to a certain atmosphere; music "helps create a place where people can come into the presence of God and worship him," and "sets the mood for praise and worship." Two respondents mention outreach or evangelism as a function. Many directors took pains to point out that music in churches was not chiefly for the entertainment of listeners.

Such attitudes toward the purpose of music shape musical practices themselves in multiple ways. Below is an excerpt from an interview with a Church of God in Christ (C.O.G.I.C.) music director, in which she explains the consequences of identifying certain purposes in the use of music:

> Janet Rollins: Gospel music in our churches is *not* considered entertainment. This is one point that I emphasize.
> Melinda Russell: The fact that it's not entertainment, does that change how you run things?
> JR: It does for me.
> MR: Can you say more about that?
> JR: I, and the reason I love my choir is because they, we're just kind of, O.K., you know, we'll never cut records, I know that. I'm glad. . . . We've got monotones, we've got people who don't know "b flat" from a "q," you know? . . . So, what I rely on, is the spirit. . . . And that is only generated through prayer, only generated through [the attitude that] "this is a ministry. This gospel music is treated like a ministry." Where we have come to be thought of as entertainment, is through the people coming. They want to be entertained. They like the sound, they like the music, they like. . . . Now, what does that do to the musicians and the choir people, if you don't have that spirit of ministry? Then you are entertainment: "Hey, we gotta get good, we gotta look sharp, we gotta be good," and "boy look at this house, we gotta really show off."[41]

This speaker alludes to the expectation of entertainment on the part of congregants and illustrates her position that entertainment is not only not a proper function of church music, but actually a destructive one, leading musicians away from prayerful intention and into narcissism. As one might expect, she does not find that the worth of a musical performance in church has a direct relationship to its musical perfection:

> You're gonna get people who can't sing in harmony, haven't been taught, they don't have anybody to teach 'em. And that is why the ministry has to come

through. I mean, I've heard choirs who can't carry a tune really, I mean, they were trying to do alto, tenor, and bass, but it was nowhere near there. Maybe one of the musicians they had was in one key, and the choir's in the other. But the spirit of God was there. . . . So it's not entertainment, it's not in whether the music is absolutely right, and all the voices have been trained, you know? It's not that. And you were touched, and people have gone away crying and the choir's standing there, tears running down, it's ministry. . . . They're being ministered to, and they're also ministering. So that is what's effective, and . . . I'm not, I'm not caught up in "You gotta sing that perfect. We gotta practice till we get everything right."[42]

The logical extension of this view is voiced by another music director, who explains that you don't need to be a singer to be in the choir. This potentially unexpected statement offers a window into the definitions of "singer" and "musician" operative in this—and some other—church contexts.

> Melinda Russell: How does somebody join the choir, do they just come up to you and say "I want to sing," or—
> Michelle Tyson: Well, they have to be a member of either the outreach ministry that we have on Friday nights, or, they have to be a member of the church.
> MR: Is that the only requirement?
> MT: Um, yeah, I mean, we, I mean a lot of times when newcomers join the church, that's the first place that they go, is the choir. There are no auditions or whatever, I mean, you don't have to be able, to be a singer to be in the choir. But most people are before they leave.
> MR: So you don't turn people down?
> MT: No, unh-unh.[43]

Here the choir is described as a kind of gateway to the church, as open as church doors themselves: No audition or particular musical status is required of potential participants. Indeed, the choir is also a gateway to musicianship itself; the statement that "most people are before they leave" indicates that belonging to the choir can transform a person into a singer.

*　*　*

A consideration of Decatur's choral music in its many manifestations prompts consideration of a number of issues or themes. The separation of local choral music into "civic or independent," "school," and "church" groups, though it reflects genuine boundaries, also artificially emphasizes them, and may obscure shared elements. In this closing section, three issues that cut across such boundaries are briefly considered: multiple musical roles in the community, the amateur/professional distinction, and race.

Perhaps the most immediate corrective to seeing local music as neatly partitioned comes from considering the involvement of individual singers and musicians. In the school example above, for instance, members of show choirs are also required be to members of curricular choirs. Even greater evidence of voluntary multiple affiliation abounds. A local man quoted earlier is a good example. The choral and music director at a local high school, he is also the director of music at his church, and the current director of Opus 24. If we look in turn at the members of Opus 24, we find that many belong to other choral groups. Some are members of their church groups, others of the Greater Decatur Chorale. Looking at the membership of other local choral groups, we would find that such multiple roles occur both concurrently and sequentially. For example, young singers belonging to either or both school and church choirs might enroll in Decatur's musical theater program in the summer, then join the Young Park Singers, designed in part as a "feeder group" for the Decatur Park Singers. Indeed, a number of singers have followed just such a course.

Another issue arising from consideration of the entire Decatur choral music scene is the distinction between professional and amateur musicians. Often, groups identified themselves as either professional or amateur, sometimes further articulating what consequences were to follow from the designation. "Professional" was used by people to signify a bewildering number of qualities or situations in choral contexts, among them being in tune, having instrumental accompaniment, being on time, paying attention to a director, having music fully learned at the time of rehearsal, and so on. Professional expectations (as with members of Opus 24 or the Park Singers groups) did not necessarily correlate with pay.

To some extent, notions of professionalism correlated with ideas or practices concerning inclusiveness and exclusivity, so that groups self-identifying as either professional or having professional aspirations tended also to have auditions, to have regular rehearsals, to use notated music, and frequently to have paid directors.

Many groups combined features that might be associated with professional or amateur status. Opus 24, for example, is self-described as a "select community chamber choir,"[44] and this, along with its name, concert dress, and program notes, connotes a certain seriousness of purpose and desire to be associated with professional groups. At the same time, the inclusion in the program notes of the non-musical "day jobs" of members highlights a status that might be called "amateur." The Decatur Park Singers have a name and a manner of performance clearly meant to evoke a casual sing-along, but they must compete for their place and are professionally contracted and paid (at least if they are "good").[45]

A third issue is that of race. Race was often cited by my consultants, often without prompting, as a major division in Decatur social life. In this example, a local African American elementary school teacher and church choir director responded to my question "What's it like to live here as a community?"

> Michelle Tyson: That depends on which neck of the woods you come from.
> Melinda Russell: Tell me about that.
> MT: O.K., first, I think: black and white. . . . There's very few mixed neighborhoods. Very few in Decatur. Very few. I'm not saying. . . . There are some, but—[46]

Another African American choir director commented that she is only a generation removed from segregation, saying, "My aunt, she's worked at Kresge's, she and her husband retired with seventy-five years of service together. . . . She can remember the time when blacks couldn't eat at the lunch counter. I mean so you go from there to where 'you can eat, but we don't want to serve you.'" "It is so subtle," she continued, "until I would not accuse [people of racism], you know what I mean?" adding that people "who've been exposed to all this don't break into things . . . always fairly or evenly."[47]

Churches in particular made formal efforts to combat racial divisions, setting up arrangements whereby predominantly white and predominantly African American churches could "fellowship" together. Some such efforts were fairly successful and continued over time, though others fizzled. Music was an important area of division or of mutuality. The elementary school teacher and church choir director quoted above discussed the experience at her church: "We've been trying to fellowship with this one white church, and it's been hard . . . just with the differences in music and the differences in culture." She acknowledged that "when we try to get 'em together, there's people from our church that won't come, and there are a lot of people from [the other] church that won't come. . . . It's kind of discouraging."[48] She cited her own inclusion of, and familiarity with, white Christian "praise" music as helpful in transcending such boundaries, indicating that some shared musical culture provides a more comfortable basis for fellowship.

These comments, and those made with reference to the repertoire in the schools, prompt some reflection on the extent to which Decatur's African

Americans are represented in the city's choral activities. While the Decatur Park Singers are the city's best-known and most prominent choral group, their membership, audience, and repertoire are not simply a representative sample of a locally unified culture. Looking to the civic musical culture, including the schools, one finds African Americans distinctly marginalized in local choral music.

* * *

Is choral music important in Decatur? By the measures of human energy, community attention, and economic resources, it certainly seems so. Such questions can be thrown into relief, as I have suggested, by events that force active assessment by the community itself, and Decatur's economic and labor woes provide such an event. The maintenance and even growth of choral music during this period argue for the central position of this mode of expression. In expressing group solidarity, choral music can also express factionalism, as when the choral traditions of whites and African Americans remain separate, or when Decatur's striking workers occasionally used choral singing to articulate their group cohesion but also their separation from the mainstream. In its diversity of context, function, style, and substance, choral music proves itself a fundamental thread in Decatur's social fabric. The continued vital presence of choral music in so many of the city's cultural institutions reflects a deep attachment to singing together in many places and many ways.

Notes

I wish to thank Carleton College for leave funding during the period in which this essay was prepared. Portions of this essay appear in different form in my dissertation, "Listening to Decatur: Musical Ethnography in an Illinois City, 1992–97" (Urbana: University of Illinois, 1999).

1. Illinois Department of Commerce and Community Affairs, *Community Profile of Decatur, Illinois* (Chicago: Illinois Department of Commerce and Community Affairs, 1996).

2. City of Decatur, *City of Decatur, Illinois 1990 Census of Population and Housing Census Atlas: General Demographic and Housing Characteristics*, vol. 1 (City of Decatur, 1991), 3.

3. Peter T. Kilborn, "In Decatur, Labor Is Put to the Test," *New York Times*, 29 January 1995: 3.

4. Mabel E. Richmond, *Centennial History of Decatur and Macon County, Illinois* (Decatur: *Decatur Review*, 1930), 218.

5. Ibid., 220.

6. Jane Martin Johns, *Personal Recollections of Early Decatur, Abraham Lincoln, Richard J. Oglesby, and the Civil War* (Decatur: Daughters of the American Revolution, 1912), 170.

7. Ibid., 171.

8. Ibid., 172.

9. Ibid., 170.

10. Ibid., 173.

11. Richmond, *Centennial History,* 220.

12. Illinois law allows the creation of Park Districts as separate governmental bodies. In Decatur, the Park District has administered (since 1967) the local Recreation Department, formerly operated by the city. The Park District choral groups are also supported by grants from federal and local sources, including some of the city's major employers. A fund-raising concert is also held by the Decatur Park Singers at the conclusion of each season.

13. David Alderman, interview with the author, 28 September 2000.

14. Ibid. Some consultants quoted in this essay are referred to by pseudonyms.

15. 1994 Decatur Park Singers Program Booklet, Decatur Recreation Department.

16. Mark Tupper, "A Green Legacy: Jerry Menz Leaves Decatur a Rich Parks Program," *Decatur Review,* 23 May 1993, A1.

17. Ibid.

18. 1994 Decatur Park Singers Program Booklet.

19. David Alderman, interview with the author, 26 July 1994.

20. Referring to "greatest hits" compilations advertised on late-night television.

21. David Alderman, interview with the author, 27 July 1994.

22. Ibid.

23. 1994 Decatur Park Singers Program Booklet.

24. Daniel Freeman, interview with the author, 25 June 1994.

25. 1994 Decatur Park Singers Program Booklet.

26. *City of Decatur,* vol. 1, 1.

27. Ruth Finnegan, *The Hidden Musicians: Music-Making in an English Town* (Cambridge: Cambridge University Press, 1989), 40.

28. Opus 24 Winter Choral Concert Program (Decatur: Westminster Presbyterian Church, 1993), 9.

29. Ibid., 9.

30. Milton Scott, interview with the author, 28 June 1994.

31. Ibid.

32. Opus 24 Concert Program, 9.

33. On this song sung by another labor chorus, see Wolensky, "'We're singin' for the Union,'" this volume, chapter 10.

34. Melinda Russell, "Listening to Decatur: Musical Ethnography in an Illinois City, 1992–97," (Ph.D. dissertation, University of Illinois, 1999), 212.

35. Marilyn Mertz, interview with the author, 26 July 1994.

36. Ken Crossley, interview with the author, 21 June 1994.

37. David Alderman, interview with the author, 26 July 1994.

38. Marilyn Mertz, interview with the author, 26 July 1994.

39. Milton Scott, interview with the author, 28 June 1994.

40. Illinois Department of Commerce and Community Affairs, *Community Profile*, 2.

41. Janet Rollins, interview with the author, 27 June 1994.

42. Ibid.

43. Michelle Tyson, interview with the author, 12 August 1994.

44. Opus 24 Concert Program, p. 10.

45. On the amateur-professional divide, see Smith, "Symphonic Choirs," this volume, chapter 13.

46. Michelle Tyson, interview with the author, 12 August 1994.

47. Janet Rollins, interview with the author, 27 June 1994.

48. Michelle Tyson, interview with the author, 12 August 1994.

3

Singing on the Steppes: Kornelius Neufeld and Choral Music among the Mennonites of Russia

WESLEY BERG

Where Russian Mennonites have settled in relatively large and con-centrated numbers in North America—Winnipeg and southern Manitoba, Kansas around Newton, Ontario around Kitchener-Waterloo, or in the Fraser Valley of British Columbia—they have become known for the excellent quality of their choral singing. It might seem a natural way for Mennonites to make music; they have traditionally emphasized close community and family ties, and the congregation occupies a central place in their religious community. Robert Shaw, the distinguished American choral conductor who enjoyed working with Mennonite choirs, remarked on the ability of Mennonites to come together from across the continent and blend almost instantly as if they had been rehearsing for weeks. He explained it in his typically down-to-earth manner as "a bunch of cousins getting together to sing."[1]

Although Mennonite choral singing has flourished especially in North America and especially in the second half of the twentieth century, in fact it began in Russia in the last decades of the nineteenth. Choral singing spread throughout the Russian Mennonite colonies as they became prosperous at the end of the nineteenth century and in the first decade of the twentieth, until the whirlwind of World War I and the Bolshevik Revolution threw all life in Russia into confusion and turmoil for more than a decade. But there were occasions before the World War and the Revolution when Mennonite choral singing in Russia took place in remote corners of the country under much more difficult circumstances. It is this story and the story of Kornelius G. Neufeld, a man who played a pioneering role in the development of choral singing in those regions, that I want to explore in this essay. It is a story reminding us that while prosperity and comfortable living conditions may be preferable for the development of cultural activities like choral singing, such activities can also play a vital and sustaining role in a community when life becomes hard. It is a story that also reminds us of the importance of the individual. Choral singing may be a communal activity, but dedicated and skillful leadership is in most cases crucial to its success. The story of Kornelius Neufeld and the Mennonite choral singers of northern Russia provides a vivid illustration of how a dedicated leader surrounded by equally dedicated singers can develop a vibrant choral music life even in less than ideal circumstances.

Mennonites living in the Vistula Delta near Danzig (Gdansk) in Prussian Poland were the descendants of Anabaptists who had fled Holland and northern Germany in the sixteenth century to escape persecution. The Anabaptist movement, sometimes called the Radical Reformation, began in 1525, only seven years after Luther's proclamation in Wittenberg. Both Catholic and Lutheran authorities saw the Anabaptists' insistence on adult rather than infant baptism, their refusal to swear an oath, and their pacifism as serious threats to the state and treated converts to the movement harshly.

A number of Swiss and south German Anabaptists found refuge in Pennsylvania in the United States; their north European counterparts were welcomed on the estates of Polish noblemen, where their farming expertise was valued. Now known as Mennonites after Menno Simons, their leader in the Lowlands, they flourished in the Danzig area in spite of the restrictions imposed on them because of their isolationist tendencies and pacifist beliefs. When the area became part of the Prussian empire in the late eighteenth century, the pressure on Mennonites to take part in an increasingly militaristic society became intolerable for many of them and they responded to the invitation contained in Catherine the Great's manifestos of 1762, 1763, and 1785 inviting foreign settlers to populate the steppes of southern Russia.[2]

The first Mennonite colonies were established in 1789 north of the Black Sea near the Dniepr River in what is now Ukraine. Part of a much larger influx of German-speaking settlers, they shared the privileges granted potential colonists by Catherine the Great, among the most important of which were the possibility of settling in self-contained colonies on large areas of land, the right to a large measure of internal self-government in these colonies, and freedom from military service.[3] After the initial difficulties that inevitably accompanied the settling of a new land, the Mennonite colonies flourished.

By the middle of the nineteenth century, a high birth rate and a Russian government policy requiring the landholdings of a Mennonite family to pass on to a single child had produced a large number of landless colonists. By the beginning of the twentieth century, a number of daughter colonies in the vicinity of the original settlements had been established, along with a number of colonies in the Kuban and Terek provinces of the Caucasus, the province of Ufa near the Ural Mountains, and after 1909 in the provinces of Tomsk and Tobolsk in Siberia.

The musical practices of the Russian Mennonites had also undergone significant changes by the end of the nineteenth century. The hymnody of the Mennonite pioneers at the beginning of the century consisted of Lutheran chorales sung in an oral tradition that produced melismatic singing in a characteristically stentorian vocal style.[4] This style of singing was offensive to some of the well-educated persons, especially teachers, who came to the colonies after 1835. A teacher named Heinrich Franz in particular set out to reform singing in the schools and churches of the Mennonite colonies. Using *Ziffern,* a system of notation using numerals to represent pitches, he published a book of chorales in four parts that became common in Russian Mennonite schools toward the end of the century, although not without considerable opposition at the beginning.

This "old way of singing" was preserved and brought to the Canadian prairies in 1874 by a conservative group of Mennonites who left Russia when the freedom from military service they had been promised was withdrawn as a part of extensive reforms the Russian government undertook after the Crimean War. In Russia, however, the musical reforms of Heinrich Franz were soon to be supplemented and complemented by religious developments among the Mennonites.

The religious life of the isolated colonies had become rigid by the middle of the nineteenth century, and there were those who perceived signs of a moral decline. The most significant response was the birth of the Mennonite Brethren Church in 1860. Influenced by Pietism, the new church emphasized personal salvation rather than the communal approach practiced by the main group. Needless to say, the hymnody of the old church did not reflect these new values either in text or in melody. As a result, the Mennonite Brethren Church turned initially toward the hymnals of the German Methodists and then to songs in German translation of the Moody and Sankey revival movement that was sweeping across North America and England at the time.

As a part of this musical revolution, the Mennonite Brethren began to organize choirs in their churches in the 1870s, both to help congregations learn the

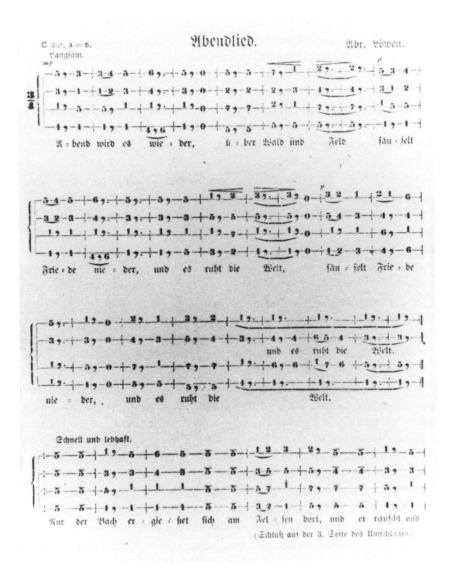

Figure 3.1 Abraham Loewen, "Abendlied," a four-part choral anthem in Ziffern (*Unser Blatt* 2 [June 1927], inside front and back covers). Loewen was a Russian Mennonite singer and choral conductor active in the 1920s.

new repertoire and to provide wholesome activities for their young people. By 1890 it was apparent that training for choir directors in the churches was urgently needed, and the first choral festival and choir directors workshop was held in the village of Rueckenau in 1893.[5]

In 1895 Mennonite church musicians formed a choral directors association that sponsored choral festivals and workshops for conductors, as well as arranging for their more experienced members to visit and work with church choirs in different regions of the country. Because of the isolation of the colonies, however, it was necessary in most cases for singers and conductors to rely on their own resources. This became even more apparent as settlements in more remote areas were established. In many cases the conductors had little more musical education than they would have received in school. They would have known how to read music in *Ziffern* and might have picked up some conducting techniques from their experiences in choirs and at the occasional conductors course.[6]

Kornelius Gerhard Neufeld was one of the rare Mennonites who were able to obtain more musical training than most of their compatriots. He was born in 1871 in Alexanderkrone in the colony of Molotschna, one of the two original colonies in southern Russia, now Ukraine. He received his initial training at the Ohrloff Secondary School, graduating in 1888, and taught for three years at the intermediate school in the village of Sagradovka. He studied at the Evangelical Theological Seminary and the University in Basel, Switzerland, from 1895 to 1897. From 1898 to 1901 he taught in a school in a colony established in the 1890s in the province of Ufa, near the Ural Mountains, and from 1902 to 1904 in Samara, in a colony established in the 1850s in the Volga region. He continued his studies in England at Spurgeon's Pastor's College in London from 1905 to 1906.[7]

Having experienced many of the best things that Europe had to offer, Neufeld, like most of the young Russian Mennonite men who left the colonies to study abroad, returned to Russia to work in communities that must from time to time have seemed isolated and unenlightened. He was one of dozens of Russian Mennonite students who attended postsecondary institutions in Russia and Europe in the period between 1880 and 1917. One survey found that of the ninety-six Mennonites who obtained university degrees between 1880 and 1917, twenty-nine were teachers and professors, twenty-four were engineers and architects, fourteen were physicians, eleven were theologians, seven were lawyers, and three were trained in forestry science. Eight others, some of whom were writers and artists, received training in various other disciplines.[8]

According to John B. Toews, the training these men received did not affect the intellectual foundations of the Russian Mennonite way of life in any fundamental way. "Here was a moderate intellectual renaissance which drew its inspiration from the best training in Russia as well as abroad, yet the importation of 'alien' culture into the Russian Mennonite communities produced little modification of traditional values. The Mennonite teacher of 1900 or 1910 spoke Russian and read Dostoevsky and Tolstoy, yet moved primarily in a minority culture and loyally upheld its values and traditions."[9] Harry Loewen examined the letters of many such men and wrote, "In reading the letters and autobiographies of these young Mennonites, one senses an air of excitement and expectancy coupled with a sense of responsibility and duty toward those who supported them financially and morally."[10] No doubt the fact that Neufeld was also a minister of the Mennonite Brethren Church played a role in his willingness not only to return to Russia but to move to the eastern frontier.

In 1908 Neufeld returned to Ufa to become the principal of the coeducational secondary school in Davlekanovo, the main village in the colony. The school was in its second year of operation when Neufeld took over. Though there must have been much to do in establishing and running a school in a new settlement, Neufeld's interest and expertise in choral music soon became evident. Although he had been trained as a theologian and pastor and was a minister of the Mennonite Brethren Church, he was also an enthusiastic and knowledgeable musician.

In January 1909 Neufeld announced that he was going to publish a magazine called *Aufwärts: Blätter für Sänger und Dirigenten und für Liebhaber des christlichen Gesanges* [Upwards: Pages for Singers and Conductors and for Lovers of Sacred Music].[11] He published it privately, but in spite of some subsidies from the Conference of Mennonite Brethren Churches, it succumbed after two years to financial difficulties and the problems of sustaining such a venture while carrying out the duties of a principal and teacher. In the second year of publication Neufeld addressed more general issues like natural science, world issues, and theology, and even included some fiction, with very little mention of musical matters, but even that change did not attract enough subscribers to keep it afloat. The first volume, however, is a rich source of information about choral activities in the eastern Russian Mennonite settlements at the end of the first decade of the twentieth century.

Some evidence of Neufeld's standing among his choral conducting colleagues in the colonies can be found in an account of a choral conductors' conference held in the village of Waldheim in May 1909.[12] Fifty conductors attended the event, arranged by the choir directors association. They came from colonies across Russia: Chortitza, Molotschna, Memrik, and Sagradovka in the southwest, Crimea and Kuban in the south, Ufa in the northeast, and Turkestan in the southeast. Neufeld was elected by the group to act as the instructor for the three-day course. An article in *Aufwärts* provides us with an insight into this remarkable man's training and experience.[13] Traveling by train on their way to a choral festival, a number of choral conductors traded stories about musical events they had experienced: "There was a certain monotony in the things most of us had to tell, since none of us had traveled very far beyond the borders of the regions where we lived. We therefore listened all the more closely as Friend N[eufeld], who has been able to get to know a sizable piece of this world, began to talk."[14]

In response to a question about the finest singing he had ever heard, he answered:

> That is not so easy to say. As a young man I heard a Russian choir sing an Easter service in the cathedral in Kharkov and thought it was heavenly. I had never thought that such singing could be possible. Later I heard the famous church choirs of cathedrals in St. Petersburg and Moscow, the choir of the cathedral in Berlin, and the singing in St. Peter's in Rome. I have attended choral festivals sponsored by Swiss choral associations. I experienced a performance of Bach's *Matthew Passion* in Basel, Switzerland, and Mendelssohn's *St. Paul* in Dresden. I have been privileged to hear the greatest living singers. . . . You can see that it is no easy task to say where I have heard the most beautiful singing. But if you ask me to tell you about the most impressive performance I have ever heard, then I can answer without hesitation that it was a performance of Handel's *Messiah* in London.

Neufeld went on to describe a performance of *Messiah* by 200 instrumentalists and 4,000 singers in the Crystal Palace in May 1906. He gave a detailed and enthusiastic account of the work, trying to give his companions an idea of a piece they would probably never get to hear in its entirety. About the last chorus he said, "It is too grand, too overpowering to describe in words. It is a seething sea of tones, intertwined and yet in perfect harmony. Now one voice takes on the melody with the others accompanying, now another takes the lead, waiting impatiently for its opportunity to take part in the joyous sound. All of these things come storming at us and leave us partially confounded."

Some of the most valuable contributions of the contents of *Aufwärts* to our knowledge of choral singing in Mennonite Russia come in the form of personal reports and reminiscences sent to the journal from its readers. A particularly poignant example can be found in the sections devoted to the colony of Terek, established in 1901. One Mennonite historian recorded its story in two dispassionate sentences, "The settlement of some fifteen villages in Terek, a province in the southeastern corner of European Russia in the Caucasus near the Caspian Sea, was a mistake. Drought, and paradoxical though it may seem, floods, famine, robbery by bandits, malaria—all these nearly liquidated the settlement by 1914; then came the war, which permitted the bandits from the foothills to drive the whole settlement back to the mother colonies."[15]

Where in this tale of woe, one might ask, is the place for choral singing, an activity that normally requires some level of stability, tranquility, and relative prosperity to flourish? Two reports in *Aufwärts* attempt to answer this question. In an article entitled "Gesang in der Wüste" [Singing in the Wilderness], J. Doerksen of Praetoria offers these memories:

> Our church (*Bethaus*) in the Terek settlement is located in Village No. 3. Sunday morning its inhabitants come together for a worship service. The worthy choir also makes its appearance. The choir members have rehearsed during the week, undergoing many hardships and traveling five to eight *verst* [one *verst* = 1.07 km or 0.663 miles] in the process. Their miserable living conditions make this very difficult for most of them. But they want to sing so badly that they were able to do what seemed to be almost impossible. During the sermon I notice that many of the singers appear pale and ill. Several have just overcome a severe fever; others have still not fully recovered. In the end they might have been better off staying at home, but they were anxious to attend the service, and perhaps they hoped that the change might do them good. One of the women had to leave her place, but the others stayed at their posts. And when the conductor beckons to them, they all stand, healthy and sick, and their singing moves me more than the most artistic singing elsewhere could have.[16]

Another perspective on life and musical activities in this troubled colony came from Johann Reimer, who visited the villages in Terek.[17] The choral directors association had decided to send out some of its more experienced members to improve choral singing in various settlements. Five choirs comprising eighty singers gathered to work on mass choir numbers and in individual sessions with Reimer over a period of three days. Reimer ends his report on the sessions with these words, "I will never forget these days, for they are oases in the wildernesses of our world, especially for the unfortunate

Terekers. Many of them were able to forget their deplorable circumstances for a few days. I have been greatly encouraged during my journey. One young man said that although he had become completely despondent, he was now prepared valiantly to sing again."

It is impossible to know what these choirs would have sounded like. But an arrangement of "Was kann es schönres geben" by Esther Wiebe sung by the Festival Chorus at the Faith and Life Choral Festival in Winnipeg in 1994 provides a glimpse into the Mennonite choir festival tradition as it might have been in Russia (CD no. 5). The choir members gathered from across the province of Manitoba, with some singers coming from other provinces as well, for a weekend of singing and socializing. Many of the participants had parents or grandparents born in Russia. Some, but not all, of the singers would have had musical training, but almost all would have had many years of experience singing in church and community choirs. The choral sound of these modern Mennonites is therefore undoubtedly more accomplished than that of their ancestors in Russia. The repertoire ranges from spirituals and gospel hymns to excerpts from oratorios by Mendelssohn, but almost always in these festivals there are references to the choral traditions of the Russian Mennonites as exemplified by this hymn.

In 1909, the year *Aufwärts* first appeared, Mennonites began to participate in the movement of settlers to Siberia that had begun just before the turn of the century.[18] A report to *Aufwärts* from a correspondent living in the settlement of Barnaul near Slavgorod presents another view of the place of choral singing in apparently forbidding circumstances.

> When we settled here one and a half years ago everything was wild and deso-late. Nothing to see far and wide, no village, no estates, just here and there a little pile of brush left over from the forests that had been cleared. Only those who have been some of the first people in a new settlement can know what this can do to one's spirits. And if one has been accustomed to gather-ing often for fellowship and music, and suddenly all that is gone, it can seem very strange indeed. In a settlement such as we have here, everything has to be built up from the beginning again. That goes for music as well. But when on the one hand such spiritual endeavors as worship services and choir practices face particular difficulties in a settlement like this, on the other hand we can say that they are appreciated in a special way. When we experience a short-age of material goods, we are that much more grateful for spiritual goods. I believe that we appreciate choral singing more here than we did before. It is therefore not surprising that we have already established ten mixed choirs in our settlement in the short space of one and one half years. . . . To be sure, the

singing is not yet very polished (*es ist ja noch kein richtiger Kunstgesang, den wir haben*), but it is our hope to make progress in our singing.

The writer goes on to describe a choir directors workshop held in the settlement. Acknowledging that no guest instructor could be invited and that none of them was an accomplished musician, they nonetheless agreed to work together to share what knowledge they had. This was the pattern more often than not. Reports of such conferences suggest that while a guest conductor might have been invited, it was often not possible for such a person to come, and the choir directors were thrown back on their own resources.

Needless to say, choirs had to work with limited resources in other ways as well. Choral music was being published by Mennonites in southern Russia; a series known as *Liederperlen* [Pearls of Song] was the best-known collection and was widely used by Mennonite choirs. But even in the less-isolated and more-affluent colonies in southern Russia choral music was often hard to find, and many families in North America still treasure a book of choral music written in the hand of a great-grandfather or great-aunt using gothic script and *Ziffern*.

In addition to keeping people across wide stretches of Russia in touch with each other, Neufeld provided various kinds of instruction in the pages of his journal: articles on notation, harmony, the qualities required of a choral singer, and instructions to the beginning choral conductor. Some of the most interesting sections are found in a series, almost certainly written by Neufeld himself, called *Aus dem Tagebuch eines Dirigenten* [From the Diary of a Choir Director], which appeared in the last four issues of the first year of the journal. The diary begins in January 1909 with these words, "Today the election of our choir director took place, since previous directors had emigrated to Siberia. I was elected. Nearly unanimously." The writer's German is clear and elegant, quite unlike the old-fashioned German, used mainly in church, spoken by most Mennonites. There is also an air of detachment and a lack of conventional pious language so common in the writing of most Mennonites of the time.

The diary allows us to follow the week-by-week activities of a choir and its capable, self-assured, but modest leader. The first few weeks are spent combating the practices of the former choir director, a good man to be sure, but whose tolerance of latecomers and whose practice of allowing the choir members to choose the repertoire at the rehearsal have produced habits that take some time to change. We also hear about the difficulty of ridding the choir of persons who simply cannot sing, especially those with considerable political influence in the congregation, and the joy of auditioning singers with excellent voices. The opening of the diary dated February 22 gives us an insight into the musical goals of the writer, as well as the efforts his singers were willing to put into the choir.

> Five weeks have passed since our first performance, [and] I have to say that I am not disappointed; indeed, I think I can say that my best hopes have been exceeded. Not so much with respect to our artistic achievements; in five weeks one can hardly conquer the world. But we have achieved some considerable goals: We no longer go so flat, we no longer sing as individuals but have achieved a better blend of voices, we are beginning to distinguish a little between *piano* and *forte*, and so on, so that on the whole I am satisfied with what we have accomplished. In any case, until we were able to do all this we have had to work very hard: two- to three-hour rehearsals twice a week.

In May and June the choir had reached the stage where it was able to invite several neighboring choirs to participate in a choral festival, after which it undertook a successful trip to a nearby village to sing with and encourage

Figure 3.2 A community choir (*Liebhaberchor*) conducted by Franz Thiessen, a student and colleague of Kornelius Neufeld, Davlekanovo, 1912. Photo courtesy of Mrs. H. F. Klassen.

the local choir. All seemed to be going so well, but the diary entry for August 14 reads:

> I don't know what I am to write today. . . . Until now it has been a pleasure to write in my diary, of pleasant experiences, of things accomplished by the choir. . . . And now, suddenly . . . I don't know what to think. I don't know what to hope for. Or if I can hope for anything at all. . . . After our trip things went on as usual. Two rehearsals during the week and a performance on Sunday. . . . We were looking forward to the autumn and winter, when we would have more leisure time for rehearsals. But it was not to be.

*   *   *

> Already in spring there had been talk in our villages of emigration. This movement had affected only a relatively small circle, but in the course of the summer it had spread quite strongly. In fact, here and there it had become an epidemic. "Barnaul" and "Pavlodar" were the watchwords among the poor; "Omsk" and "Issyk-Kul" the watchwords among the more prosperous. It seemed that such a hunger for land had broken out that it was unsettling to observe. At the next rehearsal—I had never yet approached a rehearsal with such a feeling of unease—it became apparent that my friend [who had told Neufeld that he might as well move to Siberia since that is where his choir was off to] was correct. The land deals had been made and it was only a matter of time until the journeys would begin. This meant, however, nothing more and nothing less than the complete dissolution of our choir, for among the departing families were the whole soprano section and most of the best singers in the bass section! What I experienced will be understood by those conductors who have striven to attain lofty goals in a short time, who have arrived at those goals as well as we had—only to have fallen suddenly from the heights.

In the end the choir decided to keep on singing, but the account ends there. We know that just a few years later religious and cultural activities in Russia were sharply curtailed by the onset of war and revolution. We know that in the 1920s there were a few years in which life returned to a semblance of normality and choirs were organized once again. This time the circumstances were quite different, and choral festivals became a kind of underground movement, the one place where Mennonites were able to gather as a community under a regime that prohibited all religious observances.

But Kornelius Neufeld managed to escape these difficult times. He came to the United States with his children in 1914 and settled in California, living in Fairmead, Reedley, Long Beach, Los Angeles, and finally Shafter, where he died on May 2, 1946. In California he was active as a pastor, unsuccessful as a farmer, and finally made his living as a bookkeeper. A brief biography written by a friend contains only one reference to his former life as one of Mennonite Russia's most important choral conductors. In 1929 there was to be a choral festival "of all the choirs in the state" in Los Angeles, and Neufeld, who was director of the Shafter Mennonite Brethren Church choir, took months to rehearse the "Hallelulujah Chorus." It may not have been the Crystal Palace, but it is good to know that, like a number of other Russian Mennonite musicians who managed to emigrate to North America, Kornelius Neufeld was able to make a contribution to the development of choral singing in his new home.

Notes

1. Wesley Berg, "Robert Shaw, Helmuth Rilling, and the Mennonite Festival Chorus," *Choral Journal* 32 (September 1991): 46.

2. Roger P. Bartlett, *Human Capital: The Settlement of Foreigners in Russia 1762–1894* (Cambridge: Cambridge University Press, 1979): 35–56, 121; and James W. Long, *From Privileged to Dispossessed: The Volga Germans, 1860–1917* (Lincoln and London: University of Nebraska Press, 1988). For the Mennonite story, see James Urry, *None But Saints: The Transformation of Mennonite Life in Russia 1789–1889* (Winnipeg: Hyperion Press Limited, 1989) and John Friesen, ed., *Mennonites in Russia 1788–1988: Essays in Honour of Gerhard Lohrenz* (Winnipeg: CMBC Publications, 1989).

3. Bartlett, *Human Capital,* 47–48. For a brief sketch of the relations between Mennonites and German colonists, see Urry, *None But Saints,* 260–63.

4. For a general account, see Wesley Berg, "Music among the Mennonites of Russia," in Friesen, *Mennonites in Russia.* For a detailed discussion of the singing style, see Wesley Berg, "Hymns of the Old Colony Mennonites and the Old Way of Singing," *Musical Quarterly* 80 (spring 1996): 71–117.

5. Wesley Berg, "The Development of Choral Singing among the Mennonites of Russia to 1895," *Mennonite Quarterly Review* 55 (April 1981): 131–142.

6. Wesley Berg, "Choral Singing among the Mennonites of Russia, 1895–1928," *Mennonite Quarterly Review* 56 (July 1982): 256–268.

7. Peter M. Friesen, *The Mennonite Brotherhood in Russia (1789–1910),* trans. J. B. Toews et al. (Fresno, Calif.: Board of Christian Literature, General Conference of Mennonite Brethren Churches, 1978), 769. His obituary appeared in *Zionsbote* 57 (July 10, 1946): 12.

8. Harry Loewen, "Intellectual Developments among the Mennonites of Russia: 1880–1917," *Journal of Mennonite Studies* 8 (1990): 94.

9. John B. Toews, "Cultural and Intellectual Aspects of the Mennonite Experience in Russia," *Mennonite Quarterly Review* 53 (April 1979): 154–55.

10. Loewen, "Intellectual Developments," 94.

11. Mennonite Library and Archives, Bethel College, North Newton, Kansas.

12. *Aufwärts* 1, no. 4 (1909): 20–21.

13. "Eine Gesangaufführung in London," *Aufwärts* 1, no. 3 (1909): 15–22.

14. All translations mine.

15. C. Henry Smith, *The Story of the Mennonites*, 4th ed. (Newton, Kansas: Mennonite Publication Office, 1957), 471.

16. *Aufwärts* 1, no. 4, 30–32.

17. "Eine Besuchsreise nach der Tereker Ansiedlung," *Aufwärts* 1, no. 5 (1909): 23–26.

18. James Urry, "Prologema to the Study of Mennonite Society in Russia, 1880–1914," *Journal of Mennonite Studies* 8 (1990): 53–56.

PART 2

Grassroots Aesthetics

4

Concord and Discord: Singing Together in a Sardinian Brotherhood

BERNARD LORTAT-JACOB

Translated and edited by Marc Benamou

Sacred Singing in Castelsardo

In the extreme north of Sardinia, polyphonic singing is tied to the church and its rites. In the village of Castelsardo its practice is maintained exclusively by the brotherhood of Santa Croce, a group of some sixty laymen, half of whom are competent singers who have mastered a startlingly beautiful and profoundly original repertoire.

The religious choir [*coro*] is composed of four solo voices. These are, from lowest to highest, the *bassu,* the *contra,* the *bogi,* and the *falzittu.* Generally the *bassu* and the *bogi* sing an octave apart. Despite what one might expect, the *falzittu* does not make use of his head voice. He sings a third above the *bogi,* who is in charge of the "cantus firmus." The other voices accompany the *bogi* using a technique reminiscent of fauxbourdon.[1]

Two facts are essential to any understanding of the workings of the brotherhood: (1) all year long, singing is always tied to preparing for Holy Week; (2) the singers who will perform in any given year are named by the prior, who also chooses the makeup of each choir. The prior is thus the highest official in the brotherhood and is himself elected each year by the entire membership. Naturally, all the brethren-singers have aspirations of being chosen by him for such a prestigious task.

In the scheme outlined above, one cannot sing without being chosen; that is, without being touched, in a sense, by the prior's grace. Thus it is that every year he must find twelve singers while at the same time passing over at least that many. The twelve chosen ones are called the *apostoli* [apostles], and they will make up the three ritual choirs for Holy Monday. These choirs are named respectively for one of the three songs they perform during a day-long procession, the "Miserere" (Psalm 50), the "Stabat Mater," and the "Jesu." Of these, the "Stabat Mater" ("Stabba" for short) is the most highly valued; it is the "Hammerklavier," the *Goldberg Variations* of this repertoire (CD no. 6). The entire setup—at once sacred and profane, social and political—makes for a climate of rivalry and jealousy among the singers, and contributes to the exceptional richness of the tradition.

Great attention is always paid to the personality of each *coro* [choir]. Just as blue and yellow do not result in a variegated hue but in a distinct color (i.e., green) that carries no clues as to its composite origin, so too a choir's character cannot be reduced to the individuals who constitute it. Out of multiplicity comes elemental simplicity; out of combined differences, singularity. It is nothing less than a marvel to observe each year the brethren gathering two or three times a week in the little church of Santa Maria, especially during Lent, to prepare for their *Lunissanti* [Holy Monday]. The marvel has to do with the unexpected makeup of the choirs. Even though the singers know one another and one another's respective vocal colors, nothing is as unpredictable as the commingling of voices that have never before sung together.

The brethren's singing (which is readily observable, so numerous are the occasions for it) has a definite goal—one might even call it an aesthetic project—which may be realized more or less well in each performance. They are not looking to produce a broad spectrum from their combined voices, but rather to get the most out of the different consonances available in a chord. As they sing, it is as if their attention—not to mention their intention—is focused not on a vast spectrum, but on a much narrower frequency band in which the voices suddenly double (as the singers themselves say), bringing out another voice called the *quintina*. The *quintina* is produced by the fusion of partials from different voices matching.[2] It stems from the perfect "accord"[3] of the singers, and their combined voices unite to make it fully audible.

Being a singer means many things besides skillfully controlling one's voice. It involves having a certain attitude and knowing the repertoire, for instance. But it also means knowing how to talk about singing and being able to critique it. Such critique revolves around particular performances. There is no discussion of the musical or compositional system per se, since the repertoire is entirely memorized and faithfully transmitted from singer to singer and from generation to generation, and there is no need to talk of trivial things. There is no greater pleasure the ethnomusicologist can (and should) indulge in than to step back from the immediate constraints of reciprocity that arise from the act of singing, and to listen retrospectively to his or her recordings, side by side with the singers themselves. The brethren of Santa Maria are experts: Their commentary is as precise as their singing is exact (although this does not preclude their having a rather singular relationship to truth).

Saying, Thinking, Doing

The 1980s, by and large, were a time of peace. The passage of time was punctuated by the usual small, local disputes, without which the Oratory would not be the Oratory. Back then, everyone sang with everyone, and two or three singers were unanimously admired for the quality of their voices, their experience, and their stylistic beauty. A few years later there were major problems of internal cohesion in the Oratory, which ultimately led to a schism. The very best singers are still there, but those who have gone over to the other camp deny that they're any good. The detractors never tire of pointing out the faults of the very singers they had praised to high heaven only a few years before—and who now find themselves in Hades! All of this is delivered with an air of confidentiality and regret, for no one enjoys renouncing his longtime friends. But the facts cannot be ignored: As circumstances shift, so does the truth.[4]

Truth and "beauty"—which is but truth in its aesthetic guise—have no meaning except contextually and pragmatically. They are tied to allegiances, to affective relationships, and to the shared practice of singing. Meaning is always multiple. It is a way of giving local genius its due and, ultimately, of paying homage to its intellectual acuity.

Many are the anecdotes that confirm this idea. Not the least interesting of these stories revolves around the prior's role and around recognizing his authority. Thus whenever the prior must make a decision, all of the brethren assert, "We have to leave it up to him—he's the boss." But how does this measure up to the facts? The following short interviews with a certain highly experienced singer—who was being, significantly, rather measured of speech—call that assertion into question. These were informal, private, unsolicited discussions that took place during short car rides between Castelsardo and Lu Bagnu at three distinct times of year.

On the "Thickness" of Discourse

JANUARY 19, *in other words before Lent but when rehearsals are already in full swing. It's noontime and I'm in La Pianedda (the central square of the newer part of town), hitchhiking to Lu Bagnu (a neighboring hamlet),* secure in the knowledge that I won't have long to wait. A singer from the Oratory who's out driving sees me, stops, and offers me a ride. Naturally we set in at once talking about singing, and he tells me (1) that, as far as he's concerned, he's not strongly "attached" to singing [attacato al canto], which is to say (2) that if the prior wants to choose others for the Stabba choir, that's fine by him. What's more, (3) he would even be pleased to find out that someone else had been chosen. At the last curve in the road before Lu Bagnu he tells me that, naturally, (4) if the prior wants him to sing, he's perfectly ready to do so.

PALM SUNDAY. *Same road, nearly same time, same singer. Of course we start talking about singing. It's the eve of Lunissanti, and a week since we've found out the makeup of the choirs. He was not among those chosen. He says (5) that the one who was chosen instead of him is "very attached to singing"—which means (6) that he is too attached—and he complains, after all, (7) that that singer is often chosen. The first interpretation (8) is that the other one is chosen too often; the second interpretation is (9) that he himself is not chosen often* enough. *The conversation keeps going even after we've arrived in Lu Bagnu. The car is parked by the side of the road, as if we might talk for a while yet. And when we say goodbye it feels like something is being left unsaid. Despite appearances and the sincere tone of the conversation, the polite discretion shown at leave-taking may be ascribed above all to rhetorical precaution. There had been a noticeable change in my interlocutor's position from (1) to (9), a change paralleling that in the situation. Undeniably, the reason for his initial refusal was to avoid influencing the prior (who, it seems, had felt perfectly justified in eliminating his name). But his true feelings lay elsewhere. While trying to avoid being too forward or giving the impression that he wanted to take another's place, this singer—like so many others—actually wanted/wants to sing.*

THE DAY AFTER LUNISSANTI. *Ran into him again, once more in La Pianedda. It's the happy hour at Gaston's, where we can talk in semi-confidence. Without actually coming out and saying it, this same singer lets it be known[5] (10) that he had been disappointed by the choirs that had performed the previous evening. He makes a few criticisms (11) of the* falzittu *in the* Stabba, *who, for various reasons (12), he believes is a rival; he reminds me (13) that the* Stabba *is a difficult piece to sing and (14) it's best not to be too old when taking on the* carréra[6] *(which means that the one who sang was too old, the implication being that he himself, who is younger, would have been better, etc.). In conclusion, he states (15) that it is a fault* [sbaglio] *to be (too) attached to singing (see point 5 above). The humility he had shown in the beginning has now become discreet criticism. But it has also led, ultimately, to exposing error[7] in the name of justice and rightfulness.*

The brethren say over and over—and they are uncharacteristically unanimous on this point—that "one must remain at the prior's disposal." All of them will emphatically tell you that one must not question his orders nor contest his initiatives. Be that as it may, in practice things are a bit more complicated, for no one blindly follows his decisions and, when all is said and done, few comply. Thus, for a singer who considers himself to be worthy of the name,[8] to be at the prior's disposal means to be ready to be part of a choir. For the less ambitious, a *Miserere* will do just fine; for those with slightly loftier aspirations, a *Stabba* is what they're after.

"Being at the prior's disposal" can thus mean something fairly specific, as made abundantly clear by an incident in 1973, when some *Stabba* singers refused to lower themselves to sing the *Miserere,* "that piece of shit." In fact, "being at the prior's disposal" often does not mean doing his bidding, but rather being ready to have your own desires fulfilled by him and given his stamp of authority. To say that you are "at his disposal" is a superficial declaration: By renouncing control over your fate you are really making a hidden solicitation. It can happen that this renouncing is imbued with spiritual intent and is an act of real generosity. It's a way of saving face and of steeling yourself against possible disillusion. Yet at the same time, letting the prior know that you are ready to accept not being chosen is above all a way of letting him know that you expect to be chosen.

The Affective Realm and Its Disorders

Singing does not consist merely of producing notes and melodies, however beautiful, but rather first and foremost of entering into a relationship with another. Singing means being willing to share moments of great emotional intensity. This comes with the territory, if one is to sing polyphonically. We can see this even more clearly by considering the contrapositive of this statement: To refuse such sharing makes it quite impossible to sing. In a word, to sing together you have to like each other: "And how are you going to sing with X or Y if you don't like them (*se non gli vuoi bene*)? It's impossible. . . . And if by chance you're able to do it, well, I can tell you that the song feels long—really long!"[9]

What we're talking about here is not an intellectual calculation, but rather an entirely visceral, direct reaction. It's no more explainable than, say, a dislike for certain foods, and its very intimacy is at the heart of the mechanism by which the other is accepted or rejected. Singing is an intense act, in which one cannot but get personally involved, and that's precisely why it's so satisfying . . . and so problematic.

Singing's main function is to act as a lightning rod for the emotions; it orients them and makes them meaningful by giving them an acoustic form. It thus imposes an order on the emotions while at the same time constantly turning them topsy-turvy because of the exigencies of performance. The four singers must utterly accept each other emotionally for the choir to succeed. Without that acceptance the singers would never be able to enter into the physical and acoustic proximity necessitated by song. In these affective relations all the senses are pressed into service by that organ of great sensuality, the mouth. First, there is hearing, of course. The harmonies—sustained by the *voci lunghe,* wedged in against each other and bounced back by the walls of the church, of the sacristy, or of the narrow village streets—create a sort of rapture. The singers lengthen certain notes as from sheer pleasure. At the end of each phrase each catches his breath together with the others, and, still with the others, shapes the following phrase. Thus the song is communally constructed, right up till the end, with the feeling that it's being recreated with each performance. But then there's sight: The singers watch each other from a short distance away and adjust the speed of musical and textual delivery according to what they read on the others' lips. And, finally, there's smell—the others' breath—and, sometimes, there's touch.

Naturally, during ritual performances singers do not touch each other, and one cannot but notice the propriety required by the practice of singing. It's only in other situations—during the *prove* or around a table—that relations are more relaxed, especially after a successful performance, when singers grab each other by the arm or the shoulder and embrace. Some of them show their joy directly—an almost childlike elation at having achieved something beautiful, as if they are rediscovering some of the many wonders wrapped up in song. Others are more introverted, merely smiling with the satisfaction of having trusted each other for a few minutes. In every case of successful singing, there is always a moment when one lets down one's guard. The beauty of the singing is in direct proportion to the proximity and the complicity it engenders among the singers. In this connection, if the formality of the singing creates distance, it also creates tension and emotion. The more formal and ritual the situation, the more reserved the singers are with each other, since they are more focused on the singing itself. As proof, one need only mention that with a little practice it's possible to tell just by listening whether a recording was made in a sacred, intense situation or in a more lighthearted, secular one.[10]

In any case, singing is done with the body. One can't but hear the "grain" of a singer's voice. At the same time, he picks up and accepts the other's voice, in all of its individuality. Together they build a work in the moment, whose function is to give an acoustic form to shared experiences. This form is constructed by the protagonists themselves, and it gets translated into musical harmony.

To sing is thus to offer a kind of testimony of one's self. Singers create together a communal work that is born from the intimate marriage between the heart and the body, and whose success depends on the extent to which these are relied upon. The acoustic result makes clear to the eyes and ears of all whether the project has done what it has set out to do. If the performance is a flop, it means that nothing is happening among the singers. On the other hand, musical grace is the tangible reflection of their own human grace.[11]

There is much speculation in the Oratory about why the singing doesn't always come out right. But this is a delicate question in that it involves the very people who are asking it. There's no way to ask it without implicating either oneself (which is difficult to swallow) or the other singers (which is easier to accept and more common). Often what gets blamed is none other than the song itself. This is a lot more convenient, since it is just an abstract form that has no reality except in performance; it is, in a word, a scapegoat. "That *Stabba* wasn't very good," is another way of saying (after a performance), "We didn't sing very well." And you can also throw in for good measure, "Hey, you know, that's how it always is with the *Stabba*. Sometimes it sounds great and sometimes it doesn't. . . . You just can't predict!"

When you're not blaming the song itself, you can blame the *chiave* or pitch level.[12] In fact, finding the right *chiave* is one of the skills of any competent singer, but sometimes it seems to have a life of its own. The singers may fumble around all night looking for it, as if it existed in an ideal world accessible only through inspiration or divine grace.

In practice the *chiave* is not necessarily the reason singers may be having trouble—it may just be a pretext. That is, if the singers are not happy with it, it could be that their willingness to sing together just isn't there:

> The rule is that if you consider yourself to be a real singer, you only want to sing with people you like. . . . As a case in point, not long ago I started the

song off and two of the other singers in the choir said that the *chiave* was low (too low, that is). Twice I started again, and they still said it was low. So I put it really high—as high as my *bassu* will go, and for them it was still low. So I told them to go to hell (*ho mandato un "va fanculo"*) and I said, "That's the last time you'll sing with me, because that's just how my *bassu* is—I can't change it." Actually, they were saying it was low because they didn't want to sing with me. . . . Afterwards they sang with someone else—and they even sang well!—with a *chiave* that was lower than the second one I had given!

Love, Absence, Jealousy

Singing entails interaction on a deeply emotional level; it is therefore no exaggeration to call it an act of love. It accompanies, or reveals, feelings of mutual understanding or else violent breaches, and like love, it is uncompromising in its expectations of faithfulness. Moreover, singing has all the common or incidental features of any love story: strategies of seduction, fits of jealousy, desertions, renewed seduction, dirty tricks, provocation, the game of making family alliances, offers of compromise. It is love in a nutshell—the whole gamut's there.

Such excess of emotion is an omnipresent fact, even though the brethren never mention it, or if they do it is only with the greatest discretion. But you need only observe the looks they give, the way they draw near or painfully pull back, their nostalgia, or how they can lust after a reconciliation, to know that love is indeed what this is all about: "It's been three years since I last sang with Salvatore . . . and I don't know if I'll ever sing with him again" (a singer).

Singing serves as a reminder of the date of a breakup at the same time that it points to the conditions of reconciliation. Certain remarks betray this same idea. For instance, a singer might announce to the group at large, *Sono innamorato di mio cugino!* [I'm in love with my (male) cousin!] As exaggerated as this might be—it is not meant literally—it is no less revelatory. For the cousin in question is, of course, a singer; it is inconceivable that he not be. Love and song are related metonymically. You love someone else by means of his voice, for his voice, and through his voice; no longer to stand his voice is no longer to stand him period. But love and song are also related metaphorically. "To sing with someone" is like "going out with him," so to speak. Both are intense acts, and singing bears the marks of shared love stories, which may be beautiful, sad, or tragic. They may also be tragicomic, especially if the singer makes use of the Oratory's two invincible weapons, which can always extricate a person from a difficult spot, namely humor aimed at oneself and irony aimed at others.

Singing sets up a double conquest, the one acoustic, the other human: acoustic because one must "place" one's voice then insert it into a choir of companions whom one knows well; human because one tries to get close to another through song. If this proximity does not arise naturally but is at the same time intensely desired, the attempt to get close can become a sort of hard sell.

> One night, a much-admired falzittu is working late, and afterwards, rather than going to the sacristy for the prove [rehearsals], he decides to stay in, most likely just to enjoy the comforts of home and to take care of his little daughter. He and his voice are well liked in the Oratory. The bogi are especially sad about his repeated absence. But out of discretion, they can't bring themselves to ask him to come sing with them. Would there be any justification for such an act? Isn't a brother's first priority to spend time at the Oratory? It would be unseemly to point this out. The singers wonder what to do, but actually they're hoping that the prior will pay the falzittu a visit to suggest that he come.

The emotional dimension of song only makes sense within a context of social interaction, and it feeds off of interpersonal relations that have rich histories. This is where it becomes clear that a voice doesn't just produce sound. In every performance, the resulting sound depends on pre-existing relationships. That is, the experiences of each participant with another go back many years and include long stretches of time spent together. When a quarrel arises, musical moments are remembered and they constitute proof of a friendship past. For instance, so-and-so might feel unjustly betrayed and declare, "I sang with him on Thursday, only to have him double-cross me on Saturday. Can you believe it?" Singing bears witness to what two people once meant to each other, even if things have since changed. In fact, singing is what makes the betrayal apparent in the first place, because if it hadn't been there to attest the love that one had had for another the act of betrayal would have gone unnoticed.

Not only does the voice come to life through the one who owns it, it cannot exist without him. In other words, behind every singer is a man—from a co-singer's perspective, either a companion or a rival, or perhaps the one who doted on him a few days ago or that very evening, but also possibly the one who irritated him with an unkind remark or whose behavior he finds generally intolerable.

Song takes over where everyday life leaves off, and the first cannot exist without the second. Singing is but a particularly intense moment within a larger shared narrative from which it draws its sustenance. And all it takes for it to provide absolutely nothing for the participants is for the relations between them to be mediocre, or, in the worst cases, for a singer to find nothing but shortcomings in his companion's face or voice, or a dispiritedness, or physical or mental ugliness. Admittedly, slight distance in a friendship, or partially concealed hostility, are not enough to preclude the possibility of singing together (it depends to some extent on the personalities involved). And yet someone singing under such circumstances is likely to ask himself, from the beginning to the end of the song, "What the hell are we doing here?" If that is the case, the performers might wish for the song to be over as quickly as possible, without actually saying so. But they would not have the option of stopping the song, because such an interruption would be interpreted correctly for what it was: a slap in the face. And even though a song is always finished once it's started, this is done more out of basic courtesy than for musical reasons.

But the pleasure of song is so great that it leads singers to make sure they stay on good terms with those who know how to sing. In other words, the quality of another's voice is in itself a kind of enticement, and his voice is what draws you to him. In this connection, song has the strange power of transfiguring relationships as well as faces. The voice not only makes known another's presence, but it affects the person emitting it as well, especially when it is a beautiful voice, and it confers grace upon this person. This transfiguration is written on the singers' very faces. Photographs make this quite clear: Musical expression deforms their faces, or rather re-forms them in a specific dimension, and it sometimes happens that in the tense look of a singer it becomes difficult to recognize the features of an otherwise familiar face.

Differences and Debarments

In sum, then, in order to sing one must love (one another). The obverse is also true: Discord or a lack of love renders singing impossible. And this is in fact the yardstick by which to measure commitment to singing. It is the reason singing is necessary, and it ranks first among its virtues in that it forces you to get along (well). This observation points up how singing is not only spiritual in its content, but is equally spiritual in its very nature, since bound up in the act of singing is the love for one's fellow human being. Let us not forget that this love ought not be taken for granted, or that in these disagreements the protagonists are most often singers and the apple of discord is song. Singing together amounts to seeking a state of harmony that is all the more precious in that it can never be taken for granted, and because it is rare indeed.[13]

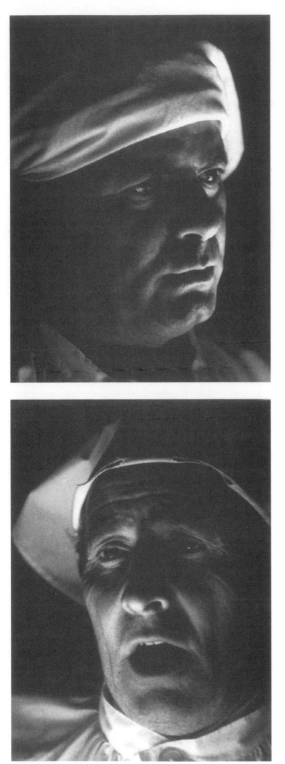

Figure 4.1 Bassu. Photos by
Bachisio Masia. Reproduced
by permission.

Figure 4.2 Falzittu.

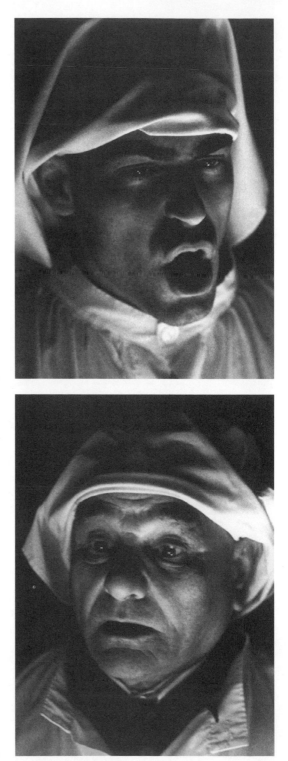

Figure 4.3 Contra.

Figure 4.4 Bogi.

One young *falzittu* was at the center of a major conflict in the Oratory. He said that he was not liked, "especially by the other *falzitti*," and added, "Hey, it's not just a coincidence that they're the ones who don't like me." No matter how much a *falzittu* might try to hide it from others or even from himself, he always tends to see other *falzitti* as rivals. The same holds true for a *bogi* and other *bogi*, a *contra* and other *contre*, etc. That is, it's only too common for men with the same vocal register to have either catty ("sweet-sour") or acerbic relations. On the other hand, men with complementary vocal registers create bonds by inviting each other to sing together. As a result, it's common to find singers with complementary voices sitting at the same table of a café. In fact, leisure time spent together is a natural prolongation of musical time during which the brethren sing together. Whereas polyphony necessarily makes use of contrasting voices, conversation takes over where habitually shared moments of intensity leave off.

This goes against the adage "birds of a feather flock together," since song encourages singers to draw together based on their dissimilarities. Song sorts singers by their sound and assigns distinct and complementary roles that have to do with technique, acoustics, and aesthetics. As for the singers, they seem to have interiorized these differences, since each voice type is clearly different from the others. This is evident in the singers' faces and in their body language. Each voice type would appear to have its own gestalt of physical traits and behavior, and with a little practice one can learn to tell if a singer is a *bassu*, a *contra*, a *bogi*, or a *falzittu* fairly reliably, even without ever hearing him sing.

> *There would seem to be a connection between a singer's voice type, his physical appearance, and his behavior. The observed data lead to generalizations rather than absolute laws. A* falzittu *tends to be nervous, lively, energetic, gaunt, and is often frugal. He is independent and always appears to hover above the fray. The* bogi's *personality seems to transfer over from the role that befalls him in singing: Like the expressivity of his voice, he is often emotional, unstable, and fragile; he is frequently described as a prima donna. By nature endowed with authority that can sometimes be coupled with conceit, the* contra *does in fact occupy a central position. He is often called the* colonna *(column) of the choir. He has a "corpulent" voice, and it is as if this timbral thickness must necessarily be reflected in the thickness of his person. A typical* bassu *has ample chest capacity; he is a heavyweight, both literally and figuratively. Often broad of frame, he is usually a bit heavy and slow in his movements—which does not necessarily mean that he is ungraceful. On the contrary, his slowness often gives him a certain theatrical quality.*

But beyond this diversity in appearance and behavior, all singers have in common the same emotional base. And just as in love, the great majority of conflicts arise from the disorders of this emotional base; these may be summed up in a single word: jealousy. Rare indeed are those singers who admit to being jealous of others. But rarer still are those who in fact are not. For in the Oratory, real and presumed behaviors do not always coincide and practice seldom agrees with theory. For instance, most singers deny ever having engaged in rejection and claim to be capable of singing with anyone. But as soon as the prior pushes them up against the wall, there emerges a different story entirely. In order to avoid singing with so-and-so, a singer will not hesitate to show insincerity; he might all of a sudden conveniently develop a sore throat, fatigue, or trouble of some kind. No one is fooled by these avoidance tactics and everyone uses them in one way or another.

We would do well to pause here and consider for a moment the malfunctions tied to singing, which are as numerous as they are revealing. Any driver knows that if you want to understand your car you have to take it to the shop, which is where it can be taken apart and the function of each "organ" looked into. Similarly, the uncertainties of a choral performance, the problems it raises, and, in the end, its failure very often point to gears that seize up or to faulty transmissions.

For if to sing is to be willing to enter into an intense relationship with someone else, to refuse to sing is to confirm that this relationship does not exist—that it cannot or should not exist. To refuse to sing is to reveal a rift. In other words, to join a choir is "to be with," while refusing to do so is "to position oneself against." Whether the rift comes as a result of singing or was already there is immaterial; what matters is the result and how it affects the group.

No prior who is worthy of the name can wholeheartedly accept rejection by singers who refuse to sing together. As a result, singing has the strange property of making public not only discord but also the very desire to negate concord. The power of song to reveal emotional truths is one measure of its importance.

Born and Raised in Song

Singing gives each brother a place and a role. But this place and this role can never be taken for granted: It's up to him to acquire them, from year to year and from choir to choir.

The first time a singer is "inserted" into a choir is a bit like a baptism. The young singer is first immersed in the voices of the others, who exert pressure on him by watching over him as they sing. He can barely hear himself; his voice is caught up in the density of the choral fabric. At the same time, he tries to find his footing. This footing consists in the basic sequence of notes making up the melody he is to utter, as well as a vocal color that can round out the wide spectrum in which the other voices of the choir are intimately amalgamated. The parallel movement is deceptively simple: At first, a beginner can have trouble finding his own part; he gets sidetracked and, without even realizing it, doubles one of the other voices he should in fact be complementing. If he does as he is asked and sings louder, he can no longer hear the others. Louder still, and he can't even hear himself anymore. Since he hasn't yet domesticated his vocal apparatus, the harder he tries the more he gets off track.

Paradoxically, by singing with his companions he discovers his own voice. He must simultaneously adjust everything in relation to them: loudness, intonation, timbre, breath control, and tempo (all along, he has been told to follow the others and to watch their mouths). Later, as he gradually finds his place in the choir, he figures out how he can contribute to the whole and he asserts himself by monitoring the sound—a skill he masters gradually. His voice then clears a swath in the overall spectrum; it renders it complete, fills it out, finds its niche in the balance as a whole. And from this he then realizes just how irreplaceable he is. If he changes his vocal production, it's not just his own voice that is affected, but the sound of the whole ensemble. At this point the novice suddenly feels fully involved and in direct contact with the others. As he masters his technique, each of his phrases acquires a pattern that gels in his consciousness and quickly takes on an ideal form he tries to reproduce. From this he realizes the role he can play and the indispensable place that thenceforth belongs to him. In this assimilation stage, as he tries to mold his style, he will learn to control his breath. This is necessary because in contrast to the spoken utterance, song demands a steady volume—or even an increase in volume—at the end of a phrase, just when the breath is petering out.

But while the young singer discovers in increments the role he must play, the musical sphere stretches before him like a field to be conquered, on which his limits are very quickly demarcated. And the others let him know, as soon as he's finished singing, that *il canto si deve ragionare sempre* [singing should always be reasoned and reasoned about], as they say in the Oratory, and that is what makes it beautiful. He will thus have to understand his faults and correct them. From then on the novice enters the maturation stage, during

which he will be expected to take initiatives, even if it means getting criticized for them, because singing is not just following others, it's constructing
a musical work as a group. He will have to listen to his companions while at
the same time asserting his authority by now adopting the personal *giru* (a
kind of ornamentation) of some prestigious singer, now suggesting an acce-
lerando, now emphasizing a particular ornamentation—in short, by finding
a style and a behavior that will be uniquely his. Rather quickly he will acquire
l'orgoglio del canto [singer's pride] in order to become a true singer; he will
be willing to enter into conflict with others, thus forgetting that humility is
necessary to the performance of sacred song.

Orgoglio del canto versus humility—this antithesis gives rise to numerous
debates. One or the other of these cultural values is invariably reflected in a
performance, and the musical sound always bears the signs of either pride
or respect for the other: The criteria for judging a choral performance center
not only on singing but also on the singers' respective moral and ideological positions, as well as on how much of a yen for supremacy they have. In
other words, when they sing, what is heard is their particular way of doing,
their particular way of being.

One of several hot topics of discussion, as it happens, has to do with
"putting oneself forward." This is not a question of good taste but rather
of self-presentation. A singer is not lightly forgiven for claiming to be that
which he is not, or for trying at all costs to exhibit an unjustified supremacy.
In order to sing loudly (that is to say, more loudly than the others), one
must be as morally deserving of it as one is physically capable: From pride
to presumption is but a small step. In a way, a singer's musical statement
refers back to his moral image and to his psychological presence. Nothing
in all of this, however, is taken for granted. The sometimes lively discussions that extend a *Stabba* or *Jesu* performance do not only revolve around
musical figures but also around what the music represents ("figures"). As
a result, if song indeed constitutes territory to be conquered, it is partly
because it is the ground where singers earn their legitimacy. Song reveals
their human and moral status and makes this status audible, as it were.
Physical prowess, that is to say singing loudly, represents moral strength,
and this is where ethics and aesthetics enter either into a harmonious or a
conflictive relationship.

It is nevertheless possible for the two antagonistic values of song—personal challenge and collective cohesion—to have points of convergence. To
be sure, a singer might take manifest pleasure in *buttando fuori* [throwing
overboard] his companions, or in *sbarcando* [disembarking] them, to use

a metaphor especially apt in this land of fishermen. But the efforts of each singer to "stay in the boat" can result in cohesion as well. The energy it takes to "limit the damage" caused by one or the other's eccentricity, as well as the desire to take up the challenge and the capacity to transform individual initiative into a global dynamic, all play a large role in determining the quality of a performance. When these elements are present there is a certain generosity of spirit that surfaces, with the result that a risk is turned into an achievement. But it can also happen that the singers will be unable to agree or to form a fine choir. The difficulties they face are complex. In the end it rests with the prior to stay on top of such perilous situations. He must take into account the individuality of each singer and then take appropriate action, not only to avoid accidents, but also to put together choirs that are both strong and harmonious.

The key to performing well thus lies precisely in the balance between the singers' loudness—intended as a kind of aural gauntlet—and the harmony they make, which is sustained by their mutual understanding. These singers may be rivals, but they are at the same time riveted to the same task, namely that of singing well. They are compelled to act in solidarity, especially in an official context (above all, for a *Lunissanti*), since in the end it is the entire choir that is being judged, and not the individual voices that make it up. As if viewed through a prism, each voice radiates an iridescence, but the overall color comes into focus only in the ensemble as a whole. This color affords pleasure, pride, and advantage to each singer. And yet the shortcomings of a single member are enough to ruin the mysterious alchemy.

This solidarity shows up, of course, on the *carréra*. If there is a problem among the members of a choir, whenever they're not singing along the processional route, they can be seen, heads down, refraining from talking to each other. The *carréra* is never a place to argue. But the day after *Lunissanti* is always a time of discussion—that's when the score is tallied up. Singers who are insecure or presumptuous—or both—don't hesitate to solicit in private the assessments of experts or of friends, expecting compliments or, more especially, a denigration of their rivals' performances. For to sing well means "to sing better than the others." It's not enough to hear that your choir was good. It has to have been better—better than the other choirs in the procession; better than what was heard over the past ten years; the best, period. Using this same logic, the other choirs must necessarily have been less good, or mediocre, or even *hanno fatto brutta figura* [have lost face] and made fools of themselves. There are no winners without losers. Such is the price of victory.

If in the Oratory there are numerous brethren who sing (about thirty in all), only a handful of these are considered to be true *cantori* [singers]. This small number, arrived at by the most rigorous criteria, serves as a reminder of just how demanding singing is. What sets these singers apart is their ability to sing "everything," even if their preferences, of course, run toward the two or three great pieces of the repertoire. In addition, they have stamina, power, beautiful voices, and especially a *portata inconfondibile* [an unmistakable phrasing, a personal imprint]. Last but not least, they are dependable, and hence are frequently chosen by the priors for the *carréra*. Their *orgoglio del canto* rests on their know-how and hallmarks their personality. For them, singing equals not holding back; it equals knowing how to associate with others while being always ready to give of themselves. For them, again, what an act means and the energy expended in carrying it out are one and the same. In other words, it is this very energy that gives meaning to what they sing. But if singing is essentially an expenditure of energy, this energy, for the true *cantori,* is best spent in favorable circumstances: between friends one can count on, when the emotional bond is strong enough to make it worthwhile; or, on the contrary, when there is a challenge to be taken up.

In the latter case—that is, in response to a challenge—singing well consists more of "squashing" one's rivals by the intensity of one's *portata* [prominence] than in trying for exact harmony and perfect balance within the choir. In accordance with the code of *la sfida* [the dare, the challenge], one must dominate one's fellow singers or even humiliate them.

> *During a conflict between two groups in the Oratory that lasted from 1990 to 1993, singers were giving reminders of their legitimacy by singing more than usual . . . and above all by keeping it no secret that they were doing so. One faction used the cathedral's sound system to broadcast a particular singer's voice to the entire town—the idea was to show that he had achieved la* padronanza *[the mastery] of the* Magnificat, *which was the specialty of a singer from the other group. This second faction rallied to the cause by getting together to sing at someone's house once or twice a week—out of sheer pleasure, naturally, but also to get the other camp riled up and to show them that they had not given up on retaking the Oratory.*

There is an obvious contradiction between the notion of a singing "challenge" and the communal or Christian rule that is built on principles of sharing. I cannot evoke this contradiction without being reminded that the word *bogi* refers as much to an individual "voice" as it does to the collective choir: *Fare una bogi* [making a *bogi*] means to make one's own voice heard as well as that of the choir in which it is inserted. The contradiction between personal vocal expression and choral participation thus takes on a meta-phorical sense. Through singing one expresses one's relation to the other, a relation in which each singer labors on behalf of the whole while at the same time listening to the others. Paradoxically, the more each singer surrenders to this relation, the stronger it is, for singing is above all a gift of oneself.

The Spiritual Dimension of Singing

This gift of oneself is a measure of singing's spiritual nature; indeed, singing taps some indefinable part of one's innermost being, a kind of intimate force that one offers selflessly to others. This process induces the singer to reveal himself to others as well as to himself. As acoustic analysis clearly shows, this particular form of polyphony does not result from a simple layering of voices, but rather from a search for a fusion in which each singer participates and is supported by the other singers to cover the acoustic spectrum as completely as possible. Polyphony thus restates in its own way the principle that the whole is greater than the sum of its parts. Whenever each singer is with his fellows he becomes larger than himself.

From this it follows that singers' personalities are necessarily paradoxical; they are extroverted (since they must give to others) and introverted (since what they give comes from within). There are those singers who are known for their "coldness" and for offering nothing in their singing for the simple reason that they find it hard to share anything of themselves in everyday life. . . . And then there are the true singers. In the Oratory true singers are judged by their aptitude for "inhabiting" song and their capacity to bring out something of themselves. Singing, it is said, is *lo spiritu diventato corpo* [spirit become body].

A young singer must frequent the Oratory for many years before what he can "give" acoustically as well as spiritually can be evaluated. Singing is not merely aligning musical notes but being able to share them with others and to fill them with meaning. This is why it takes so long to evaluate his aptitude for becoming a *cantore*.

The role of the prior in this spiritual organization, which is intimately linked to the practice of singing, cannot be overemphasized. Ethics and aes-thetics, spirituality and acoustics—these all blend together in his various responsibilities. On the one hand he is in charge of all essential activities of the Oratory and directs the sacrifices (in both the literal and symbolic senses of the term). Yet he himself seems to be at the center of this sacrifice, for not only does he give of himself unstintingly, he is constantly being put to the test, constantly subject to the contradictory rumors spread by some, to the irritation shown by others, to cooked-up commotion, to secret acts of petty revenge, etc. In short, he is there to suffer, as if he had to serve the sentence he would seem to have accepted along with his ecclesiastical charge. On the other hand, he is the symbolic representative of God the Father, in charge of the brotherhood and of its primary means of expression, song, which he dispenses as if it were a favor [literally "grace"] to be granted to "his" brethren according to their merit.

The brethren, for their part, are constantly seeking an inaccessible truth while consecrating themselves (the word could not be more apt) to their art. They strive to fuse their voices together while calling forth the hidden surface of their melodies, the *quintina*. The *quintina* has the purity of divine grace while at the same time inviting rapture. When it does "come out," it happens so strangely that it seems to belong to the supernatural realm.[14] This only occurs when the singing is perfect, and the *quintina* is indeed the manifestation of this perfection.

In discussing this metaphysico-sonic search, I must mention as well the incessant questioning about the notion of *chiave* or key. This *chiave* must always be exact. It bears the stamp of truth. Finding the right chiave is no mean responsibility, to the point that some singers are reluctant to start the song off because they say they can never get it right. Choosing the exact key means putting the choir on the right track; conversely, the wrong key will unfailingly lead everyone into error and—worse yet—make the blunder apparent, that is to say fully audible. The way to fix the mistake is by starting the song over from the beginning, sometimes several times in a row, until the right *chiave* is found. Or else the error is compensated for by commenting on and discussing it. In either case, everyone is abruptly brought back to earth. A finger is pointed, so to speak, at whoever slipped up. What this explicit condemnation of error accomplishes is to remind everyone where the path of justness lies.

Lest I have overemphasized the pleasures of song, let us not forget its penitential function. For singing is also a "sacrifice," in both meanings of the word: secular because the singers sacrifice time and energy, and sacred because song is a ritual offering. In order to earn the pleasurable privilege of taking center stage in the chapel and in the street, especially during Holy Week, a brother must have shown humility and abnegation, he must have buried a good fifty people, and he must have taken part in some twenty feast days throughout the year, all at the expense of his leisure activities, his rest, or his spare time. And yet, pleasure is paradoxically manifested in the songs for the dead (Psalm 50 primarily), such that the gift of oneself entails pleasure in return as well as pain. The function of this magnificent repertoire is thus fundamentally reconciliatory. It is a provider of both secret and public spiritual gratification; it is an object of personal seeking as well as a confirmation of one's own existence; and finally, it is a voicing of the ineffable.

Translator's Note

A note is in order on the use of certain words. The most fundamental of all is *le chant.* In an ordinary context, this may mean either "song," "the song," or "the act of singing." I have tried to choose the most appropriate translation for each context, but the reader should bear in mind the built-in ambiguity. In addition, most of the time, when Lortat-Jacob talks about *le chant,* he clearly means singing as it is practiced in Castelsardo. His statements of a general nature are thus not necessarily meant to apply to all human singing.

Another fundamental word is *choeur.* I have chosen to translate this as "choir," even though most English-speaking musicians would call these small ensembles "vocal quartets."

Yet another possible point of confusion lies in the various ways of designating the musical brotherhood in question. The brethren themselves refer to their organization as Santa Croce (the name of the brotherhood), or metonymically as the Oratory, the sacristy, or Santa Maria (short for Santa Maria delle Grazie, the name of the church).

The word "thickness" [*épaisseur*] deserves special mention, especially as it is applied to "meaning" [*sens*] and related concepts. This is a specialized and fairly subtle use of the word, and it is missing from most dictionary entries. Among the many definitions given by the immense *Trésor de la Langue Française* for *épaisseur* is the following: "The quality of that which appears to be imbued with a third dimension (relief, depth) and made up of numerous and varied elements that give it richness, texture (or viscosity), and density." I have variously translated the adjective *épais* as "thickly layered," "dense," or simply "thick" (with corresponding noun forms for *épaisseur*). In one case, where it is applied to the sound of a singer's voice, I have chosen "corpulent," but some of the above-mentioned quality also applies.

Interspersed throughout the chapter are quotes taken from oral conversations with members of the brotherhood. Finally, because a number of local terms are used repeatedly, we have decided to provide a short glossary. The definitions are based on the glossary entries in Lortat-Jacob's larger study on this topic, a portion of which serves as the basis of this essay.[15]

Glossary

bassu—the lowest of the four voices of the *coro*.

bogi—"voice," (1) of the four voices of the *coro*, the second highest, and the one which carries the cantus firmus; (2) the entire vocal ensemble or a song performed by it (as in *tirare una bogi*, "to strike up a song").

carréra—"the street," where processions take place—above all, the procession for Holy Week.

chiave—"key," the specific pitch level set by the *bogi* (or sometimes the *bassu*) at the beginning of each performance (see note 12).

contra (pl., *contre*)—the second lowest of the four voices of the *coro*.

coro—"choir," an ensemble of four singers, each with his own separate part. For certain items in the repertoire, and on certain occasions, a larger ensemble sings in four parts.

falzittu (pl., *falzitti*)—the highest of the four voices of a *coro*.

Lunissanti—the Monday before Easter, the feast day par excellence, the first day of Holy Week.

Miserere—Psalm 50, the most important of the songs in the brotherhood's repertoire, for which there are four musical settings (three for Holy Week, one for funerals).

orgoglio del canto—singer's pride.

portata—a personal imprint given by a singer to a song every time he sings, consisting of phrasing in general, but especially of timing.

quintina—"small fifth," "fifth voice," an acoustic phenomenon resulting from the fusion of partials of at least two different fundamentals, giving the impression of a fifth voice.

Stabba—"Stabat Mater," one of the three great songs for Holy Week, considered by many to be the most beautiful.

voci lunghe—"long voices;" the repertoire of songs associated with the Oratory (characterized by sustained notes).

Notes

1. See Ignazio Machiarella's book *Il falsobordone* on the relationship between the *falsobordone* and the oral traditions of polyphonic singing in Sicily and Sardinia (Lucca: Libreria musicale italiana, 1995).

2. For instance, the third partial of the *bassu* generally matches the second partial of the *contra*. In Castelsardo, *quintina* ["little fifth"] is a generic term used for any fusion of partials in the upper part of the spectrum. Despite the name, the *quintina*

is not necessarily a fifth above one or another of the voices that produce it. For an interactive illustration of the phenomenon, see www.ethnomus.org. (Trans.)

3. In French, the word *accord* means both "agreement/understanding/social harmony" and "musical chord." Both senses are meant here, since singers must be perfectly in tune with each other, both musically and emotively, for the *quintina* to come into focus. (Trans.)

4. Audio recordings can serve as a useful corrective here. In this particular case, they show just how beautiful the choirs were at the end of the 1980s and remind the listener how well the singers were still getting along.

5. I am distinguishing here between merely implying something [*sous-entendre*] and letting something be known [*laisser entendre*]. The latter involves a greater degree of intentional clarification.

6. "The street"—the place where religious processions are held. (Trans.)

7. The error [*sbaglio*] in this case belongs as much to the prior as to the disappointing singer.

8. But who is not necessarily so. In this connection one ought to distinguish between *uno che "si sente" cantore* [someone who thinks he's a singer] and *uno che è veramente cantore* [someone who really is a singer].

9. On the other hand, liking each other too much leads to exclusivity—a situation where singers refuse to sing with anyone else. This can get in the way of the prior's choosing "his" choirs.

10. Like seasonal fruit, singing is cultivated each year in time for it to be ripe for Holy Week. There is always an obvious difference in quality, and especially in emotional investment, between recordings made during the first rehearsals—at the end of winter—and those made just before Easter. A similar jump in quality may be perceived between the rehearsals and the actual performance for *Lunissanti*. Those for *Lunissanti* are always the densest.

11. I am reminded here of the felicitous expression "grace notes" to designate melodic ornamentation.

12. The pitch level in question (*diapason* in French and other Romance languages) has to do with the absolute pitch of any particular note and not the "key" in the sense of tonality. The range of variability of this pitch level for any given song is roughly a whole tone. Differences of less than a semitone can have a noticeable effect on the musical experience. (Trans.)

13. Cf. the words of a singer: "*Santa Maria non ha mai conosciuto pace*" [Santa Maria has never known peace]. Or, even more eloquently put, "*Santa Maria non fu mai stata in pace*" [Santa Maria has never stayed peaceful]. The change of verb in the second version indicated a permanent state, as if "non-peace" were integral to the very nature of the Oratory.

14. Once during a lecture/discussion held in Castelsardo, in which I had presented a technical analysis of the *quintina* [resultant voice], a singer from the Oratory summed up my thoughts on the matter by contrasting "physical" sounds, which are emitted

by the singers, with "metaphysical" sounds, which are not. As the etymology of the word "metaphysical" implies, this second category of sounds encompasses the first.

15. Bernard Lortat-Jacob, *Chants de Passion: Au Coeur d'une confrérie de Sardaigne* (Paris: le Cerf, 1998). Thanks to Laurence Rondinet and Jean-Claude Lévy for facilitating the publication of this essay.

5

Music and Morality: John Curwen's Tonic Sol-fa, the Temperance Movement, and the Oratorios of Edward Elgar

CHARLES EDWARD McGUIRE

Starting in the mid-nineteenth century, the rise of amateur singing revitalized English music festivals, leading in turn to what has been called the English Musical Renaissance. While the veneration of Handel's and Mendelssohn's oratorios enabled the provincial music festival to continue at this time, successful British composition only began to flourish when a variety of sight-singing methods, including Tonic Sol-fa, increased overall musical literacy for the working classes. Yet the emergence of this new musical culture was only a fortuitous by-product of the sight-singing movement. The primary goal of sight-singing's proponents was to increase the moral character of individual singers by guiding them toward greater ease in singing religious hymns. A strong secondary goal was to give the middle and working classes rational recreation: a morally edifying leisure-time activity that would both strengthen domestic ties and provide a distraction from possible vice-ridden pursuits.[1]

John Curwen (1816–1880), a Congregational minister, initially promoted Tonic Sol-fa throughout Great Britain as such a distraction from vice, embracing the contemporary evangelical Christian reform agenda. As Tonic Sol-fa spread, Curwen began envisioning it as an active aid to reform organizations. He sought to emulate one of the largest contemporary reform movements, temperance, to create a more active role for Tonic Sol-fa in uplifting society. Using Tonic Sol-fa to promote temperance, he attempted to link the aims of both causes.

Curwen's Tonic Sol-fa also implicitly adopted another major political issue of nineteenth-century Great Britain: anti-Catholicism. However, Tonic Sol-fa's didactic power ultimately frustrated Curwen's anti-Catholic biases by providing the music education infrastructure that propelled to fame the English composer Edward Elgar's consummately Catholic oratorio, *The Dream of Gerontius.*

The history of the temperance movement illuminates the evangelical agenda of Tonic Sol-fa. Even before Curwen attempted to merge the two, Tonic Sol-fa imitated temperance organizations. Both movements originated as middle-class paternalistic attempts to reform the working class, envisioned and fulfilled by Evangelical Dissenters and Low-Church Anglicans. To the middle-class leadership, "temperance" was an attempt to lead the working class toward moderation in drink by showing that excessive drinking decreased efficiency in work, corrupted morals, and damaged health.[2]

Early temperance often focused so narrowly on Protestant aims that Catholic participation was nearly impossible. The Dissenters and Low-Church Anglicans who led and populated the temperance movement were also usually the most vocal critics of Catholicism, in many cases stating outright that Catholics were not Christians.[3] Catholics were consequently not welcome in this predominantly Protestant movement. For example, early temperance associations in Ireland drew the great majority of their leadership and membership from the middle-class Protestant ranks. Since temperance leaders treated intemperance as a personal moral failing of the Irish rather than a broader societal problem, negative beliefs drove potential working-class Catholic members away.[4] Religious enmity further created negative views of Catholics as undisciplined inebriates. Following their middle-class leaders, the Protestant working class living in the developing urban centers such as Liverpool, Birmingham, Manchester, Sheffield, and Leeds derided Irish Catholics both for their embrace of the papacy and their great love of drink.[5] Such views spilled first into the popular media, as Catholics were often presented as drunkards in popular English literature and caricature, and then into civil justice, as Irish Catholics were arrested more often than their Protestant English counterparts for drunk and disorderly conduct.[6] Even later in the century, after the successful temperance crusades of Catholic priests such as Father Matthew, Catholics refrained from joining the organizations of the Dissenters and the Established Anglican Church.[7] Some Protestant temperance workers called for religious unification on the issue, but this never occurred, since many prominent temperance leaders remained staunch anti-Catholics.[8]

Between 1835 and 1880, the working classes gradually gained control of temperance as part of a wider societal movement toward self-improvement.

This period coincided with the founding of many workers' self-aid organizations, such as friendly societies, mechanics' halls, and cooperatives. In the hands of working-class members, temperance shifted from a desire to encourage moderation in drinking to a demand for total abstinence from alcohol. In many areas, local temperance organizations began with evangelical "missions," which might include scientific lectures on the evils of drink from respected doctors, sermons about the moral problems drink caused, and testimonials of reformed drinkers. At the end of the mission, those interested would surrender themselves to teetotalism, often signing a pledge. Organizers punctuated the missions with entertainment, presenting choirs and bands to reinforce the edifying sermons and testimonials.

In the wake of such missions, many communities formed their own temperance societies and built permanent halls, which became social and education centers. To rival the strong pull of the public house, typically the only source of affordable local entertainment for the working classes, temperance halls held Sunday picnics, sponsored scientific and literary lectures, built cheap lending libraries, and gave classes on a wide variety of subjects, including music. For many permanent temperance associations, music's rational recreation let the working classes form social circles, replacing those found at the pub. For instance, annual picnics of the Birstall's Heavy Woolen District Temperance Union culminated with the members singing Handel's *Messiah*. This was not considered a performance, just entertainment for the singers and non-singers alike.[9] Such associations typically formed choirs and bands and organized subscription concerts. As the temperance movement evolved during the second half of the nineteenth century, so too did the type and amount of music used at temperance meetings. Initially, music was simply a means to interest people in temperance meetings—free entertainment to capture a potentially larger audience. This was certainly the desired effect of the original middle-class temperance workers, who included a few singers or instrumentalists within their gatherings to punctuate the speeches about moderation. The large evangelical temperance meetings of the 1870s (often called "Gospel" temperance) usually featured large choirs, bands, and even the occasional orchestra. For instance, the massive temperance meetings held annually in the Crystal Palace from the 1860s on always included choral contests open only to temperance choirs.

As the movement grew, music was moved from simple entertainment to a central thrust of temperance organizations because it aided recruitment of members, especially children. By the 1860s, a prominent children's offshoot of the main temperance movement known as the "Band of Hope" was formed, in the belief that successful temperance required preventive alcoholic abstinence in children. Most Bands of Hope prominently included children's singing classes. Even though temperance remained a predominantly volunteer movement, music was considered so essential to these organizations that a substantial part of the Band of Hope's budget would be used to hire someone to teach the children to sing and lead the children's choir formed through singing classes. Such a music teacher was usually one of only two paid employees within any local Band of Hope organization.[10]

Through this musical promotion, Bands of Hope became one of the best advertisements for the temperance movement. Between 1862 and 1886, annual competitions of the Bands of Hope choirs from the entire nation were held in the Crystal Palace. These competitions blossomed from presenting concerts of 1,000 singers to eventually spacing three "monster" combined concerts over a single day, including a total of 15,000 child singers.[11] Such concerts gave the movement publicity, as they were widely reported in the press. Finally, temperance organizers believed that Band of Hope children were the best possible influence to promote temperance within the home, thinking that the sight of children practicing temperance songs and hymns would turn intemperate parents from the evils of drink. It was strongly believed that such moral music, sung by adults and children alike, would spread throughout society and consequently win both popular and domestic support for the temperance cause.

A concern with promoting moral music for children and adults also lay at the heart of the Tonic Sol-fa movement. Sarah Glover, the daughter of a church rector from Norwich, initially developed Tonic Sol-fa as an easy method to teach singing. Glover successfully tested the system on children at several schools, a small church choir, and a number of teachers-in-training. In her 1835 instruction manual, *Scheme for Rendering Psalmody Congregational,* and her 1839 *Tonic Sol-fa Tune Book,* Glover's examples were hymns and other songs of high moral character. Glover's vision for her Tonic Sol-fa was always the improvement of congregational singing. To this end, she advised singing teachers to avoid criticizing musical performances, believing that any harsh sentiment might discourage the musical worship she espoused. And in contrast with Curwen's later beliefs about Tonic Sol-fa, Glover did not acknowledge that music could bring about moral improvement except that which came automatically with the formation of a singing community.[12]

Glover's books went through relatively modest printings and few editions. She had no major patron or benefactor to help support her efforts, and her Norwich publishers did little to advertise Tonic Sol-fa outside the local community. But in 1841, Curwen received a copy of Glover's *Scheme* while under a commission by the national Sunday School Union to find a suitable method of children's musical instruction.[13] He immediately began teaching Glover's method to his Sunday School of poor students at Plaistow. Entranced by its simplicity, he quickly recognized its potential for congregational singing, children's singing, and the moral improvement of society in general. Unlike Glover, who relied primarily on word of mouth to advertise her method, Curwen carefully built a publicity machine. He disseminated Tonic Sol-fa through a series of lectures and articles in the *Independent Magazine,* which he briefly edited in the early 1840s. He published further articles on the method in the influential journal *Cassell's Popular Educator.* In 1851, he founded the Tonic Sol-fa Association and soon after began editing the monthly *Tonic Sol-fa Reporter,* which promoted the method through articles emphasizing its ease and efficiency and effectively provided a larger repertory by publishing eight pages of Tonic Sol-fa music in every issue.

The *Reporter* was many things: promotional material to be sent to potential singers and teachers of the system; an organ to enlist aid in the political causes of the Tonic Sol-fa movement (such as the desire to promote teaching of singing in government-aided children's schools); and a social newsletter and calendar, presenting biographies of prominent movement members, dates of concerts to come, and reviews of previous concerts. The magazine, started in 1853, was at times a monthly or a bimonthly publication, increased gradually from sixteen to thirty-two pages of music and news, and even published for a time a complicated four-tiered system of music for different Tonic Sol-fa audiences, based on skill level and interest. Curwen edited the publication until his death in 1880. Continually advertised within the *Reporter* were a steady stream of Tonic Sol-fa instruction books Curwen wrote for both students and teachers, as well as published transcriptions of oratorio choruses, hymn tunes, and other compositions through the in-house firm of the Tonic Sol-fa Agency (later called Curwen and Sons).

Progress was initially slow, partially because there were many other sight-singing methods to choose from at the time, including those of John Hullah and Joseph Mainzer.[14] But Curwen invested a great deal of his time, energy, and personal financial resources into the movement. His early experiences teaching children coupled with an understanding of factory assembly-line and business methods gave Tonic Sol-fa the ability to expand quickly. Following the success at his first classes in Plaistow, Curwen and a few others instructed adults with the specific purpose of using them as teachers to spread the Tonic Sol-fa method. In weekly lessons, one teacher would instruct a large group of between twenty and thirty adults, gradually taking them through the basic steps of learning how to sing, just as an assembly line would form a product. After the course of lessons was complete, Curwen or another instructor would personally inspect each singer individually, either passing them and allowing them to go onto further studies, or recommending more practice. Aided by Curwen's step-by-step instruction books, the successfully tested teachers would then evangelize the method in the cities and countryside.

Linking evangelical ardor with assembly-line methods of instruction was extremely efficient. By 1870, Tonic Sol-fa eclipsed its competitors and dominated the British sight-singing movement. Other publishers began producing music in Tonic Sol-fa, including Novello and W. G. McNaught. At the century's close, the major choral works in the British festival canon, including as the oratorios of Handel, Haydn, and Mendelssohn, had been published in Tonic Sol-fa notation, and most new oratorios and cantatas were published in both Tonic Sol-fa and standard notation simultaneously.[15] During Curwen's lifetime, the Tonic Sol-fa Association concentrated on producing church music, philanthropic music, oratorios, and cantatas. Other publishers began using Tonic Sol-fa for a number of other genres, including opera by 1870. The notation was popular enough that transcriptions of any sort of vocal music were always in demand until the beginning of the First World War.

Certainly one reason Tonic Sol-fa spread quickly throughout the country was its cheap cost of reproduction. Tonic Sol-fa graphically adapted solmization, using single letters to represent pitches and punctuation marks for rhythms (Example 5.1). It required no special musical type for printing, which greatly aided its use by foreign and domestic missionary societies. Tonic Sol-fa was not diaschematic, so large musical scores could be printed on small pieces of paper, making it cheaper than standard notation. Most Tonic Sol-fa scores print only the vocal parts, omitting any accompaniment, allowing even further condensation. For instance, the four-part chorus "And He Shall Purify" from Handel's *Messiah,* presented in this example, is only an inch high. The same passage in the standard Novello octavo vocal scores of the time (with piano accompaniment) is about four inches high. Further, standard-notation scores for oratorios and cantatas usually cost between three and seven shillings apiece in 1900. Full Tonic Sol-fa scores were normally about half the size of the octavo editions, and usually cost between one shilling and one shilling sixpence.

While the advancement of congregational psalmody was the primary goal of Curwen's Tonic Sol-fa, as the movement gained momentum, Curwen increasingly viewed it as a moralizing panacea for the working class. Not only

Example 5.1 George Frideric Handel, "And He Shall Purify," from *Messiah*, Tonic Sol-fa edition transcribed by W. G. McNaught (London: Novello, Ewer and Co., [c. 1890]), mm. 20–23.

would Tonic Sol-fa provide a method of rational recreation for the individual worker, it would also strengthen him by distracting him from vice (including, but not limited to, alcohol, smoking, and gambling), create stronger family units, and increase worker productivity by putting the singer into an automatic frame of mind conducive to factory work.[16] In virtually every issue of the *Reporter,* Curwen published editorials, articles, and testimonials that propagated this active social vision for Tonic Sol-fa and called repeatedly for continuing the struggle against alcohol: "To counteract the evil influence of the public house needs the united efforts of the legislator, the Christian preacher, and the musical reformer. It must be gratefully acknowledged that Tonic Sol-fa has already done much good in this direction, still I think much ground yet remains unoccupied."[17]

Despite Curwen's belief in music's potential for good in the domestic, philanthropic, and church spheres, he also acknowledged its power to aid vice. Within the *Reporter*'s pages, he lambasted any music or musical activity he saw as a corrupting moral influence. To this end, he republished Robert Carlyle's famous article on the degeneracy of opera.[18] He also noted continually the damaging effects of questionable music on both morals and individual health: "Where music has no other purpose than to please and excite you, what do you think will be the result of that enervating state of body in which such music will have put you? Your mind will also be enervated, it will soon lose its balance, and be unable to distinguish what is pure and noble, until you have become one of that large class of society which lives only by animal instincts, and unprincipled and often even unlawful means of satisfying them."[19] During Curwen's tenure as editor, the *Reporter* also vigilantly spoke out against music at public houses (the so-called "Free and Easy" concerts) and music halls, stating that such gatherings generally introduced young men to drinking and included indecent language and references.[20] To mitigate these potentially damaging influences, Curwen repeatedly advanced choral compositions with religious or some other "proper" texts, including ones that promoted a love of work, patriotism, domesticity, or pastoralic ideals.

Though Curwen's initial efforts focused on children's singing, it was clear from the outset that adults would use Tonic Sol-fa for their own instruction. Curwen thus positioned the machinery of the Tonic Sol-fa movement into the musical reform of the working classes. From the beginning of its publication, the *Reporter* chronicled Tonic Sol-fa classes made up of members of mechanics' halls, church choirs, and workingmen's groups. Special attention was placed on those courses that were either run by a member of the middle class donating his time to the improvement of the working class or groups run entirely by members of the working class itself. Space for six months of music within the issues of the *Reporter* was given over to "The Working Man's Singing Lessons"—a Tonic Sol-fa course aimed specifically at quickly teaching singing to the working classes.[21] One theme continually emphasized was that the Tonic Sol-fa movement sought to create a moral "People's Music" that would elevate the tastes and state of the workers. To this end, the Tonic Sol-fa Association promoted a series of "People's Concerts" throughout England.[22] Championing such concerts, Curwen also responded to the specific threat of drunkenness that the temperance movement sought to eliminate, believing that the People's Concerts and Tonic Sol-fa singing as rational recreation would protect such vulnerable working-class men and women from the dangers of the public house.[23]

Curwen only occasionally tempered his zeal for using Tonic Sol-fa as an agent of morality and reform with a concern for appearing moderate. In a reply to a letter sent to the *Reporter,* Curwen declared that anyone could use Tonic Sol-fa:

> As editor of the *Reporter* he is neither a Dissenter, a Churchman, a Catholic, nor a Protestant. . . . On the other hand, let it be understood that the Editor of this *Reporter* will never publish music which he does not believe in. If, therefore, his Roman Catholic friends wish to publish hymns of worshipful praise to the Virgin; if Mr. Neale desires to put into Sol-fa language his songs of dissent and schism; if any Temperance advocates desire to set forth in Sol-fa music the glories of the Maine Law, these various parties must do the work themselves. Mr. Curwen will give them free permission to use the Tonic Sol-fa notation, for that belongs to "mankind," and not to "a party."

But he himself, as *a man,* must hold his own conscience, rejoicing heartily when others do the same.[24]

In asserting that he would not impede the publication of Catholic compositions, Curwen was disingenuous, given his antipathy toward Catholicism. Similarly, his self-conscious posture of neutrality toward temperance belied his efforts to link Tonic Sol-fa and temperance in both methodology and goal. Curwen's own views on drinking mirrored the general ideological progression of the temperance movement. Biographical accounts state that he was always abstemious and emphasize that he gave up drinking entirely for the last eight years of his life.[25]

Unsurprisingly, therefore, Curwen appropriated many of temperance's methods to spread Tonic Sol-fa. The Tonic Sol-fa Association embarked on a series of exhibitions in London and throughout the country to demonstrate the ease of the method, imitating the successful missions of temperance lecturers. These exhibitions featured demonstrations by a choir of Tonic Sol-fa singers and speeches about its moral usefulness, concluding with a public trial of the system. All present would receive a sample lesson to experience its moral uplift. Local Tonic Sol-fa classes were the ultimate aim of the exhibitions, just as community temperance associations were formed after missions converted members in the area. Similarly, as new teetotalers signed pledges of abstinence from alcohol, Tonic Sol-fa singers received certificates denoting their status as trained singers upon successful completion of a class. Both organizations reserved the right to revoke the pledge or certificate if the individual behaved in a way contrary to the views of the movements.

Curwen also adopted the use of testimonials within the *Reporter.* Especially in early issues, part of each "Correspondence" or "Intelligence" column featured communications from individuals who were either won over by the system or stories of how Tonic Sol-fa built a better community. The testimonials in the *Reporter* usually resembled those testimonials of former drinkers converted to temperance. First, they described the confusion and dissatisfaction the old notation engendered. Then, the simple and scientific appeal of the notation sparked their conversion to Tonic Sol-fa. After this, success followed in evangelizing the method to others, who, in turn, used it for their own improvement—in this case, going on to comprehend standard notation.[26] Such testimonials appear immediately in the first issues of the *Reporter* and became part of a regular column by 1865.

To promote its moralizing power more widely, Curwen began explicitly advancing Tonic Sol-fa as an agent of reform, once stating outright that

Tonic Sol-fa was utterly necessary to all contemporary reform movements.[27] Curwen believed music to be a particular aid to any sort of philanthropic work because it associated pleasure with moral and religious poetry, brought attention to the words and sayings of the reform movements, made the repetition of those words agreeable, and created comradeship through the uniting of voices for a good purpose.[28] At times Curwen advocated the use of Tonic Sol-fa for advancing the cause of Ragged, Reform, and Industrial Schools; the anti-slavery movement; urban missions; and work among the mentally and physically handicapped.[29] Curwen's aid to such movements sometimes entailed just an article about a prominent member of the reform organization or a call for donations to the cause within the pages of the *Reporter*,[30] but it usually included at least a lengthy editorial on its necessity if not an offer of Tonic Sol-fa music and method books at a greatly reduced price to aid specific organizations.[31]

Yet even with this plethora of other reform possibilities, the *Reporter* maintained its strongest links to the temperance movement. The *Reporter* printed news of Tonic Sol-fa classes that were held at temperance halls, ones that comprised members of temperance societies, or were formed solely for the purpose of temperance, such as the London Tonic Sol-fa Temperance Choir and the Edinburgh Temperance Choral Union.[32] It also often mentioned Tonic Sol-fa choirs that performed specifically to aid temperance organizations.[33] Curwen noted when temperance songs were sung at national or local gatherings of temperance or non-temperance singers. For example, an advertisement in the *Reporter* stated that the annual Juvenile Choral Festival of 1869, held in the Crystal Palace, would include the temperance song "Drink Water" on the program.[34] And just as he had advocated editing or omitting music on general moral grounds, Curwen also favored severely pruning compositions with intemperate texts.[35]

Further, Curwen published a large amount of temperance music in Tonic Sol-fa notation, both in stand-alone editions and in the *Reporter*. Its first volume contained *Temperance Songs, No. 1*, a collection of four-part tunes including "Water for Me" and "The Crystal Spring." One-quarter of the musical side of volume VI—the largest amount of space Curwen ever devoted to a single topic—contains "A Temperance Course Of Exercises On The Tonic Sol-Fa Method Of Teaching To Sing."[36] He condensed the entire Tonic Sol-fa method into forty-eight pages, including both standard exercises and many two-, three-, and four-part temperance songs, some traditional, and some newly composed for the course. Curwen justified his focus in an article that detailed temperance's biblical roots and its compelling need in British society, explaining how Tonic Sol-fa was the best means to convey this message.[37] Outside the *Reporter,* Curwen published separate methods, including *The Templar's Course* (1874) and a number of collections of temperance songs, including *The Templar's Lyre* (1872), as well as a monthly series of single songs published as "Temperance Leaflets."[38] Curwen promoted this music with full-page advertisements aimed toward temperance workers; the names of the Tonic Sol-fa Agency or of Curwen and Sons were prominently featured within them.[39] In abbreviating the Tonic Sol-fa method for easy comprehension by temperance advocates and providing a generous selection of music for such groups to sing, Curwen strengthened the connections between the two movements.

In a similar fashion, Curwen also acknowledged and encouraged the work of the Band of Hope movement. Curwen published announcements of classes and concerts given by such organizations, often noting with pride their moral usefulness.[40] He found or composed simple songs specifically aimed at children's voices and abilities on temperance subjects, publishing them either independently or within the *Reporter* in sections devoted to songs for children—as he did with "The Crystal Spring" in a collection called *Songs for Young People.*[41] While Curwen did not initially create a method specifically for the Band of Hope movement, he did encourage and advertise the publication of *The Band Of Hope Harmonist,* an early selection of temperance melodies in Tonic Sol-fa notation edited by W. M. Miller.[42] Later, the press of Curwen and Sons printed both its own *Band of Hope Tune Book* and a method book to teach Tonic Sol-fa to Band of Hope children.[43] Within the magazine, reports about local Bands of Hope were ubiquitous, and Curwen emphasized the strong connections between the two movements. He enthusiastically noted that at the 1871 annual Band of Hope mass meeting and choral competition in the Crystal Palace, the children singers used more than 10,000 Tonic Sol-fa scores (as opposed to about 1,000 standard notation ones). He also continually published articles and papers linking the Band of Hope to Tonic Sol-fa, including Frederic Smith's "Singing in Connection with Band of Hope Work."[44]

Within his temperance music publications, Curwen strove to present simple, four-part hymns like "Friends of Temperance" (Example 5.2a [in original Tonic Sol-fa notation] and 2b [transcription into staff notation]). The first line of this composition presents a wholly homophonic texture; the second line has the two lower parts continuing within the simple rhythmic and harmonic structure, punctuated by the trumpet-like triadic call of the two upper parts. The text of the excerpt is also quite typical for a temperance hymn: Temperance and religion are linked absolutely ("God and truth are on your side"), and both the drunkard and the moderate drinker are warned that they face dire consequences if they continue to drink ("Touch not, taste not, lest they die"). The simplicity of the music was a conscious design: Such tunes and hymns were meant to be sung without accompaniment, if necessary, and have a rhythmic gait suitable to marching.

The temperance songs on the recorded selection ("Drink Water," "O Come

Example 5.2a Beginning of "Friends of Temperance" in Tonic Sol-fa notation, from *Temperance Songs No. 1* (*Tonic Sol-fa Reporter*, March 1856): 152.

Example 5.2b Beginning of "Friends of Temperance" transcribed into staff notation.

and Sign the Pledge," and "Truth Shall be Victorious" (CD nos. 7–9) all fall
into the same patterns: They are mostly homophonic (with the occasional
passing tone on a subdivision in one part), usually in four-part harmony,
hymn-like, and all published in multiple sources. The three selections also
show other typical characteristics of temperance music of the time: They
are in bright, major keys (F major, A major, B-flat major, and G major), are
mostly diatonic ("Truth Shall Be Victorious" contains only three accidentals
in a twenty-four-measure composition), and come from a variety of sources.
As temperance was a public political movement, temperance music collec-
tors often drew one or two successful songs from other collections for their
own compilation, used music written by amateurs, or reworked older, well-
known compositions into temperance songs (such is the case of "Truth Shall
Be Victorious," which is a hymn by Franz Joseph Haydn).

Curwen acknowledged that temperance singing, while robust and enthusiastic, would not necessarily be of high quality. When temperance choirs
sang well, he was always quick to praise them, as he did a massed concert of
Tonic Sol-fa Band of Hope singers at the Crystal Palace in 1874: "Temperance
Societies cultivate music not so much for its own sake as for its valuable aid
to their own special work. It is therefore creditable to them that the singing
of this great Choir was so effective . . ."[45] And while he constantly required
at least the most basic level of Tonic Sol-fa certificate to be earned by all who
would sing in public (outside of classes), Curwen noted many times that
temperance workers and Band of Hope singers should not be held to the
same standard, because their real work was not music, but temperance.[46]

In the 1870s, the Tonic Sol-fa Agency began publishing a number of "Temperance Stories," "Temperance Services," and "Temperance Cantatas." These
compositions, either pastiches of older choral music with a newly written
temperance lyric or entirely newly composed, were produced with increasing
frequency after Curwen's death in 1880. But even during the 1870s, Curwen
repeatedly published both advertisements of these compositions as well as
notices of Tonic Sol-fa choirs performing them.[47]

Indirectly, the *Reporter*'s advertisements of lodgings and descriptions of
refreshments served at Tonic Sol-fa gatherings also reflect Curwen's desire
to merge the Tonic Sol-fa and temperance movements. Until the late 1870s,
the only non-musical advertisement seen in the pages of the *Reporter* was for
Eaton's Temperance Hotel, a hostelry where no alcohol was served and the
intemperate forbidden entry. The *Reporter* never failed to mention that tea,
not alcohol, was served at breaks of Tonic Sol-fa classes or choral rehearsals. Sometimes such implicit descriptions could turn explicit, with direct

references to temperance quotations. A report of a meeting in Amersham noted, "After the company had partaken of 'the cup which cheers, but not inebriates,' a Catholic Chant and a German Chorale were very nicely sung by the class."[48] In placing Catholic and Protestant musical selections on the same level, this passage is unique within the *Reporter*. However, its message of shared morality is not, as Curwen consistently identified Tonic Sol-fa with temperance. Consequently, despite his disingenuous statement to the contrary, he rooted the Tonic Sol-fa movement firmly in the temperance cause, thus making Tonic Sol-fa an active reform institution.

Just as Curwen falsely denied a direct connection between temperance and Tonic Sol-fa, his claim that he welcomed Catholics to use the method was also untrue. The *Reporter*'s pages bristle with anti-Catholic bias. Curwen revealed his prejudice most tellingly in assailing the morality of Protestants and Catholics singing together. A concert in Heidelberg prompted him to print the following warning in the *Reporter:*

> As an illustration of the want of *a real faith* among these people—of the *infi-del* spirit with which they peruse art—I may mention that here were a mixed company, young citizens, Catholic and Protestant, singing, "Holy Mary, pray for us," and "A true body of Christ,"—referring to the bread in the Lord's supper. If they *meant* the words, it was, for the Protestants, an awful profanation; if they meant them not, it was a sin of untruth, which we can none of us commit without injury to our moral characters. If you trifle with truth, she forsakes you. I would not *frequent* a singing society thus conducted for the sake of the finest music in the world. I hope that our Tonic Sol-fa Association will always protest against the fearful amount of infidelity and untruth with which art has been connected.[49]

Curwen makes no direct judgment of the Catholics who sing such words, but harshly condemns the Protestants for "awful profanation."

As the *Reporter* had close ties to British evangelical Christianity, articles and reports about all aspects of Christian life continuously appeared within the magazine. Many articles praised ecumenical Christian groups that excluded Catholics, either directly or indirectly. Statements and selections of articles that directly separated Catholics from Christians and even condemned their faith as heretical also appeared frequently: "Perhaps there are some of you here who would not allow that the religion of the 13th century was Christianity. Be it so, still is the statement true which is all that is necessary for me now to prove, that art was great because it was devoted to such religion as then existed. Grant that Roman Catholicism was not Christianity—grant it, if you will, to the same thing as old heathenism."[50] Curwen further perpetuated anti-Catholicism by virtually excluding any positive mention of Catholics and Catholicism in the *Reporter*.[51] The first ten years of issues of the *Reporter* have no sacred music by Catholic composers other than Palestrina or Mozart. Palestrina's compositions appear divested of their Latin titles and translated into tepid English, and for the first two decades of the *Reporter*'s publication, Mozart's *Twelfth Mass* was protestantized into a "Service."[52] The first eight years of *Reporter* issues contain no articles about the use of Tonic Sol-fa by Catholic associations or churches. When the *Reporter* printed intelligence from Ireland, Protestant organizations alone received notice, even though the country was predominantly Catholic.

Only when the national English paper *The Standard* specifically identified Tonic Sol-fa with "the dissenting interest" in 1861 did news of Catholics begin to appear in the *Reporter*.[53] After this comment, Curwen again claimed in print that Tonic Sol-fa was for all, including "Jews, Mormons, Mohammedans, Roman Catholics, and all branches of Protestants."[54] Yet the Catholic Tonic Sol-fa classes mentioned in the magazine from this time—only one in 1861 and four in 1862, compared to hundreds of reports from Protestant organizations—were either separated from the intelligence reports about Protestants or emphasized the fact that a Protestant teacher instructed the Catholics.[55] Similarly, an 1862 year-end report on the great progress of Tonic Sol-fa throughout British society mentioned the publication of Tonic Sol-fa methods and books for a number of Protestant organizations, but neglected to mention that the firm of Burns and Lambert published a *Tonic Sol-fa Vespers Book* earlier that year.[56] This report also strongly emphasized that "the [Protestant] Christian Life in England is that to which our Tonic Sol-fa must cling."[57]

This pattern was repeated in 1872. When the *Guardian*, the *Musical Times*, and the *Athenaeum* all identified Tonic Sol-fa in general and Curwen in particular with the Nonconformists, a brief attempt was made to make the *Reporter* more inclusive.[58] By August of that year, an advertisement within the *Reporter* noted that Frederic Smith, a Tonic Sol-fa official, would travel to Ireland to promote the movement and check on its success in that country. The advertisement calls on "Irish friends Catholic as well as Protestant," but states unequivocally that Smith would meet the two groups separately.[59] When reports of Smith's journey were later recounted within the *Reporter*, few of them mentioned Catholics at all. Most of the meetings in Ireland took place in Protestant schoolrooms and church halls.[60] A small report about "Catholic Music" was also given in the 1 December 1872 issue of the *Reporter*, noting that the conductor of a student choir at a Catholic college in Hammersmith used Tonic Sol-fa and had even transcribed and printed a number of Catholic mass compositions into Tonic Sol-fa notation, but these pieces were not sold by the Tonic Sol-fa Agency, and Curwen never provided details on how one might acquire them.[61] After this, the *Reporter* reverted to its older policy of simply mentioning Catholic Tonic Sol-fa singers briefly, if at all.

Curwen promoted Tonic Sol-fa by borrowing the publicity methods of the temperance movement, even to the point of constructing Tonic Sol-fa as a necessary component of temperance and evangelical reform. Both types of reform hinged on removing the working-class individual from the public house and returning him either to his home or to a Protestant church that deeply distrusted Catholicism. Consequently, Catholics were either left to form their own associations—as was the case with temperance—or mostly ignored, as occurred in the Tonic Sol-fa movement.

However, the power of this connection was fleeting at best. Historical and cultural forces doomed Curwen's narrow reformist aims for Tonic Sol-fa. Following the defeat of the Liberal Party in the election of 1895, temperance ceased to be an important political issue in Great Britain. By that point in the century, Tonic Sol-fa had trained a large body of educated singers who, contrary to Curwen's ambitions, sang less in church and in the home than in amateur choral organizations and provincial music festivals, such as the annual Three Choirs Festival at Hereford, Gloucester, and Worcester, or the semi-annual civic music festivals at Birmingham, Norwich, and Leeds.

The popularity of music festivals in England throughout the period of Tonic Sol-fa's ascendancy is unquestionable. The festivals began in the eighteenth century as charity organizations, usually with philanthropic aims similar to what Curwen espoused. The annual Three Choirs Festivals gave all their profits to a fund devoted to the widows and orphans of the clergy. The Birmingham Festival's profits went to the operating budget of the Birmingham General Hospital. Even those festivals founded in the nineteenth century as extensions of civic pride, such as Norwich, Leeds, Sheffield, or Brighton, were ostensibly charitable undertakings. The focus of these festivals was the performance of oratorios. Though presentations of secular and instrumental music at such festivals had made inroads by 1860 and would increase in importance throughout the rest of the century, the production of Handel's *Messiah* and Mendelssohn's *Elijah* were the highlights of any festival, the concerts that would consistently have the highest attendance and make the most money for the charities. The festival was also the only regular source for compositional commissions—and until the end of the nineteenth century, solely for oratorios or cantatas.[62] It further remained the easiest way for a foreign or domestic composer to gain recognition and publishing contracts within England.

Oratorios were increasingly heard in other venues as well. Just after the Tonic Sol-fa era began, the conductor and composer Michael Costa instituted a semi-annual Handel Festival at the Crystal Palace in London. Scholars Howard Smither and Michael Musgrave noted the phenomenally huge forces used for the presentation of *Messiah* and other oratorios: thousands of singers and audiences in the tens of thousands.[63] It is certain that Tonic Sol-fa was the introduction to choral music and Handel for a great number of these amateur singers and probably many in the audience as well. The Handel festivals always received notice and often a review within the *Reporter*. Concerts of *Messiah, Elijah,* and a number of other oratorios could be further heard in a variety of venues—from churches to lecture halls to civic theaters—weekly and sometimes even daily throughout Great Britain.

Curwen himself was not averse to using the popularity of oratorios and cantatas to aid the growth of Tonic Sol-fa. Promoting oratorios within the Tonic Sol-fa method ensured attracting a large middle-class following for the movement. Further, since one goal of Tonic Sol-fa was to increase the general musical taste of all of Britain's working classes, and oratorios were considered to be the most sublime musical genre in Great Britain at the time, it is only natural that Curwen would mine them for Tonic Sol-fa transcriptions. For instance, the composition published in the initial issue of the *Reporter* was the "Hallelujah Chorus" from Handel's *Messiah*.[64] Other choruses followed, from *Messiah, Israel in Egypt, Elijah,* and *St. Paul.* The Tonic Sol-fa Agency had taken up publishing complete oratorio scores in Tonic Sol-fa transcriptions by 1854. Novello and other publishers soon followed suit. A number of cantatas were even composed expressly for the use of Tonic Sol-fa choirs and released only in Tonic Sol-fa notation. Tonic Sol-fa classes and choirs first sang oratorio excerpts published in the *Reporter,* but by 1860 they had already presented a number of complete oratorios in concert and from the late 1860s, such concerts became increasingly common. This was partially by design: The *Reporter* began to review new oratorios and cantatas, or at least advertise them within its pages, and at one point even seriously entertained creating a system of grants drawn from class dues and fees to ensure the production of oratorios and what the editors considered to be other "high-class" music by Tonic Sol-fa singers in poorer districts.[65]

While many Tonic Sol-fa singers sang only within their own organizations, a good number joined other amateur choruses then flourishing throughout Britain. Some of these singers progressed to reading standard notation (always the ultimate aim of the Tonic Sol-fa method), but many did not, causing the creation of "bilingual" choruses. Such was the case of a Staffordshire chorus in 1903, three-quarters of whose singers used Tonic Sol-fa either exclusively or with a better facility than standard notation.[66] Many amateur choirs had a significant number of Tonic Sol-fa singers well into the second decade of the twentieth century.

Even though Curwen accepted the use of oratorios for Tonic Sol-fa purposes, he still tried to put the stamp of humility and evangelical Christian mores on their performance. In the mid-1850s, Tonic Sol-fa classes often sang or presented choruses from *Messiah* without any instrumental accompaniment whatsoever, the given reason being that though "the instruments enrich and beautify the composition, they are far from essential to its power."[67] He authorized ensemble changes in compositions as well. A concert of *Israel in Egypt* sanctioned by Curwen used several singers for the solo parts in order to avoid the "vanity" of individual singing.[68] And when he mentioned oratorio concerts within the *Reporter,* he always made sure to emphasize the religious nature of these performances, speaking with disapproval about any applause heard at such a concert. Cautioning a group of Tonic Sol-fa singers in Burnselm preparing to present *Messiah,* he admonished that productions not to be presented as concerts: "I hope that Tonic Sol-faists will try to strip it of everything like mere 'performance'; especially that they will take care to avoid anything in dress or manner that would be inconsistent with a place and a season of worship. The 'Messiah' has, in London, been so often prostituted for amusement, that our Christian Sol-faists here would rather sing any Oratorio than that which is the most sacred and the most soul-inspiring of all."[69] To Curwen, any "mere performance" would cheapen and degrade the religious meaning of the text to treat it like a "vulgar, profane entertainment," a sentiment that appeared many times within the *Reporter.*

*   *   *

The world of Tonic Sol-fa was one of which the composer Edward Elgar was always aware. Born in 1857, he was never conscious of a time when Tonic Sol-fa did not exist. Elgar's gradual rise to fame followed the typical path open to an English composer: He played violin in or conducted a number of ensembles, including the Three Choirs Festival orchestra at his home city of Worcester, the choir of his own Catholic parish church, St. George's (where he was also the organist), as well as the amateur choral and instrumental Worcestershire Philharmonic Society.[70] Provincial festivals or amateur choral societies premiered all of Elgar's first major compositions in the 1890s, many of which were choral works. Most of these compositions were published shortly after their premieres in Tonic Sol-fa notation; all had at least choral selections published.[71] These compositions gave Elgar a modest reputation as a provincial composer, though one who had the potential to do great things.

Elgar realized that potential in 1899. His first internationally successful composition, the opus 36 *Variations on an Original Theme* ("Enigma") premiered to almost universal applause. He also received a commission for an oratorio from the Birmingham Music Festival. After the premiere of Mendelssohn's *Elijah* in 1846, the Birmingham Festival garnered the reputation as the most prestigious in England. Its commissions imported a number of great foreign composers and their works to England (such as Dvořák and Gounod), and at the end of the century it was directed by Hans Richter, the great Wagnerian conductor. A Birmingham commission was a sure way to have one's work published by Novello, the pre-eminent English firm. Like those of the other provincial festivals, the Birmingham chorus increased greatly in size over the second half of the nineteenth century, partially because of the huge number of singers trained through Curwen's Tonic Sol-fa method. The better-trained singers were also able to learn and perform increasingly difficult compositions.

Such a large and well-trained chorus was completely necessary for Elgar's Birmingham commission composition, *The Dream of Gerontius.* Like most narrative oratorios of the nineteenth century, *Gerontius* relies on the chorus to represent a number of characters. The singers must emulate in rapid succession servants, priests, angels, and demons. Each choral character portrayed has a distinct musical style. Elgar's choral writing is complex, and while he mostly concentrates on straightforward four-part settings, he often divides the singers into a chorus and a semi-chorus, presenting up to nine separate parts at a time. His writing is also extremely contrapuntal, requiring a talented and secure ensemble for successful performance.

Perhaps the most brilliant stroke of irony is that *Gerontius* completely rejected Curwen's evangelical agenda and implicit anti-Catholicism. *Gerontius*'s text was drawn from a poem by the infamous Catholic convert Cardinal John Henry Newman. The Roman Catholic conversion and ensuing domination of Catholic intellectual life by this former member of the Oxford Movement and Anglican vicar made him one of the most famous converts of the era. Newman's poem *The Dream of Gerontius,* while not widely known today for any reason other than Elgar's oratorio, was incredibly popular through the end of the nineteenth century. The poem had a special place for Elgar, who was born a Catholic. He gave a copy of it to console his future wife, Alice Roberts, on the death of her mother.[72] While Elgar's adapted libretto de-emphasized some Catholic aspects of Newman's poem and shifted the weight of the philosophical message from Gerontius's journey of discovery in heaven to his final human suffering on Earth, the ultimate Catholic message is unmistakable.[73] Elgar's and Newman's interpretation of death, based on Catholic eschatology, includes a presentation of the "Kyrie eleison" in Latin, pleas to the Virgin Mary and the Communion of Saints, as well as detailed references to Purgatory and the sacrament of Reconciliation.

Because of the narrative structure of the oratorio, Elgar's chorus plays a vital role in the presentation of Catholic ideas. For instance, when Gerontius first asks his assistants to pray for his faltering health, the chorus responds by invoking "Holy Mary, all Holy Angels, Apostles, Disciples, Confessors, and Martyrs." The final climactic chorus of Gerontius's first part presents an even stronger statement of Catholic dogma. This section contains a long prayer to God wherein a priest and the chorus of assistants act as intercessors for Gerontius's soul, delivering it up to God. Responding to the direct statement of the priest, the chorus of assistants sends the soul to God with a Catholic blessing in the "name of Angels and Archangels, Thrones and Dominations, Princedoms and Powers and in the name of Cherubim and Seraphim." Newman's original text (which Elgar retained in his libretto) includes the priest proclaiming the prayer first in Latin (as a Catholic priest would do at the time for a deathbed prayer) before translating the entire segment into English—more for increased power through repetition than textual necessity.

Heretofore in Gerontius, the chorus responded in an occasional series of prayers that occurred only when Gerontius himself asked for them. The chorus's third entrance is typical (Example 5.3): After Gerontius begs intercession from Jesus and Mary, the chorus responds by singing the phrase "Rescue him, O Lord, in this evil hour, / As of old so many by Thy gracious power," continuing with invocations to Job, Moses, and other Old Testament figures. The opening of this chorus is briefly imitative and includes occasional flashes of homophony, but stays predominantly within polyphony.

The moment of the chorus's intercession (Example 5.4) differs sharply from the other choral entrances, which focused on Gerontius's state of health rather than the infinite potential his death now brings. First, Gerontius has now faltered to the point where he can no longer ask for any intercession himself. The priest must do it for him. Second, the writing is presented in an

Example 5.3 Edward Elgar, "Rescue him," from *The Dream of Gerontius* (London: Novello, 1900), part I, rehearsal 63, mm. 1–9. Author's collection.

Example 5.4 Edward Elgar, "Go forth," from *The Dream of Gerontius,* part I, rehearsal 72, mm. 2–10, rehearsal 73, mm. 1–2.

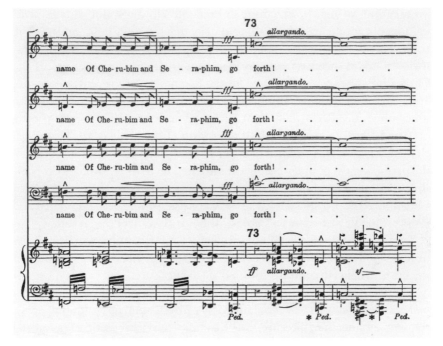

Example 5.4 Continued.

energetic and even enthusiastic way: For eight measures, the chorus blasts a
series of homophonic chords, descending each measure by half-step, until
dramatically launching the final unison "Go forth," by leaping up an octave
on C in all the voice parts. The triumphant fervor this passage is meant to
impart is unmistakable. And it succinctly expresses Catholic dogma through
the required intercession on behalf of the soul, which would be especially
troubling to Curwen, since the evangelical Christianity he espoused held
that people should communicate directly with God. The intercession of a
surpliced individual was regarded as unnecessary and perhaps even arrogant.
Yet the power of this passage is undeniable. It is the most powerful chorus
of the first part of the oratorio, and it directly echoes the stepwise descent
initially presented by the priest. A more positive and affirming presentation
of Catholicism is hard to imagine.

Acceptance of *Gerontius* was slow. The premiere performance was a near-
disaster due to time pressures caused mainly by Elgar's delay in finishing the
work. It took a successful performance in Düsseldorf, at the Lower Rhine
Festival, and universal acclaim on the part of German critics to garner enough

momentum for new productions in England. However, not all were willing to embrace the composition, primarily due to its Catholic subject. The composer Charles Villiers Stanford contemptuously observed that the oratorio "stank of incense."[74] Its presentation at Gloucester meetings of the Three Choirs Festival was banned for the first decade of the century because authorities regarded the Catholic subject as "inappropriate" for performance in a cathedral.[75] Performances at Hereford and Worcester meetings only occurred after the expurgation or alteration of the text's more "Catholic" elements. However, *Gerontius* overcame these prejudices and soon became the period's most popular oratorio, compared favorably with the compositions of Handel and Mendelssohn. Between 1909 and 1914, performances of *Gerontius* at the provincial festivals were consistently the best-populated and most profitable. It remains a staple of the British festival canon today.

Temperance ultimately did not succeed as a reform movement because its fundamental evangelical approach of castigating drinkers alienated it from the British public. In contrast, Tonic Sol-fa did not succeed to Curwen's specifications because it became too popular. The efficacy of the system created a vast number of singers who, not limited by Curwen's aim of promoting music for reform rather than pleasure, struck out into the larger world of organized amateur singing. The provincial music festival choirs eagerly accepted these singers into their ranks, as did many other amateur musical organizations. The choirs' growth, combined with the incipient musical nationalism of the late nineteenth century, led to a new emphasis on native English composition, starting with the oratorio. Consequently, *Gerontius*'s existence and success occurred because of the training of Tonic Sol-fa singers that Curwen strove to promote throughout his life. *Gerontius,* however, not only transcended but subverted Curwen's narrow vision of moral uplift, harnessing the power of Tonic Sol-fa to present a distinctively Catholic message.

Notes

I would like to thank the staffs of the Royal College of Music, the Royal Institute of Education, the Curwen Institute, the John Curwen Society, and the British Library for their generous assistance in obtaining archival sources for this study, and Reinhold Brinkmann, Karen Painter, Byron Adams, and Christina Fuhrmann for their helpful comments and suggestions on earlier drafts. Phyllis Weliver, with her detailed knowledge of English Victorian literature and history, provided invaluable assistance during the final stages of writing. Versions of this essay were delivered at the 1998 annual meeting of the American Musicological Society in Boston and the 1999 Richard Murphy Colloquium at Oberlin College Conservatory of Music.

1. "Rational entertainment" or "rational recreation" was a common nineteenth-century designation for any activity that would keep a member of the working or middle class away from potential morally damaging pursuits. The term was first used in relation to the Tonic Sol-fa movement in the *Tonic Sol-fa Reporter* (hereafter the *Reporter*) on 30 June 1854, 30. Since the format of the *Reporter* changed so often in the period under consideration (it was at times a monthly periodical, and at times a bimonthly one), when the journal is cited, only dates, not volume or series numbers, will be given (e.g. January 1857 or 1 April 1871).

2. Lilian Lewis Shiman, *Crusade Against Drink in Victorian England* (New York: St. Martin's Press, 1988), 11.

3. D. G. Paz, *Popular Anti-Catholicism in Mid-Victorian England* (Stanford, Calif.: Stanford University Press, 1992), 36, n67.

4. Elizabeth Malcolm, "Temperance and Irish Nationalism," in *Ireland Under the Union: Varieties of Tension—Essays in Honour of T. W. Moody,* ed. F. S. L. Lyons and R. A. Hawkins (Oxford: Clarendon Press, 1980), 70.

5. Colin Holmes, *John Bull's Island: Immigration and British Society, 1871–1971* (London: Macmillan Education Ltd, 1988), 59.

6. L. Perry Curtis Jr., *Apes and Angels: The Irishman in Victorian Caricature* (Washington, D.C.: Smithsonian Institution Press, 1971), vii, and Paz, *Popular Anti-Catholicism,* 72 and 260.

7. Shiman notes that Catholics often felt "uncomfortable" joining any but their own organizations, since most temperance associations were strongly identified with Protestantism. See Shiman, *Crusade Against Drink,* 61.

8. Brian Harrison, *Drink and the Victorians: The Temperance Question in England 1815–1872* (Pittsburgh, Pa.: University of Pittsburgh Press, 1971), 165.

9. Shiman, *Crusade against Drink,* 164.

10. Shiman, *Crusade against Drink,* 141.

11. Shiman, *Crusade against Drink,* 141–42. For a detailed discussion of the Band of Hope, see Shiman's "The Band of Hope Movement: Respectable Recreation of Working-Class Children," in *Victorian Studies* 17, no. 1 (1973), 49–74.

12. Sarah Glover, *Scheme for Rendering Psalmody Congregational* (original edition 1835); reprint, introduced by Bernarr Rainbow and reproduced under the direction of Leslie Hewitt (Clarabricken, Ireland: Boethius Press, 1982), 67 [reprint 85].

13. Bernarr Rainbow, *The Land without Music* (London: Novello, 1967), 53.

14. For details on Hullah and Mainzer, see Percy Scholes, *The Mirror of Music, 1844–1944: A Century of Musical Life in Britain as Reflected in the Pages of the Musical Times* (London: Novello; Oxford: Oxford University Press, 1947), 1–21.

15. Charles Edward McGuire, "Epic Narration: The Oratorios of Edward Elgar" (Ph.D. dissertation, Harvard University, 1998), 2–6, and *Elgar's Oratorios: The Creation of an Epic Narrative* (Aldershot: Ashgate Press, Ltd., 2002), 5–6.

16. For Curwen's views on these ideas, see the *Reporter,* 15 March 1872, 2; 1 August 1871, 227 (a reprint of an article from the July 1871 issue of the *Quarterly Review*);

and his *Singing for Schools and Congregations: A Grammar of Vocal Music* (London: Tonic Sol-fa Agency, 1852 reprint of 1843 edition), [xi]. A longer discussion of these tenets may be found in McGuire, *Elgar's Oratorios,* esp. 17–20.

17. *Reporter,* 15 June 1871, 189.

18. *Reporter,* September 1857, 102–4.

19. *Reporter,* September 1857, 104.

20. *Reporter,* August 1858, 261–62, and March 1865, 43.

21. *Reporter* 1, 45ff.

22. *Reporter,* April 1855, 30.

23. *Reporter,* 1851, [2].

24. *Reporter,* December 1859; Curwen's emphasis. An abbreviated version of this passage was also printed in John Spencer Curwen, *Memorials of John Curwen* (compiled by his son, J. Spencer Curwen, with a chapter on his home life by his daughter, Mrs. Banks; London: J. Curwen & Sons, 1882), 79.

25. Curwen, *Memorials,* 108.

26. See, for instance, the testimonials in the *Reporter,* March 1856, 115.

27. *Memorials,* 218.

28. Curwen, *The Teacher's Manual of the Tonic Sol-fa Method* (reprint of the tenth edition, 1875; introduced by Bernarr Rainbow and reproduced under the direction of Leslie Hewitt; Boethius Press, 1986), 312.

29. Curwen, *Teacher's Manual,* 312–17; mentions for such aid abound within the *Reporter.* See, for instance, November 1858, 301; January 1860, 194; and February 1860, 210.

30. See, for instance, the call for donations to relieve those suffering from the Lancashire cotton famine (*Reporter,* October 1864, 323).

31. The Ragged Schools movement (gratis institutions opened in the middle of the century for the education of poor children working in factories) was one of the principal benefactors of Tonic Sol-fa materials in the early 1860s. See the *Reporter,* January 1860, 194; February 1860, 210; and March 1860, 234.

32. Such reports of temperance choirs were legion within the *Reporter* and its later incarnation, the *Musical Herald.* See, for instance, the *Reporter,* May 1855, 36 ("Wolverhampton Temperance Society"); July 1856, 146; December 1856, 90; January 1857, 5–6; September 1863, 121; and November 1859, 132.

33. In just one of many cases, the *Reporter* of July 1862, 303, describes how a temperance hall was built in Nottingham partially with funds raised by a Tonic Sol-fa choir under the leadership of J. W. Kent.

34. *Reporter,* 1 June 1860, [81].

35. For an example, see the *Reporter,* 1 July 1871, 201.

36. *Reporter,* musical section 6 (1864), 1–48.

37. *Reporter,* January 1863, 3–4.

38. Curwen, *Teacher's Manual,* 316; *Reporter,* 15 September 1872, 288; and 1 March 1873, 73. The "Temperance Leaflets" were advertised in the *Reporter* beginning in the 1870s.

39. *Reporter,* 1 March 1874, 70. Such advertisements were a regular feature of the *Reporter* and the *Musical Herald.*

40. *Reporter,* November 1859, 136, and October 1864, 324–25.

41. *Reporter* 1, 130.

42. *Reporter,* August 1861, 105.

43. *Reporter,* September 1864, 318, and 15 August 1871, 241.

44. *Reporter,* 1 September 1871, 265, and 15 January 1872, 20–21.

45. *Reporter,* 1 August 1874, 234.

46. *Reporter,* 15 February 1870, 249.

47. See, for instance, the *Reporter,* 1 January 1875, 14, advertising John Nash's *The Start in Life,* which Curwen noted was performed three times in three months.

48. *Reporter,* May 1856, 131. A similar quotation may be found in the *Reporter,* July 1861, 62.

49. *Reporter,* July 1856, 151. Emphasis Curwen's.

50. *Reporter,* July 1855, 54.

51. Other than the report mentioned previously on p. 124 that a "Catholic chant" was sung at a Tonic Sol-fa meeting in Amersham, no mention of anything Catholic appears in the *Reporter* until 1860.

52. *Reporter,* February 1861, 18.

53. *Reporter,* August 1861, 106.

54. *Reporter,* August 1861, 106. It should be noted that the Tonic Sol-fa movement also had difficulties with the established Church of England, especially with so-called "High-Church" advocates. Yet while the relationship between the mostly evangelical Tonic Sol-fa movement and the Church of England was often strained, it was in no way filled with as much obvious animosity as Curwen's beliefs about Catholics.

55. See, for instance, the *Reporter,* February 1862, 112, and September 1862, 338.

56. *Reporter,* July 1863, 97.

57. *Reporter,* January 1864, 186.

58. *Reporter,* 15 June 1872, 184.

59. *Reporter,* 15 August 1872, 255.

60. *Reporter,* 1 September 1872, 265, and 1 October 1872, 301.

61. *Reporter,* 1 December 1872, 362.

62. However, instrumental music (especially the symphony) became an increasingly important part of many music festivals, perhaps partially because oratorios and cantatas became the bulwark of the working class through such methods as Tonic Sol-fa. At the turn of the century, all the major festivals were commissioning instrumental works, and the Three Choirs Festival presented symphonies within the cathedrals as "preludes" to other works. See Charles Edward McGuire, "1910, Vaughan Williams, and the English Music Festival," in *Vaughan Williams Essays,* ed. Byron Adams and Robin Wells (Aldershot: Ashgate Publishing, Ltd., 2002).

63. Howard Smither, "*Messiah* and Progress in Victorian England," *Early Music* 13 (1985), 339–48, and Michael Musgrave, *The Musical Life of the Crystal Palace* (Cambridge: Cambridge University Press, 1995), esp. 52.

64. *Reporter,* April 1851, 8–12.

65. *Reporter,* 1 June 1870, 372.

66. Fred Muir to Novello & Co., 2 August 1903, collection of the City of Birmingham Archive MS 2067. Letter transcribed in McGuire, *Elgar's Oratorios,* 8.

67. *Reporter,* January 1855, 5.

68. *Reporter,* August 1862, 320. Curwen published a humorous fictional account by J. Proudman, entitled "Miss Sonata Silvertone: Soloist" as the lead article to the 1 April 1870 issue of the *Reporter* (291–95); Proudman's central point is that as a solo singer, Silvertone did not produce music, but artifice. Only when she began to sing in a chorus did she become a real musician singing real music, and her vanity gave way to humility.

69. *Reporter,* January 1861, 197.

70. Jerrold Northrup Moore, *Edward Elgar: A Creative Life* (Oxford: Oxford University Press, 1984), 227–28.

71. See Christopher Kent, *Edward Elgar: A Guide to Research* (New York and London: Garland, 1993), 122, 137, 141, 144, 149, and 156.

72. Moore, *Edward Elgar,* 119.

73. See McGuire, "One Story, Two Visions: Textual Differences Between Elgar's and Newman's *The Dream of Gerontius,*" in the *Elgar Society Journal* 11, no. 2 (July 1999), 75–88; reprinted in *The Best of Me: A Gerontius Centenary Companion,* ed. Geoffrey Hodgkins (Rickmansworth: Elgar Editions, 1999), 84–101.

74. Michael Kennedy, *Portrait of Elgar,* 3rd ed. (Oxford: Clarendon Press, 1987), 151.

75. *The Yorkshire Post,* 20 November 1903.

6

Accounting for Taste: Choral Circles in Early Soviet Workers' Clubs

AMY NELSON

Writing in a Soviet trade union journal in 1924, Sarra Krylova, voice student at the Moscow conservatory, Communist Party member, and long-time activist in popular musical education, identified three main objectives of musical activities, especially choral circles, in workers' clubs. First of all, the choral circles provided a means to develop the artistic and cultural sensibilities of the working class. Secondly, singing offered workers a creative outlet and a way for them to express their collective aspirations and struggles. Finally, and most importantly from Krylova's perspective, music in the club served an important agitational function. It should be used "to awaken collective feelings, articulate the heroism of the working class and summon the proletariat to a new way of life."[1]

Through the fog of Krylova's rhetoric, we can identify a diverse and somewhat contradictory agenda for the choral circles. In the period bounded by the Bolshevik Revolution of 1917 on the one hand and by the completion of "Stalin's Revolution" and the collectivization and industrialization drives in 1932 on the other, workers' clubs attracted attention from cultural activists such as Krylova, who saw the clubs variously as "schools of communism," "forges of proletarian culture," or simply as forums for "raising" the cultural level of previously disadvantaged social groups by fostering an appreciation for "bourgeois" cultural and artistic traditions. These perspectives reflected the challenges inherent in formulating a coherent response to political and social upheaval in the cultural sphere. They also indicate the dilemmas confronting the Bolsheviks on what became known as the "third" or "cultural" front, a term that emerged as the revolutionaries consolidated their political and military victories in 1920–21. With the transition from war to peace, the task of "building socialism" in Russia began to focus on the cultural arena, where the enemies were the old intelligentsia and, even more importantly, the backwardness of the masses.

At a time when Soviet cultural policies were evolving and much contested, the artistic divisions of the workers' clubs, such as the music and drama circles, offered reformers distinctive arenas for exploring the mutability and intransigence of popular preferences. This essay examines the activities and repertoire of the choral circles in the 1920s, as well as reformers' efforts to cultivate and change popular taste.

Among the many influences on the clubs' choral circles, the orientations of the pre-revolutionary adult education movement and the Russian labor movement played a particularly prominent role. Contradictory attitudes about the aesthetic merits and cultural value of urban popular music, traditional folksongs, and the classic tradition informed the choral circles' repertoire, as did the tension between the reformist aims of many chorus directors and advisors who saw the choruses as vehicles for cultural, moral, and political education, and chorus members, who often participated in the choral circle for recreation and because they liked to sing. Debates over what "amateur" musical activities such as the choral circles should entail and how the choruses should differ from "professional" ensembles persisted throughout the decade. For the most part, reformers' efforts to mold popular taste succeeded only to the extent that they accommodated singers' musical preferences.

As a meeting place between ordinary citizens, state authority, and the diverse currents of urban culture, workers' clubs provided a unique venue where the cultural policies of the young Soviet state encountered the cultural marketplace.[2] Examining the activities of the choral circles thus affords new insights on the process of cultural change in the early Soviet period. It suggests that popular preferences figured prominently in the evolution of Stalinist musical culture and points to the limited capacity of even the most authoritarian political regime to dictate and regulate creative expression.

The musical activities sponsored by Soviet workers' clubs were direct descendants of the pre-revolutionary adult education movement and of the workers' clubs established by trade unions in the aftermath of the 1905 revolution. Before 1917, clubs provided a range of educational, cultural, and recreational opportunities to their members, as well as a screen for political activism and revolutionary agitation. From the beginning, the clubs' activities depended heavily on the participation of intellectuals who gave lectures and public readings and often promoted a particular political agenda.[3]

Reform-minded intellectuals would continue to play a prominent role after the revolution, as would pre-revolutionary efforts to use music to develop the aesthetic sensibilities and thus raise the cultural level of the Russian people. Fueled by educated Russians' perceived debt to the underprivileged and uneducated, in the nineteenth century this mission had dovetailed both with the reform agenda of Liberalism, which considered education a necessary vehicle for the democratization of society, and with more diffuse longings for a unified culture, constructed and imposed from above.[4] The objectives of the People's Conservatory, which used a curriculum based on choral singing to acquaint adult students with the finer achievements of Russian and European art music typified the kind of adult education activities often referred to by reformers themselves as *kul'turtregerstvo* [bringing culture].[5]

The number of workers' clubs mushroomed during the Civil War that engulfed Russia after the Bolsheviks' seizure of power in October 1917. Much of this growth reflected the tremendous creative energy and organizational initiative of the proletarian cultural organizations known as *Proletkul't,* a movement often associated with the philosophical orientations of Alexander Bogdanov.[6] Proponents of what has been called "revolutionary romanticism" encouraged artistic creativity by, for, and about workers, drawing on the images and experiences of modern industrial life and the revolutionary struggle. But Bogdanov's belief that the *Proletkul't*'s clubs and studios would provide workers with the possibility of developing a unique "proletarian culture," distinct from and superior to the "bourgeois" culture of the past, was just one of the perspectives informing the activities of the choral and instrumental circles that formed in many workers' clubs and comparable organizations in the Red Army. Clubs attracted support from representatives of the iconoclastic wing of the artistic avant-garde, as well as from those seeking to instill workers and soldiers with an appreciation of Russia's pre-revolutionary cultural heritage.[7]

Proletkul't activists also appropriated selected aspects of cultural institutions that were implacably hostile to Bolshevism. Dmitrii Vasil'ev-Buglai used members of a former church choir as the foundation for a ninety-voice *Proletkul't* chorus that toured the front lines agitating for the Bolshevik cause. A graduate of the Moscow Synodal School, Vasil'ev-Buglai used the melodic conventions of liturgical music and traditional folksongs for the agitational and anti-religious songs and skits that made up his choir's repertoire.[8]

Veterans of the People's Conservatory, such as the former head of the Moscow Synodal School, Alexander Kastalsky, and the theorists Boleslav Yavorsky and Nadezhda Briusova, saw the choral circles as an ideal forum for continuing their campaign to "bring culture" to the masses. The peasant folksong provided the cornerstone for their efforts to develop people's musical sensibilities.[9] At a *Proletkul't* conference in 1918, Kastalsky praised the folksong's "healthy" and "unique" musical language that was completely understandable to the "people" (*narod*).[10] Using the folksong as a foundation, they would then proceed to "more complex" examples of Russian and Western "cultured" [*kul'turnaia*] music.[11]

The apolitical thrust of this program prompted some communists in the *Proletkul't* and the cultural organizations of the Red Army to denounce it as the ill-conceived project of bourgeois intellectuals who wanted "only" to bring the treasures of elite culture to uneducated workers and peasants without engaging in political agitation. Continuing a critique formulated in the pre-revolutionary adult education movement, militant activists opposed "abstract enlightenment activity" and "culture for culture's sake" as the remnants of Liberal and Populist agendas that denied the need for education in the class struggle.[12]

Tensions between proponents of "education," "enlightenment," and "agitation" would be a critical and recurring issue in the development of official cultural policy throughout the twenties. In music, however, criticism of *kul'turtregerstvo* was always somewhat muted. Indeed, a commitment to "bringing culture" to the proletarian heirs of the revolution informed many agendas and cut across other political and aesthetic divisions.

This was because many revolutionaries, including Lenin, felt that the Party's campaign on the cultural front was primarily about the acquisition of culture rather than its transformation.[13] Faced with the daunting task of governing in the name of a largely illiterate proletariat and dependent on the cooperation, if not support, of "bourgeois specialists" to maintain the country's economy, social institutions, and bureaucracy, the Bolsheviks attached signal importance to educating Russia's toiling masses. The struggle for "culture" focused on education, and especially literacy, as well as "civilized" behavior, including comportment, hygiene, sobriety, and even such "bourgeois" habits as appreciating classical music.[14] During the period of the New Economic Policy (1921–1928), official cultural policy focused on achieving these goals by democratizing access to the "bourgeois" cultural legacy, enlisting the support of the pre-revolutionary intelligentsia, accommodating multiple artistic factions, and encouraging competition and debate among them.[15] The choral circles thus provided reformers with an ideal laboratory for evaluating their programs for cultural transformation.[16]

Although they existed primarily to provide cultural services to the urban proletariat, clubs were more than simply a venue for entertainment and leisure pursuits. Amidst acute shortages of housing, heat, and food during the Civil War, clubs became "social hearths" and welcome havens from the grim realities of urban life.[17] Clubs with heated premises or a cafeteria found their services particularly in demand. With the return of some semblance of stability in the early twenties, a club's popularity depended less on the creature comforts it was able to provide and more on the variety and quality of its activities. By the end of the decade, there were more than 4,000 clubs and membership had reached 1.5 million.[18] Most clubs were affiliated with a trade union, but many were sponsored by local Party organizations, city councils [sovety], and individual factories. Club premises ranged from custom-built "palaces," with auditoria, meeting rooms, cafeterias, and libraries, to a couple of small rooms appropriated in the cellar of a factory or office building. The diversity of club programs varied accordingly, but usually included films, artistic activities such as theater and music, reading rooms, and chess clubs, as well as political and educational lectures.

While films and theatrical performances were the most well-attended club programs, music groups were also very popular. Many clubs supported instrumental circles as well as vocal groups, but the choral circles were far more numerous, probably because participation did not require access to an instrument or much in the way of formal instruction. The choral groups attracted music lovers and men and women who liked to sing, but who usually knew little about music.

The repertoire adopted by the choral circles was divided into three main categories: "Revolutionary music," including old revolutionary and prison songs, as well as newly composed "agitational" music [agitki] made up a large portion of the choruses' fare. The second category consisted of an eclectic assortment of "classics," which included choral settings of pieces by Bach, Haydn, Mozart, Beethoven, and Schubert, many choral works by nineteenth-century Russian composers, and a number of pieces for smaller ensembles (duets and trios) by Dargomyzhsky, Tchaikovsky, Rachmaninov, and Rimsky-Korsakov. Folksongs, especially "artistic" arrangements of well-known melodies (by Glazunov, Tchaikovsky, Borodin, Musorgsky, etc.) rounded out the choral circles' repertoire.[19]

Some music circles also fell under the influence of the "mass singing" movement. Promoted by reformers such as K. Postavnichev, mass singing was intended to counter the "professional" orientation that had developed in many choral circles during the Civil War. Rather than trying to emulate professional choruses (or church choirs), proponents of mass singing asserted that choral singing was a "natural" form of musical expression that required little, if any, special preparation.[20] A leader with a strong voice could lead, or even quickly teach, large group renditions of songs at club meetings, political rallies, and holiday demonstrations. This kind of "spontaneous" performance mode had the advantage of eliminating the traditional divide between performers and audience. But by the mid-twenties, mass singing largely vanished in favor of more conventional performances by modestly sized choirs singing in two or four parts.

In the early twenties, the choral circles' programs were fairly self-contained. The choruses performed for other club members and gave recitals, sometimes in conjunction with political meetings, demonstrations, or other club-sponsored events. As the decade unfolded, circle organizers focused more on providing music for other club activities and less on trying to emulate professional music making in the form of independent concerts. In part this shift reflected evolving attitudes about the nature of amateur [samodeiatel'nyi] artistic programs in the clubs.[21] But it was also a response to the fact that club members who most liked to sing and listen to music usually joined the choral circles, leaving few appreciative listeners in the audience.[22] By 1925 choruses were often enlisted to provide music for skits, plays, and "living newspapers" (dramatic commentary on current events) put on by the clubs' drama circles.

This shift in the nature of the choruses' activities paralleled changes in the broader orientation of the clubs. As John Hatch has shown, during 1924 the *Proletkul't's* conception of the clubs as "the 'forges' of a new proletarian culture" gave way to the more tutelary objectives of the Party and trade unions, which viewed them as "instruments" of communist education.[23] The scope of these changes is evident in the way reformers described the objectives of the clubs' music circles after 1924. The purpose of the club, they acknowledged, was one of political education [vospitanie]. But the club should also help workers mold a new way of life [byt] and overcome the old one.

This meant that musical activities were not merely entertainment or a means of relaxation for tired workers. Rather, the objective of the choral and instrumental circles was to prepare politically conscious citizens and to overcome bourgeois musical tastes as well as bourgeois ideology.[24] Music was to awaken collective feelings, glorify the heroism of the working class, and help emancipate workers from the grip of religion, alcohol, and degenerate musical taste.[25] In the choral circle workers would acquire musical, as well as political, literacy. The music circle would provide musical education and upbringing [vospitanie] for backward workers, bring "joy and liveliness" to the club's overall work, and support the activities of its other divisions. Outside the club, the choral circle was also to be a conduit of musical culture out into the masses by spreading healthy, proletarian music.[26]

Most of the activists who embraced and promoted this ambitious vision of the music circles' objectives belonged to one of the three groups that made up the left wing of the Soviet musical scene: the Russian Association of Proletarian Musicians (RAPM), the Organization of Revolutionary Composers (ORK) and the Production Collective of students at the Moscow Conservatory (*Prokoll*). Although the tactics of these groups varied, all three shared a commitment to overcoming the gap between the musical life of the previously privileged social elite and that of the workers and peasants in whose name the revolution had been won. They all devoted considerable energy to eliminating this divide, hoping to cultivate a new kind of musical culture by working in popular music education programs and writing music that would have mass appeal and further the cause of the revolution.[27] Although their orientation was explicitly Marxist, they generally shared the veneration for the classical legacy and peasant folksong that figured so prominently in *kul'turtregerstvo.* They were also united by a deep-seated hostility to urban popular music and other cultural forms intellectuals scorned as degenerate and petty bourgeois.

The most well-known of these groups was the Russian Association of Proletarian Musicians.[28] Young ideologues, many of them communists and musicology majors at the Moscow conservatory, formed the core of this group. Rejecting both modernism and urban popular music, RAPM saw the nineteenth-century classical repertoire, especially the music of Beethoven, as well as certain kinds of peasant folksongs, as the foundations for proletarian music, which they freely admitted did not yet exist. They developed elaborate if not entirely coherent ideological justifications for championing both the music of the bourgeoisie (Beethoven) and that of the politically backward peasantry. In the twenties, RAPM members made few efforts to actually write music, focusing their energies on working with the club music circles, reforming music education, and polemical exchanges with other musicians.

The only composer of note to support RAPM was the aging Alexander Kastalsky. While Kastalsky's distinguished career as a composer of religious music made him an unlikely ally of a militantly communist group, he supported the Proletarian Musicians out of sympathy for their democratic orientation and because they shared his interest in using Russian folk music as the source for a new mass revolutionary art.[29] Before his death in 1926, Kastalsky composed several choral pieces on revolutionary themes, including "Pesnia pro Lenina" [Song about Lenin] and "V. I. Leninu" [To V. I. Lenin], which commemorated Lenin's death, as well as the *Sel'skokhoziaistvennaia simfoniia* [Agricultural Symphony] (1923). In pieces such as "Troika" (Example 6.1), he experimented with unusual vocal effects and instrumentation, while in others, such as "Rybolov" [The Angler] and "Sten'ka Razin," he employed his more customary style of adapting folk melodies to a choral setting.

A splinter group of RAPM, the Organization of Revolutionary Composers, has received far less scholarly attention and opprobrium than its more notorious parent organization.[30] The Revolutionary Composers shared the Proletarian Musicians' veneration of selected portions of the classical musical legacy and their objections to the "decadence" of most recently composed art music. But unlike RAPM, the Revolutionary Composers felt that composing and disseminating music on revolutionary themes was essential to the development of a new musical culture. From their base at the music division of the State Publishing House, the Revolutionary Composers churned out the "agitational" music [*agitki*] which provided an important portion of the choral circles' repertoire. Like the Proletarian Musicians, they also worked as directors of club music circles and participated in other popular music education programs.

The Revolutionary Composers acknowledged the distinction between their "agitational" pieces, almost all of which were for solo voice or vocal ensembles, and music promoted as "artistic literature." Indeed the group's leader, Lev Shul'gin, claimed that the purpose of these pieces was simply "to rivet attention to certain themes and moods, . . . and to play a certain musical-educational (*vospitatel'naia*) role for the proletariat."[31]

The Revolutionary Composers favored romantic, revolutionary themes for their music. Hymns extolling the glory of the revolution, visions of happiness for all, or the joys of free labor often used verses by Demian Bednyi, Vladimir Maiakovsky, and Aleksandr Bezymensky, as well as the texts of the so-called "peasant poets" such as Vladimir Kirillov. Their music was usually festive and often bombastic and overwrought.

Mikhail Krasev was by far the most prolific member of the group, publishing more than 250 choruses in five years. Also among the organization's more active composers were Grigorii Lobachev, who published folksong arrangements as well as martial agitational songs, and Klimentii Korchmarev, a conservatory graduate who wrote "artistic" as well as agitational music.

The scorn this kind of musical propaganda later elicited from Soviet and Western observers echoed concerns raised at the time by other musicians, RAPM, and even communist bureaucrats.[32] In 1926, Anatoly Lunacharsky,

Example 6.1 A. Kastalsky, "Troika," from *Krasnyi Oktiabr'* (Moscow: Muzykal'nyi sector gosudarstvennogo izdatel'stva, 1923). Composed on a text by the peasant poet Petr Oreshin and published in an anthology of revolutionary music commemorating the sixth anniversary of the revolution, "Troika" calls for mixed chorus, three trumpets in C, triangle, and cymbals. Kastalsky uses vocal glissandi and hissing to evoke the winds that sweep a speeding Russian troika to a great destiny.

Example 6.1 Continued.

the head of the Commissariat of Education, mocked *agitki* as "homebred simplifications" that either "forged" old music or flaunted inappropriate decoration, "like wearing earrings in one's nose."[33]

The one Revolutionary Composer whose work escaped the brunt of this criticism was the *Proletkul't* veteran, Dmitrii Vasil'ev-Buglai. In the twenties he continued to compose on revolutionary themes and work with amateur choruses, directing the musical activities of the clubs affiliated with the All-Russian Central Executive Committee. The experiences of the Civil War provided a common theme for many of his pieces, such as his famous arrangement of the satirical recruitment song "Provody" [Send Off] (Example 6.2), "Pliasovaia" [Dancing Song], and "Krasnaia molodezh'" [Red Youth]. He also continued to write anti-religious, satirical songs such as "Popy-trutni zhivut na plutni" [Priest-Drones Living by Cheating] and "Tserkovnaia sluzhba" [The Church Service], an extended musical "fresco" based on cartoons and poetry by Demian Bednyi published on the front page of *Pravda* on January 6, 1923.

The final group on the musical "Left" consisted of students at the Moscow

Example 6.2 D. Vasil'ev Buglai, "Provody" (Moscow, n.d.). Text by Dem'ian Bednyi. Vasil'ev Buglai's music is an adaptation of the Ukrainian folk tune "Oi, shcho zh to za uchinivsia."

Conservatory who formed a "production collective" [*Prokoll*] to write songs and marches with a broad popular appeal.[34] Led by Aleksandr Davidenko, *Prokoll* members rejected the distinction between "agitational" and "artistic" music. Unlike the Revolutionary Composers, they avoided deliberate simplification, insisting that the mass audience deserved music that incorporated the best qualities of contemporary art music as well as the classical legacy. Like the ORK's *agitki,* the *Prokoll*'s compositions dealt with a discrete set of themes: the revolution and its heroes, the Civil War, building socialism, and the country's "new heroes," Soviet youth. *Prokoll* members drew on a diverse range of sources for their music, including contemporary (anonymous) revolutionary songs, rhymed ditties called *chastushki,* contemporary art music, the aural palette of the modern urban environment, and songs from the Red Army.

The musical Left's program for developing a new musical culture depended in large part on successfully instilling workers with an appreciation for their own compositions, folksongs, or selections from the classical repertoire. The flip side of this effort to cultivate an appreciation for some kinds of music was a determination to eradicate others. Choral circle activists displayed particular hostility toward songs and dance tunes published under the category of the "light genre," a catch-all designation for the "gypsy genre" [*tsyganshchina*], dance tunes, and "songs of the new way of life." Asserting that this music promoted petty-bourgeois banality and philistinism ([*poshlost'*] and [*meshchanstvo*]), reformers claimed it corrupted the sensibilities of workers and peasants. In the capitalist economic environment of the twenties, light genre music enjoyed wide distribution through sheet music, on records, from the stages of variety [*estrada*] theaters, and in restaurants, cafes, and bars.

Most popular were "gypsy" romances or *tsyganshchina.* Although their lyrics sometimes referred to gypsies, horses, or gypsy camps, these pieces were only distant cousins of the authentic songs of gypsies. A free, emotional style and often frank sensuality made *tsyganshchina* more accessible than the salon romance from which they descended. These pieces generally conveyed one of two ranges of emotions—a feeling of abandon, recklessness, or lawlessness, or one of disappointment in love, spiritual crisis, jealousy, and hopelessness.[35] Among the most popular "gypsy" songs in the twenties were "Tsyganochka" [Gypsy girl], "Bubentsy" [Little bells], and "Stakanchiki granenye" [Cut-glass tumblers].[36]

"Songs of the new way of life" sometimes used the musical style of *tsyganshchina,* but took the revolution or its impact on everyday life as a theme. Most were written by composers who began their careers working for the variety stage, often in southern Russia or Ukraine. Among the most popular songs about the revolution were three written by *estrada* musicians during the Civil War: "Krasnye kavaleristy" [Red Cavalrymen] by Dmitrii Pokrass, "Krasnaia armiia vsekh sil'nei" [The Red Army is stronger than all] by his brother Samuil, and the future anthem of the Soviet air force, "Aviamarsh" (better known as "Vse vyshe" [Ever Higher]) by Iulii Khait.[37]

In the twenties, songwriters such as Khait, the Pokrass brothers, Matvei Blanter, and Valentin Kruchinin published much of their work with the

Association of Moscow Authors, which became a primary source of light genre music. The mood of many of their songs continued the *tsyganshchina* tradition of restlessness, melancholy, and disillusionment with love. Other pieces evoked the hopes and travails of a distinctly Soviet context and became widely popular with a range of audiences. Most emblematic of this second type of song was Kruchinin and Pavel German's "Kirpichiki" [Little bricks], a lively, pro-Soviet ditty about love and revolution in a brick factory, which swept the popular music scene in the mid-twenties.[38]

"Kirpichiki" and its success typified just about everything that reformers thought was wrong with urban popular music. Because they regarded music as an ideological weapon that not only reflected but also influenced its environment, club activists from the musical Left attributed a range of defects in working-class life to light genre music. Just as nineteenth-century intellectuals had denounced the penny novel as "poison" to the common people's sensibilities, the musical Left maintained that light genre music had a subtle, narcotic effect on those who sang it, listened to it, and danced to it.[39] *Tsyganshchina* and foxtrots provided diversion and entertainment for workers and Young Communist League members, but dulled their militant, revolutionary aspirations and dampened their enthusiasm for "social work." To the musical Left, the popularity of "Kirpichiki," with its sentimental lyrics and lilting waltz tune, indicated how susceptible the masses were to petit-bourgeois "survivals" [*perezhitki*] masquerading as revolutionary music.[40] Reformers complained that light genre music often promoted "narrow individualism" and dealt with "base feelings" or "naked sensuality." Banal, sentimental lyrics or simple coarseness made these songs very "accessible," and thus prevented people from searching out more sophisticated musical material.[41]

Lyrics of unrequited love, revenge, and melancholy that typified *tsyganshchina* were incompatible with the wholesomeness that the Proletarian Musicians and other cultural puritans associated with building socialism. But the musical Left found the music even more harmful, because it intensified the effect of the text. Activists criticized pieces that employed harmonies with suspensions, movement from a major key to its parallel minor, and particular melodic conventions [*oborota*], pointing out that these musical devices were hallmarks of the *tsyganshchina* style.[42] They especially disliked melodic chromaticism, which they identified as the musical component of the sentimentality they found so objectionable in *tsyganshchina*. By the end of the twenties, this musical critique expanded to include a denunciation of syncopation, "monotonous rhythms," and melodic fragments that began and ended on the same note. For example, RAPM maintained that "'Kirpichiki' stifled a person's aspirations" because the song's basic melodic unit used only three ascending step-wise notes that then returned, also by steps, to the starting tone: "[The melody] dulls the will, discourages striving and development, and brings everything back to the starting point."[43] The *tsyganshchina* "sound" even made reformers suspicious of pieces with impeccable political pedigrees. They condemned pieces such as "Ever Higher" and "Pesnia kommuny" [Song of the Commune] as "pseudo-revolutionary music," insisting that "bad" music undermined, and even sabotaged, the meaning of the words.[44] A similar critique informed objections to the common practice of "updating" an old familiar melody by setting it to a revolutionary text. The Left particularly loathed a favorite fighting song-hymn of the Red Army, "Smelo my v boi poidem" [We go to battle boldly], whose melody bore audible debts to a pre-revolutionary "gypsy" romance.

Reformers appreciated the difficulty of the task they had undertaken and considered proper education an indispensable component of their campaign to change popular musical taste. They placed heavy emphasis on the importance of "musical literacy" to the overall objective of developing workers' musical preferences as well as their "general cultural literacy."[45] The task of the circle leader was to train [*vospitivat'*] workers' tastes so that they could distinguish between bad, bourgeois urban music and music that was "fresh, healthy and valuable."[46] What "musical literacy" meant varied. It often included the ability to read music and proficiency at the rudiments of ear training such as recognizing intervals, cadences, and scales, and taking rhythmic dictation. The Left's programs for teaching musical literacy in the clubs emphasized active learning using familiar tunes, especially folksongs and revolutionary songs.[47] Boleslav Yavorsky's method for "listening to music" [*slushanie muzyki*], which taught people to follow the phrasing and respond to the mood of a given piece, was also widely used and served as the curricular foundation for the Krasnaia Presnia School of Musical Instructors.[48] Some activists even staged demonstrations that compared "good" revolutionary music with *tsyganshchina* and "pseudo-revolutionary" music. Whatever the method, the objective and underlying assumptions were the same: Knowledge was essential to overcoming a liking for music that was too sentimental, trite, sensual, or coarse. Directed listening, a basic awareness of the mechanics of musical language and exposure to "good music," would make workers more discriminating in their musical preferences.[49]

This program to develop a new musical culture in the choral circles was as ambitious as it was perilous, and would-be reformers confronted an array of obstacles in their efforts to eradicate the bad musical culture of the past and nurture the healthy "proletarian" music of the future. Among the most significant of these problems were the motivations of the people who joined the choral circles. For regardless of what the organizers intended, many people participated in music circles because they wanted to sing and enjoyed public performance, not to become more politically literate and culturally sophisticated.[50]

The second problem was the instructors of these groups, who had to have the appropriate musical skills and political orientation if the music circles were to spread musical literacy, develop socialist values, and raise political awareness among their members.[51] Outside the ranks of the musical Left, however, such circle leaders were in critically short supply. Indeed, activists from the musical Left constantly bemoaned the fact that many choral circle leaders either shared the same "bad" musical tastes as the circle members or were former directors of church choirs.[52] Courses offered by the Moscow Trade Union Soviet, the Krasnia Presnia School of Music Instructors, and the Moscow Conservatory tried to address this problem, but the deficit of "good" music instructors persisted throughout the decade.[53]

Intractable as they were, problems with the training and motivations of instructors paled in comparison to the difficulties reformers encountered with the choruses' repertoire. While chorus members and audiences often responded positively to folk music and "classics," they rejected most new "revolutionary" music and continued to favor light genre music. Their favorite pieces included arrangements of folksongs such as Liadov's "Kolodets" [Ring dance] and Glazunov's setting of "Ei ukhnem." Old revolutionary songs and Civil War hits like "Provody" were still popular in many quarters, but people became bored with them as the immediacy of the war years faded. New "revolutionary music" that the choruses did like, such as Davidenko's "Konnaia Budennogo" [Budennyi's Cavalry, CD no. 10], Vasil'ev-Buglai's "Krov' i sneg" [Blood and snow], and his "O proshlom" [About the past] invoked the style of a folksong.

Activists constantly struggled to regulate the choruses' repertoire for performances at club-sponsored events such as political meetings and demonstrations, as well as for the circles' independent performances, trying to balance the musical preferences of the singers and audiences against their own sense of appropriate music. The Left urged club leaders to select and prepare the music for any activity in advance, since spontaneous music making in the club or choral circle inevitably consisted largely of songs like "Kirpichiki" and other music reformers found objectionable.[54]

But despite these efforts, it became clear that singers and audiences found much of the "new" revolutionary music too hard, too clichéd, or just not very interesting. In emulating "artistic" vocal music, the Revolutionary Composers (and many *Prokoll* members) made their pieces too difficult and lost the opportunity to engage a "mass" audience. Most of their compositions were four-part choruses with moderately difficult piano accompaniments. Many of Aleksandr Davidenko's pieces were well-received in clubs and the Red Army, but most of the *Prokoll*'s vocal pieces were too complex and too closely tied to the recital hall to allow for quick assimilation by the uninitiated. As for the ORK's *agitki,* singers complained that they "all sounded alike," and rejected newly composed pieces as "the same old stuff."[55]

By the mid-twenties, activists from the musical Left began to acknowledge the failure of the *agitki* and call for more accessible "mass songs," a concept that had been used in the most general way since the early days of the revolution.[56] Criticisms of the *agitki* began to appear even in the ORK's journal, where choral circle members called for "bold, revolutionary songs" with simple melodic lines and no accompaniment.[57] These requests echoed other calls for better, easier pieces that would truly be "mass songs" at the same time official agencies began to show some interest in musical affairs.[58]

In March 1926, *Glavpolitprosvet,* the state agency for political education, convened a conference on mass musical work in Moscow to address the problems facing activists in the club music circles. More than half of the 150 participants were leaders of local music circles. These activists worked with delegates from various musical institutions and the musical Left to formulate a more effective program for the music circles and the choral groups in particular. While much of this program was never realized, the conference resolutions were significant because for the first time they conferred official approval on certain musical qualities and disapproval on others.[59] In particular, they outlined the characteristics of the "mass song," which would become the backbone of state-sponsored popular music in the 1930s.

The conference resolutions described the "proletarian-soviet mass song" as one that correctly portrayed the life and was "saturated with the mood and ideas of its class." It would provide the foundation of mass musical culture and the opportunity to replace musical deformities [*urodstva*] with genuine artistic compositions. Addressing the difficulty and poor quality of much agitational music, the resolutions stipulated that a mass song could be assimilated by the broad masses "without special effort" [*bez spetsial'nykh usilii*] and be performed in everyday life. Mass songs often served a particular social function and could be closely connected with activities such as work, dancing, or festivals. The resolutions also stipulated that a mass song must have an appropriate text, use accessible musical language that clearly expressed the song's mood (sorrow, joy, heroism, etc.), have a clear, singable melody, as well as simple, lively rhythm, and an affinity with the "harmonic conventions (*oborota*) employed by the masses until now."

Despite the popularity of peasant folksongs in the music circles, however, the conference resolutions suggested that the folksong's contribution to the music of the future needed to be carefully circumscribed. A much-debated resolution stipulated that while mass songs should use "familiar" harmonic conventions, they were not to imitate the traditional peasant folksong,[60] because this music was too closely bound to pre-revolutionary peasant ideology. The resolution further warned that the "despair, passivity and ignorance" reflected in the folksong could harm the psyche of the modern worker.[61] Here were the first signs of the (short-lived) hostility to traditional folk music that would come into full flower during the Cultural Revolution.[62]

Resolutions notwithstanding, reformers noted little change in the club music scene in the later part of the twenties. Qualified instructors remained in short supply, and the problem of finding songs with ideologically acceptable texts and music that could rival "Kirpichiki" for popularity persisted, despite the continued efforts of the Revolutionary Composers and *Prokoll* to produce appealing alternatives to *tsyganshchina* and "pseudo-revolutionary" songs. The acuteness of this situation became painfully evident in 1928 when the jury of the First All-Union Mass Song Competition chose not to award a first prize to any of the 600 entries.[63]

With the adoption of Stalin's five-year plan for rapid economic modernization in 1928, the gradualist and pluralist cultural policies of the twenties gave way to more militant and authoritarian programs for cultural revolution.[64] In the musical sphere this period was marked by aggressive efforts to "proletarianize" the conservatories, heightened criticism and censorship of most "modern" music as well as of jazz and *tsyganshchina*, the end of private music publishing, and the consolidation of the musical Left under the leadership of the Proletarian Musicians' organization, RAPM.[65] But although it now had at least some of the official backing it had long lobbied for, RAPM found its own agendas overshadowed by broader political objectives, as the Party enjoined all creative artists to mobilize their creative efforts on behalf of the campaigns for rapid industrialization and the collectivization of agriculture.

During these years of the Cultural Revolution, many choral circles' activities moved out of the clubs and into the countryside or onto construction sites. Just as Vasil'ev-Buglai's *proletkul't* choir had toured the battlefront during the

Civil War, now musical activists worked in the front lines of the First Five Year Plan where choral "brigades" exhorted steel workers to exceed their production quotas and urged peasants to join collective farms ("Harvest Dance," CD no. 11). These years also witnessed a revival of the mass singing movement, as an organization called *Muzyka-massam* ["Music to the masses"] enrolled thousands of workers in amateur singing activities.[66] RAPM also approved the use of mass singing at demonstrations and political meetings.[67]

Bowing to directives "from above" to mobilize all creative resources for the fulfillment of the First Five Year Plan, RAPM enjoined all of its members to write "mass songs" for the collectivization and industrialization campaigns. Under pressure to work and disseminate their music quickly, many composers finally employed a simpler musical language with more unison sections and a minimal or optional accompaniment. Their efforts to produce music that was "bold" and "infused with brave emotion" made generous use of fanfares, dotted rhythms, duple meter, and predictable uplifting modulations from a minor verse to a major refrain.[68]

Even now, however, the musical Left's offerings remained unappealing and generally too difficult. Virtually none of the "mass songs" from this period achieved genuine popularity. When a decree by the Party's Central Committee dissolved RAPM and marked the official end of the Cultural Revolution in April 1932, most of RAPM's members ceased to compose the short vocal and choral pieces that had been the focus of their creative energies for the past decade.

But while the musical Left was officially dead, choral circles and mass songs were not. As the political and social upheaval of the First Five Year Plan abated, workers' clubs continued to provide the resources and physical space for organized leisure, including choral groups, while "mass songs" became one of the most ubiquitous forms of a mass culture that was both manipulated by political authorities and genuinely popular and universal.[69]

The musical Left's campaign to sanitize popular musical forms succeeded, at least partially, in that "*Kirpichiki*" and other light genre hits from the twenties fell under a virtual ban for the next forty years.[70] But the mass songs of the thirties also incorporated elements of the *tsyganshchina* tradition, as well as influences from Jewish folk music, the Russian folksong, old revolutionary and prison songs, and other urban genres. Unlike their predecessors in the twenties, which had focused almost exclusively on topics related to the revolution, the mass songs of the thirties dealt with a broader range of human experience. Although both the personal and the political received a carefully optimistic treatment that was often widely divergent from the realities of

Soviet life, millions of Russians embraced the catchy tunes and compelling strains of songs such as "Pesnia o rodine" [Song of the Motherland] and "Sportivnyi marsh" (Sportsman's March) by Vasilii Lebedev-Kumach and Isaac Dunaevsky. The fact that many of the light genre composers stigmatized by the musical Left in the twenties emerged as the "kings" of mass song in the thirties highlights both the extent to which individual composers were able to adapt to evolving political circumstances and the importance of popular preferences in the melange that was Stalinist culture.

Efforts to change musical preferences in the twenties often foundered when reformers rejected genuinely popular forms at the same time they sought to use music as a vehicle for political mobilization. These experiences highlight the ways in which popular taste asserted itself even in the repressive conditions of Stalinism. The popular songs of the thirties accommodated many of the preferences reformers found so objectionable in the first decade after the revolution. At the same time, these songs placed less emphasis on the divisive rhetoric of class war that had figured so prominently in the political discourse of the twenties. In keeping with a broader shift in Soviet culture, the songs of the thirties stressed common purpose and celebrated the feats of new Soviet heroes and the promise of a bright socialist future.[71] The experiences of the twenties conditioned the musical style of this emerging mass culture in significant ways. For if the authoritarian voice of the state often made itself heard in the popular song of the thirties, so were the musical tastes of Russia's urban masses rarely out of range.

Notes

1. S. Krylova, "Muzyka v rabochem klube," *Prizyv* 1924 no. 7: 35.

2. John Hatch, "Hangouts and Hangovers: State, Class, and Culture in Moscow's Workers' Club Movement, 1925–1928," *Russian Review* 53 (January 1994): 98.

3. Victoria Bonnell, *Roots of Rebellion: Workers' Politics and Organization in St. Petersburg and Moscow, 1900–1914* (Berkeley: University of California Press, 1983), 328–34.

4. Jeffrey Brooks, *When Russia Learned to Read: Literacy and Popular Literature, 1861–1917* (Princeton, N.J.: Princeton University Press, 1985), 318–33; Joan Neuberger, *Hooliganism: Crime, Culture and Power in St. Petersburg, 1900–1914* (Berkeley: University of California Press, 1993), 139, 253–54.

5. A. D. Kastal'skii, *Stat'i, vospominaniia, materialy* (Moscow: Gosudarstvennoe muzykal'noe izdatel'stvo, 1960), 39; Nadezhda Briusova, "Muzykal'noe prosveshchenie i obrazovanie za gody revoliutsii," *Muzyka i revoliutsiia* 1926 no. 1: 25; Vladimir Morosan, *Choral Performance in Pre-Revolutionary Russia* (Ann Arbor, Mich.: UMI Research Press, 1986), 117–26.

6. Zinovia Sochor, *Revolution and Culture: The Bogdanov-Lenin Controversy* (Ithaca, N.Y.: Cornell University Press, 1988); Gabriele Gorzka, "Proletarian Culture in Practice: Workers' Clubs, 1917–1921," in *Essays on Revolutionary Culture and Stalinism*, ed. John W. Strong (Columbus, Ohio: Slavica, 1990), 29–55; Lynn Mally, *Culture of the Future: The Proletkul't Movement in Revolutionary Russia* (Berkeley: University of California Press, 1990), 183–91; John Hatch, "The Formation of Working-Class Cultural Institutions during NEP: The Workers' Club Movement in Moscow, 1921–1923," *The Carl Beck Papers in Russian and East European Studies* 806 (1990): 15–32.

7. Mally, *Culture of the Future*, 122–23; Mark von Hagen, *Soldiers in the Proletarian Dictatorship: The Red Army and the Soviet Socialist State, 1917–1930* (Ithaca, N.Y.: Cornell University Press, 1990), 88–114.

8. D. L. Lokshin, *D. S. Vasil'ev-Buglai* (Moscow: Sovetskii kompozitor, 1958), 6–7.

9. A. D. Kastal'skii, "K voprosu ob organizatsii muzykal'nykh zaniatii v Tsentral'noi studii Moskovskogo proletkul'takh" (1918?), in *Muzykal'naia zhizn' Moskvy v pervye gody posle Oktiabria,* ed. S. R. Stepanova (Moscow: Sovetskii kompozitor, 1972), 283–84; Nadezhda Briusova, *Zadachi narodnogo muzykal'nogo obrazovaniia. Doklad prochitanyi na konferentsii kul't.-pros. proletarskykh organizatsii* (Moscow: Vscrossiiskik proletkul't, 1919), 6, 14.

10. Kastal'skii, "K voprosu," 284.

11. Briusova, *Zadachi narodnogo muzykal'nogo obrazovaniia,* 7, 10.

12. K. Postavnichev, *Massovoe penie* (Moscow: Vserossiiskii proletkul't, 1925), 4–5; von Hagen, *Soldiers in the Proletarian Dictatorship,* 94, 153.

13. Carmen Claudin-Urondo, *Lenin and the Cultural Revolution,* trans. Brian Pearce (Atlantic Highlands, N.J.: Harvester Press and Humanities Press, 1977), 11–24.

14. William G. Rosenberg, ed., *Bolshevik Visions: The First Phase of the Cultural Revolution in Soviet Russia* (Ann Arbor, Mich.: Ardis, 1984); Michael David-Fox, *Revolution of the Mind: Higher Learning Among the Bolsheviks* (Ithaca, N.Y.: Cornell University Press, 1997); Stefan Plaggenborg, *Revolutionskultur: Menschenbilder und Kulturelle Praxis in Sowjetrussland zwischen Oktoberrevolution und Stalinismus* (Cologne: Böhlau, 1996).

15. Sheila Fitzpatrick, "The 'Soft-Line' on Culture and Its Enemies," in *The Cultural Front: Power and Culture in Revolutionary Russia* (Ithaca, N.Y.: Cornell University Press, 1992), 91–114.

16. Leon Trotsky, "Leninism and Workers' Clubs," *Problems of Everyday Life and Other Writings on Culture and Science* (New York: Monad Press, 1973), 288–319.

17. Lynn Mally, *Revolutionary Acts: Amateur Theater and the Soviet State, 1917–1938* (Ithaca, N.Y.: Cornell University Press, 2000), 25.

18. Vance Kepley Jr., "Cinema and Everyday Life: Soviet Worker Clubs of the 1920s," in *Resisting Images: Essays on Cinema and History,* ed. Robert Sklar and Charles Musser (Philadelphia: Temple University Press, 1990), 111; Neil Edmunds, *The Soviet Proletarian Music Movement* (Oxford: Peter Lang, 2000), 112.

19. N. D., "O muzykal'no-khorovoi kruzhkovoi rabote v klubakh Mosraikoma

VSRM," *Muzyka i revoliutsiia* 1926 no. 1: 39; Georgii Polianovskii, "Khorovaia rabota v soiuz shveinikov," *Muzyka i revoliutsiia* 1926 no. 2: 31–32; N. Dem'ianov, "Semeinye vechera v rabochykh klubakh," *Muzyka i revoliutsiia* 1926 no. 3: 9–12; L. "Rabota muzykal'nykh kruzhkov v soiuze stroitelei," *Muzyka i revoliutsiia* 1926 no. 4: 24.

20. Postavnichev, *Massovoe penie,* 54.

21. L. Kaltat, "K voprosu o klubno-muzykal'noi rabote," *Muzyka i Oktriabr* 1926 no. 4–5: 24; Katerina Clark, *Petersburg: Crucible of Cultural Revolution* (Cambridge, Mass.: Harvard University Press, 1995), 146; Mally, *Revolutionary Acts,* 94–101.

22. L. Kaltat, "Klub imeni t. Stalina pri Sekretariate Ts. K. V. K. P. (b)," *Muzyka i Oktiabr'* 1926 no. 2: 20.

23. John Hatch, "The Politics of Mass Culture: Workers, Communists, and Proletkul't in the Development of Workers' Clubs, 1921–25," *Russian History/Histoire Russe* 13, nos. 2–3 (1986): 119.

24. Sergei Bugoslavskii, "Metodika muzykal'noi raboty v klube," *Prizyv* 1925 no. 1: 52.

25. S. Krylova, "Muzyka v rabochem klube," *Prizyv* 1924 no. 7: 35.

26. Ts. Ratskaia, "Muzykal'naia rabota v khorkruzhkakh," *Muzykal'naia nov'* 1924 no. 11: 6–7.

27. Amy Nelson, *Music for the Revolution: Russian Musicians and Soviet Power, 1917–1932,* (University Park: Pennsylvania State University Press, 2004) 67–93; Edmunds, *Soviet Proletarian Music.*

28. Amy Nelson, "The Struggle for Proletarian Music: RAPM and the Cultural Revolution," *Slavic Review* 59 no. 1 (spring 2000): 101–32; Sheila Fitzpatrick, "The Lady Macbeth Affair: Shostakovich and the Soviet Puritans," in *The Cultural Front,* 183–215; Neil Edmunds, "Music and Politics: The Case of the Russian Association of Proletarian Musicians," *Slavonic and East European Review* 78 no. 1 (January 2000): 66–89; Richard Taruskin, *Defining Russia Musically: Historical and Hermeneutical Essays* (Princeton, N.J.: Princeton University Press, 1997), 92–94; *Istoriia sovremennoi otechestvennoi muzyki* 1 (Moscow: Muzyka, 1995), 30–33; *Istoriia russkoi sovetskoi muzyki* 1 (Moscow: Gosudarstvennoe muzkay'noe izdatel'stvo, 1956), 39; *Istoriia muzyki narodov SSSR* 1 (Moscow: Sovetskii kompozitor, 1970), 135–36; Boris Schwarz, *Music and Musical Life in Soviet Russia* (Bloomington: Indiana University Press, 1983), 55; Stanley Dale Krebs, *Soviet Composers and the Development of Soviet Music* (New York: Norton, 1970), 49–50; Gordon McQuere, ed., *Russian Theoretical Thought in Music* (Ann Arbor, Mich.: UMI Research Press, 1983), 50.

29. A. Kastal'skii, O vechere narodnostei v Bol'sh. teatr," *Muzykal'naia nov'* 1923 no. 2: 25–26; L. Kaltat, "O podlinno-burzhuaznoi ideologii gr. Roslavtsa," *Muzykal'noe obrazovanie* 1927 no. 3–4: 40–41.

30. A. Sokhor, *Russkaia sovetskaia pesnia* (Leningrad: Sovetskii kompozitor, 1959), 109–14; Edmunds, *Soviet Proletarian Music,* 153–210.

31. Lev Shul'gin, "Sovremennoe muzykal'noe tvorchestvo i predposylki nashei tvorcheskoi raboty," *Muzykal'naia nov'* 1924 no. 4: 16.

32. Vladimir Frumkin, "Tekhnologiia ubezhdeniia: zametki o politicheskoi pesne," *Obozrenie* no. 6 (September 1983): 24; M. Ivanov-Boretskii, "Agitatsionno-prosvetitel'naia muzykal'naia literatura," *Muzykal'naia nov'* 1924 no. 8: 27; Gosudarstvennyi arkhiv rossiiskoi federatsii (GARF) f. 298, op. 1, d. 129, l. 1580b; Iurii Keldysh, "Problema proletarskogo muzykal'nogo tvorchestva i poputnichestvo," *Proletarskii muzykant* 1929 no. 1: 19.

33. A. Lunacharskii, *V mire muzyke. Stat'i i rechi,* 2nd ed. (Moscow: Sovetskii kompozitor, 1971), 186–87.

34. Edmunds, *Soviet Proletarian Music,* 211–88; Edmunds, "Alexander Davidenko and Prokoll," *Tempo* 182 (1992): 1–5; Valentina Zarudko, "Istoriia muzyki. Iz proshlogo sovetskoi muzykal'noi kul'tury,' in *Moskovskii muzykoved* vyp. 1 (1990), ed. M. E. Tarakanov, 5–19.

35. Galina Soboleva, *Russkii sovetskii romans* (Moscow: Znanie, 1985), 18.

36. Soboleva, *Russkii sovetskii romans,* 3–44; Gerald Stanton Smith, *Songs to Seven Strings: Russian Guitar Poetry and Soviet Mass Song* (Bloomington: Indiana University Press, 1984), 60–64; Robert Rothstein, "The Quiet Rehabilitation of the Brick Factory: Early Soviet Popular Music and its Critics," *Slavic Review* 39, no.3 (1980): 375–76; Robert Rothstein, "Popular Song in the NEP Era," in *Russia in the Era of NEP,* ed. Sheila Fitzpatrick, Alexander Rabinowitch, and Richard Stites (Bloomington: Indiana University Press, 1991), 271–73; Richard Stites, *Russian Popular Culture. Entertainment and Society since 1900* (Cambridge: Cambridge University Press, 1992), 12–15.

37. M. F. Leonova, *Dmitrii Pokrass* (Moscow: Sovetskii kompozitor, 1981), 36; M. I. Zil'berbrandt, "Pesnia na estrade," *Russkaia sovetskaia estrada 1917–1929 gg. Ocherki istorii* (Moscow: Iskusstvo, 1976), 209–10.

38. Rothstein, "Quiet Rehabilitation"; Sokhor, *Russkaia sovetskaia pesnia,* 98–99; Zil'berbrandt, "Pesnia na estrade," 236–37; Iurii Sokolov, *Russian Folklore,* trans. Catherine Ruth Smith (New York: Macmillan, 1950), 627–29; A. Groman, "O muzyke dlia derevni," *Muzyka i Oktiabr'* 1926 no. 1: 7; P. Bosh, "O chem poet molodaia derevnia," *Zhizn' iskusstva* 1926 no. 15: 14; Richard Stites and James von Geldern, eds., *Mass Culture in Soviet Russia* (Bloomington: Indiana University Press, 1995), 69–70 (also recording on companion cassette).

39. Nikolai Shuvalov, "Muzykal'noe prosveshchenie prezhde i teper'," *Muzykal'naia nov'* 1923 no. 1: 24; Brooks, *When Russia Learned to Read,* 331.

40. Groman, "O muzyke," 7; "Nekotorye voprosy muzykal'noi revoliutsii," *Muzyka i revoliutsiia* 1926 no. 4: 13; L. Lebedinskii, "K voprosu o proletarskoi muzyke," *Muzyka i Oktiabr'* 1926, no. 2: 1; Sarra Krylova, "Po povudu stat'i tov. Paskhalov," *Muzyka i Oktiabr'* 1926, no. 2: 8.

41. Lev Shul'gin, "Massovaia pesnia," *Muzyka i revoliutsiia* 1926 no. 2: 19.

42. Sergei Bugoslavskii, "Vasil'ev-Buglai," *Muzykal'naia nov'* 1923 no. 2: 23.

43. L. Lebedinskii, "Vazhneishshee zveno nashei raboty," *Dovesti do kontsa bor'bu s NEPmanskoi muzyki* (Moscow: Gosudarstvennoe muzkal'noe izdatel'stvo, 1931), 4–5;

N. Briusova, "Na bor'bu s muzykal'nym durmanom," *Protiv Nepmanskoi muzykoi* (Moscow: Gosudarstvennoe muzykal'noe izdatel'stvo, 1930), 17.

44. Lev Shul'gin, *L. V. Shul'gin. Stat'i, vospominaniia* (Moscow: Sovetskii kompozitor, 1977), 26.

45. R. "V Moskovskoi Gos. Konservatorii. Pedagogicheskii otdel," *Muzykal'naia nov'* 1924 no. 10: 26.

46. Bugoslavskii, "Metodika muzykal'noi raboty," 53.

47. N. Demianov, "Formy i metody raboty khor-kruzhka," *Muzykal'naia nov'* 1924 no. 5: 14; Ratskaia, "Muzykal'naia rabota v khorkruzhkakh," 11–12; A. Kastal'skii, "Pervye shagi," *Muzykal'naia nov'* 1924 no. 11: 8–10; A. Kastal'skii, "Posleduiushchie shagi," *Muzykal'naia nov'* 1924 no. 12: 9–10; Bugoslavskii, "Metodika muzykal'noi raboty," 52–56; I. Dubovskii, "Besedy po muzykal'noi gramote," *Muzyka i Oktiabr'* 1926 no. 2: 11–15.

48. M. Pekelis, "O slushanii muzyki," *Muzyka i Oktiabr'* 1926 no. 1: 11–15; A. D. "Muzykal'naia shkola instruktorov imeni Krasnoi Presni,' *Muzyka i revoliutsiia* 1926 no. 1: 41; GARF f. 2306 op. 25 d. 77 ll.1–2.

49. Lev Shul'gin, "K postanovke voprosa o slushanii muzyki v kruzhkakh," *Muzyka i revoliutsiia* 1926 no. 1: 19–22; Gr. Avlov, "V bor'be za pesniu," *Zhizn' iskusstva* 1927 no. 5: 7.

50. Polianovskii, "Khorovaia i muzykal'naia rabota," 31; N. Demianov, "Novaia ustanovka klubno-khorovoi raboty," *Muzyka i revoliutsiia* 1927 no. 4: 9.

51. S. Abakumov, "V Moskovskoi Gos. Konservatorii. Khorovoi otdel," *Muzykal'naia nov'* 1924 no. 12: 28.

52. Ivan Lipaev, "Tserkovniki ili obshchestvenniki," *Muzykal'naia nov'* 1924 no. 11: 7; Krylova, "Muzyka v rabochem klube," 34; V. Furman, "Kontserty v rabochykh klubakh," *Muzyka i revoliutsiia* 1926 no. 3: 29.

53. Rybinskii, "Kursy dlia klubnykh rukovoditelei," *Pravda* January 16, 1924: 7; "Khorovaia rabota v soiuze tekstil'shchikov," *Muzyka i revoliutsiia* 1926 no. 1: 36; N. Dem'ianov, "Muzykal'naia samodeiatel'naia rabota i professional'noe muzykal'noe iskusstvo," *Muzyka i revoliutsiia* 1929 no. 4: 11; V. A. Dasmanov, "Derevenskie instrumental'nye kruzhki," *Muzyka i revoliutsiia* 1929 no. 4: 14.

54. Dem'ianov, "Semeinye vechera," 10.

55. Dem'ianov, "Semeinye vechera," 10.

56. Dem'ianov, "Semeinye vechera," 10; Sokhor, *Russkaia sovetskaia pesnia*, 113.

57. "Khorovaia rabota v soiuze tekstil'shchikov," 37; D. Rovynskii, "O massovykh pesniakh," *Muzyka i revoliutsiia* 1926 no. 2: 33.

58. "O repertuare muzykal'no-professional'nykh uchebnykh zavedenii," *Muzykal'noe obrazovanie* 1926 no. 5–6: 54; GARF f. 298, op. 1, d. 128, ll. 194–940b.

59. "Resoliutsiia I konferentsii po muzykal'noi politprosvetrabote," *Sovetskoe iskusstvo* 1926 no. 6: 75–78; "Konferentsiia," *Muzyka i Oktiabr'* 1926 no. 2: 10–12; "S'ezdy, konferentsii, soveshchaniia," *Muzyka i revoliutsiia* 1926 no. 4: 30–31.

60. Nikolai Roslavets, "O psevdo-proletarskoi muzyki," *Na putiakh iskusstva*.

sbornik statei, eds. V. M. Blumenfeld, V. F. Pletnev, and N. F. Chuzhak (Moscow: Moskovskii proletkul't, 1926), 180–92; Simon Korev, "Pervyi kamen," *Sovetskoe iskusstvo* 1926 no. 4: 35–37.

61. "Konferentsiia," 11.

62. Stites, *Russian Popular Culture,* 72–73; Susannah Lockwood Smith, "Soviet Arts Policy, Folk Music, and National Identity: The Piatnitskii State Russian Folk Choir, 1927–1945" (Ph.D. dissertation, University of Minnesota, 1997), 43–84.

63. Sokhor, *Russkaia sovetskaia pesnia,* 117.

64. Sheila Fitzpatrick, ed., *Cultural Revolution in Russia, 1928–1931* (Bloomington: Indiana University Press, 1978); Michael David-Fox, "What is Cultural Revolution?" *Russian Review* 58 (April 1999): 181–201.

65. Nelson, "The Struggle for Proletarian Music"; Nelson, *Music for the Revolution,* 207–40; Fitzpatrick, "The Lady Macbeth Affair," *The Cultural Front,* 192–94; Edmunds, "Music and Politics"; Schwarz, *Music and Musical Life,* 102–3; Taruskin, *Defining Russia Musically,* 93; *Istoriia russkoi sovetskoi muzyki* 1, 38–39, 58–59; *Istoriia muzyki narodov SSSR* 1, 145–47.

66. E. Braudo, "Muzyka-massam," *Pravda,* March 27, 1929: 6; "K polozheniiu v o-ve, Muzyka-massam," *Proletarskii muzykant* 1930 no. 7: 26–30; B. Shteinpress, "Vserossiiskaia Assotsiatsiia Proletarskykh Muzykantov (RAPM) i obshchestvo 'Muzyka-massam'," *Za proletarskuiu muzyku* 1930 no. 1: 6–8.

67. N. Demianov, "Kak provodit' massovoe penie," *Za proletarskuiu muzyku* 1930 no. 1: 10–13.

68. Rossiiskaia assotsiatsiia proletarskykh muzykantov, *Tvorcheskii sbornik 1* (Moscow: Gosudarstvennoe muzykal'noe izdatel'stvo, 1931).

69. Lewis Siegelbaum, "The Shaping of Workers' Leisure: Workers' Clubs and Palaces of Culture in the 1930s," *International Labor and Working-Class History* 56 (fall 1999): 78–92; Stites, *Russian Popular Culture,* 76–78.

70. Rothstein, "Quiet Rehabilitation," 383.

71. James van Geldern, "The Centre and Periphery: Cultural and Social Geography in the Mass Culture of the Thirties," in *New Directions in Soviet History,* ed. Stephen White (Cambridge: Cambridge University Press, 1992), 62–80.

PART 3

Minority Identities

7

Spiritual Singing Brings in the Money: The Fisk Jubilee Singers Tour Holland in 1877

HELEN METZELAAR

In their first foray onto the European continent, the Fisk Jubilee Singers toured Holland in 1877. Besides proving a stunning success, the Singers caused considerable stir, bringing to the fore a number of critical issues for their Dutch audiences. The Singers and their concerts confronted listeners with their own role in slavery, with religious tensions, with constructions of "high" and "low" culture, with conceptions of civilization, and with their own jealousy at the Singers' success. Indeed, as musically accomplished, university-educated Americans of African descent, the Jubilee Singers triggered vehement reactions.

One of the first priorities for the four to five million slaves freed at the end of the American Civil War in 1865 was to learn how to read and write. Progress was so rapid that within a few short years many African Americans were ready for further education. In 1867 the American Missionary Association opened Fisk University in Nashville, Tennessee. The school struggled with many problems, not the least being a shortage of funds, which by 1871 endangered its very survival. Students were often unable to pay tuition and teachers were unable to collect salaries. After noticing that many of his students were exceedingly gifted singers, George L. White, treasurer and music teacher at Fisk University, came up with a novel idea: why not form a chorus and try to raise funds by touring the northern states?

After rehearsing in the summer of 1871, White set off for the North with twelve young students. Success was not immediate; never before had white audiences heard singing like this. Until then, the only black musicians they were acquainted with were minstrels. As a highly schooled chorus, the Jubilee Singers eschewed the music hall circuit, instead concentrating on professional performances in churches. As in church services, they relied upon proceeds through collections, and although they fervently hoped to earn a profit, the results of the first concerts were dismal.

It was soon clear that what touched audiences most were the slave songs, spirituals with a strong melancholic vein. These songs, previously sung by slaves among themselves, were often beautiful melodies echoing their trials and longing for freedom. In 1872 the Reverend Theodore L. Cuyler wrote to the *New York Tribune,* "I never saw a cultivated Brooklyn assemblage so moved and melted under the magnetism of music before. The wild melodies of these emancipated slaves touched the fount of tears, and gray-haired men wept like children."[1]

The chorus began to earn much more after deciding to concentrate on this genre and to adopt the name of Jubilee Singers, inspired by the Old Testament (Lev. 25), where in the Jubilee year Jewish slaves were freed to start life anew. Within three months in the spring of 1872, they had earned $20,000, enabling them to purchase twenty-five acres for the university.

Their next step was to venture abroad. In 1874 nine singers and their pianist sailed for Britain, where success was immediate and overwhelming. Audience members included distinguished upper-class citizens such as the Duke and Duchess of Argyll and the Earl of Shaftesbury. Prime Minister Gladstone honored them by inviting them to his mansion for breakfast. After they sang for Queen Victoria, she commissioned their portrait as a gift to the university. They continued their travels up through Scotland and over to Ireland, concertizing in Belfast and Londonderry. With invitations for more performances and a relentless schedule, their first British tour was immensely profitable. They took home nearly $50,000, enabling them to pay for the construction of the first brick building, appropriately called Jubilee Hall. Dutch newspapers described its architecture as Victorian, with six stories and 120 rooms.[2]

Two years later, in the fall of 1876, they embarked on a second tour of Britain to raise funds for another building, to be called Livingstone Hall in honor of the famous explorer and missionary David Livingstone. During this tour, even more successful than the first, a new opportunity presented itself. According to J. B. T. Marsh, an eminent Christian gentleman of Rotterdam, G. P. Ittman Jr., heard them in London and urged them to visit Holland.[3]

At first they were hesitant—would Dutch audiences respond to songs in a foreign language? After extensive deliberation, they set sail for Rotterdam at the end of February 1877. Within two months they had given approximately thirty concerts in the Netherlands, returning to England on 20 April 1877. Then, to rest up and prepare themselves for the next leg of their journey, they spent the following summer in Geneva, Switzerland. In the fall of 1877 they briefly concertized again in Holland before embarking on a strenuous eight-month tour of Germany.

The Singers' worries were unfounded. Dutch audiences were eager to become acquainted with these young African Americans. Harriet Beecher Stowe's novel *Uncle Tom's Cabin* had long been an absolute bestseller in the Netherlands, and since the 1850s various acting companies regularly staged successful theatrical versions of her novel.[4] Dutch audiences were also acquainted with black-painted minstrels, such as the Lantum Ethiopian Serenaders, who had performed from 1847 through 1849.[5] Just as in the United States, minstrels generally appeared at fairs and in the more popular halls with a repertory of light, humorous songs, often with instrumental accompaniment, including Dutch favorites such as "Buffalo Gals" by John Hodges and the sentimental "Farewell, Mary Blanc" by Francis Germon.

With an entirely new repertory, the Jubilee Singers were something altogether novel. Moreover, as in the United States and Britain, they chose to perform in churches and public concert halls, thus attracting the ruling classes. The ten singers the Dutch heard in 1877 consisted of four sopranos, two contraltos, two tenors, and two basses, plus their pianist, Ella Sheppard. Dutch newspapers identified them as seven former slaves and three freemen, accompanied by director Theodore F. Seward and professor Erastus M. Cravath, one of the founders and president of Fisk University.[6]

The Jubilee Singers presented a program of some eighteen songs in various settings, planned to ensure variety. Many of the spirituals related to biblical themes, describing the anguish, woe, and sadness felt by the slaves and the hope that one day they would be freed. The word "spiritual" was never used during their tour of the Netherlands; the songs were simply called slave songs. Each program seems to have opened with "Steal away to Jesus," followed by the Lord's Prayer. Dutch author C. S. Adama van Scheltema explained the title of this song as follows: because the slaves had been prohibited from worshipping openly, they had to steal away from their work for a short prayer.[7]

Most Dutch reviews were highly appreciative of the music. The a cappella spirituals were praised for their simplicity, naturalness, and purity, and the Singers were especially complimented for their use of dynamics. Reviews often commended the bass Frederick Loudin, who frequently gave a solo performance: "Their choral songs are beautiful: they set in without any accompaniment, an organ-like sound rolling from their lips, their crescendos,

Figure 7.1 The Fisk Jubilee Singers. Seated from left: Jennie Jackson, Mabel Lewis, Ella Sheppard, Maggie Carnes, and America W. Robinson. Standing from left: Maggie Porter, Edmund W. Watkins, Hilton D. Alexander, Frederick J. Loudin, and Thomas Rutling. Source:

727

DE GESCHIEDENIS

VAN DE

JUBILEE-ZANGERS

MET HUNNE LIEDEREN,

VERTAALD DOOR

C. S. ADAMA VAN SCHELTEMA.

Met twee Platen.

𝔗𝔴𝔢𝔢𝔡𝔢 𝔇𝔲𝔦𝔷𝔢𝔫𝔡.

AMSTERDAM,

HET EVANGELISCH VERBOND.

1877.

De geschiedenis van de Jubilee-zangers met hunne liederen, trans. C. S. Adama van Scheltema. Amsterdam: Het Evangelisch Verbond, 1877. Opposite title page. Author's collection. Not included in this photo is Georgia Gordon, a soprano who took part in the Dutch tour.

diminuendos and whispering pianissimos are excellent. There is no question of shouting, drowning out, or being out of tune. Many a choir here and elsewhere can take this well-rounded singing as an example. Mister Loudin, who sang a solo, has a beautiful, deep bass sound with a great range; many a professional singer would be jealous of him."[8] Tenor Thomas Rutling also occasionally sang a solo number.

The program in Utrecht on 7 March 1877 follows below. Other works on this Dutch tour included "Keep Me From Sinking Down" and "Home, Sweet Home." In Goes they also sang "O Restless Sea" and "Bright Sparkles in the Churchyard." A frequent encore number was "John Brown's Body," honoring the famous abolitionist at Harper's Ferry.

Jubilee program in Utrecht on 7 March 1877:
1. Steal away to Jesus + Lord's Prayer (in a simple choral setting)
2. Gwine to ride up in the Chariot
3. I'm troubled in mind
4. I'm rolling thro' an unfriendly world
5. We shall walk through the valley
6. Trio: Three Distant Chimes! (by Glover)
7. In bright mansions above
8. The angel's waiting at the door
9. Turn back Pharaoh's army

Second half:
10. Bells (by Theo[dore] F. Seward)
11. Mary and Martha
12. Vocal Medley
13. I've been redeem'd
14. Wrestling Jacob
15. Rise and Shine
16. solo by Mr. Loudin
17. Oh! Wasn't that a wide river?
18. Wait a little while, then we'll sing the new song

The 1877 tour of the Netherlands can be reconstructed in part (see Table 7.1). It is probable that the Jubilee Singers also gave concerts in Dordrecht, Zwolle, Arnhem, Haarlem, Leiden, and Delft, as these cities each formed an introductory committee for the choir. The seventh edition of *The Story of the Jubilee Singers* also mentions a concert at Alkmaar, while a recent publication names Kampen and Zutphen.[9] Thus the Singers probably gave some thirty concerts during their two-month tour. In addition, after departing to

Table 7.1. The Fisk Jubilee Singers' Performances in the Netherlands, 1877

Date	City	Venue	Public or Private
Mon. 26 Feb.	Rotterdam	Miss Deutschmann	private
Tues. 27 Feb.	Rotterdam	Zuiderkerk	public
Fri. 2 March	Amsterdam	?	private
Sat. 3 March	The Hague	Baron van Wassenaer Catwijck	private
Mon. 5 March	The Hague	Gebouwr Kunst and Wetenschap	public
Tues. 6 March	Rotterdam	Zuiderkerk	public
Wed. 7 March	Utrecht	Tivoli	public
Thurs. 8 March	Apeldoorn	Loo Palace, 9–10 P.M.	private for King William III
Fri. 9 March	Amsterdam	Parkzaal	public
Mon. 12 March	The Hague	Gebouwr Kunst and Wetenschap	public
Tues. 13 March	Schiedam	Groote Kerk	public
Mon. 26 March	Amsterdam	Hersteld Evang. Luthersche Kerk	public
Mon. 26 March	Leeuwarden	Groote Kerk	public
Tues. 27 March	Sneek	Martinikerk	public
Wed. 28 March	Harlingen	Nieuwe Kerk	public
Thurs. 29 March	Groningen	Harmonie	public
Tues. 3 April	Amsterdam	Westerkerk	public
Sat. 5 April	Utrecht	Dom or Tivoli	public
Sun. 6 April	Zeist	?	public
Thurs. 10 April	Rotterdam	Zuiderkerk	public
Tues. 17 April	Amsterdam	Parkzaal	public
Thurs. 19 April	Rotterdam	Zuiderkerk	public
Tues. 23 Oct.	Goes	Reformed Church	public

England from Rotterdam on 20 April, the Singers returned to give a concert in Goes in the autumn; it is not known whether they gave more concerts in Holland before their eight-month tour of Germany.

The Jubilee tour of Holland was extremely well organized, with careful attention paid to public relations. Besides announcing venues and dates of concerts, newspaper advertisements took care to add that the Singers would be introduced by gentlemen of considerable social standing and by members of Dutch upper circles. In each city a committee of leading citizens, including numerous barons and dukes, welcomed the Singers. In addition, committee members included dignitaries of various foreign countries, such as Hendrik Muller, consul general of Liberia; Friedrich Schutz, the American consul; and Alexander Turing, consul of Great Britain. A German advertisement for a concert in Darmstadt stated that the Singers enjoyed "the very highest commendation of His Highness the Grand Duke."[10] Associating the chorus with influential members of society not only lent the performances an air of gentility, but assured higher revenues.

In addition to being introduced by prestigious foreign and Dutch notables, the Jubilee Singers also greatly benefited from a Dutch translation of J. B. T. Marsh's *Story of the Jubilee Singers with their Songs.* The translator, the Reverend C. S. Adama van Scheltema (1815–1897), a liberal Protestant already well known for his translations of gospel hymns, wanted to reach as many people as possible through this inexpensive publication. He had often visited revival meetings in Britain and modeled his own work on English publications of religious songs. His translation of Marsh's book, which included 104 songs, appeared without citing Marsh's name.[11] Adama van Scheltema's publication, *De geschiedenis van de Jubilee-zangers met hunne liederen,* was timed to accompany the Jubilee Singers' tour and was printed in runs of 1,000 copies. Demand in the Netherlands was sufficient to warrant at least three runs.[12]

In each city concert tickets were to be purchased beforehand at a local bookstore. Ticket sales for the Park Hall concert in Amsterdam were so successful that a seating system was implemented. The *Algemeen Handelsblad* announced, "It has been determined that the first purchasers will be given the front rows. The red tickets are meant for the first 600 chairs immediately behind the seats reserved for the Committee. The yellow tickets are for the next 600 seats. On the evening of the concert, the price of the remaining tickets will be raised."[13] Holders of orange, red, and committee tickets were directed to one entrance, while those with yellow and white tickets used another. This streamlined admissions system reminds one of pop concerts today, and it indicates that the Jubilee Singers were pulling huge crowds.

In Schiedam tickets cost Dfl 1.50, 1.00, and 0.50, an amount many people could ill afford. In at least two instances organizers were considerate of the less well-to-do. In Goes a newspaper stated that the local Reformed Church Council would give free tickets to the needy.[14] After learning that admission for the first Jubilee concert in Rotterdam had been too expensive for many, for their second appearance in Rotterdam the organizing committee decided to offer tickets at fifty cents. Apparently, this sorely tempted those well off, as the committee hoped that "this arrangement would not be thwarted by those for whom Dfl 1.50 is not an obstacle."[15]

A phenomenal number of people attended the concerts: 1,500 in Rotterdam, 1,400 in Schiedam, 1,270 in Sneek. The *Rotterdamsche Courant* noted that at the Singers' second appearance in Rotterdam the church was filled "as we have seldom seen, not only the nave of the church, but the alcoves and galleries were also packed, so that many had to be satisfied with standing room only."[16] The *Leeuwarder Courant* stated, "The surge of people was so great that the roomy church building could hardly hold everyone." For concerts in smaller towns such as Sneek, Harlingen, and Zeist, farming families came in from the countryside, with ministers accompanying their flocks. Because there were no reserved seats for the general public in Sneek, people arrived an hour early to secure good places. One report noted that a servant had been posted to guard seats reserved for members of the welcoming committee with their wives and children.[17]

Several Dutch church councils let the Singers use their churches without charging rent, so that net profits were higher. Newspapers report that the Zuiderkerk in Rotterdam, for which no rent was charged, was packed with 1,500 listeners. A local newspaper reports that their concert in Leeuwarden brought in more than 1,300 guilders.[18] In 1877 one Dutch guilder was equivalent to approximately forty cents, so in Leeuwarden the Singers pulled in at least $520. For their performance in Goes, the Singers charged a fee of 500 guilders. In order to come up with this sum, tickets were priced at a guilder or half a guilder. Luckily, hundreds flocked to this concert, with proceeds totaling 516 guilders.[19]

Additional income sources included the sale of programs, sheet music, and perhaps also a percentage from the sales of the Dutch translation of the spirituals. In Schiedam young girls were enlisted to sell more than 1,000 programs at four cents each.[20] At some church concerts donations were made, either by passing a basket or by collecting at the exit door. As discussed below, conservative Dutch Protestants soon became upset with what they viewed as commercial activities in places of worship.

Newspapers notified the public that it was also possible to send money to local committees. Advance publicity urged generosity: "May there be not a single city or village in the Netherlands that does not show its appreciation of freedom and civilization by contributing at least one stone to the construction of Livingstone Hall."[21] It is not known how much money was raised this way.

As in the northern states of the United States, the phenomenon of the "colored race" appearing as professional musicians excited considerable attention. Dutch royalty was also interested in the Jubilee Singers. Because the king and queen were living separately, each attended a different concert. A local newspaper records that Queen Sophie and her sons Willem Hendrik and Alexander were so enthusiastic about a private concert at Baron van Wassenaar Catwijck's home in The Hague that they also attended the public concert in The Hague two days later.[22]

The Dutch Royal Archives still has a letter written by the king's private secretary with typical royal decorum, in which he notified King William that the

American consulate would like to relay that the Jubilee Singers would like to perform for His Majesty.[23] The *Dagblad van 's Gravenhage* reported that after hearing the Jubilee Singers in Rotterdam on 27 February 1877, His Majesty invited them to his palace in Apeldoorn. After their Rotterdam performance King William donated 500 guilders, and after the concert at the Loo Palace in Apeldoorn he donated another 500 guilders, a total of about $400.[24]

The purpose of their tour was, as one Dutch newspaper put it, "to sing money out of people's pockets." How much did the Jubilee Singers raise in Holland? Although a lack of information precludes an exact answer, an approximation may be made. If their earnings for some thirty concerts in Holland averaged roughly $300 per concert, this would mean a total of about $9,000. Together with King William's gift, proceeds from programs, plus basket donations, their two-month tour in Holland may have yielded a net profit of about $10,000, a figure also cited by J. B. T. Marsh.[25]

One other type of income should be mentioned. The program of the concert in Zeist noted that people could also donate 100 guilders or more directly to the university. In return, their names would be inscribed in a special Founders' Book at Fisk and they would receive a yearly Fisk University report.

＊　　＊　　＊

The appearance of the Jubilee Singers in Holland raised a number of issues. The first question pertains to how audiences related to the Singers in light of the leading role the Dutch had historically played in the slave trade. And what about slavery in their own colonies? Whereas the English abolished slavery in 1834 and the French in 1848, it took the Dutch until 1863 to pass a law against slavery in the Antilles and Surinam. Not only was *Uncle Tom's Cabin* a favorite novel in Holland, in 1860 Multatuli (the pen name for Dutch author Edward Douwes Dekker) had awakened many to the stark realities of forced labor in the Dutch East Indies (present-day Indonesia) through his novel *Max Havelaar.* But it was not until 1870 that the so-called culture system was abolished in the East Indies, a system by which instead of paying taxes, natives were required to work for the Dutch colonial government.

Indeed, the Jubilee Singers awakened feelings of deep-seated guilt. The program booklet for their concert in Zeist urged financial generosity, asking, "Will they fruitlessly hope for Dutch support and cooperation? Is any nation in the world more guilty of Africa's suffering than ours?" The *Leeuwarder Courant* noted that "the Netherlands is to be blamed for the slaves because in 1620 [*sic*] the first slaves disembarked from a Dutch boat on the coast of Virginia."[26]

A curious parallel was drawn by the Reverend E. F. Kruijff, who saw similarities in the struggle of the newly freed slaves and the American colonial struggle for independence against Great Britain. Just as in the eighteenth century, when the colonists had sailed to Europe to seek financial backing, so now inhabitants of the New World were again seeking help from the Old World in their fight against ignorance and superstition.[27]

The sheer novelty of the Jubilee Singers' appearance gave rise to much commentary in the Dutch press. Waling Dijkstra, a well-known Frisian, spent much of his article comparing this chorus to other crowd-pullers, such as the Tirolian singers, Auerbach's operetta group, and an American horse show. He commented that when foreign attractions were well advertised, everyone rushed to spend their money, feeling bad about spending so much the next day. He added that all these groups were good for one time only; they wouldn't attract much attention a second time. A successful tour by the European Ladies' Orchestra in Holland in the fall of 1876 was ascribed to this same hunger for things new and sensational.[28]

Clearly it was not only their singing that attracted such large audiences; many people in Holland were simply eager to see people with a darker skin. Some critics were even let down: "I was disappointed that they were not blacker. Two women were as white as I am, although their hair and thick lips revealed their descent."[29] When the Original American Jubilee Singers returned to Goes in 1880, advertisements detailed the mixed ancestry of the twenty-four performers as "freed slaves, negroes, mulattos, mestizos, quadroons, etc."[30] For the 1883 World Exhibition, "bush negroes, redskins, and city negroes" were brought over to Amsterdam from Surinam and exhibited in a large round tent.[31] When the Jubilee Singers returned to Holland in 1897, the well-known music critic Frans Coenen Jr. noted, "Five gentlemen and two women, whose color varied from the shining sallow black of Negroes to the light yellow-brown known to us from our Dutch East Indies, entered the stage two by two, and clad in simple European clothing, positioned themselves around a small organ, upon which one of the gentlemen accompanied."[32] In 1901 Coenen again reviewed them: "The Jubilee Singers always seem to be a really nice type of people, especially because they are brown-black, which contrasts so well with their tails and white ties, but also because they sing so well, especially their own songs."[33]

All these reactions to skin color do not mean the Jubilee Singers encountered malignant racial discrimination in Holland. On the contrary, their Dutch hosts were eager to make them feel welcome, and various newspaper articles wished the Singers a successful trip through Holland. At several concerts the Dutch were inspired to noble speeches about America, emphasizing that now that slavery had been abolished, closer ties could be developed. At the end of their concert in Leeuwarden, J. W. Kramers thanked church wardens for use of their church and the audience for their interest and appreciation: "And when the delicious sounds of their songs reverberate in our memory, let us remember that only freedom can lead to brotherhood. America is proof of this. Before the abolition of slavery the coloreds crept and labored for the whites. . . . If everyone is free to work for the highest and holiest purposes of mankind, each according to his own conviction, then the dividing walls shall be pulled down, the cloves that now separate shall be closed, the oceans lying between the various parties shall be removed."[34]

However, the reaction of the Dutch Roman Catholics to the abolition of slavery in the United States was quite hostile. At the beginning of 1878 a Catholic periodical ran a cartoon plus a short, unsigned racist article referring to African Americans as "niggers." Entitled "Coming Back from the University," the article clarifies this textless cartoon of a family welcoming a proud young black as follows: "The old Nigger hopes for a better future for his children and has sent his eldest son to the university to become a doctor or a professor. The young Nigger has come home, wearing his cap at a rakish angle and holding a cigar. The whole family is filled with admiration, ecstatically gazing at the savior of their race. Tonight there will be a feast, but what will happen in the future? Because he is too dull-witted to be a scholar and too learned to do any other work, this student will probably have to be supported by his race."[35]

The attitude of European Roman Catholics toward blacks in the nineteenth century needs further investigation. In any case, the Jubilee Singers, who were Protestant, did not perform in the Catholic southern provinces of the Netherlands, and attendance was noticeably poorer at concerts given in the Roman Catholic south of Germany.

The Singers' tour also brought to the fore religious tensions between orthodox Protestants (Gereformeerd) and the more liberal Protestants (Hervormd). In the 1830s orthodox Christians had split off from the liberals, founding their own Reformed denomination. In the second half of the nineteenth century these two Protestant camps were engaged in a far-reaching struggle to mark out their respective spheres of influence. Both groups spent much time and energy competing with each other to civilize the working classes. To forge social harmony and discourage the spread of socialism, liberal Protestants organized lectures, concerts, theatrical performances, and sporting events.

This contrasted sharply with the Reformed Church, where almost all forms of entertainment were considered sinful. Reformed ministers steadfastly warned their flocks against frivolous amusements, condemning to damnation those who were tempted. In order to provide at least something to occupy the leisure time of their flocks, more Christian events such as revival meetings were organized. Under the leadership of Abraham Kuyper, the Reformed Protestants enjoyed considerable growth in the 1870s.

Were the Jubilee Singers welcomed by the liberal or by the orthodox Protestants? Most larger cities were dominated by liberal Protestants, so it was they who hosted the Singers. In Amsterdam the Jubilee Singers satisfied three camps, giving one concert in a public venue for liberal Protestants, another in the Westerkerk for Reformed listeners, and a third in a Lutheran church.

Because the Singers were closely affiliated with the American Missionary Association, whose objective was evangelization, a number of Dutch Reformed churches considered hosting them. After extensive deliberation the Reformed Church Council in Goes, a town of some 6,000 inhabitants in the south of Holland, decided to host the Jubilee Singers as an "exceptional case." Upon arrival by train, the Singers were welcomed by leading civic authorities and members of the church. The Reformed viewed their choral singing not as entertainment, but as a form of evangelizing; the spirituals would bring the Good News to their flock and their performance was incorporated into a service-like gathering. Nevertheless, the congregation had to be requested to refrain from clapping, which was considered inappropriate behavior in a place of worship.

However, even the liberal Protestants raised their brows, with a reviewer of the concert in Sneek noting, "What would Jesus have thought of all this selling, hand-clapping and foot-stamping?"[36] In a number of Dutch cities, singing in a church for the purpose of raising funds was met with strong disapproval, even though the Singers enjoyed official church council sanction.

The success of the Jubilee Singers also gave rise to quite jealous reactions by devout Christians. In Amsterdam a bitter letter was sent to the *Weekblad de Vrijheid*, complaining that the Westerkerk had hosted "unknown blackies," while this same church had refused to host the yearly meeting of a Dutch Bible Society. The writer also disapproved of the special stage built in the church, the use of a piano, of songs "you couldn't understand if you didn't speak English," and of the fact that you had to pay to get in, which meant that "business was being done in God's house." He wrote, "See here, mister editor, if the orthodox can degrade a church into a café, . . . and the non-orthodox can't even use the church to make their yearly report on spreading the Bible, where everything is orderly and no entry is charged, then I call that biased and unchristian to the highest degree. . . ."[37]

And there were more jealous reactions. The success of this foreign chorus was painful in light of the fact that fund-raising by Protestants for their own Protestant schools was not doing well. In the north of Holland a journalist complained that the Dutch were not as generous when donating to their own Christian schools. According to him, "black children from Africa" had been sent to Europe for "our money," "a real American discovery."[38] The Reverend Tinholt, editor of a newspaper in Workum, wrote, "We Dutch are so clever. Full of enthusiasm we contribute to a Christian academy for the freed slaves in America, moved by the songs of these poor people, but in the meantime we . . . rob the Christian character of our own academies and schools."[39]

The appearance of the Jubilee Singers in Holland also brought to light the then-dominant construction in which civilization was conceived as a linear evolutionary process and European civilization was seen as the highest degree on this ladder. Meant as a compliment, Dutch newspapers reported that the music these African Americans brought to Europe proved that they were not heathens, that their songs were not inferior to songs of the civilized world, and that they, too, were civilized and could ascend the ladder of white gentility. A Rotterdam critic noted that during intermission audience members could mingle with the singers so as to convince themselves of their "highly advanced degree of civilization."[40] A critic for the *Schiedamsche Courant* wrote that now that the slaves were free, they were proud of their African heritage. At the same time he hoped that listeners would be convinced that the Negro race was suited for the "highest development."[41]

The Jubilee Singers challenged the construction that so-called civilized people produced art music, while the non-civilized brought forth "primitive" music. One reviewer noted with surprise, "While no one knows . . . where and how these songs were created by these uncivilized slave peoples, the melodies, whose moving vigor is alternated with lovely softness, are often so rich that they are not inferior to songs of the civilized world."[42] On the other hand, the critic Frans Coenen Jr. stuck to the trusted dichotomy. In one review he noted that their pianissimo was widely hailed, which seemed to him to be "slightly exaggerated," because "the choice of songs and the manner of singing do not always stay within the boundaries of High Music."[43] He deemed the songs not fit for "friends of the arts," but more for those who wanted to be carried away by their sweet, melancholic sounds. Yet Coenen mulled over their appropriate performance arena, feeling the Singers neither suited for the concert hall, which was meant for "high" music, nor for cafés, meant for "low" music.

The Jubilee Singers and their managers were fully aware of this demarcation line between "art" and "folk" music, and they soon expanded their programs to include "a few selections of more artistic composition . . . for the purpose of demonstrating . . . that the students have been educated to the appreciation of the higher grades of vocalization."[44]

Negative Dutch criticism generally found the spirituals to be too simple. A reporter in the *Goesche Courant* wrote that most songs were "monotonous, often raw or boring."[45] Although he did not attend the concerts, Waling Dijkstra made fun of the repeated phrases, mocking the nineteen repetitions of "I've been saved." Dijkstra was clearly not familiar with the verse and chorus form of these spirituals, in which a lead singer is answered with a short repeated refrain. Besides, Dijkstra asked, why were learned university students singing simple songs like these?[46] A newspaper review of recent concerts in Utrecht simply dismissed the Jubilee Singers: "From a musical standpoint the Negro singers were only a curiosity."[47]

After one of their concerts in Britain, a British critic yearned for something more authentic: "We should have expected the conditions [of] Negro life to have developed something more [of a] race-character than that which is found in the music Mr. Seward has collected and arranged which [*sic*] belongs entirely to the highly artificial diatonic scale of modern Europe. The only exception we noticed were the absence of accidental semitones and the plagal cadence, and the infrequency of fourths and sevenths."[44] This critic's conclusion echoes that of a number of Dutch reviewers: "Indeed, much of the music, as music, was very thin and devoid of character." Theodore Seward, who directed the Singers on their Dutch tour, addressed this criticism: "One criticism has been made on the singing of the Jubilee Band, which deserves notice. It has been frequently said, especially by persons who have been at the South, and heard the singing of camp-meetings. 'This music is too good. It is too refined. There is too nice a balancing of parts, and too much delicate shading to be a genuine representation of slave-music.'"[49]

Seward went on to praise the Singers for their musical aptitude and for their ability to "adopt improvements" from "cultivated music": "The objection is easily answered, in this wise. The manner and style of singing at the South depends entirely upon the degree of culture in the congregation. There is a very great difference between the lowest and the highest, in this respect. It cannot be thought strange that the musical feeling which is so prolific in original melodies should soon find its way to the enjoyment of harmony in the singing of various parts. The Jubilee Singers, no doubt, represent the highest average of culture among the colored people, but the singing of these songs is all their own, and the quickness with which they have received impressions and adopted improvements from the cultivated music they have heard, only affords an additional illustration of the high capabilities of the race."[50]

Another theme related to the issue of race and civilization, and one continually emphasized in the Dutch press, was that the Jubilee Singers were presented as the future saviors of uncivilized Africa. Both articles in Dutch newspapers and the program booklets emphasized that the purpose of Fisk University was to educate and civilize blacks in America so that they could go back to Africa to evangelize and educate the blacks there. The Zeist program booklet even stated that the Jubilee Singers did not want to be heard as practitioners of art, but as representatives of Africa. In Friesland a local newspaper noted that it was good to contribute "to the true civilizing of 200 million inhabitants of Africa."[51] The *Schiedamsche Courant* elaborated: "Their selfless and persevering endeavor is meant for AFRICA, meant for the maltreated part of the world, which for centuries has been robbed of millions of its children in the deepest inland, as a disgrace to civilized nations for whom they [the Singers] have accomplished the heaviest unrewarded work, suffering as exiles: *no contribution can atone* [italics original] for, much less erase this. As children fighting for the honor and rights of a mother, they strive to work to help raise Africa out of its humiliation to the level of civilized peoples."[52]

Lastly, although the Jubilee Singers were among the first to begin popularizing black music within white European music culture, the songs Dutch audiences heard in 1877 had little lasting influence on Dutch music repertory. The translations by Adama van Scheltema did not take hold in Holland. An expert in this field, Jan Smelik, surmises that this may have been because the melody type differed considerably from that familiar to the public. Although roughly 20 percent of all Protestant songs published between 1866 and 1938 were either English translations or based on British and American melodies, only one Dutch collection included a few Jubilee songs.[53] The English and American songs that did find their way into Dutch publications were gospel hymns, first introduced by Adama van Scheltema.[54]

The appearance in the Netherlands of the Jubilee Singers raised a number of significant issues. The Singers clearly awakened feelings of guilt because of the major role the Dutch had formerly played in the slave trade. Organizers in Holland knew well how to exploit these feelings and urged generous financial support. Another specific Dutch situation is the different role assigned to the Singers by strict Reformed Protestants and the more liberal Protestants.

When singing for the strict Reformed, the Singers were incorporated into a service-like setting, while for more liberal Protestants, the Singers' concerts were considered to be fund-raising entertainment. In both Protestant camps questions arose as to the suitability of this fund-raising in places of worship. As noted, the Singers' success also gave rise to various envious reactions.

At a more general level, the spirituals triggered discussions on the concept of civilization, with European culture placed at the top of the evolutionary ladder. The Singers were urged to keep up their hard work, so that they too might one day reach the top. It was continually emphasized that the very purpose of their education at Fisk University was to return to Africa to help its peoples become civilized.

Because this original Jubilee tour was such a triumph, other African American choral groups soon followed in their footsteps, albeit with a lighter repertoire. However, the meteoric success of the Jubilee Singers in Holland was never again matched.

* * *

All translations are by the author. The first research results were presented at the conference "Black American Music in Europe: Past and Present," 15–16 May 1998, under the auspices of the Research Institute for History and Culture OGC of Utrecht University. An earlier version of this article, entitled "A Hefty Confrontation: The Fisk Jubilee Singers Tour the Netherlands in 1877," appeared in *Tÿdschrift van de Koninklÿke Vereniging voor Nederlandse Muziekgeschiedenis* 55/1 (2005), 67–86. I would like to thank Herman Openneer of the Dutch Jazz Archive for his generous assistance, and Emile Wennekes for providing me with two reviews by Frans Coenen Jr. My thanks also to John Helsloot for two reviews of the concerts in Goes and René Kunst for reviews of concerts in Friesland.

Notes

1. James M. Trotter, *Music and Some Highly Musical People*, 7th ed. (Boston: Lee and Shepard; New York: Charles T. Dillingham, 1885), 260–61.

2. *Nieuwe Rotterdamsche Courant*, 27 February 1877.

3. J. B. T. Marsh, *The Story of the Jubilee Singers with their Songs*, rev. ed. (Boston: Houghton, Mifflin and Co., 1881), 87.

4. Irene Visser, "American Women Writers in the Dutch Literary World, 1824–1900," in *"I Have Heard about You." Foreign Women's Writing Crossing the Dutch Border. From Sappho to Selma Lagerlöf*, ed. Susan van Dijk et al. (Hilversum: Verloren, 2004), 287–290.

5. Albert Kramer, "Lantum Ethiopian Serenaders," in *Nederlands Jazz Archief Bulletin* 21 (September 1996): 25–27.

6. Seward's middle name, Freylinghuysen, is Dutch, which means he may have had connections in the Netherlands. In 1877 he was listed as "professor of music" in the *Catalogue of Fisk University.* See Dena J. Epstein, "The Story of the Jubilee Singers: An Introduction to its Bibliographic History," in *New Perspectives on Music: Essays in Honor of Eileen Southern,* ed. Josephine Wright (Detroit: Harmonie Park Press, 1992), 153, 156, n. 24.

7. John Wesley Work gives another account; see his *Folk Song of the American Negro* ([Nashville, 1915] New York: Negro Universities Press, 1969).

8. *Leeuwarder Courant,* 1 April 1877.

9. Andrew Ward, *Dark Midnight When I Rise: The Story of the Jubilee Singers Who Introduced the World to the Music of Black America* (New York: Farrar, Straus and Giroux, 2000), 335.

10. *Darmstädter Tagblatt,* 8 February 1878.

11. It was only after the Civil War that efforts were made to notate various slave songs, which until then had been passed on orally. The first publication was a thin volume by William Francis Allen, Charles Pickard Ware, and Lucy McKim Garrison, *Slave Songs of the United States,* which appeared in 1867. Marsh's *Story of the Jubilee Singers* was an abridgment of two works by the Reverend G. D. Pike. In 1872 T. F. S. Seward published a book entitled *Jubilee Songs as Sung by the Jubilee Singers* (Nashville). See Epstein, "Story of the Jubilee Singers."

12. Amsterdam: Het Evangelisch Verbond, 1877. This publication includes the translation of a seven-stanza poem, "The Song of the Jubilee Singers" by Marianne Farningham, plus a two-page introduction to the songs by Seward, followed by a preface by the translator. C. S. Adama van Scheltema also published a separate collection, which was likewise reprinted several times: *Keur van Slavenzangen door Negers in de Zuidelijke Staten van Amerika in hunnen staat van dienstbaarheid gezongen* (Amsterdam, 1877). When the Singers were lodged in private homes, their hosts were often given the English edition as a token of thanks. See Casper Höweler, *Negro Spirituals en hun beeldspraak* (Bussum: Unieboek, 1970), preface, n.p.

13. Advertisement in the *Algemeen Handelsblad,* 8 March 1877.

14. *Goesche Courant,* 20 October 1877.

15. *Nieuwe Rotterdamsche Courant,* 2 March 1877.

16. *Rotterdamsche Courant,* as quoted in the *Schiedamsche Courant,* 11 March 1877.

17. *Friesch Volksblad,* 8 April 1877.

18. *Leeuwarder Courant,* 1 April 1877.

19. *Goesche Courant,* 25 October 1877.

20. *Schiedamsche Courant,* 11 March 1877.

21. *Schiedamsche Courant,* 7 March 1877.

22. *Dagblad van Zuidholland en 's-Gravenhage,* 6 March 1877.

23. Koninklijk Huisarchief, A45–XIVc-81 (160).

24. Koninklijk Huisarchief, receipts dated 28 February and 8 March 1877, E8-IVa-164^I (February IXc-3).

25. Marsh, *Story of the Jubilee Singers,* 89.

26. In 1619 a Dutch man-of-war sailed up the James River, docked at Jamestown, Virginia, and bartered some twenty Africans in exchange for provisions. However, the slave trade was not new in the Americas. After millions of native Indians had died in Central and South America in the fifteenth and sixteenth centuries, Spain and Portugal began sending African slaves over to their colonies. By 1623 the Dutch West Indies Company, formed in 1621, had transported some 15,430 slaves to Brazil. In turn, blacks from Brazil were shipped up to New Amsterdam (New York), the first shipment arriving for sale in 1649.

27. *Leeuwarder Courant,* 1 April 1877.

28. *Leeuwarder Courant,* 12 November 1876.

29. N. N. [Geertruida Jentink] in *Friesch Volksblad,* 8 April 1877.

30. A quadroon is someone with three white grandparents and one black grandparent.

31. *De Volkskrant,* 22 August 1997.

32. *Oprechtsche Haarlemmer Courant,* 22 January 1897.

33. *Oprechtsche Haarlemmer Courant,* 8 February 1901.

34. *Leeuwarder Courant,* 1 April 1877.

35. *Katholieke Illustratie* 11, no. 32 (January 1878).

36. *Friesch Volksblad,* 8 April 1877.

37. *Weekblad de Vrijheid,* as quoted in the *Schiedamsche Courant,* 14 April 1877.

38. *Friesch Volksblad,* 1 April 1877. H. Kingmans discusses coverage of the Jubilee Singers in Friesland in his article "'Iets is meer dan niets': Leeuwarder cultureel leven in 1877" in *De Vrije Fries* 57 (1977): 91–97.

39. *De Banier,* 21 March 1877, as quoted in *Friesch Volksblad,* 15 April 1877.

40. *Nieuw Rotterdamsche Courant,* 27 February 1877.

41. *Schiedamsche Courant,* 14 March 1877.

42. *Schiedamsche Courant,* 14 March 1877.

43. *Oprechtsche Haarlemmer Courant,* 22 January 1877.

44. Ibid.

45. *Goesche Courant,* 25 October 1877.

46. *Friesch Volksblad,* 15 April 1877.

47. *Utrechtsch Provinciaal en Stedelijk Dagblad,* 14 March 1877.

48. *Paddington Kensington and Bayswater Chronicle,* 27 May 1876, as quoted in Epstein, "Story of the Jubilee Singers," 153, n. 6.

49. Quoted in Epstein, "Story of the Jubilee Singers," 154.

50. Ibid.

51. N. N. [Geertruida Jentink] in *Friesche Volksblad,* 8 April 1877.

52. *Schiedamsche Courant,* 7 March 1877.

53. *Liederen en Solo's,* published by Stads-Evangelistatie "Jeruël" in Rotterdam, cited in Jan Smelik, *Eén in lied en leven: het stichtelijke lied bij Nederlandsche Protestanten tussen 1866 en 1938* (The Hague: Sdu Uitgevers 1997), 157, n. 145.

54. The first popular collection was *In het land der vreemdelingschap,* also translated by Adama van Scheltema. Published in 1871 and enjoying more than ten editions, this collection included popular songs such as a translation of "Shall we gather at the river." See Smelik, *Eén in lied en leven,* 167.

8

The "New Negro" Choral Legacy of Hall Johnson

MARVA GRIFFIN CARTER

African Americans in the 1920s created art, literature, and music in a climate of aesthetic expression known as the Harlem Renaissance, the Negro Renaissance, or the New Negro Movement. Many social and cultural factors helped to foster the environment for this phenomenon. Blacks were changing from rural to city life and migrating from the South to the North. They were aspiring to dismantle the Uncle Tom- and Mammy-like images in favor of ones that were self-assured, racially proud, and demanding of full citizenship. The Urban League, the National Association for the Advancement of Colored People, and their respective journals, *Opportunity* and *The Crisis,* boldly articulated their opposition to lynching and acts of racial discrimination, while at the same time they encouraged superior artistic creations from the Black Talented Tenth. An increased interest in African American history led to the formulation of historical societies and journals. Positive identification with Africa as the ancestral homeland intensified as Marcus Garvey and his "Back-to-Africa" movement gained momentum. Likewise, blacks began to bond with others of African descent from around the world, creating a climate for pan-African platforms to address mutual concerns. In short, in a society merely two generations from slavery, African Americans were coming of age, moving from the southern plantations to the northern urban centers, reflecting positive images, and revealing themselves more realistically as the New Negro.

One northern urban center where many migrated was Harlem, the city within a city, and not merely the largest black community in the world, but the first historical concentration of diverse people of color. It attracted the

African, the West Indian, and the African American. It brought together black Americans from the North with those from the South, those from the city with those from the town and village; it brought the peasant, the student, and the businessman together with the artist, the poet, and the musician.

The mid-1920s marked the appearance of a special Harlem edition of *Survey Graphic,* edited by Alain Locke, the nation's first black Rhodes scholar. This publication was recast and enlarged into *The New Negro,* an anthology of articles, stories, and poems that aimed "to register the transformations of the inner and outer life of the Negro in America."[1] Included was Locke's essay "The Negro Spirituals," in which he characterized this genre as an ingenious classic folk expression: "[The] universality of the Spirituals looms more and more as they stand the test of time. They have outlived the particular generation and the peculiar conditions which produced them."[2] He further argued, "In its disingenuous simplicity, folk art is always despised and rejected at first, but generations after, it flowers again and transcends the level of its origin. The slave songs are no exception."[3]

Indeed, this African American song repertoire had been initially disregarded when the Fisk Jubilee Singers began their concert tours in 1871. Only after the singing of European sacred anthems, southern popular tunes, and American patriotic songs did George White (the white choral director and university treasurer) finally persuade the Singers to perform the songs of their heritage. The Jubilee Singers conveyed their reluctance:

> It was our own expectation at that time to sing the more difficult music—composed by educated & talented artists, and our practice consisted chiefly in rehearsing these pieces. It was not common for us to spend much time singing slaves song [sic]—the tendencies of the freedmen being to leave them behind in the grave of slavery—indeed some seemed almost to regard them as signs of their former disgrace & to shun them as one would the prison clothes of the days of his incarceration. We did not realize how precious they would be held by those who had prayed for us, and with us till we were delivered from slavery, & how these were the genuine jewels we brought from our bondage. It was our fear that the colored people would be grieved to have us expose the ignorance & weakness incident to the days of their degradation—not know [sic] that our songs would be regarded as born of God—and sweet & touching as angels lifes [sic] might sing.[4]

Spreading these "genuine jewels" of song caused the Jubilee Singers' popularity to soar and to result in national and international exposure. Their coffers increased by $150,000, which financed the construction of Jubilee Hall on the fledgling Fisk University campus.

Singing songs from their cultural heritage led the Jubilee Singers to acknowledge their history and identity. These twin preoccupations were also utmost in the minds of the New Negroes who desired to be known for their *true* selves and their *true* ancestral heritage. They were cognizant of belonging to a minority set apart by its unique cultural memory and traditions. The plantation, the slave quarters, the proscriptions even in freedom, the lynchings and the riots, and the segregation and discrimination created a body of common experiences that helped to promote the idea of a distinct and authentic cultural community. While this community envisioned social and economic freedom, it cherished the unhappy experiences that had drawn it closer together.

As Nathan Huggins has suggested, the New Negroes thought "of themselves as actors and creators of a people's birth (or rebirth)."[5] They began to re-examine their relationship to the continent of Africa: The Motherland was used as an artistic source first among the poets, who knew very little about the *real* Africa. Countee Cullen's poem "Heritage," for example, inquired, "What is Africa to me?"—a rhetorical question that pervaded the consciousness of the New Negro. Africa was not so much a place, but a glorified symbol, an ideal land where blacks had once been happy, kingly, and free.[6]

Not only were Renaissance poets preoccupied with Africa, so were anthropologists, sociologists, and scholars of other disciplines. Similarly, they investigated which artistic and cultural traits could be attributed to African origins. The writings of prominent anthropologist Melville Herskovits in *The Myth of the Negro Past* and New Negro philosophical architect Alain Locke in "The Legacy of the Ancestral Arts" both maintained that there *were* African survivals in the culture and artistic expression of the American Negro.[7]

A notable New Negro who ventured to Harlem in the early 1900s and recaptured Africanisms as well as the *unique* spirit of African American folksongs was choral conductor Hall Johnson (1888–1970).[8] He achieved remarkable success in arranging, performing, and creating original compositions inspired by the slave songs. Johnson said, "I felt that the work and folk songs of my people and their spirituals offered a rich and untapped field. I wanted to give that music to the world."[9]

Having grown up in Athens, Georgia, with direct exposure to the singing of songs by family and church members who had been slaves, Johnson believed that he had been "born at the right time and in the right place ideally suited for years of study of the Negro musical idiom as expressed in the spirituals."[10] From his maternal grandmother, Mary Hall Jones (a slave until thirty years of age), Hall received his Christian name and his love for African American songs and stories. She was the most powerful single influence upon his youth, one that directed him into what was to become his life's work. She incessantly sang the old slave songs. Hall Johnson said of his grandmother, "Every night, she would sing the beautiful old songs to us as all day long at work she would sing them, half consciously to herself." As a young lad of seven, he sat in his grandmother's kitchen "and heard her sing as she did up the white folks' laundry." She sang "He Heahs All You Says and He Sees All You Do—My Lawd's A-Writin' All de Time," "Rise and Shine, and Give God de Glory, Glory," and "I Want to Shout Glory When Dis World's on Fire." Some of the most successful songs later performed by his choir were songs he had never heard from any lips other than those of his grandmother.[11]

Hall Johnson was reared in an educated family of art, letters, and music. His father, the Reverend William Decker Johnson, was born of free parents in Baltimore, Maryland, and took advantage of every educational opportunity available to blacks. He was the first African American to graduate from Lincoln University in Pennsylvania and until his death was one of its best-known alumni pastors in the African Methodist Episcopal Church. His father introduced Hall to solfège and to French and German phonetics. His mother, Alice Sansom, was a slave until the age of eight (when slavery was abolished) and later attended Atlanta University soon after it was established in 1865.[12] Hall studied piano with his oldest sister, Mary Elizabeth, and began to compose miniature melodies during his youth. He was inspired to perform after hearing Frederick Douglass's son Joseph Douglass concertize on the violin. As a boy, he was also exposed to operatic arias and ensembles as sung by Sissieretta Jones with her traveling Black Patti's Troubadours (named after the Italian prima donna Adelina Patti).[13]

When Johnson's father became president of Allen University in Columbia, South Carolina, Hall matriculated there from 1905 to 1908. He later transferred and earned a bachelor of arts degree from the University of Pennsylvania in 1910, where he studied composition with Hugh A. Clark and received the annual Senior Simon Haessler Prize for best composition for chorus and orchestra. While remaining in Philadelphia, he continued his studies with Frederick Hahn, formerly a first violinist with the Boston Symphony Orchestra and founder of the Hahn School of Music, and attended weekly concerts given by the Philadelphia Orchestra.[14] More than a decade later, he returned to compositional studies with Percy Goetschius, chair of theory and composition at the Juilliard School of Music.

In 1914 Johnson moved to New York City, where there was a growing demand for black musicians to play in dance orchestras. He joined James Reese Europe's Society Orchestra and became known as the "tallest viola player in New York," standing an imposing six-feet-two-and-a-half inches tall.[15] He soon traveled with dancers Irene and Vernon Castle, performing Irving Berlin's first musical, *Watch Your Step.* After four years, he united with Will Marion Cook's Southern Syncopated Orchestra and toured the United States playing African American folk music, blues, syncopated songs, and classics. In 1921 Johnson performed in the orchestra of Eubie Blake and Noble Sissle's Broadway hit *Shuffle Along,* one of the longest-running musicals of its time. He also played in its sequel, *Runnin' Wild,* in 1923, which introduced the Charleston to the stage.

Dance and theater venues were not sufficiently satisfying to Johnson, who then decided to form the Negro String Quartet with Felix Weir, first violin; Arthur Boyd, second violin; and Marion Cumbo, cello. This ensemble concertized principally along the eastern seaboard, performing the classic chamber literature and compositions by contemporary black composers. The quartet appeared with Marian Anderson and accompanied Roland Hayes in a group of Negro spiritual arrangements at a Carnegie Hall recital in 1925. Cumbo later recalled, "Hall was an exceptionally fine player [and] a wizard on the viola. He had terrific technique."[16] Johnson believed that the constant practice of chamber music was of inestimable value to his later choral work. He would attempt to achieve string sounds when he had his choir hum a certain way, and the high sopranos were used as piccolos for intermittent tonal effects.[17] A 1933 review reported, "Hall Johnson not only thinks of the choir in terms of an orchestra, but he uses it as an orchestra, drawing from each voice not the quality of song but an instrumental quality or some needed tonal color. Under his direction female voices become 'tenor,' as they do in the group singing of the South, baritones sing falsetto where the soprano quality 'would never do.' And singers with near perfect pitch are taught to render off key the sharp staccato 'cries' which build up the harmony of that chorale. By this slight distortion of the voice timbre the composer gives his choral 'orchestra' new instruments."[18]

Johnson's instrumental career was short lived, however, because of his decision to revisit the haunting folksongs of his youth. He believed that "in a few years any spirituals remaining would be found only in the libraries—and nobody would know how to sing them." This dilemma led him to assemble a group of eight black singers to preserve and present traditional Negro music in the style of its original creators. He soon discovered that

Figure 8.1 The Hall Johnson Choir. Author's collection.

eight voices could not reproduce the spirit and fervor of the camp meeting; consequently, the ensemble was increased to twenty in order to create the desired lush harmonies and syncopated counterpoint. With a larger mixed group, he endeavored to reproduce the vocal timbre of the folk spirituals, and on September 8, 1925, the Hall Johnson Choir was born.[19]

The choir began as a musical family with intense rehearsals for two years, awaiting the optimum opportunity to perform for the general public, which occurred on February 26, 1926, at the Roxy Theatre in downtown Manhattan. Nearly two years later, on November 1, 1927, the choir was invited to sing at the funeral of Florence Mills, the singer-dancer of *Shuffle Along* fame. There were reportedly 5,000 inside the Mother Zion Church and 150,000 outside for the largest funeral in Harlem's history.[20] Two months later, a rich, retired singer, Cobina Wright, invited Johnson and his choir, among others, to entertain her guests at a party in honor of the French composer Maurice Ravel.[21] Many of the influential musicians of New York were there, and the group was able to obtain its long-desired exposure.

The choir was soon brought to the attention of concert manager William

C. Gassner, who financed its first formal appearance at the Pythian Temple on February 29, 1928. One critic wrote, "American negro 'spirituals'. . . are rarely presented with the fidelity that marked this ensemble. . . . In natural harmony of humble religious expression, as in spontaneous attack, dying pianissimo and, above all, communicative diction, the compact chorus distinguished itself and its leader."[22] Subsequently, there were appearances "to a full and fashionable house" at Town Hall, where the singers showed "devotion to their leader and instinctive sentiment for the old camp-meeting croons."[23]

During the summer of 1928, the Hall Johnson Choir appeared with the New York Philharmonic at Lewisohn Stadium. Their reception was so favorable that this became the first of six consecutive summer appearances. In these performances the choir displayed "characteristics of unity, marked expressiveness and infectious spirit"[24] "under the spell of Mr. Johnson's serpentine fingers and rubbery wrists."[25] Audiences were so impressed that in every review critics referred to their demand for encores, which sometimes specified selections. One writer stated, "If the conductor, Hall Johnson, had led his choir through every item requested by various voices in the Stadium, the concert would have lasted far into the night."[26]

For more than three decades, the Hall Johnson Choir staged concerts in Carnegie Hall, Town Hall, Pythian Temple, and many other concert venues in New York City. It was the first professional choral group of its kind to win national and international acclaim in its demonstration of how Negro spirituals should be sung on the concert stage, on Broadway, and in Hollywood films, including *Hearts Divided* (1936), *The Bowery Princess* (1936), *Banjo on my Knee* (1936), *Lost Horizons* (1937), *Way Down South* (1939), *Swanee River* (1941), and *Cabin in the Sky* (1943).

The Hall Johnson Choir was devoted to preserving the oral literature and performance practices of the black folk tradition, yet polishing them into an acculturated style acceptable and aesthetically pleasing to black and white audiences alike. In an interview Johnson describes his method for acquiring the choir's repertoire: "The songs come from all sorts of sources. Of our several hundred singers, each is a committee of one, in constant search for fresh but authentic tunes. Sometimes we hear about a tune that is being sung at such and such a meeting in Brooklyn or rural New Jersey and the next Sunday some of us will hustle out on the quest. In this way 'John de Revelator,' and 'Elijah Rock!' were dug up in Keyport, N.J. revivals."[27]

Johnson is believed to have arranged between 400 and 500 songs for his singers and to have known of nearly 100 more that he wanted them to learn.[28] According to one of his choir members, Helen Duceburg, Johnson remembered many original melodies that had never been published. He engaged in oral research and drew from his massive library of history, folklore, literature, and languages. He was against using harmonies that were "too cute or too modern." In attempting to recreate the folksongs as he thought they were originally sung, he would sometimes allow his singers to improvise and instinctively "read *into* the music." They were not allowed to use musical scores, however, but were trained instead by rote. Johnson was a perfectionist and a wonderful teacher, sometimes repeating phrases over and over to get the desired accent, breath control, and phrasing. It was not uncommon for rehearsals to last six or seven hours every night during the week.[29] His policy was, "No matter how fine the voice or how well trained, *every* singer must be in *every* rehearsal to study the old techniques together."[30] Further, "When I want a certain effect, I first explain the musical side, painting a word-picture at the same time and they, having been brought up with Negro stories and songs and having lived among revivals and camp-meetings, immediately grasp the emotional intention and rise to the mood with a spontaneity which gives me effects that I could not possibly get from singers who did not know and feel the atmosphere in which the spirituals originated."[31]

Johnson wrote choral arrangements that embodied the traditional folk characteristics of call-and-response patterns, pentatonic scales, blue notes, heterophonic textures, syncopated rhythms, obbligatos, and a wide range of vocal embellishments and tonal effects. In his arrangements, he aimed to preserve "the conscious and intentional *alterations* of *pitch* often made. . . . The unconscious, but amazing and bewildering *counterpoint* produced by so many voices in *individual improvisation. The absolute insistence* upon the pulsing, *overall rhythm,* combining many varying subordinate rhythms."[32]

Johnson incorporated dramatic shouts in the well-known arrangement of "Elijah Rock!" which depicts the biblical prophet Elijah being carried to heaven by a whirlwind in a fiery horse-drawn chariot (CD no. 12).[33] The adopted ancestral spirit of Elijah was called upon to bring humanity closer to God. Whenever the presence of God was felt, the human reaction was often to shout. Thus, "When the ark of the covenant of the Lord came into the camp, all Israel gave a mighty shout, so that the earth resounded" (1 Sam. 4:5). During the dramatic peak of "Elijah Rock!" Johnson utilizes a choral sonority of twelve-part *divisi* and obbligato voices that provide a rhythmic and melodic contrast to the lower voices. The blue notes in the soprano obbligato create a tonal blend and intensify the exclamatory shout common in the black folk tradition.

The ejaculatory shouts in Johnson's spiritual arrangements were recog-

Example 8.1 "Elijah Rock!" spiritual arrangement by Hall Johnson, mm. 74–77. ©1965 (Renewed) by G. Schirmer, Inc. (ASCAP). International copyright secured. All rights reserved. Reprinted by permission.

nized by his choir as "authentic" and representative of their true culture in its off-keyed, blue-noted splendor. These and other unique musical nuances displayed throughout Johnson's works helped to portray the race in its complexity to a wider audience.

The engagement that gave the Hall Johnson Choir its greatest exposure was its integral role in the dramatization of the Old Negro/New Negro allegory, *The Green Pastures* (1930). This play, written by Marc Connelly after Roark Bradford's "Ol' Man Adam an' His Chillun" (1928), attempted to transform the stories of ancient biblical figures (i.e., Adam and Eve, Moses, Noah, and the like) into characterizations of contemporary southern Negroes in attire, vernacular, and customs. The ten-cent-cigar–smoking God descended from his heaven of fish-fries and walked the earth like a "natchel man" in order to monitor humanity's behavior. The singers were concealed in the orchestra pit beneath a canopy of leaves, performing Negro spirituals. As the scenes were changed, the musical selections helped to carry the mood forward to the next episode. The spirituals brought out the meaning of the dialogue with remarkable effect and provided a vital soundscape for the drama. Their role was not unlike that of the chorus in Greek dramas, serving as "articulate spectator," voicing the response to the events portrayed in the action, remonstrating, warning, or sympathizing with De Lawd, in this case.[34] One reviewer of the production reported, "The mixed choir . . . sings often, and always with thrilling effect."[35] Another commented, "At no point does the choir force itself upon the audience, but the music it gives forth is powerful."[36]

This Negro folk fable was dramatized, directed, and produced by whites and performed by an all-black cast of ninety-five actors and singers. The role of De Lawd was played by the Shakespeare elocutionist Richard B. Harrison. Canadian born, he was unfamiliar with Negro dialect and was tutored by a white actor who had played several black roles. In addition, Harrison used dark makeup to blacken his mulatto features. Connelly took Bradford's mixed cast of southerners and blackened all the biblical characters for commercial reasons. In spite of these circumstances, the work had a certain charm and actors who could give the play a quasi-authentic folk feeling. Consequently, *The Green Pastures* was an enormously successful play. It ran on Broadway for 640 performances and was revived in 1935 and 1951. The production won a Pulitzer Prize in the 1929–30 theatrical season and was recast in a film version by Warner Brothers in 1936.

One commentator maintained, however, that even though the movie was "well intentioned, it merely gave filmgoers once more the happy, religious, hymn-singing black man whose idea of heaven seems to consist mainly of long white nightgowns, hymn-shouting and fish-fries."[37] Journalist Mel Watkins further asserted, "Humor in *The Green Pastures* is derived from the underlying premise that a black Heaven is a cosmic absurdity. In many ways the movie is comparable to nineteenth-century blackface parodies of politicians, preachers, and pundits."[38] Yet just as the portrayal of blacks in the film production was characteristic of the stereotypical Old Negro, there were also elements that personified the racial pride of the New. Particularly, they were evident in Johnson's accompanying choral music, which was essential to the drama.

The opening spiritual in *The Green Pastures* film, "Walk Together Chillun, Don't You Get Weary," suggests the ideas of group solidarity and persistence toward progress. Indeed, "the slaves always seem to be on the move in the spirituals," as in "We Are Climbing Jacob's Ladder."[39] The next spiritual, "Cert'n'y Lord," frames the entire film's beginning, middle, and end with musical dramatizations of the exuberant, emotional experiences surrounding a conversion experience. The "Preacher" asks, "Have you got *good* religion?"—the implication is that everybody talk'n 'bout heaven ain't goin' there. The congregation responds in the affirmative—"Cert'n'y Lord." Reinforced confirmation occurs as this question-and-answer dialogue is repeated three times. One poignant verse queries the "parishioners," "Have you been baptized?" This ritual connotes a metamorphosis from an old circumstance to a new one, purified by water and symbolized by the shift from Old to New Negro status.

One of the most potent biblical scenes in *The Green Pastures* portrays the encounter of Moses with Pharaoh and his court. The commanding spiritual "Go Down, Moses" accompanies the sudden death of Pharaoh's and others' firstborn sons in the land. The proclamation "Let my people go" rings out through time from Egypt (ironically, the cradle of African civilization) to the United States (caustically, the cradle of American liberty). Religious scholar Albert Raboteau writes that the transplanted Africans "increasingly turned to the language, symbols, and worldview of the Christian holy book. There they found a theology of history that helped them to make sense of their enslavement. One story in particular caught their attention and fascinated them with its implications and potential applications to their own situation: the story of Exodus."[40] He continues, "No single symbol captures more clearly the distinctiveness of Afro-American Christianity than the symbol of Exodus. From the earliest days of colonization, white Christians had represented their journey across the Atlantic to America as the exodus of a New Israel from the bondage of Egypt into the Promised Land of milk and honey. For black Christians, the imagery was reversed: the Middle Passage had brought them to Egypt land, where they suffered bondage under a new Pharaoh."[41]

The extended ramifications of that bondage were addressed in a critic's analysis of one of the final scenes featuring the New Negro Hezdrel, a soldier, "barechested, fighting in a smoky battle against a nameless and presumably godless enemy who can only be racism. It was a powerful denouement for a movie that had opened in a Paradise framed as a grand fishfry."[42]

Although there were various interpretations of *The Green Pastures,* the most overarching portrayed an evolution from the Old Testament God of wrath, judgment, and vengeance to a New Testament God of love, mercy, and forgiveness. In the first Testament, God speaks through miracles of nature in the firmament, clouds, and creation and punishes Adam and Eve after the Fall in the Garden of Eden. Musically, Hall Johnson's choir comments through the spiritual "Doncher Let Nobody Turn You Roun.'" As God continues to show disappointment in the disobedience of humankind, he sends the devastating flood, followed by the scene-changing interlude, "De Ole Ark's A Movin.'" Johnson weaves twenty-five Negro spirituals into the drama and inserts at the finale one of his original compositions, "Hallelujah! King Jesus," reiterating "God of Mercy, Lord of Love!" These pregnant lyrics reinforce the conclusion of the 23rd Psalm (from which the title *The Green Pastures* originates), "Surely Goodness and Mercy shall follow me, all the days of my life."[43] God manifests love by sending his son to earth to demonstrate, even while on the cross, how one should live and forgive. These biblically based messages in song and word were convincingly dramatized on the stage and screen in the productions of *The Green Pastures*.

Hall Johnson was committed to intimately studying black folk culture in order to portray it more *authentically*. Thus he could be a harsh critic if he believed the authenticity of the folk traditions had not been maintained. In a 1936 review of *Porgy and Bess,* he criticized George Gershwin for having depicted black folk in a superficial manner. He argued that "a good Negro opera . . . must be not only good opera but must be written in an authentic Negro musical language and sung and acted in a characteristic Negro style."[44] Johnson believed that "a *few* visits to Negro revivals and funerals" during field work excursions to Charleston were not sufficient for Gershwin to move beyond the superficial: "The obvious sights and sounds are only the foam that has no meaning without the beer. And here let it be said that it is not the color nor the aloofness of the white investigator that keeps him on the outside. It is the powerful tang and thrill of the 'foam' that excites him prematurely and makes him rush away too soon,—to write books and music on a subject of which he has not even begun to scratch the surface."[45] Johnson maintained that *Porgy and Bess* was more Gershwin's *idea* of what a Negro opera should be, rather than *being* a Negro opera.[46]

Hall Johnson demonstrated his skill with this genre in his creation of the folk drama *Run, Little Chillun,* which opened at the Lyric Theatre on March 1, 1933, the day after the banks closed. It ran for four months on Broadway despite the Depression. The play represented a milestone in the history of Negro folk opera in that it was the only one of the successful stage works of the time (e.g., *Four Saints in Three Acts, Porgy and Bess, The Green Pastures, The Emperor Jones*) to be written by a black man.[47] It was revived in New York a decade later and performed in Los Angeles for a year and in San Francisco for a few months during the late 1930s by the Federal Theater.

Run, Little Chillun's plot takes place in a southern town and involves a conflict between the Old Negro pagan moon-worshiping cult known as the Pilgrims and the New Negroes of the Baptist faith. The lead character, Jim, neglects his wife and the Baptist religion to pursue the enticing Sulamai, who wants to become a Pilgrim convert and pleads with Jim to join her. He finally decides to reject her and the Pilgrim religion and return to his Baptist tradition. Jim "testifies" and asks for prayer as Sulamai enters to entice him once again and is struck by lightning in the process.[48] The New Negro denominational religion triumphs over the Old pagan cult.

The play is in two acts with four scenes that integrate music, dance, and drama. Its musical scenes consist of the Pilgrims' religious orgy in the woods and the revival meeting of the Baptists. The choreography of the orgy was so "masterfully" executed by Doris Humphrey that "it looked as if it had not been staged at all, which is the highest praise for any sort of folk dancing across a set of footlights."[49] Morton Eustis described the revival meeting in a southern Negro church as "so true and so stirringly expressed that it took the audience completely out of the theatre into the black belt."[50]

The music, which featured the Hall Johnson Choir, was hailed as the most outstanding aspect of the play, and the renditions were deemed realistic. *The New York Times* reported that some of the spirituals "deserve—without the usual equivocation—the adjective superb, and all of them are more than good." Arthur Ruhl stated that "the singing was so good, and its immediate background so interesting, that once in the last act the first-nighters seemed quite to forget that they were watching a play at all, and nearly 'stopped the show' with their demand for an encore."[51]

Despite his success on stage and screen, Johnson maintained his substantial concert and festival choral activity. In January of 1946, he organized the Festival Negro Chorus of New York City in order to "strengthen racial unity and to promote racial harmony." This message was also taken abroad when in 1951 Johnson and his choir represented the United States at the International Festival of Fine Arts in Berlin. (Other American participants included the Juilliard String Quartet, a Theatre Guild production of *Oklahoma*, and a production of *Medea* featuring opera singer Astrid Varney and actress Judith Anderson.) According to Robert C. Schnitzer, the Hall Johnson Choir was "the most successful of all the American attractions, not only because of their novelty and personal appeal, but also because of their musicianship. Even the critics could find nothing to criticize and the audiences refused to leave the hall, demanding encore after encore."[52] Johnson lectured and wrote program notes in German on the Negro folksong and spiritual. Additionally, radio and television broadcasts were made of the choir as they toured West Germany and Vienna following the festival.

The European tour may have been reconciliatory regarding German-American relations. It enhanced cultural understanding, both interracially and internationally, almost a generation after the 1936 Olympic Games in

Berlin, where Hitler had refused to shake hands with black athlete Jesse Owens after Owens had won the gold medal in the 100– and 200–meter dash events.[53]

During his lifetime, Johnson received many honors and awards for his achievements, including the Holstein Prizes for composition (1925, 1927), the Harmon Award (1931), an honorary doctorate in music from the Philadelphia Academy of Music (1934), a citation from the city of New York (1954), and the Handel Award (1970).

Hall Johnson's New Negro choral legacy may be best described as a "call to action." Choir member Madeline Preston recalled that Johnson's *raison d'être* was "to get America singing. He always thought that people who could sing together, live together, and love together, would not create wars."[54] The refrain in his song "Sing Out America" summarizes this philosophy:

SING OUT, AMERICA!
Let the whole world hear you singing.
SING OUT, AMERICA!
Sing the GOOD NEWS you're bringing!
Sing it strong and clear and brave,
Over ev'ry land and sea;
Sing that ev'ry man's a slave
Until ev'ry man is free!
So, SING LOUD, AMERICA!!
And the world will sing with you![55]

Moreover, Johnson interpreted the power of chorus and community in an unpublished memoir: "After nearly thirty years of constant work with choral groups, I am now more than ever convinced that nothing *brings* people together and *holds* them together in good fellowship like the singing *together* of *good* songs. . . . Furthermore, singing together not only creates and promotes good will among the *participants* but communicates the same kindly feelings to *all* within listening range of the song."[56]

From the Harlem Renaissance of the 1920s to the civil rights movement of the 1960s, a rich legacy has been maintained through the creative genius of Hall Johnson, his choral leadership, and his commitment to the re-creation of Negro folksong through *authentic* performance practice and "skeletal" published arrangements. He instinctively knew the power of this repertoire, which echoed the sentiments of the African ancestors and the African American slaves. He concluded that one cannot chain human thought: "So if you do not want your slave to *speak* freely you should also forbid him to sing—

even without words."[57] Johnson and his choir were able to perpetuate the slave's words, groans, moans, and shouts and to bring about powerful, unifying psychological effects as the Old Negro progressed from minstrel stage entertainment to the New Negro's acculturated image in concert, film, and theater. Johnson had a deep appreciation for the importance of the *old* Negro spiritual, having lived for nearly a century as an eyewitness to the evolution of the multiple musical progeny of this genre: work songs, game songs, and later chain-gang songs, blues, and, much later, jazz and gospel. Because many of the qualities of performing spirituals defy notation, he dedicated his life to recreating that *traditional* sound through his choir. Hall Johnson helped to elevate the Negro folksong genre from the cotton field to the concert hall in the societal advancement of a people from slavery to freedom.

Notes

1. Alain Locke, ed., *The New Negro: An Interpretation* (New York: Albert and Charles Boni, 1925), ix.

2. Ibid., 199.

3. Ibid.

4. Unsigned handwritten note found on the back of a monthly statement dated March 26, 1873. Researchers Doug Seroff and Toni Anderson believe that this was probably the text of a speech made by one of the Jubilee Singers. Located in the Jubilee Singers Archives, Fisk University Special Collections. Quoted by Toni Passmore Anderson in "The Fisk Jubilee Singers: Performing Ambassadors for the Survival of an American Treasure, 1871–1878" (Ph.D. dissertation, Georgia State University, 1997), 85.

5. John Hope Franklin and Alfred A. Moss Jr., *From Slavery to Freedom: A History of African Americans,* 7th ed. (New York: McGraw Hill, 1994), 363.

6. Arthur P. Davis and Michael W. Peplow, *The New Negro Renaissance: An Anthology* (New York: Holt, Rinehart and Winston, 1975), 203.

7. Reprinted articles by Melville J. Herskovits in *The New World Negro,* ed. Frances S. Herskovits (Bloomington: Indiana University Press, 1966); Locke, *New Negro,* 254–70.

8. According to a letter from Sara Jo Granade, Supervisor of Vital Records, March 7, 1975, the practice of filing birth certificates did not begin in Georgia until January 1, 1919. Alice Foster, the sister of Hall Johnson, informed the author (March 6, 1975) that her brother was christened Francis Hall Johnson.

9. Hall Johnson, quoted by Alexander Kahn, *Daily Worker* (New York), November 8, 1939, 7.

10. Hall Johnson, "Notes on the Negro Spiritual," in *Readings in Black American Music,* ed. Eileen Southern (New York: W. W. Norton, 1971), 272.

11. Floyd J. Calvin, *Pittsburgh Courier,* August 1, 1931, 8.

12. Hall Johnson, "Biographical and General Notes," September 7, 1943, Hall Johnson Clipping File, Library for the Performing Arts Theatre Division, New York Public Library. All ensuing biographical data are from this source unless otherwise indicated.

13. Verna Arvey, "Hall Johnson and His Choir," *Opportunity* 19, no. 5 (May 1941): 151.

14. "Hall Johnson," *Current Biography* 6 (January 1945), 22; *Philadelphia Musical Academy Catalogue,* 1935–36, 5.

15. Arvey, "Hall Johnson and His Choir," 151.

16. Marion Cumbo, interview with the author, August 3, 1974, New York City.

17. In an interview, Madeline Preston, a Hall Johnson Choir member, stated, "I think he would try to get string sounds when he wanted us to hum a certain way." Moreover, "high sopranos [were used] not for solos but for little high pitches here and there, like a piccolo."

18. *World Telegram,* May 29, 1933.

19. Johnson, "Notes on the Negro Spiritual," 272.

20. James Weldon Johnson, *Black Manhattan* (New York: Knopf, 1930), 200; Richard Newman, "Florence Mills," in *Black Women in America: An Historical Encyclopedia,* ed. Darlene Clark Hine (Brooklyn: Carlson Publishing, 1993), vol. 2, 798–99.

21. *Pittsburgh Courier,* August 1, 1931, Sect. 2, 8.

22. *New York Times,* March 1, 1928, 29.

23. *New York Times,* March 21, 1928, 30.

24. *New York Herald Tribune,* August 2, 1933, 10.

25. *New York Times,* July 6, 1938, 21.

26. *The New York Times,* July 13, 1931, 12.

27. *The New York Times,* July 30, 1933, Sect. 2, 4.

28. *Washington Tribune,* July 7, 1936.

29. Helen Duceburg, interview with the author, March 19, 1976, New York City.

30. Johnson, "Notes on the Negro Spiritual," 273.

31. *Afro-American* (Baltimore), April 16, 1932, 19.

32. Quotation from Johnson, "Notes on the Negro Spiritual," 271–72.

33. Story based on 2 Kings 2:9–13.

34. Donald Jay Grout, *A Short History of Opera,* 2nd ed. (New York: Columbia University Press, 1965), 12.

35. *Boston Herald,* September 6, 1932, 12.

36. *Norfolk Journal and Guide,* March 26, 1932.

37. Quoted in Mel Watkins, *The Real Side: Laughing, Lying, and Signifying—The Underground Tradition of African-American Humor That Transformed American Culture, From Slavery to Richard Pryor* (New York: Simon & Schuster, 1994), 213.

38. Ibid.

39. Charles Joyner, "'Believer I Know'—The Emergence of African-American

Christianity," in *African-American Christianity: Essays in History,* ed. Paul E. Johnson (Berkeley: University of California Press, 1994), 28.

40. Albert J. Raboteau, "African-Americans, Exodus, and the American Israel," in *African-American Christianity,* 1.

41. Ibid., 9.

42. Thomas Cripps, *Slow Fade to Black: The Negro in American Film, 1900–1942* (New York: Oxford University Press, 1977), 260.

43. See Hall Johnson, *The Green Pastures Spirituals Arranged for Voice and Piano* (New York: Carl Fischer, 1930).

44. Hall Johnson, "*Porgy and Bess*—A Folk Opera: A Review," *Opportunity* 14, no. 1 (January 1936): 25.

45. Johnson, "*Porgy and Bess,*" 26.

46. Ibid., 28.

47. Eileen Southern, *The Music of Black Americans: A History* (New York: W. W. Norton, 1971), 432.

48. Hall Johnson, *Run, Little Chillun, A Play in 2 Acts* (New York Public Library, Schomburg Collection, n.d. [carbon copy]).

49. *New York Times,* March 12, 1933, Sect. 9, 7.

50. Morton Eustis, "The Optimist on Broadway," *Theatre Arts Monthly* 18 (May 17, 1933): 338.

51. Arthur Ruhl, *New York Herald Tribune,* March 2, 1933: 10.

52. See Robert C. Schnitzer, "Report on United States Contributions to the Berlin Festival," U. S. Department of State, Bureau of Educational and Cultural Affairs, October 17, 1951.

53. Jesse Owens set a new world record in the 200–meter dash and also won a gold medal for the 400–meter relay. He also won the gold medal in the long jump with a leap of 26 feet, 5 inches, and his world record (set in 1935) of 26 feet, 8¼ inches stood for a quarter-century. See Henry Louis Gates Jr. and Cornel West, *The African-American Century: How Black Americans Have Shaped Our Country* (New York: The Free Press, 2000), 141.

54. Madeline Preston, interview with the author, March 19, 1976, New York City.

55. Hall Johnson, "Sing Out, America!!!" words by Johnson. Unpublished ms. in author's collection acquired from Olive Ball, a former Hall Johnson Choir member. In his later years, Johnson organized numerous festivals from coast to coast with thousands of singers performing together in hopes of bringing about a world of peace and harmony.

56. Untitled typewritten four-page document, n.d., secured by author from Olive Ball.

57. Johnson, "Notes on the Negro Spiritual," 269.

9

From Communism to Yiddishism: The Reinvention of the Jewish People's Philharmonic Chorus of New York City

MARION S. JACOBSON

It is a Monday night in the spring of 2001 and members of the Jewish People's Philharmonic Chorus (JPPC), founded in 1923 by Jewish immigrant garment workers in New York City, are preparing for a concert in the Upper West Side of Manhattan. The thirty-seven-year-old conductor-composer, Binyumen Schaechter, is coaching the singers on a well-known labor song in Yiddish. Although Yiddish was the vernacular language of the chorus's founders, many in the chorus have only recently become students of the language, enrolling in Yiddish classes at the YIVO Institute for Jewish Research or the Workmen's Circle. The conductor is striving for a brisk and staccato march tempo, but the chorus responds instead with shapely lyrical phrasing and a subtle crescendo led by some especially strong soprano voices. The conductor is not pleased. As the chorus sings the words "*mir vern dershosn, derhangen!*" he stops the group and comments, "That was a *lovely* version of 'we've been shot and we've been hanged.'"

In the 1930s and 1940s it had been possible to find dozens of Yiddish choruses in New York and other major cities in America. Founded by Jewish workers in their left-leaning social movements (communist, socialist, and Labor Zionist), they performed songs at rallies and demonstrations, earning widespread admiration as the "voice of Jewish labor."[1] Following the social upheavals affecting Jewish American life in the 1950s, the choruses lost membership, merged, and/or disappeared entirely. Today, the Jewish People's Philharmonic is one of two surviving movement choruses (the other, the Workmen's Chorus, remains affiliated with the fraternal benefit society founded by socialist-leaning Jews). At forty members, the JPPC is one-fourth the size it was during the 1930s and 1940s, and its founding organization, the Jewish People's Fraternal Order, has been defunct since 1958.[2]

However, as a result of "outreach concerts" and because of widening interest in Yiddish music, the contemporary chorus has brought the music beyond the bounds of the earlier social movements that had supported it. It has found a reliable audience at Yiddish weekends, Yiddish camps, and the Holocaust memorials that have proliferated at synagogues and Jewish cultural and community centers in the last few decades. Its concerts and projects have even engaged people interested in Jewish liturgical music—a radical departure from its secular heritage. As such, the JPPC has been involved in the Yiddish revival scene ("*Yiddishvelt*").

When I joined the JPPC in 2000 to begin my research, my aim was to look at Yiddish choruses, which may be defined as vocal ensembles of lay singers, modeled on European immigrant philharmonic societies and maintained as symbols of progressive or leftist Jewish identity in America. I assumed that the continuation of the folk choir tradition represented a kind of alternative culture to that of mainstream denominational Judaism and its accompanying preoccupations with the religious aspects of Jewish identity, its Zionist ideology, and its focus on Hebrew.

This supposition proved to be inadequate. It did not account for the dynamic, tangled collection of ideologies, musical concepts, attitudes, and personal experiences I encountered in weekly rehearsals and presentation of concerts. What I found was a more complicated situation that placed folk choruses within a web of symbolic discourses, one that illuminated questions of authority regarding the interpretation of labor song, the contradiction between the conductor's calling his chorus a "Yiddish" chorus and the reality of its radical past, and the superimpositions of post-Holocaust worldviews shaping American Jewish culture (some of which reflected the Zionist tendencies I had assumed the chorus to have rejected). It also linked questions of style and aesthetics to formulations of Jewish identity in a contemporary American context.

The composer and conductor Binyumen Schaechter, hired in 1997 to direct the JPPC, added unexpected dimensions to my research. The new members he recruited and the changes he implemented in style and repertory prompted heated discussions about the purpose and mission of a Jewish folk chorus and were accompanied by the abrupt departures of long-time members. The singers' interest in exploring the chorus's past, and the texts of the songs themselves, disclosed a relatively unknown chapter of Jewish

American life, one in which "we lived and breathed our struggles," in the words of one member. Here I analyze some ways in which singers in a contemporary Yiddish chorus make sense of the connections among traditions of labor choruses, *Yiddishkeyt* [Yiddish culture], and contemporary choral aesthetics. I address ideology, ideals, and strategies by which people organize and explain their local musical knowledge—in sum, I discuss creativity, productivity, and making and experiencing the emotion of singing as kind of cultural work.

People's perceptions of their past and present are a significant issue. The realities of life in the early garment factories are distant from the experiences of the white-collar professionals and students now singing in the chorus. But their perceptions of history shape their performances, becoming basic assumptions. Different though the concerns of these singers and their working-class counterparts more than fifty years ago are, one of their basic assumptions is the notion that labor songs—the musical creations of social movements long gone—are *real*, and that they have unique powers to affect the consciousness of singers and listeners. Although not often so explicitly stated, another understanding about the nature of labor song conditions much of the contemporary performance of the genre: the reconceptualization of labor song as a "Yiddish" musical genre. As the conductor's sarcastic comment makes clear, these understandings of the violence of struggle can conflict with the desire to make the song sound pleasing. In short, I seek an understanding of labor song as an ideology, if we understand ideology to be a "rich system of representations" worked up in specific material practices that help form individuals into social subjects who "freely internalize a picture of their social world and their place in it."[3]

Like many ideologies, that of the labor song's unique power draws our attention to certain aspects of the objects it presents, but it obscures others. In this essay, I explore how that ideology works by continuing a discussion of the song that opened it, David Edelstadt's "In Kamf," written in 1898, from a perspective informed by ethnographic research and by an interpretive focus on a community that has drawn on this kind of music to shape its self-understanding—upwardly mobile Jewish Americans. How might such a song both reinforce and be interpreted through the terms it establishes? Such an undertaking requires attention to two different perspectives emerging at different points in Jewish history: first, the role of music as a marker of collective identity and self-definition—a perspective intimately related to the culture in which the song was composed; and second, the experience of music as it addresses the needs of 1990s Jewish Americans with a well-developed awareness of Yiddish culture and the Holocaust. In brief, I seek to interpret the "work" of a labor song in the Yiddish choral tradition and the ideological filters that help to define it.

* * *

The popularity of Yiddish folk choruses surged in the urban centers of the 1920s and 1930s. The aim of such groups was to cultivate an awareness of "Yiddish music," a broad category that embraced "labor song"—anthems and sweatshop poems arranged and composed by proletarian Jews—as well a highly developed tradition of art song in Yiddish and European choral music (the repertories of these choruses included works by Beethoven, Handel, and Bach, all sung in Yiddish).[4] By providing such access, as well as basic musical and vocal training, these groups confirmed one's sense of belonging to the larger American society while supporting the culture of the Jewish voluntary movements.

Of the most vital choruses was the Freiheit Gezangfarein, which later changed its name to the Jewish People's Philharmonic, established by communist-leaning garment workers who lived in the Coops on Allerton Avenue in the Bronx. The Freiheit became widely visible in the New York City Jewish left community, performing thirty times a year at rallies, concerts, and political functions aimed at a locally based movement audience. To the Yiddish press, which covered the concerts regularly, the Freiheit symbolized the accomplishments of everyday singers who devoted themselves to the highest artistic standards without concern for financial remuneration.[5] Singing in the Freiheit, a group of 100–150 singers, was a mark of status within the community. "If you sang in that chorus, you were really somebody," notes one singer whose mother sang in it.[6]

In the 1940s the worlds of the left choruses were caught up in the political upheavals of the Red Scare, and the Industrial Workers Organization (IWO), the Jewish People's Fraternal Order (JFPO), and its Camp Kinderland were targeted on a list of subversive organizations. In 1947, the IWO was liquidated, its assets were taken over, and the JPFO lost its license to sell insurance in New York State, thus losing its livelihood.[7] Within the ranks of the JPPC, many members who were afraid that their affiliation would jeopardize their children's chances of getting into college began dropping out of the chorus.[8] Those who stayed urged their fellow singers to drop such leftist anthems as "Unfurl the Red Flag."[9] By 1981, the JPPC had dwindled to eighteen members, many of whom assumed that the chorus would soon die out.[10] Some simply came to rehearsals because they were "old soldiers" who felt bound to continue despite their feeling that there was no longer a next generation to take their places in the group.[11]

It was in this context that the JPPC began its transformation from a "leftist" chorus to a "Yiddish chorus." In 1997, when conductor Peter Schlosser retired, Schaechter took over the JPPC. Schaechter was born in 1963 in New York City to one of the elite Yiddishist families in the United States. His father, Mordkhe Schaechter, is a prominent Yiddish linguist and teacher at the YIVO Summer Program in Yiddish Language and Literature, and his aunt Beyle Schaechter-Gottesman has published books of her Yiddish poetry and songs. The Schaechters were active within the Sholem Aleichem movement, a Jewish social movement that distanced itself from partisan politics and embraced Yiddish with quasi-religious fervor. The major thrust of the movement was establishing Yiddish schools for children and encouraging families to speak exclusively Yiddish within the family and network of movement cohorts. In keeping with this ideal, Schaechter's family spoke only Yiddish in the home.[12] As an undergraduate, Schaechter studied composition and piano at Manhattan School of Music, where he took classes in conducting, after which he worked as an accompanist, arranger, and composer of musical revues. Among his credits are the off-Broadway musicals *Too Jewish* and *Naked Boys Singing*.[13] He also sang with the Zamir Chorale, a Hebrew liturgical chorus in New York City, a connection that later became significant for the JPPC.

Schaechter's mission for the JPPC began when he found out the group would be celebrating its seventy-fifth anniversary in 1998—a moment he felt was an opportune time to revitalize the chorus by preparing for a special concert in June of that year. He realized he could not do it with the chorus he had. It was weak in volume and pitch and consisted of mostly older people; the average age was sixty-five or seventy.[14] He decided to assume personal responsibility for the situation and began to recruit students from the Uriel Weinreich Summer Program in Yiddish Language and Literature at Columbia University and from *Yugntruf* Youth for Yiddish, a cultural club co-founded by his father. *Yugntruf* presents a variety of Yiddish cultural activities in and around New York City, including a week-long intergenerational summer camp and language-immersion program where such activities as yoga classes and softball games are conducted in Yiddish. Calling everyone he knew who might be musical, like Yiddish, and have time to sing, within a year's time he had doubled the JPPC in size.[15] Most of the new members are under fifty.[16]

Schaechter's single-minded enthusiasm was not the only factor in generating interest in a Yiddish chorus. Some JPPC recruits pursued Yiddish song as a result of finding themselves caught in the momentum of the klezmer revival, set in motion in the 1980s and offering new possibilities for restoration and reform in the cultural activities of the JPPC.[17] In the midst of the unprecedented and unpredicted widespread interest in Yiddish dance music, new forces emerged that energized Yiddish choruses and allowed them to play a more visible role than before. This sentiment is captured in a recent fundraising letter, which describes the group as "inspiring audiences" with the "voices of sweatshop laborers, immigrants, mothers, partisans, *khalutsim*,[18] *tumlers*,[19] and lovers" that "sing out through us in every Chorus concert—all in our warm, eloquent *mame-loshn* (mother tongue)."[20]

As the letter suggests, the appeal of Yiddish song sparked an immediate change in the chorus's repertory from the staples of the progressive left to a new menu of songs and performances that would serve as the foundation of the JPPC's concerts over the next few years. One major shift was the abandonment of songs in English (songs like "Union Maid" had been a staple of this chorus in its communist days).[21] The transformation of the JPPC from a labor chorus affiliated with communist politics into a Yiddish chorus did not occur overnight; rather, it had to be negotiated, member by member, song by song. As we will see, a rehearsal and performance of the song "In Kamf" in 2000–2001 was an important turning point.

*   *   *

Since the peak of their activity during the 1930s and 1940s, the "signature" pieces of labor choruses have been hymns and anthems, pieces composed to poems by revered folk intellectuals such as David Edelshtat and Morris Rosenfeld. Documenting the hardships of factory life and often written from a first-person perspective, these songs became a central element in the choral repertory during the 1930s, when conductor-composers such as Jacob Schafer and Lazar Weiner set out to collect and arrange them.[22] After 1946, Hirsh Glik's "Zog Nit Keynmol" [Never Say Never] was widely circulated as the "Hymn of the Partisan Fighters" at choral concerts, particularly those held in observance of Yom HaShoah [Holocaust Remembrance Day]. Such songs are often presented at the ends of programs, with the audience spontaneously standing up and joining in.

Edelstadt's "In Kamf" (CD no. 13) was composed in 1889 and, according to the folklorist Chana Mlotek, "became the beloved hymn of Jewish workers everywhere. . . . It was absorbed into the Yiddish folksong and later sung in the *shules* (Yiddish schools)." Mlotek also describes a memorable incident in London in which Jewish workers sang "In Kamf" in a large-scale protest march in 1903.[23] Its focus, like that of many labor songs, is unquestionably collective struggle. It reflects the vitality of the "sweatshop poets" by addressing a community of workers. Its relative technical simplicity and its marked similarity to the "Marseillaise," the well-known French anthem (to which it has been compared), marks it as a "singable" tune. Indeed, the song appears on dozens of concert programs from the 1930s to the 1950s in the files of dozens of movement choruses available in the YIVO archives.

In 1996, Mark Zuckerman, a composer, computer programmer, and Yiddish enthusiast, enrolled in the YIVO Summer Program, where folksinging in Yiddish was a part of the curriculum. Students are urged to purchase the "Mlotek songbooks" (three-volume collections of folksongs by Chana and Joseph Mlotek) and participate in regular singing workshops with prominent Yiddish vocalists such as Paula Teitelbaum, Adrienne Cooper, and Michael Alpert. Zuckerman discovered "In Kamf" in the second volume, *Mir Trogn a Gezang* [We Bring a Song], published in 1977. The grandson of a Yiddish-speaking immigrant and member of the Jewish Labor Bund, Zuckerman was struck by the song's subject matter and decided to arrange it for the Jewish People's Philharmonic to sing. Zuckerman notes that while he approaches the song through a strong connection to the labor tradition and ensures that his harmonization maintains the "folklike character of the underlying song and melody," his strongest musical commitments lie elsewhere—in the field of atonal music. "I had hoped initially that there might be some cross-fertilization, that performers and audiences for the arrangements (of Yiddish songs) might develop an interest in my 'atonal' compositions."[24]

In the early fall of 2000, sheet music in hand, singers rehearsing "In Kamf" for the first time reveal different kinds of knowledge of the song and the history of the genre. Many of the elder members of the chorus recall singing it—in rousing unison—in their Yiddish schools or in the Holocaust memorial celebrations organized by the Workmen's Circle, as well as in synagogues and community centers. The younger singers, however, have encountered few songs like this. At least one person thinks it is from the old country, Jewish eastern Europe, and others express surprise that its arranger is alive and well in New Jersey.

Singers who have practiced at home with Schaechter's "part tapes" prepared for all four sections read through the music confidently; those who "know" the song from their Yiddish schools sing confidently through the first eight bars, where the melody resounds in unison (Example 9.1). But Zuckerman has varied the texture. The men's voices take over for the song's most graphic lyrics (Example 9.2, m. 21). Tonight, the men's section consists of six singers, creating a notable imbalance (there are twenty-five women

Example 9.1 David Edelstadt, "In kamf," arranged by Mark Zuckerman, mm. 1–8. Music ©by E. C. Schirmer Music Company, a division of ECS. Reprinted by permission.

in the chorus). Two voices, S.'s and C.'s, prevail, as if to compensate for the thin textures. The women's voices re-enter a little hesitantly (Example 9.2, m. 30). "Watch me!" urges Schaechter. The altos are late with their little motif (Example 9.2, m. 34), momentarily losing focus.

When it is time for the parts to split at the cadence (Example 9.2, m. 30), Schaechter wants to know who will sing the high A-sharp and G. Need he ask? Judy Bro, a lyric soprano who has performed professionally with the touring company of *Annie,* is one of only two members who "have" those notes, and she exults in singing "*di gantse velt vet vern bafrayt*" [the whole world will be liberated] (Example 9.2, mm. 38–40). Completing this run-through, Schaechter moves on to fine-tuning. All the sections have solos and they all needed to be heard clearly. In the chorus, a cappella performance is the norm. All of Zuckerman's arrangements are a cappella, a sound that both Schaechter and Zuckerman have described as more "direct," "emotional," and authentic. Interestingly, in the past, Yiddish choruses (like most mainstream non-Jewish philharmonic societies) performed most frequently with piano or orchestra.

Schaechter has worked on these pieces (along with others) throughout the year, drilling the chorus repeatedly in their sections. When satisfied that most everyone in the choir knows their parts and can hold them against the other sections singing together, he works on the combination, striving for a homogenous sound. Several rehearsals later, singers who are not familiar with Yiddish begin to grapple with the meaning of the text. While he is meticulous about diction, pronunciation, and the use of Yiddish in performance, he does not always provide a translation.

Schaechter has frequently discussed with his chorus the dynamics of musical communication, urging singers to identity points of personal emotional engagement with labor song. When rehearsing a lullaby he instructs the chorus along the lines of a drama coach invoking Stanislavsky's acting "method," asking the singers to imagine the saddest thing they could, and then imagine themselves singing it to a child.[25] J., a young professor of classics at Columbia, needs no prodding to interpret "In Kamf" on an emotional level. Her interest in Yiddish music is an extension of her abiding interest in workers' songs from many cultures (she once sang with a lesbian-feminist chorus specializing in world music) and with the various political causes she supports. Later in the year, she proposes that the choruses present "In Kamf" at an anti-sweatshop rally by one of the UNITE! Union locals. Another woman, a publications editor at a university, identifies with "In Kamf" in a directly personal way. "I spend eleven hours a day chained to my computer, so I can

Example 9.2 David Edelstadt, "In kamf," arranged by Mark Zuckerman, mm. 21–40.

Example 9.2 Continued.

relate to sweatshop songs," she says. Other singers are less delighted with "In Kamf." "It's ridiculous for us to sing so many labor songs," says another singer. "What's the relevance now?" Says another singer, the true value of "In Kamf" is—like all the other songs in its repertory—that it is a Yiddish song, "I know we used to do all these lefty songs, spirituals, whatever. But Yiddish music really needs its own place. I really believe that we have to be *the* chorus devoted to Yiddish. Who else is out there but us to do that?"[26]

As the rehearsals progress and the chorus begins preparing for concerts, discussion about the meaning of the song gives way to *musical* issues (tempo, dynamics, and tuning) that are crucial to ensuring a good performance of the song. A transformation occurs in their interpretation of "In Kamf." The group no longer sings lyrically, but in a forceful manner that renders the words clear and comprehensible. At that point, Schaechter decides that the JPPC is ready to present "In Kamf" onstage.

* * *

When it was most vital, in the 1930s and 1940s, the JPPC performed concerts primarily within a "movement culture," appearing throughout the year at rallies, marches, and events associated with particular political causes.[27] The group would conclude its season with a festive concert at Town Hall, performed for five hundred listeners. Subsequently, Peter Schlosser curtailed the group's public appearances because of the difficulty of new repertory and the decline in the skills of its aging membership.

Remarkably, in the mid-1990s the JPPC's invigorated leadership ended a ten-year lull in concertizing and filled the calendar with concerts. But without a movement culture to support it, the JPPC circulates within a milieu that layers the principles of the free market onto an earlier tradition of social service and "giving back" to the community through public performance. Since revitalizing its membership in the early 1990s, the JPPC has performed about ten to twelve concerts per year, an impressive schedule compared with the handful of annual appearances made by its counterpart in the Workmen's Circle. The JPPC owes its visibility to the efforts of chorus members Judy Bro and Jo Abrams, who have volunteered their time to book concerts and raise funds. Abrams makes a claim that is novel in the JPPC's history, "We'll perform anywhere that'll pay us."[28] Indeed, Abrams does a kind of informal target marketing to Jewish organizations, museums, and cultural institutions whose constituents are interested in Yiddish culture: the Museum of the Jewish Heritage, the Holocaust Center on Long Island, the Queens College Jewish Lecture and Concert Series, as well as several senior centers in Manhattan.[29] Most of the concerts are free and open to the public and are funded by grants from private and non-profit foundations. For these events, known as "outreach concerts,"[30] the chorus usually collaborates with the presenters to carry out advance publicity, an e-mailing by Schaechter, and preparation of programs with English translations of all the songs. For these concerts Schaechter selects twelve to fifteen songs from his "wish list" from a variety of sources, running the gamut of genres and expressive forms—labor songs, theater songs, religious pieces, satirical songs, children's songs, and contemporary popular music in Yiddish—while attempting to make them seem effortlessly blended into a coherent program. In performance Schaechter acts as emcee as well as conductor, engaging with the audience in a strategy of his own making: translating lyrics, providing historical background on the songs, cracking jokes, and on the whole striving to put people at ease with Yiddish.

Schaechter often introduces the chorus in the context of an emerging Yiddish-speaking community, particularly when introducing a group that usually performs at JPPC concerts: the Pripetshik Choir.[31] A few years ago, he organized a singing group among the children attending the Pripetshik School, a Sunday-morning Yiddish program that meets at the Workmen's Circle in Manhattan. It has since become a fixture at all JPPC concerts. Under

Schaechter's leadership, the children's group has presented a small repertory of children's songs, including "Ikh Bin A Kleyne Chaynik" [I'm a Little
Teapot] (Figure 9.1). The children are always a big hit, and Schaechter seems
to understand what mileage he can get from their success. As the children
take their bow, he explains that his family, as well as those of others in the
chorus, speaks only Yiddish at home and are part of a thriving movement
to promote Yiddish as a living language.

Schaechter always notes that the group has celebrated its seventy-fifth
anniversary, doubled in size, and given a dozen concerts in a single year. This
testimony never fails to elicit hearty applause and cheers from the audience.[32]
Indeed, JPPC concerts are more than competent performances of Yiddish
songs; they are also a show of strength to the Jewish community beyond the
confines of the *Yiddishvelt*. The JPPC cultivates a "Holocaust song" repertory, a core selection of songs that document Jewish suffering and heroism
in the ghettoes and camps from the perspective of firsthand witnesses. Songs
whose lyrics deal with appropriately tragic material have been adopted into

Figure 9.1 The Jewish People's Philharmonic Chorus in concert, April 15, 2001, Sholem
Aleichem Cultural Center, Bronx, N. Y. Binyumen Schaechter at the piano with Reyna
Schaechter (his daughter) performing "I'm a Little Teapot" in Yiddish. Photo by Marion
Jacobson.

it.[33] While "In Kamf" predates the Holocaust by a half-century, it has become associated with the Holocaust song repertory and is performed in numerous memorial ceremonies by the various Yiddish choruses.

Of the dozen or so concerts the JPPC gave that year, one of the most significant was the North American Jewish Choral Festival (JCF). This gathering of hundreds of synagogue and Jewish community center choirs was organized by the prestigious Zamir Chorale. The festival is primarily concerned with sacred music; the JPPC is one of only two choruses in it that sings Yiddish secular music.[34] For the Jewish People's Philharmonic, the choral festival is a significant mode of musical production, charged with new meaning. In the past twenty years, festivals have made up a crucial element of the subculture of American Jewish lay choral singing. The accumulation of new repertory, commissioning of works, and the cultivation of a blended and clean sound have become the primary elements of an emerging vocal practice among these singers. People make an investment in their choruses and the development of their voices by taking part in such festivals, which despite the name more are serious than festive in tone. The JCF offers voice lessons, workshops in sight reading, and other kinds of musically enriching and demanding activities. Performance is a major part of choral festivals, for they serve as the evening entertainment as well as the primary showcase of the participating groups (groups are usually invited to participate based on the musical competence of the singers and their conductor).

For two years in a row, the JPPC has participated in this festival. Among the twenty-two singers who self-selected to attend were many of the younger and more musically skilled members, people recruited by Schaechter from Yugntruf. The festival was thus an opportunity to showcase new acquisitions: trained young singers with strong voices and new repertory. For this performance, Schaechter has prepared one of his own compositions, "Bay di taykhn fun Bovl" [By the Waters of Babylon], based on a Yiddish translation of Psalm 137 by the poet Yehoash, author of a noted Yiddish translation of the Five Books of Moses. "Bay di taykhn" struck many members as dead-on for the audience at the festival. "Those synagogue choir people can relate to this music," commented one soprano. When Schaechter introduced the song in rehearsal, several of the "old-guard" members, one of whom described his family heritage as "anarchist," became incensed at the notion of the JPPC performing a "religious song" and demanded that it be dropped. One of these members ultimately left the chorus. Following this dispute, Schaechter never addressed the controversy over "Bay di taykhn" in any official way; rather, he established a "mini-chorus" (a self-selected subgroup) and assigned the composition to this group to rehearse separately. Hence, the JPPC split itself into two choruses: a "folk chorus" modeled after the traditional chorus, and a chorale made up primarily of younger singers with trained voices.

On a warm August evening in 2001, the JPPC faced an audience of 1,000 people, mainly Jewish choral singers and their conductors, in a large ballroom at the Nevele Hotel in the Catskills. The chorus had spent the earlier part of the evening rehearsing and listening to a few other choruses' performances, including Kol Zimrah from Chicago, who gave a polished performance of contemporary settings of Jewish (Hebrew) texts by Chicago-based composers commissioned by the synagogue for use in the Friday night Sabbath liturgy. The JPPC singers who listened to this part of the program commented admiringly on the powerful, resonant voice of their soloist, an operatic mezzo-soprano. Before they took the stage, some expressed their concern that they "wouldn't be as good as the pro singers"; others noted that most choruses wore snazzy matching evening ensembles, while the uniformless JPPC looked like a motley crew in various black and white outfits ranging from business suits to guayaberas. Professionalism had suddenly become a glaring concern. As a strategic approach to impressing audiences at the festival, Schaechter had selected six pieces, each representing a different musical style. He also made some remarks about the history of the JPPC and Yiddish choirs in general. His off-the-cuff comments seemed casual, lighthearted, and a bit haphazard. Coming on the heels of the somewhat stiff and formal presentations of the synagogue choirs, who had hardly interacted with the audience at all, this commentary seemed to elicit a warm response. And so did the music.

"In Kamf" was performed much as Schaechter had coached the performers in rehearsal, but it did not elicit a particularly strong response. As many in the chorus predicted, "Bay di taykhn" worked beautifully as a centerpiece for this program, flowing with the festival's liturgical focus (the Zemer Chai Chorus had also sung Hebrew Psalm texts). After Schaechter took his bows and the JPPC filed off stage, many people in the audience nodded their approval. One elderly woman tugged at my shirt to tell me how good we were, and we had a brief conversation in Yiddish. Now that we were free for the rest of the evening, many stayed to hear Zemer Chai ("Washington, D.C.'s Jewish Community Chorus") sing about God and angels in an upbeat gospel style.

Following the performance, all in the JPPC, except for those who stayed to take advantage of the NAJCF's programs, boarded the bus with their conductor. In high spirits after a successful performance, the chorus began to sing various Yiddish songs in keys and harmonies of their own choosing. Schaechter did not join in, but proceeded to share some larger thoughts on his mind. He wanted to know, should the JPPC become an auditioned chorus? Indeed, Schaechter's question embodied the fear of some of the elder JPPC members that he would take drastic measures to achieve the sound quality he desires. According to the old-guard members, Schaechter has expressed frustration over the inability of some singers to sing difficult lines or remain on key and has hinted to some that he would consider asking some of them to leave. Recently, he faced the dilemma of deciding how to deal with one elderly singer who was facing musical difficulties. This particular singer, who grew up in a communist household, endured the McCarthy persecutions and remained devoted to the chorus for twenty years. But she could not read music and she frequently sang off key, despite many hours of practicing with the tapes. Concerned about her effect on the overall sound, Schaechter eventually asked her to leave.

Quality-control measures like these alarm the old guard. "It's fine to tell someone 'I don't think you're ready to sing this or that piece,' but don't tell them they can't come. This is a folk chorus, which means that anyone can sing," said a long-time singer with the JPPC. Eventually, Schaechter backed down over this issue, instead addressing difficulties singers were having by scheduling special rehearsals for certain sections. Indeed, Schaechter had already made his decision known through the performance of "Bay di taykhn," the most harmonically complex of any in the chorus's entire repertory. He explained that this smaller group was geared toward those who feel ready for the challenge of singing more difficult music. The virtuosic potential of a chamber chorus, which could potentially go beyond single numbers to perform concerts on its own, raises other questions about the relationship between the traditions of a folk chorus and its ambitions to improve its sound. Is the Jewish Choral Festival a rite of passage that signifies its budding maturity as a more "pro" chorus? The set-apart qualities of the chamber chorus, along with its special role in making an impression at the festival, serves as a frame for altering the dynamics of this left chorus, spacing it farther from the taken-for-granted habitus of earlier left traditions.

* * *

If the JPPC is no longer a labor chorus, what work does it do? At the beginning of the twenty-first century, the agenda and repertory of the JPPC represent a dramatic departure from those of the 1930s and 1940s. At that time, participation in such choruses promised participation in a total social movement defined by the values of Jewish immigrant workers. Singing Yiddish song alongside labor song in English (as well as Russian, Spanish, and Chinese) and European art music enacted the international vision of the Jewish People's Fraternal Order and its faith in the potential of art music to elevate the sensibilities of proletarian workers. Ultimately, however, the JPPC merged with the value system of the klezmer revival by making the preservation of *Yiddishkeyt* its primary aim. In addition, it has internalized a post-Holocaust sensibility by shouldering the symbolic weight of presenting evidence of Jewish martyrdom and heroism at memorial concerts.

Likewise, the presentation of Yiddish labor songs as artistic products shaped by Zuckerman and Schaechter places the performative element of labor song in the foreground. Just how one sings "we've been shot and we've been hanged" is an issue that has yet to be resolved at the JPPC. In stating his intention to resist singing labor song in a manner that is simply "pretty," but wanting to compete with semi-professional choirs in a festival, Schaechter wrestles with the tensions between choral aesthetics and historical ideological commitments. Nevertheless, an embrace of labor song as a labor of love for Yiddish has contributed to the vitality of Yiddish song in New York and beyond and its move toward creating real and convincing images of Jewish life. Such a stance should not be taken as a rejection of politics or a desire to replace labor song with leisure song. To the contrary, I would suggest that contemporary Yiddish singers' idiosyncratic engagements with labor song have stayed true to the creative and humanistic values of their own core community, the *Yiddishvelt*. By declining to reproduce the voices of their communist predecessors, the Yiddish singers should not necessarily be seen as apolitical. Instead, they might be said to be doing significant and risky cultural work: insisting that Yiddish song is terrain on which Jewishness can and should take form.

In its musical variety and in its disaffection with both the present and its own radical past, the JPPC turns the notion of "political music" on its head. To most for whom Yiddish song is clearly "political" in its historical referents, its subject matter, and the settings in which it was sung, the JPPC troubles the waters. If a piece is presented at a choral festival where the conductor introduces the chorus as a former lefty chorus, one is pushed to ask what (if anything) makes music sound political and why. If the Yiddish chorus leaves a legacy beyond its alternately frustrating, enlightening, inspiring, and puzzling rehearsals, it may be this: Such questions are worth struggling with again and again, one song and one performance at a time.

Notes

1. Melech Epstein, *Jewish Labor in the United States* (New York: Trade Union Sponsoring Committee, 1969 [1943]), vol. 1, 51.

2. Paul Mishler, *Raising Reds: Young Pioneers, Radical Summer Camps and Communist Political Culture in the United States* (New York: Columbia University Press), 111.

3. James H. Kavanagh, "Ideology," in *Critical Terms for Literary Study,* ed. Frank Lentrichia and Thomas McLaughlin (Chicago and London: University of Chicago Press, 1990), 310.

4. In New York City a variety of organizations encouraged people's participation in Western choral art music, for example the People's Choral Union and the People's Chorus of New York, founded and conducted by Lorenzo Camilieri. Both groups assembled choirs of 1,000 singers. Within the Jewish community, the growing cosmopolitan aspirations of the workforce demanded a deeper association with art music. The development of Jewish choral societies was also linked to the identification of middle-class Jews with Germanic art music, a phenomenon that is discussed in Philip Bohlman, *"The Land Where Two Streams Flow": Music in the German-Jewish Community of Israel* (Urbana: University of Illinois Press, 1989).

5. "They Don't Sing For Money," *Morning Freiheit,* January 26, 1936, n.p.

6. Conversations with Seymour and Pearl Graiver, December–January 2000–1.

7. Mishler, *Raising Reds,* 197.

8. Madeline Simon, past conductor of the JPPC, interview with the author, August 10, 2000.

9. Ibid.

10. Robert Snyder, unpublished ethnography of the Jewish People's Philharmonic Chorus conducted in 1981.

11. Ibid.

12. Binyumen Schaechter, interview with the author, May 6, 1999.

13. Ibid.

14. Ibid.

15. Ibid.

16. Survey of JPPC members completed December 4, 2000.

17. The 1980s and 1990s, a time of renewed attention to ethnicity in the United States, was also a time when Yiddish music was suddenly recognized by mainstream audiences and the musical establishment. Bands like the Klezmatics, Kapelye, Brave Old World, and the Klezmer Conservatory Band toured across two continents promoting their albums. Yiddish dance music dominated the American Jewish musical world, prompting what is popularly known as the klezmer revival or renaissance. The phrase captures both a narrow importance (tied to the popularity of bands) and a wider significance for Yiddish choruses and the everyday singers who perform in them: It was both a resurgence of interest in Yiddish vernacular musical expressions

and folk traditions and a larger awakening of interest in Yiddish literature, language, and song. It marked an opening of a movement in Jewish culture, the first act in a larger renaissance that stamped an indelible imprint on American culture. See Mark Slobin, *American Klezmer: Its Roots and Offshoots* (Berkeley: University of California Press, 2001).

18. Jewish pioneers in Palestine.

19. Jewish entertainers, such as those commonly found in summer camps and Catskills resorts in the first half of the twentieth century.

20. Jewish People's Philharmonic Chorus letter, received January 1, 2003.

21. Madeline Simon, conversations with the author, August 1999.

22. For example, Schafer's collections *Mit Gezang Tsum Kamf* [With Song to the Struggle] (New York: IWO, 1930) and *Gezang un Kamf* [Song and Struggle]; and Lazar Weiner, *Songs for Chorus,* 2 vols. (New York: Workmen's Circle, 1938 and 1941).

23. Eleanor Gordon Mlotek, *Mir Trogn a Gezang,* 2nd. ed. [We bring a song] (New York: Workmen's Circle, 1977), 80.

24. Correspondence dated August 22, 2002.

25. Field notes, Jewish People's Philharmonic, December 2000.

26. Ibid.

27. Jewish People's Philharmonic Chorus concert programs, 1945–50, Jewish Music Alliance collection, YIVO Institute Archives, New York.

28. Jo Abrams, interview with the author, November 11, 2000.

29. Ibid.

30. Jo Abrams and Judy Bro, conversations with the author, October and November 2000.

31. Pripetshik, meaning "fireplace" in Yiddish, is a reference to the popular Goldfaden song, "Oyfn Pripetshik," which opens with the image of a rebbe teaching children the Hebrew alphabet.

32. Field notes from JPPC concerts, September–December 2000.

33. See Marion Jacobson, "We Sing It Like We Say It: The Yiddish Folk Chorus Tradition in New York City" (Ph.D. dissertation, New York University, 2003); and Gila Flam, *Singing for Survival: Songs of the Lodz Ghetto, 1940–45* (Urbana: University of Illinois Press, 1992).

34. The other Yiddish chorus appearing at the festival was the auditioned Yiddish chorale founded by Zalmen Mlotek, The New Yiddish Chorale, formerly Di Goldene Keyt [Golden Chain].

PART 4

The Activist Chorus

10

"We're Singin' for the Union": The ILGWU Chorus in Pennsylvania Coal Country, 1947–2000

KENNETH C. WOLENSKY

During the Great Depression American clothing manufacturers fled Manhattan's garment district to secure inexpensive non-union labor in places such as the remote Appalachian mountains of northeastern Pennsylvania where the decline of coal mining devastated local communities, leaving people desperate for jobs. The International Ladies' Garment Workers' Union (ILGWU) countered these "runaway" sweatshops in Pennsylvania's Wyoming Valley by organizing women garment workers into one of the largest and most influential labor organizations in American history.

Part of the infrastructure built by the ILGWU in its organizing drive included a chorus created in 1947. The chorus played an integral role in transforming women garment workers into a powerful community-conscious alliance. It also anchored the union as an important and highly recognized part of the community, the labor movement, and the political scene. The chorus is testimonial to the creative capacity of the American labor movement to use entertainment for social and political enlightenment.

At the end of the nineteenth century the manufacture of clothing in the United States shifted from artisan shops, individual homes, and immigrant-occupied tenements of urban industrial areas such as New York's Lower East Side to a growing number of factories. The factory system expanded in the early twentieth century as tens of thousands of Russian and eastern European Jews and Italians provided a ready pool of labor to the garment industry. Many immigrants were employed in so-called "inside shops," owned by a manufacturer, where fabrics were cut, sewed, pressed, and shipped to retail markets.

Manhattan's "garment district" emerged as the leading locale for the pro-duction of clothing in the United States. In June 1900, delegates from several unions met in Manhattan to form the International Ladies' Garment Workers' Union (ILGWU), representing workers who made clothing for women and children. The ILGWU affiliated with the American Federation of Labor.[1]

To avoid the ILGWU and its demands for higher wages, "jobbers" or inde-pendent manufacturers secured orders from retailers, then contracted work to small, highly competitive producers. The contractors paid low wages and demanded long hours from their employees who, in turn, worked at frantic paces in cramped, unsafe, and unsanitary conditions. The process gave rise to the industrial "sweatshop."

Contracting became more prevalent during hard economic times. By the time David Dubinsky assumed the ILGWU presidency in 1932, the union's future appeared grim. The Great Depression had caused a significant indus-trial slowdown. ILGWU membership plummeted to fewer than 25,000, down from more than 100,000 a decade earlier. As the nation's economy stalled, competition among jobbers put tremendous pressure on contractors, who were played against one another for even the smallest margins. Contractors responded by ignoring union agreements, paying below-market wages, break-ing the union altogether, and seeking the cheapest labor possible by "running away" to remote areas. At its 1932 Philadelphia convention, the ILGWU board explained, "[This] problem is closely tied up with the situation in New York both in the cloak and dress industries. The number of shops in the suburban territory grows when it becomes profitable for the New York cloak and dress jobbers to encourage their contractors to move their shops or open new shops out-of-town. There are, according to figures obtained by us, not less than 150 dress shops located within a radius of 70 miles from New York employing several thousand workers at unbelievably low wages."[2]

The exodus of contractors to distant areas was well-known to those who followed industry trends. According to Frances Perkins, labor secretary to President Franklin D. Roosevelt, "Since he [the contractor] cannot hope to meet union conditions or the requirements of labor law, he goes to some out-lying suburb where garment factories are not a feature of the local picture and where state inspectors are not on the lookout for him. Or perhaps he goes to a nearby state—New Jersey, Connecticut, Pennsylvania, Massachusetts—where he believes labor laws are less stringent or that he will escape attention. . . . His work force is made up of daughters and wives of local wage earners who have been out of work for months or even years and whose family situation is desperate. The boss sets the wage rates, figures the pay slips, determines the hours of work. His reply to complaints is, 'Quit if you don't like it.'"[3] At the height of the Great Depression the ILGWU found more than 25,000 workers employed in a "sweatshop swamp" in New Jersey, Connecticut, and parts of Pennsylvania. Pennsylvania's anthracite or "hard" coal region and, in particular, its northernmost reaches around Wilkes-Barre and Scranton was one such locale.

For most of the nineteenth and early twentieth centuries, coal was central to the economy of northeastern Pennsylvania. American industrialization was born in this 500-square-mile region of the northern Appalachians with its enormous deposits of anthracite or "hard" coal. A clean, low-ash, high-carbon-content coal, anthracite fueled American industry, heated homes, and powered the country's railroads. The industry drew immigrants from the British Isles and eastern and southern Europe by the tens of thousands. Anthracite reached its peak in 1917 when 175,000 workers produced seventeen million tons of coal.

By the later 1920s the single-industry economy of the area began a downward spiral from which it would never fully recover. By the end of the 1950s deep mining virtually ceased following the Knox Mine Disaster.[4] Scranton and Wilkes-Barre, the region's two main cities, were the only urban areas in the United States with unemployment rates greater than 12 percent. Fluctuations in the national economy, competition from alternative energy sources, lack of investment by coal companies in new technologies, industry and union corruption, mine disasters, and years of labor-management conflict had taken their toll.[5]

With few employment alternatives, thousands of struggling families turned to permanent out-migration, long-distance commuting, and employment by mothers and daughters in the growing garment industry. Clothing factories mushroomed in the area, manufacturers attracted by a pool of female labor willing to work for low wages to support desperate families. In the mid-1930s David Dubinsky set out to organize garment factories in the Wyoming Valley, a large and populous urban/suburban area located about 100 miles west of New York City. Dubinsky was particularly concerned because many local factories had fled Manhattan's garment district to hire non-union labor and produce apparel on a per-contract basis. Another problem was that organized crime owned or influenced some of the runaway factories, particularly in Pittston, a coal town at the northern end of the valley.

Early organizing efforts were unsuccessful. In 1944 Dubinsky enhanced the effort by creating the Wyoming Valley District and administratively housing it within the ILGWU's vast Northeast Department, which covered the

Figure 10.1 Bill and Min Matheson in 1960. Reproduced by permission of UNITE! Union.

mid-Atlantic and part of New England. He charged the task of organizing Wyoming Valley factories to Minnie (Min) Lurye Matheson and her husband Wilfred (Bill) Matheson. Min, the daughter of Russian-Jewish socialists, assumed the role of director of the newly established district. Bill, a Canadian labor activist of Scottish heritage, directed the district's educational programs.

The couple relocated to the Wyoming Valley in early 1944 to begin organizing. Min described the situation upon her arrival:

> All the mines were down. Men weren't working. We organized in New York and surrounding areas. The wages were getting higher. Employers were looking for low wages and areas where they could produce garments at the lowest level possible so they went to the coalfields of Pennsylvania. [Organized crime]

in New York [was] having their legal problems. So they wanted a front for their illicit activities. They had really set up a [garment] center in Pittston. They needed a legal front and the dress industry was easy. You need very little capital and all you have to do is have a handful of machines and you're in business. And all these manufacturers in New York who were looking for cheap labor outlets loved it. Work was coming in plentifully and these shops were growing, mushrooming.[6]

As Min studied the situation she was struck by the subservience and pow-erlessness of women: "The atmosphere in the town was that everything was controlled and the women had no say at all. They did the cooking and the sewing and taking care of the lunches and getting the men out to work in the mines and the kids out to school. They were active in their churches. Many went to work in garment factories. This was their life. They [shop owners] told the women, 'We'll teach you to sew.' They worked for weeks for noth-ing. And the hours! You know there were [labor] laws in the land but they weren't carrying out any of the laws. They made it easy for the women to come in any time of the day or night. Double, triple shifts."[7]

Minnie Caputo, a garment worker and Matheson contemporary, described conditions in the early days: "I started when I was 16 or 17 years old, non-union. I think I got around 10 cents an hour. They were like sweatshops. They [bosses] stood behind you and timed you and if one girl did eight operations he would say, 'Why not you?' But, you know, not everyone had the same speed. If they didn't want you they got rid of you fast. You were out. They were really sweatshops. But the factories kept this town going. There was nothing for the men."[8]

The Mathesons found about 650 union members in a handful of organized shops when they arrived in 1944. Remarkably, by the time they departed in 1963 the Wyoming Valley District of the ILGWU consisted of 11,000 members in 168 organized factories. Yet their legacy stretched far beyond organizing garment factories.

To counter the growth of the runaways, the Mathesons did more than construct a pay-and-benefits organization. They built an infrastructure to serve members and their needs. In 1948, the union opened a health care center in Wilkes-Barre. Garment workers and their families received medi-cal checkups, x-rays, immunizations, examinations, and screenings free of charge. The ILGWU set up a workers' education program on subjects that included union organizing, factory health and safety, federal and state leg-islation, and topics in history and the humanities. Min and Bill engaged the

Figure 10.2 Wyoming Valley garment workers, early 1940s. Reproduced by permission of UNITE! Union.

union politically by forming a political education club, holding voter registration drives, endorsing selected candidates for local, state, and national office, and involving rank-and-file members in lobbying in Harrisburg (the state capital) and Washington, D.C.

By the late 1940s the ILGWU had gained momentum. Min had recruited about 3,000 members and the Wyoming Valley District consisted of locals at Wilkes-Barre, Pittston, and Nanticoke. Contracts were negotiated with employers, even some with unscrupulous reputations. Workers joined the ranks. The community was increasingly aware of Min Matheson and the ILGWU.

The health care center and the union's workers' education programs had successfully demonstrated that the ILGWU did more than arouse workers regarding conditions in the workplace. Min and Bill's decision to create a chorus modeled after a New York–based ILGWU theater performance group was another crucial step to securing the union's presence and tapping into the artistic creativity of workers to advance the causes of the labor movement—notions familiar to the ILGWU.

In the mid-1930s, the union purchased and operated the Labor Stage theater in midtown Manhattan and assembled a collection of singers, dancers, and other performers drawn from its rank and file. The group debuted with a play entitled *Steel,* which dramatized life as an American steelworker. The play coincided with the efforts of the Steel Workers' Organizing Committee, which would later become the United Steelworkers of America, to organize the industry's employees. By 1938 the group produced and performed a pro-labor musical known as *Pins and Needles,* which depicted historical and contemporary aspects of the American labor movement and working-class life.

The popularity of the troupe and *Pins and Needles* grew quickly as it received accolades from the labor movement and the New York theater community. Two traveling companies ensued. Hollywood performances were booked. One company was invited to give the revue in the East Room of the White House for President Roosevelt and selected federal officials. Bolstered by favorable reviews and a high-profile performance in the nation's capital, by the early 1940s *Pins and Needles* had become the longest-running Broadway musical up to its time. It had successfully launched the ILGWU's long-term commitment to entertainment to espouse the causes of working people and the labor movement.[9]

The Mathesons believed it was important to engage Wyoming Valley workers in cultural and artistic aspects that had become a hallmark of the ILGWU. They also recognized the relevance of providing social outlets to boost esprit de corps, encourage mutual association, and promote a positive and creative union image. Min and Bill recruited local residents Jim Corbett, Bill Gable, and Clementine Lyons to help organize their version of the New York troupe. In the coming years the Wyoming Valley chorus—referred to interchangeably as the Northeast Department chorus—would be recognized as the pre-eminent ILGWU performing group. According to Clem Lyons, a garment worker who enlisted as an ILGWU activist:

> In 1947 we got the shows going. . . . New York, of course, had the Labor Stage. We soon followed. . . . Min Matheson came to me to try and find people to go to the first meeting for the chorus. And you'd go into the shops [factories] and sit beside them on the lunch hour and coax them out. But it was very difficult to get them interested because, in some cases, they were afraid. And their husbands wouldn't let them participate. So I got about eight or ten to go and, sure enough, they put on the [first] show down at the Armory. And Jim Corbett [a fellow ILGer] had me do a number. We put on a kiddie show, called it the *Lollipop Revue.* So in 1954, when it came time to go into rehearsals for the regular annual musical, Mrs. Matheson let me and Billy

Gable do the shows for her. Every year [we had these shows] from 1947 to 1976. I had been in them from 1947.

* * *

The shows began to be a part of the social calendar around the area. People said, "When are they going to have another show? We'll buy tickets." In fact one year we sent $450—at that time $450 was a lot of money, I think they charged 50 cents to get in to see the show—and then we sent the money up to St. Michael's [a local school for orphans] to buy athletic equipment for the kids up there. Some [performances] would be, maybe, popular shows that were on Broadway at the time, but most of them would be union flavor.

* * *

We used to go to the Veteran's Hospital every Thursday night for years. Around '52 we helped the American Italian Association with their show. [We performed] at the American Legion. [We had] a medley, "I Could Have Danced All Night," "Darkness on the Delta," "Buttons and Bows." We had maybe 48 people in that group.[10]

The first large-scale musical narrative performed by the chorus was entitled *My Name is Mary Brown.* It debuted in 1950 and featured music and lyrics written by ILGWU organizer Michael Johnson and chorus co-director Jim Corbett with the assistance of Bill Matheson and New York–based ILGer Leon Stein. It opened with a solo introduction of Mary Brown, a fictional character representative of any number of women garment workers employed a runaway factory:

I am Mary Brown.
I come from Pennsylvania,
Vermont and Massachusetts,
New Hampshire and Rhode Island,
From Delaware and New York State,
From Maine and from New Jersey.
My Name is Mary Brown.[11]

The musical married history with the contemporary state of affairs in the American garment industry to tell the story of how Mary Brown, like New York garment workers of an earlier era, worked long hours in horrid conditions in a non-union factory. Songs such as "Won't You Come Along" and "This is a Strike!" (CD no. 14) told how Mary and her co-workers grew disillusioned with working conditions, banded together with ILGWU organizers, and went on strike for higher wages and shorter hours. The story continued

Figure 10.3 Chorus rehearsal, 1954, Clementine Lyons at right. Reproduced by permission of UNITE! Union.

with songs explaining that not only did conditions improve following the strike, but life as union member yielded benefits that went beyond the shop floor. "Here's to Your Health" explained how ILGWU members benefited from the services of the union-sponsored health care center. And "Up at Unity House" celebrated the virtues of the ILGWU's vacation resort and workers' education center nestled in Pennsylvania's Pocono Mountains, the only union-owned facility of its kind in the United States.[12] The musical concluded with "Help Us to Organize!" which called on garment workers to unionize runaway factories and build the ILGWU to ensure not only better pay and benefits, but to advance fairness and equity for working people.

My Name Is Mary Brown was performed in numerous community settings. The chorus traveled to locales in the northeastern United States where runaway factories had become a problem and where the Northeast Department had set out to organize, such as Binghamton, New York, and several locales in Massachusetts. The program was also performed at Unity House and at community theaters in Allentown, Scranton, Philadelphia, and Johnstown, Pennsylvania.

The chorus quickly gained recognition within the ILGWU and grew in popularity in its hometown area thanks to *My Name Is Mary Brown*. Before long it was performing for local ethnic and civic clubs, churches, political events (usually for the Democratic Party and Democratic candidates or incumbents), garment factory parties, hospitals, and community agencies. Holidays were always busy. Memorial Day, Labor Day, Fourth of July, and December–January holiday events brought numerous invitations. By the mid-1950s it was common for the chorus to perform at least once monthly. By the end of the decade performances grew more frequent. In December 1959 the group headlined for sixteen community affairs in addition to staging performances exclusively for district members and participating in the ILGWU's annual holiday program in New York City.[13]

Initially its productions consisted of songs from *My Name Is Mary Brown*. By 1952 varied annual musical revues became a regular feature. Such revues were typically rooted within the larger contexts of social justice, workers' rights, and political activism. They also drew upon the history of the American garment industry and its leading union. In early 1952, for example, the chorus staged a revue entitled *Meet the Girls*. Held at the Shriner's Irem Temple auditorium in Wilkes-Barre, the revue cast sixty and featured music, song, and dance that depicted garment factory work, described the mission of the ILGWU, and linked the union's agenda with the larger goals of the labor movement and progressive American politics. The troupe staged a special performance for delegates to the Pennsylvania Federation of Labor's annual convention.[14]

Reflecting the union's growing community involvement, the chorus staged a benefit revue entitled *Everything Goes* in 1959. Here performers mixed popular Broadway melodies with union-flavored songs in both solo and group renditions. Staged before successive sellout crowds at a local theater, it earned proceeds to be donated to the families of twelve coal miners who lost their lives in the January 1959 Knox Mine Disaster.[15]

In recognition and celebration of the ILGWU's twenty-five-year presence in northeastern Pennsylvania (1937–1962), Jim Corbett, Bill Gable, Mike Johnson, and the Mathesons created a program entitled *Make Way for Tomorrow*. This revue drew on themes familiar to ILGWU history to demonstrate the union's progress in organizing 450,000 workers nationwide and securing benefits that included vacation pay, sick benefits, and a thirty-five-hour work week. Original songs such as "It's So Different With A Union" championed the labor movement as the best assurance among working people for a future of security and prosperity:[16]

> It's so different since we got the Union,
> It's so different than it used to be.
> We're half-a-million strong
> As we proudly march along.
> What a feeling to be free!
>
> It's so different since we got the Union,
> Now the days don't seem to be so long.
> Everybody's treated fair,
> Everybody gets a share—
> What a feeling to be strong.
>
> * * *
>
> It's so different since we got the Union,
> As we march along in unity.
> And we want you all to know
> That we're gonna keep it so
> With the good old ILG!

The troupe also became a medium through which the union advocated its larger political agenda. Among its first political bookings was an invitation from the local Democratic Party to perform on Public Square in Wilkes-Barre during a 1948 welcoming ceremony for President Harry Truman. By the mid-1950s the chorus had gained the recognition of the Pennsylvania Democratic Party when it was invited to the State Capitol in Harrisburg to open a rally for visiting presidential hopeful Adlai Stevenson. Its specially designed songs drew the attention of the press, which mentioned special political campaign songs "We're for Adlai," "You Gotta Know the Score," "On for Stevenson," and "You Must Be There."[17]

Bill Matheson worked with chorus members to choreograph their work, and he wrote songs for political events. Some of them supported local, state, and national politicians friendly to the union's cause, such as Pennsylvania congressman and Washington legend Daniel J. Flood, who was always on the dais for such events.[18] The song for Flood was sung to the tune of "The Yellow Rose of Texas."

There's a Congressman for Luzerne
Who serves both you and me,
No other one can match him
On that we all agree.
We won with him many times before
And how we're here to say
That Dan goes back to Congress
On the next Election Day.

He's the servant of the people,
The best we ever knew,
He works for us from early morn
Until the day is through.
They may talk of other Congressmen
In states from sea to sea,
But we have a friend in Dan Flood,
He's the only one for me.[19]

Another politically oriented song encouraged union members to remain informed about political issues and support selected candidates for public office. Shouting over an accompanying vamp, the singers rally the troops:

Working gals and working guys,
Every one got to know the score.
Ev'ry one come lend an ear, 'cause
This is an election year.
It's time we all knew where we stood,
Time to pick the bad from the good.
They've had us fooled for quite a while,
But know we're wise to their style.
They're pretty sharp with double talk,
But, it's time we made a squawk.
We know the bills they voted for,
They're not for us, that's for sure.

Then they break into song:

You gotta know the score.
You gotta know the score.
So don't give in—cause you're bound to win
When you know the score.

(verse) So, tell your friends and your neighbors that
Every worker must go to bat.
Tell them all to get out and vote.
If you don't then you're the goat.
If your senator or congressman
Doesn't vote for the working man.
If he doesn't prove that he's labor's friend
You vote will get him in the end.
(chorus)
(verse) We need more supporters for LBJ
Men who think of a better day.
Men who'll battle with you and me
To build this great society.
We need better housing, a better wage,
Better schools in this day and age.
Rights for ev'ry one, rights for all,
Join with us and heed the call.[20]

Complementing its political overtones, the chorus performed songs to foster solidarity and sustain workers during organizing campaigns, strikes, pickets, and other related actions. One was the familiar "We Shall Not Be Moved":[21]

Chorus:
We shall not be moved.
We shall not be moved.
Just like a tree that's planted by the water,
We shall not be moved.

1. The union is behind us
We shall not be moved.
The union is behind us
We shall not be moved.
Just like a tree that's planted by the water,
We shall not be moved.
2. We're fighting for our freedom.
3. We're fighting for our children.
4. We'll fight for compensation.
5. We'll build a mighty union.

New York ILGWU officials credited the chorus with bolstering the union's community image and promoting a worthwhile and visible agenda. According to Northeast Department vice president David Gingold, "Changes in community attitudes particularly in Pennsylvania were heavily influenced by live revues featuring lyrics, music, and sets and acting by members as part of the Northeast Department's educational activities. Proceeds from numerous performances are contributed to worthy local agencies and causes thus strengthening the union's ties with communities and expanding local respect for the union. Some of those aided at that time were . . . the Hospital for Crippled Children in Wilkes-Barre."[22]

In December 1953, more than 500 individuals attended a testimonial dinner honoring Min Matheson at Wilkes-Barre's Hotel Redington. Speakers included ILGWU vice president Charles Zimmerman, chairman of the Greater Wilkes-Barre Chamber of Commerce William Sword, president of the Pennsylvania Dress Manufacturers Association Abraham Glassberg, Pennsylvania AFL-CIO officials, local clergy, and ILGWU rank-and-file members. The testimonial, which included several songs by the chorus, recognized that in a few short years Min Matheson had built a reputable organization that had earned the community's respect and admiration. In her remarks to the audience Min noted that while the union had accomplished much, a great deal was yet to be done. And, according to Min, the union's institutions—including its chorus—had and would continue to play key roles in building a garment workers' movement.[23]

In 1957 more than 1,000 area garment workers assembled in the gymnasium of Wilkes-Barre's Kings College to celebrate the ILGWU's success in improving their lives and livelihoods. Introduced by David Dubinsky, Governor George M. Leader of Pennsylvania (1955–1959) gave the keynote address followed by a chorus performance that included a number of political songs highlighting the ILGWU's commitment to the Democratic Party and its leaders, including the young and popular governor for whom it had campaigned and helped elect.[24]

For the remainder of the 1950s and the 1960s, the chorus continued performing its annual musical revues. It sang and raised money for community organizations and institutions including the Knights of Columbus, Salvation Army, Boy Scouts, March of Dimes, Little League baseball, and local hospitals. The ILGWU leadership showcased the chorus at the union's holiday festivities and at its triennial conventions that drew several thousand members to places such as Madison Square Garden and Miami Beach. Chorus members also participated in annual spring fashion parades through New York's gar-

Figure 10.4 ILGWU chorus campaigns with gubernatorial candidate George M. Leader, 1954 (George M. Leader Papers, Pennsylvania State Archives).

ment district dubbed with flashy titles such as "Fashion Goes to Broadway." On numerous occasions the troupe was invited by ILGWU leadership to stage performances at Unity House that by the mid-1950s drew 10,000 union members during its summer operating seasons. Political bookings continued as well. A few weeks before the 1960 election, the chorus opened a rally on Public Square in Wilkes-Barre for visiting presidential candidate John F. Kennedy.[25]

By 1962 the Wyoming Valley District of the ILGWU consisted of more than 10,000 members in 168 unionized factories. It ranked among the largest in Pennsylvania and the union's multistate Northeast Department.[26] The following year, however, was one of transition for the district. The Mathesons accepted positions with the Union Label Department at ILGWU New York headquarters near Times Square. They helped to create and promote a new label design that by the late 1960s was familiar to millions of American consumers who heard the song and saw the "Look for the Union Label" print and television ads. The song became a key anthem of the ILGWU and was adopted by the chorus as the finale of virtually every performance for the remainder of the twentieth century:

> Look for the Union Label
> When you are buying a coat, dress or blouse.
> Remember somewhere our Union's sewing,
> Our wages going to feed the kids and run the house.
> We work hard, but who's complaining?
> Thanks to the I.L.G. we're paying our way!
> So always look for the Union Label.
> It says we're able to make it in the U.S.A.![27]

Members protested the Mathesons' move, but gave their approval. According to one newspaper account, "In view of the storm in the wake of the announcement that Mrs. Matheson had been named Director of the Union Label Department in New York, the farewell dinner for her and her husband should be a memorable affair. Never has greater Wilkes-Barre witnessed a demonstration such as the transfer of Mrs. Matheson evoked. The reaction has not only attested to the loyalty she commanded from the rank-and-file of the union, but the esteem in which she was held in the community after two decades of service."[28]

In advance of their departure, more than 700 people attended a gathering for the Mathesons. Rank-and-file members and representatives from the union's hierarchy joined with elected officials, judges, clergy, media representatives, heads of local colleges and businesses, and friends who knew and worked with the guests of honor. The chorus gave a moving tribute to Min and Bill. The editor of a local newspaper, also present at the event, commented:

> Mrs. Matheson is quite a woman. She has been controversial but, at the same time, held the affection of thousands of workers whose standard of living was raised and whose working conditions were bettered through [her] concentrated and devoted efforts.
>
> Never did we see a woman work so hard at a picket line. . . . She became so enthusiastic for the cause of the workers. She became overly vigorous at times. To say she didn't make any enemies in the battle would be naive—because "enemies" were never a problem for her. Mrs. Matheson would be on the picket line ordering, demanding, blocking for an entire day. And, that night she would go out of her way to raise funds for some needy family or spark some worthy cause to success.

When it came to the good of the area, Min was smart, vigorous and determined. We could list a hundred occasions when we witnessed Mrs. Matheson
do good for the region. But space will not permit.[29]

By the time of their departure the Mathesons had successfully institution-
alized the health care center, workers' education programs, and the chorus,
which continued to play a leading role in the union's activities. In 1965 the
chorus expanded its membership to include garment workers from other
locals in the Northeast Department and produced an LP recording of its performance at the thirty-second convention of the ILGWU held in Miami Beach.
The ethnic mix of the chorus was reflected in the surnames of its members
who performed live before 1,000 convention delegates: Suriano, Wasko, Weiss,
Castiglia, De Annuntis, Trigiana, Pickett, Philips, and Pingitore.

The revue told the story of the rise of the union from the sweatshops of
New York's Lower East Side to its 1965 membership roster of 460,000. The
performance, which ran forty minutes, alternated narration with fourteen
musical numbers, some ("It's Different With the Union" and "You Gotta
Know the Score") previously used, others new. For example, after the narra-
tor exhorts the workers (the chorus) to strike, the chorus sings the strikers'
anthem, "This is a Strike," from *Mary Brown*. According to the album liner
notes, "Actual working members of the Northeast Department created every
song, every lyric, every note of music" in the performance.[30] In fact, however,
several melodies were taken from familiar songs including the "Battle Hymn
of the Republic" ("Solidarity Forever"), and "Sweet Betsy from Pike" (the
verse section of "Look for the Union Label"). Other melodies, while not direct
quotations, evoke familiar musical styles such as Tin Pan Alley and Broadway.
Good examples are the two songs in minor keys, both of which represent
negative aspects of the workers' lives. "Little Machine"—that is, a garment
worker's sewing machine—has a "Jewish" flavor reminiscent of *Fiddler on
the Roof* (1964). With a descant that evokes "Summertime," "Mr. Boss," on
the other hand, could equally have come out of *Porgy and Bess* (1935).

And in fact, simplicity and familiarity of style, along with clever word-
smithing, may have contributed most to the success of the show and the
chorus's work as a whole. A song such as "This is a Strike!" is typical, with a
catchy, singable melody performed mostly in unison, a melodic "hook" on
the title words, clear structure and text declamation, and an equally clear message (CD no. 14). Accompanied by piano, guitar, bass, and light percussion,
the chorus sings with energy and gusto. The arrangement is simple and the

ensemble—clearly an amateur group—has no trouble pulling it off, down to the small bit of four-part singing at the end on the word "halleluia."

The chorus closed its show with a finale that boasted of the progress of the ILGWU and the Northeast Department (CD no. 15). The first song, "Northeast Department," identifies the group's geographical origin in an energetic march typical of the faster songs in the show:

We're from the Northeast Department
And today we're proud we're thirty years of age.
Here in the Northeast Department
We've got good conditions and a decent wage.
For thirty years we have been working,
Now we've narrowed the gap,
In 1935 we started, now we're on the map, we're shouting
We're from the Northeast Department,
And today we're proudly thirty years of age.

A brief transition then brings on the contrasting grandeur of "Solidarity Forever," closing the show with artistic flourishes such as modulation and a descant. This last song, on the "Battle Hymn" tune, become another of the chorus's trademarks, thereby adding a political double entendre that was probably intentional: "The union/Union makes us strong."

(transition) We all must stand together and be ready to fight
To guarantee each citizen his God given right!
Make sure indeed for race and creed to live in dignity.
Organizing hand in hand in Solidarity.
("Battle Hymn" melody) When the Union's inspiration through the
        workers' blood shall run,
There can be no power greater anywhere beneath the sun,
Yet what force on earth is weaker than the feeble strength of one,
But the union makes us strong!
Solidarity forever! Solidarity forever!
Solidarity forever! For the union makes us strong.

As throughout the recording, the singers come off as well-prepared, proud of their show, and eager to put its message across. The creative team had judged the singers' capabilities astutely.

From its founding to 1965 the ILGWU the chorus performed in sixty-five cities and towns reaching an estimated live audience of 150,000 people. It had raised $160,000 for charitable organizations including hospitals, orphanages, civic clubs, and community groups. According to co-director and pianist Bill Gable, whose work with the chorus dates back to the 1950s, "There was a time when the chorus performed for almost every community event. There wasn't a parade, a holiday, an important [political or social] event, or a union convention that went by where we didn't perform. We practiced a few nights every week and performed at least twice a month—sometimes more. Min or Sam Bianco [Matheson's successor] would always say to me 'Bill, we have this or that event coming up or this important dignitary coming to town. Could you put something together for us?' Those really were our heydays."[31] Like its parent organization, which boasted nearly a half-million members in the late 1960s, the chorus was enjoying the prime of its life.

As with other manufacturing sectors of the U.S. economy over the past several decades—from televisions to automobile components to children's toys—the amount of apparel manufactured overseas and sold in the domestic marketplace has grown exponentially. American garment workers, like their counterparts in steel, autos, electronics, and other industries, have been "downsized," unemployed, underemployed—in short, "deindustrialized" as the American economy has evolved from manufacturing to service and technology. Clothing was among the first consumer products to have its manufacturing base shift offshore.

By the late 1960s ILGWU membership reached a peak of 470,000 members. However, it soon began a downward spiral from which it has not recovered. Its decline can be directly traced to a familiar problem. For years, terms like the "runaway" shop had come to apply mainly to contractors who produced away from Manhattan. Today these terms refer to contractors that produce apparel beyond U.S. borders and sell those products to American consumers.

In 1955 apparel imports amounted to a mere 3 percent of the total U.S. market. By the mid-1960s they had grown to 12 percent. In the mid-1970s the percentage stood at 31 percent and, by the early 1990s, sales of imports surpassed domestic-made apparel, claiming more than 70 percent of the total market. Put another way, in the early 1960s, about five out of every 100 garments sold in the United States were made in foreign nations. By the 1990s the number had climbed to more than 70 out of every 100.[32]

The total number of women's and children's apparel workers nationwide stood at more than 660,000 when David Dubinsky retired as ILGWU president in 1966. When Jay Mazur took office as the union's leader twenty years later, total industry employment had fallen to fewer than a half million and ILGWU membership to 196,000. As the century drew to a close, domestic employment continued its decline. On average, the United States has lost nearly 40,000 combined apparel and textile jobs annually since 1979, or about 3,400 jobs each month. The ILGWU's 1995 merger with the Amalgamated Clothing and Textile Workers (ACTWU) to form the Union of Needletrades Industrial and Textile Employees or UNITE! resulted in total membership of 200,000.

Pennsylvania is no longer a large center of clothing manufacturing. The total number of combined apparel and textile workers statewide peaked at nearly 200,000 in the late 1960s. By 1984 the number dropped to 102,000. By the mid-1990s it had fallen to fewer than 50,000. By the early 1990s the state continued to lose 2,000–plus apparel jobs annually. The Pennsylvania Department of Labor and Industry counted about 20,000 workers in various segments of women's, misses', and children's apparel making in 1994. The agency estimated that this sector of the industry will continue to lose approximately 5 percent of its workforce annually and projects that fewer than 2,000 jobs will remain by 2010.[33]

In Pennsylvania's anthracite region the effects of deindustrialization in the garment industry have been equally apparent. The ILGWU's Wyoming Valley District no longer exists, having been consolidated with other regional locals and districts. Only a few hundred active union members remain. So do several thousand retirees, but their numbers are dwindling as well; it is rare to read the obituaries in the local and regional newspapers and not find "former member of the ILGWU" in biographical notations.

Garment factories are few. In 2001 a half dozen remained in the Wyoming Valley District's original territory, down from more than two hundred factories thirty years prior. The union's institutions have, likewise, been affected. The health care center closed in the mid-1980s. Workers' education programs are infrequent. The union has far less political clout than it once had. However, the chorus remains, now consisting entirely of retiree volunteers. It still performs an annual musical revue, donating the proceeds to charity, and occasionally sings for community institutions such as hospitals and nursing homes. Members travel at times for special events such as statewide labor conferences, the occasional strike or picket line, and to perform at political rallies in places like Harrisburg.

After having returned to the Wyoming Valley in 1972 to live out her retirement years, Min Matheson passed away in 1992. Bill Matheson preceded her in death in 1987. Both the chorus and its founder have had their place in history recognized. On September 24, 1999, the Pennsylvania Historical and Museum Commission and the Pennsylvania Labor History Society

Figure 10.5 Chorus members at Pennsylvania state historical marker dedication to Min Matheson, Public Square, Wilkes-Barre, September 1999. Photo by George E. Zorgo, Jr., Zorgo Printing Service. Reproduced by permission.

dedicated a state historical marker on Wilkes-Barre's Public Square to Min Matheson. The marker recognizes the contributions of both Min and Bill in building among the most active and community-spirited ILGWU districts anywhere in the nation. It memorializes the Mathesons' tireless dedication to the working people of Pennsylvania's anthracite coal region.

The historical marker also highlights the Wyoming Valley District chorus. The chorus was at the dedication ceremony and included many of the members originally recruited by Min in the late 1940s. In a fitting tribute they performed several tunes in posthumous honor of their friend and founder.[34]

Throughout its more than fifty-year history, the chorus has reflected a multifaceted agenda. Members have been provided with the opportunity to mutually associate and sharpen and deliver a message of unity and common purpose. Performers bolstered their self-esteem while strengthening the image of organized labor in the community and exploring talents and skills that remained largely untapped in the daily routine of the garment factory.

Within the community the chorus had both an entertainment and an ideological value. It exposed its members and observers alike to political messages in support of working-class causes. Such causes were familiar to area residents with their long history of cantankerous relations with coal companies; they, too, had shared a familiarity with organized labor through the United Mine Workers of America (UMWA). The chorus became an important and popular means through which the ILGWU advocated its progressive political agenda, an agenda shared by many that had come to admire and follow its performances.

The chorus also played a key role in anchoring the ILGWU as a vital and highly recognized part of the labor movement and political scene, not just locally, but across Pennsylvania and throughout the ILGWU. As former governor George M. Leader explained, "The ILGWU was located in other parts of the state, but they weren't a force like they were in the Wyoming Valley. Min wasn't just a labor organizer. She was a political organizer. She was an educator. She had a fantastic relationship with her membership. It really was extraordinary to observe. There is no doubt about the fact that Min had mobilized the ILGWU as a political and community force that had to be reckoned with. The members knew that. I knew that. And, Min knew that."[35]

The creation and tenure of the ILGWU chorus reflects an era in which the American labor movement learned to use tools and techniques—other than strikes, protests, and violence—to establish a presence, deliver ideological messages, and align itself with progressive politicians and social policies. The chorus presents a positive and creative side of a movement that is, unfortunately, all too often known only for its corruption, scandal, latter-day decline, and relative powerlessness in a globalized economy.

Notes

1. On ILGWU history, see Max Danish, *The World of David Dubinsky* (Cleveland: World Publishing, 1957); David Dubinsky, *A Life with Labor* (New York: Simon and Schuster, 1977); Philip Foner, *History of the Labor Movement in the United States,* vol. 9 (New York: International Publishers, 1991); International Ladies' Garment Workers' Union, *ILGWU News History: The Story of the Ladies' Garment Workers, 1900–1950* (New York: ILGWU, 1950); Lewis Lorwin, *The Women's Garment Workers* (New York: Arno, 1969); Leon Stein, ed., *Out of the Sweatshop: The Struggle for Industrial Democracy* (New York: Quadrangle, 1977); Benjamin Stolberg, *Tailor's Progress: The Story of a Famous Union and the Men Who Made It* (New York: Doran, Doubleday, and Company, 1944); Gus Tyler, *Look for the Union Label: A History of the International Ladies' Garment Workers Union* (Armonk, New York: M. E. Sharpe, 1995); and Kenneth C. Wolensky, Nicole H. Wolensky, and Robert P. Wolensky, *Fighting for the Union Label: The Women's Garment Industry and the ILGWU in Pennsylvania* (University Park: Pennsylvania State University Press, 2002).

2. Report of the General Executive Board to the Twenty-First Convention of the ILGWU, May 2, 1932 (New York: ILGWU, 1932).

3. Frances Perkins, "The Cost of a Five-Dollar Dress" (1933), in *Out of the Sweatshop*, 224–25.

4. At the direction of the Knox Coal Company miners had illegally burrowed under the Susquehanna River at the River Slope Mine to reach a pristine vein of coal. On January 22, 1959, miners came within a few feet of the riverbed. The river caved into the mine in a massive whirlpool. Eighty-one mine workers were trapped while more than ten billion gallons of water flooded the Wyoming Valley's mines in a catastrophe that riveted the nation. While the majority of mineworkers eventually found their way to safety, twelve never escaped and remain entombed. On the Knox Mine Disaster, see Robert Wolensky and Kenneth Wolensky, "Disaster—or Murder?—in the Mines," *Pennsylvania Heritage* 24, no. 2 (spring 1998): 4–11; and Robert Wolensky, Kenneth Wolensky, and Nicole Wolensky, *The Knox Mine Disaster: The Final Years of the Northern Anthracite Industry and the Effort to Rebuild a Regional Economy* (Harrisburg, Pa.: Pennsylvania Historical and Museum Commission, 1999).

5. For further discussion of the anthracite industry and ethnicity and immigration in the anthracite region, see Harold Aurand, *From the Mollie Maguires to the United Mine Workers: The Social Ecology of an Industrial Union* (Philadelphia: Temple University Press, 1971); John Bodnar, *Anthracite People: Families, Work and Unions, 1900–1940* (Harrisburg, Pa.: Pennsylvania Historical and Museum Commission, 1983); Edward Davies, *The Anthracite Aristocracy: Leadership and Social Change in the Hard Coal Regions of Northeastern Pennsylvania, 1800–1930* (DeKalb: Northern Illinois University Press, 1985); Thomas Dublin, *When the Mines Closed* (Ithaca, N.Y.: Cornell University Press, 1998); Donald Miller and Richard Sharpless, *The Kingdom of Coal: Work, Enterprise, and Ethnic Communities in the Mine Fields* (Philadelphia: University of Pennsylvania Press, 1985); Ellis Roberts, *The Breaker Whistle Blows: Mining Disasters and Labor Leaders in the Anthracite Region* (Scranton, Pa.: Anthracite Museum Press, 1984); Zenin Wasyliw, "European Identities of East Slavic Settlements in Northeastern Pennsylvania during the late 19th and early 20th Centuries," in *Proceedings of the Sixth Annual Conference on the History of Northeastern Pennsylvania*, ed. Robert Janosov (Nanticoke, Pa.: Luzerne County Community College, 1994), 116–32; and Anthony F. C. Wallace, *St. Clair: A Nineteenth-Century Coal Town's Experience with a Disaster Prone Industry* (New York: Knopf, 1987).

6. Min Matheson, oral history interview, November 30, 1982, Northeastern Pennsylvania Oral History Project, University of Wisconsin, Stevens Point, tape 1, side 1. Also see Min Matheson, oral history interview, September 7, 1983, Pennsylvania State University Oral History Collection, Historical Collections and Labor Archives, Paterno Library, University Park, Pa., tape 1, side 1.

7. Min Matheson, oral history interview, November 30, 1982, tape 1, side 1.

8. Minnie Caputo, oral history interview, July 22, 1983, Northeastern Pennsylvania Oral History Project, University of Wisconsin, Stevens Point, tape 1, side 1.

9. On *Pins and Needles* and the ILGWU's Labor Stage, see H. Broun, "Pins and Needles," in Stein, *Out of the Sweatshop*, 249–51. See also *ILGWU News History; Report of the Educational Department, ILGWU*, June 1, 1944, to December 31, 1946 (New York: ILGWU, 1947); *Report of the General Executive Board to the Twenty-Fourth Convention of the ILGWU*, May 27 to June 8, 1940 (New York: ABCO Press, 1940), 142–44; and Gus Tyler, *Look for the Union Label*, chapter 15.

10. Clementine Lyons, oral history interview, July 5, 1990, tape 1, side 1; July 24, 1993, tape 1, side 2. Northeastern Pennsylvania Oral History Project, University of Wisconsin, Stevens Point.

11. Program for *My Name Is Mary Brown, A Musical Narrative*, presented by the Northeast Department, ILGWU, 1950. Copy of program given to the author by ILGWU member Helen Weiss.

12. On Unity House, see Kenneth C. Wolensky, "Unity House: A Worker's Shangri La," *Pennsylvania Heritage* 24, no. 3 (summer 1998): 21–29.

13. *Needlepoint* 53 (February 1960). *Needlepoint* was the newsletter of the Wyoming Valley District of the ILGWU.

14. *Needlepoint* 16 (May 1952).

15. *Needlepoint* 49 (April 1959). See also note 4.

16. *Needlepoint* 63 (May 1962).

17. "ILGWU Chorus Sings at Stevenson Rally," *Wilkes-Barre Record,* September 14, 1956: 8.

18. Known for his handlebar mustache, flashy dress, passionate speeches, and pork-barrel politics, Flood represented Pennsylvania's 11th congressional district from 1944 to 1946, 1948 to 1952, and 1954 to 1980. He was a prime sponsor of legislation that created the Commerce Department's Area Redevelopment Administration and the Appalachian Regional Commission. He was also a prime sponsor of the landmark 1969 Coal Mine Health and Safety Act. See William Kashatus, "Dapper Dan Flood: Pennsylvania's Legendary Congressman," *Pennsylvania Heritage* 21, no. 3 (summer 1995): 4–11; and George Crille, "The Best Congressman," *Harper's* 250, no. 1 (January 1975): 11–16.

19. Lyrics provided by founding chorus member Clementine Lyons.

20. *Northeast Department Anniversary 1935–1965, presented at the thirty-second convention of the ILGWU,* May 17, 1965 (New York: Astoria Press, 1965). This version of the song was introduced in the early 1960s and was edited from an earlier version that referred to Adlai Stevenson and Estes Kefauver. Later versions mentioned Democratic presidential candidates through Michael Dukakis.

21. Lyrics provided by Clementine Lyons.

22. Quoted in Harry Crone, *35 Northeast: A Short History of the Northeast Department of the ILGWU, 1935–1970* (New York: ILGWU, 1970).

23. "500 at Testimonial Hail Min Matheson in Wilkes-Barre," *Justice* 35, no. 24 (December 15, 1953): 1.

24. A liberal Democrat, George M. Leader served as governor of Pennsylvania from 1955 to 1959. See Kenneth C. Wolensky, "Born a Leader for Pennsylvania," *Pennsylvania Heritage* 28, no. 1 (winter 2002): 22–29. On the anniversary and speech, see *Needlepoint* 40 (December 1957).

25. *Needlepoint* 19 (May 1955), 26 (January 1956), 45 (September 1958), 56 (June 1960). On the chorus's political performances, including an October 1960 rally on Wilkes-Barre's Public Square for John F. Kennedy, see *ILGWU Silver Jubilee—Wyoming Valley District Council, Northeast Department* (New York: ILGWU, 1962).

26. *Report of the General Executive Board,* May 23, 1962 (New York: ABCO Press, 1962).

27. There are variants of the song "Look for the Union Label." This version (sung to the tune of "Look for the Silver Lining") is taken from *Northeast Department Anniversary.*

28. "Impressive Tribute to Min L. Matheson," *Pittston Sunday Dispatch,* January 27, 1963: 6.

29. "Mrs. Matheson Key Figure in Area," *The Times Leader,* Wilkes-Barre, Pa., February 4, 1963: 2A.

30. David Gingold, liner notes to *The Northeast Sings,* LP of performance by the Northeast Department chorus at the thirty-second convention of the ILGWU, Miami, May 17, 1965 (New York: Ralph R. Reuter, 1965).

31. William Gable, oral history interview, December 3, 1999, Northeastern Pennsylvania Oral History Project, University of Wisconsin, Stevens Point, tape 1, side 1.

32. For statistics on the growth of imports and changing ILGWU membership, see Sol C. Chaikin, *A Labor Viewpoint: Another Opinion* (Monroe, N.Y.: Library Research Associates, 1980), 32; State Senate Apparel Industry Caucus, *The Pennsylvania Garment Industry: Foreign Competition Costing Garment Workers' Jobs* (Harrisburg, Commonwealth of Pennsylvania, 1985), 4–5; "Don't Let Another U.S. Industry Be Destroyed," *Citizens' Voice,* October 24, 1984: 14; *Report of the General Executive Board Report to the Forty-Second Convention of the ILGWU,* June 1995, 30.

33. Apparel Industry Caucus, *Pennsylvania Garment Industry,* 4–12; Kevin Miller and Susan Smith, *Update on Pennsylvania: The Economy—Jobs, Forecasts, and Telecommunication* (University Park: Pennsylvania State University Department of Agricultural Economics and Rural Sociology and Bell Atlantic-Pennsylvania, 1997); "Garment Makers Suffer in Sales of Imported Clothes," *Philadelphia Evening Bulletin,* June 24, 1977: 34; Pennsylvania Department of Labor and Industry, Bureau of Research and Statistics, Pennsylvania Labor Market Information Database System (www.lmi.state.pa.us).

34. "Plaque Honoring Min Matheson Unveiled," *Citizens' Voice,* Wilkes-Barre, Pa., September 25, 1999: 1.

35. George M. Leader, oral history interview, Northeastern Pennsylvania Oral History Project, University of Wisconsin, Stevens Point, May 30, 1995, tape 1, side 1.

11

The Voice Empowered:
Harmonic Convergence of Music and
Politics in the GLBT Choral Movement

JILL STRACHAN

Through the common ground of singing, the gay, lesbian, bisexual, and transgendered (glbt) choral movement has empowered numerous individuals to come forth and declare their identities in a safe environment. The movement has been transforming on many levels—translating into heightened awareness of the glbt population, burgeoning of commissioned choral works, and economic power.[1]

The origins, purpose, and history of the glbt choral movement are documented in part in the history of the Gay and Lesbian Association (GALA)[2] of Choruses and its members, which formerly included the Lesbian and Gay Chorus of Washington, D.C. (LGCW). In 1996, 5,000 delegates attended GALA Choruses' Festival V and spent $20 million in Tampa while attending one of the largest conventions ever hosted there. From 1992 to 1996, GALA Choruses awarded more than $11,000 in commission matching grants to its member choruses and funded nine commissions for performance at Festival V. Festival 2000—the sixth Festival—occurred July 22–29, 2000, in San Jose, California. This festival attracted about 6,000 singers from around the world, representing 125 choruses and 30 smaller ensembles. The festival commissioned four works. GALA Choruses then represented more than 190 choruses and 10,000 singers on four continents. Its 1999 operating budget was more than a million dollars (U.S.).

GALA Choruses' vision statement—Our Voices Win Freedom—telegraphs a universal message. The vision statement, adopted in 1996, is a clear belief statement that links the act of singing with social and political justice.

GALA Choruses' statement of purpose of October 2000 is provided to its members for inclusion in concert programs: "[Individual chorus name] is a member of GALA Choruses, the international association of the lesbian and gay choral movement. Founded in 1982, GALA Choruses represents 190 choruses, their 10,000 singers and 750,000 patrons in Australia, Europe, South America, and North America. The Association's programs and services include annual conferences, matching grants to support the creation of new works, publication of reference materials, a resource center, training programs and music festivals."

The original context for GALA Choruses was gay male culture. Although women's music was already a growing phenomenon in the 1970s, it did not provide the immediate backdrop for the creation of GALA Choruses. (The contributions of women's music are discussed below.) In his essay "Authority and Freedom/Toward a Sociology of the Gay Choruses," Paul Attinello wrote that the gay subculture "is a complex field of values and relationships that is suffused with both traditional American middle-class values and intense reactions against those values."[3] For his empirical study, Attinello chose choruses—all gay men's—in Los Angeles, Chicago, and San Francisco.

The beginning of the glbt choral movement is often tied by popular anecdote to the formation in 1978 of the San Francisco Gay Men's Chorus (SFGMC), although Philadelphia's Anna Crusis Women's Choir was already three years old in that year. The first night of auditions for the SFGMC was scheduled for November 27, 1978. No one could have known that this would also be the day that Dan White would murder San Francisco mayor George Moscone and supervisor Harvey Milk. Instead of auditions on that night, a collection of singers sang a hymn on the steps of San Francisco's City Hall. The SFGMC's subsequent tour (1981) to twelve U.S. cities inspired the founding of other lesbian and gay choruses, including men's, women's, and mixed (SATB).

Dennis Coleman, artistic director of the Seattle Men's Chorus since 1981, suggests that the genesis of the movement was socio-political as gays and lesbians began to receive more public recognition. He writes that the member choruses of GALA Choruses generally articulate several non-musical priorities: "(1) to structure a musical community that provides emotional and spiritual support for its members, (2) to nurture positive self-esteem and pride within the chorus and the lesbian and gay community, (3) to care for member singers affected by HIV/AIDS and other traumatic life experiences, and (4) to build bridges of understanding, respect, and cooperation between the lesbian and gay community and society as a whole."[4]

Before the arrival of the SFGMC and the formal, legal establishment of the GALA Choruses network in 1982, there was "women's music." The existence of women's music was communicated primarily by word-of-mouth and for many a woman, the expression "women's music" was understood to mean "lesbians are found here." The Sister Singers' Network—a network of women's choruses—had its roots in the mid-1970s when women's choruses began to form, fueled by feminism and the women's music movement. Women found their voices expressed in a new, exciting way, first through the music of Alix Dobkin, Kay Gardner, and Meg Christian, whose first releases came out in 1974, and later through Holly Near, Margie Adam, and Cris Williamson.

Dr. Catherine Roma is the founding director of Anna Crusis Women's Choir, current music director of MUSE: Cincinnati's Women's Choir, and a longtime cultural activist. In an interview published in the GALA Choruses newsletter, *GALAgram,* Roma describes women's music as encompassing "all types of music by, for and about women from all eras of history and all cultures. What these different iterations of this nebulous thing called 'women's music' have in common is that the music gives women a voice they otherwise would not have. In general, the experiences of women are, historically and cross-culturally, not substantiated in ways that we are taught are legitimate."[5] Women's choruses embraced the stories of lesbian and heterosexual women. They sang about women's experience and women's history in ways that were not embodied by traditional choral repertoire. As women's choruses became more active members of the GALA Choruses network, their voices had a profound, and not always comfortable, impact on the network's gay male culture. The most obvious results were the broadening of potential choral repertoire and an increasing legitimizing of women's experiences within the network. Because many women's choruses also focused on other marginalized voices in the broader culture, their voices have been an important impetus for the glbt choral movement to look beyond itself.

The Denver Women's Chorus was the first women's chorus to perform at a GALA Choruses festival when it participated in Festival II in 1986 in Minneapolis. No mixed chorus performed and sixteen men's choruses performed. At the 1989 Festival III in Seattle, forty-four choruses and about 2,500 delegates attended. Eight women's choruses (25 percent) and five mixed choruses (11 percent) performed.

Mixed choruses, as in choruses welcoming lesbians and gay men, began to surface more visibly at the 1989 GALA Choruses' festival in Seattle. The music and politics of these choruses bridge the gaps that exist between gay men and lesbians and present an instructive and creative model of cooperation and understanding.

As with women's choruses, the history of some mixed glbt choruses predates the establishment of the legal entity of GALA Choruses. The Stonewall Chorale in New York City was founded in 1979. The Lesbian/Gay Chorus of San Francisco (LGCSF) was founded in 1980. LGCSF member Linda Rhode participated in the 1982 GALA Choruses "constituting meeting," which followed the 1982 Gay Games in San Francisco, and signed the incorporation papers for GALA Choruses in 1983. The other signers giving birth to GALA Choruses represented six men's choruses: Gay Men's Chorus of Los Angeles, Seattle Men's Chorus, Denver Gay Men's Chorus, San Francisco Gay Men's Chorus, Windy City Gay Men's Chorus, and New York City Gay Men's Chorus.

Since mixed choruses express the voices of men and women, they could not, and do not, present the same cultural and social messages of gay men's or women's choruses, although they draw on those sources for strength and community. The mixed choruses unveiled yet another message for the glbt choral movement, combining the voices of glbt pride and feminism while drawing on traditional and new choral repertoire. In mixed choruses, men and women experienced increased interaction that produced—not without hard work and some strife—increased understanding as men and women learned from each other.

*　*　*

In the Lesbian and Gay Chorus of Washington, D.C. (LGCW), this message has been honed through organizational structure and repertoire. The LGCW is a non-auditioned, community-based chorus that draws about fifty singers per season. In addition to presenting two major concerts annually, the LGCW also appears at other community events, sometimes represented by one of its three ensembles.

In eighteen years, the LGCW has raised more than $25,000 for community groups. Its repertoire draws from a wide range of choral music from renaissance to popular music. Under the direction of Ray Killian, LGCW's fourth music director, the LGCW performed Gian Carlo Menotti's *The Unicorn, the Gorgon and the Manticore* (1998), Vincent Persichetti's *Celebrations* (in collaboration with D.C.'s Different Drummers and the Unitarian Universalist Church of Arlington Choir in 1999), and Robert Convery's *Songs of Children* (2000). The LGCW has released three CDs, its most recent, *LGCW LIVE!* in 1999.

As a member of GALA Choruses beginning in 1988, the Lesbian and Gay Chorus of Washington, D.C. has made a strong commitment to the glbt choral movement, performing at Festivals III through VI, attending all Leadership Conferences, and assisting LGCW members in their work on the GALA Choruses board and committees. A member of the LGCW served on the GALA Choruses Board of Directors continuously from 1993 to 2002. In 1999, the LGCW hosted the Leadership Conference and Singers' Weekend.

LGCW ensembles—two mixed groups and one group of three tenors—are self-forming and self-directed. The ensembles are both a marketing and outreach tool for the LGCW. The ensembles sometimes arrange their own gigs but they often are asked by the chorus to appear when the chorus cannot. The decisions to accept smaller gigs and which group will perform are made by the music director and the general manager with obvious attention to the individual ensemble's logistical and performance constraints. In 2000, the oldest LGCW ensemble, Not What You Think, cut its own retrospective CD of ten years. The ensemble provided its own funding for this project.

When the LGCW was founded, its members were not fully cognizant of the glbt choral movement or of the rich choral tradition of Washington, D.C. The opening LGCW scenes—often repeated in many grass-roots movements—involved a small gathering of singers who responded to flyers, posted at local gay and women's bookstores and other community hangouts, announcing the creation of a gay and lesbian chorus. The first eight to gather and sing met at a drag bar, the Rogue, in a borderline area of Washington, D.C., in the early fall of 1983. The "closet" was an active parameter of glbt life in Washington, D.C. in the early 1980s.

After several meetings at the Rogue, the group decided to move to a location that would be more conducive to prospective choristers. The group became the guest of the William Penn House on Capitol Hill, which sported a "tonier" address, but which functioned as a Quaker youth hostel or B&B of sorts. The William Penn House proved to be a comfortable, rent-free home for several years.

The LGCW's first two years were rocky from both organizational and musical perspectives. The idea of an organization where gay men and lesbians worked together was relatively novel in the D.C. gay and lesbian community of the early 1980s.[6] LGCW founder Diana Wilcox was also a trumpet player in D.C.'s Different Drummers (DCDD), a marching band of gay men and lesbians founded in 1980. Her positive experience in the band gave her the idea to start a gay and lesbian chorus. In spite of Wilcox's experience with DCDD, the D.C. gay and lesbian community was not particularly interested in the birth of a gay and lesbian chorus.

Other glbt community music groups were already up and running, including the Federal City Performing Arts, which housed the Gay Men's Chorus of Washington (GMCW), founded in 1981, and the D.C. Area Feminist Chorus (DCAFC) founded in 1978. (DCAFC became Bread & Roses Feminist Singers in 1994.) The GMCW's vision statement "affirms the gay experience and promotes a culture of diversity through musical and performance excellence."[7] The Bread & Roses Feminist Singers (BRFS) statement of purpose says that the group "is committed to promoting women's culture and projecting a musical message of peace and social justice. . . . The group focuses on improving personal musical skills, performing, and providing support within the group, and raising social consciousness."[8] In the early 1980s, both the GMCW and the DCAFC had hearty, but different, constituencies based on their separate identities. In the larger Washington, D.C., metropolitan choral community, the LGCW's birth went unnoticed.

Washington, D.C., is a "chorally saturated city," to borrow an expression from J. Reilly Lewis, music director of the Cathedral Choral Society.[9] Lewis comments in the September 1997 issue of *Washingtonian* magazine, "The start of Washington's classical choral tradition can be dated precisely. On December 1, 1941, . . . 30–year old Paul Callaway presided over the first rehearsal of the Cathedral Choral Society."[10] The *Washingtonian* article provides a non-inclusive list of twenty-five choral groups, segmented into (1) large mixed choruses, such as the Cathedral Choral Society and the Choral Arts Society of Washington (100–200 singers), (2) smaller mixed choruses, such as the Alexandria Choral Society, the Friday Morning Music Club Chorale, and the LGCW (40–100 singers), (3) chamber music (fewer than 40 singers), and (4) men's choruses (55–200 singers). The Gay Men's Chorus of Washington is listed here. The article discusses D.C.'s African American vocal music tradition, which is intertwined with religious music (gospel began to appear in about 1920). Also covered are close harmony groups (men's and women's), folksingers, and children's choruses. D.C. supports two groups, Hexagon and the Washington Revels, that are managed on and off stage by volunteers alone. The article makes no mention of D.C.'s Sweet Honey in the Rock, a highly successful, professional *a cappella* group of seven African American women (including a signer), which draws its music from spirituals, hymns, and gospel music from nineteenth- and twentieth-century Baptist, Methodist, and Pentecostal traditions. Sweet Honey in the Rock is more than a quarter-century old and its musical message of inclusion has become very special to many choruses in the glbt choral movement, including the LGCW (for example, "We Are" and "We Want the Vote!" by Sweet Honey member Ysaye M. Barnwell, CD nos. 16 and 17).

The first name of the LGCW was "Capital City Chorale," which suggested a stronger identification with place than with a political movement. After a short time, the group selected the name "Gay and Lesbian Chorus" and performed in D.C. and Baltimore in 1983 with that name under the direction of Tess Garcia. Later, the group changed its name to "Lesbian and Gay Chorus of Washington, D.C." and was incorporated as such in 1990.

It is worth documenting how the final name, which places "lesbian" at the front, came about. The idea for the name change arose from the LGCW men, including LGCW's second music director, Mark Bowman. It was their premise that the chorus should change its name to put women first because society often does not recognize women's experiences. The LGCW men believed that the name "Lesbian and Gay Chorus of Washington" would highlight women's participation in the organization and would be a constantly visible stand for social justice.

In its first two years, the group strongly resisted formalizing itself, deciding to put off adoption of bylaws—the first step toward incorporation—and filing for non-profit tax-exempt status. All business was carried out in a half-hour pre-rehearsal meeting once a month.

Musically, its first selections were chosen by Garcia, who had been a church musician. Beginning with the summer of 1984, the LGCW was without a permanent conductor until February 1986 when Mark Bowman agreed to become the music director. In the interim, Dave Hughes, a chorus member with band experience, conducted rehearsals, but there was no guiding musical or organizational plan. Members shared music. Rehearsal selections could run the gamut from Gilbert and Sullivan to PDQ Bach to camp songs.

There was a clear turning away from singing traditional classical choral repertoire. Singers did not want to sing overtly sacred or Christian choral music, although this music was certainly a defining aspect of the musical heritage of many members. These early members expressed their discomfort and distaste for singing music that was hurtful in its exclusion and that did not specifically honor their lives. Three members were enthusiastic members of D.C.'s glbt synagogue, Bet Mishpachah, which was developing a more inclusive liturgy and where the LGCW made several early appearances. Two early members were practicing Quakers and one a pagan. Evidence that these early themes remain strong is indicated in a recent concert program statement of a current LGCW member, "I really enjoy singing but could not find a church that would *accept*—not just tolerate—me."[11]

Although the group was not formally organized, it did have a compelling spirit of commitment and purpose, qualities Mark Bowman admired the first time he heard the group at a Twelfth Night celebration. Bowman had studied music at Oberlin College. He was forced to give up his dream of becoming a Methodist minister when he was asked to leave the seminary after his life as a gay man was revealed. Before getting involved with the LGCW, Bowman had been the choir director of a Methodist church.

In addition to his credentials in music, Bowman brought a strong sense of personal pride, a capacity for grass-roots organizing, a deep commitment to social justice, and a vision of what the group could become. Bowman agreed to conduct one rehearsal as a favor to one of the charter members, and he stayed for six years. Of particular interest to Bowman was the commitment of gay men and lesbians to work together. Bowman's political thinking encompassed feminist principles and alternative concepts of organizing power. His perspective was shaped by his activism in the Methodist Church. His values were a perfect match for the group and helped the chorus build more inclusively on its inherent diversity and make thoughtful choices about its music and organization.

Bowman's concept of the position of music director was non-traditional. Although he possessed powerful leadership qualities and the competence to create the organization himself, he used a collegial approach with the singers. The conductor's traditional central role prevailed in rehearsal and performance, but LGCW members actively chose and shaped the organization's structure and its music choices. Bowman encouraged the LGCW members to stake their dreams for the organization on its mission rather than around the personality of the music director.

In an interview in August 2000, Bowman discussed his relationship with the LGCW and his first observations of how the group was operating. "My recollection is when I came the Chorus was already making decisions as a whole. . . . I don't have a clear recollection of exactly when we decided we were going to continue the consensus decision-making. It was always there."[12]

Shortly after Bowman's arrival, LGCW members—now numbering closer to twenty than ten—articulated the following mission statement.

> The purpose of the LGCW is to:
> Make quality music
> Foster gender cooperation
> Demonstrate lesbian and gay pride
> Develop talent, and
> Have fun.

To create the mission statement, the group used a process based on consensus. The process was rooted in the Quaker tradition, as explained by the two Quaker members. A facilitator managed the process and agreed to reflect the views and concerns of all present. For their part, all participants agreed to listen and to work together to craft a statement that was acceptable to all. The elements of the mission statement have been reaffirmed through subsequent visioning and long-range planning processes.[13]

From this major successful and exciting experience with consensus, the group made a formal commitment to use a consensus process for its governance. This choice reflected the members' vision of an egalitarian and just approach to all issues the chorus might face—allowing for each voice to be expressed and eliminating volatile situations of winners and losers. In particular, this decision was a feminist choice because the members believed that an alternative structure would be more likely to engender sharing of power within the organization. The choice reflected a high degree of active trust within the organization. The trust was based on a common purpose—to sing—and a group consciousness of what lay behind that purpose—to change the world. Chorus members were immediately passionately and actively invested in the group.

In our interview, Bowman reflected on the chorus's decision to use consensus: "Consensus is not only helpful because it's a more equitable and fair way of making decisions but it gives people greater investment within the chorus and I think that's really important. In so many choruses you sort of show up and do what you're told. You don't always understand why things are done or the difficult decisions that go into deciding to do something. The gift of the chorus was it built people's investment to the chorus."[14]

Within the LGCW's understanding of consensus, the role of facilitator is special but not more powerful than anyone else's in shaping the organization's plan. Facilitators first alternated between male and female members. As the business of the chorus became more complicated, two facilitators began to serve together for one or two years. Co-facilitators organize internal affairs and represent the LGCW to the outside world, as well as functioning as internal ears for the LGCW members and, when necessary, as interpreters.

About 1990, the LGCW created a second paid, contractual position—business manager, now general manager. (The music director was the first.) The functions of the co-facilitators remained essentially the same, but the general manager was empowered by the chorus to conduct general operations, a responsibility once shared by the co-facilitators and other volunteers.

The concept of empowering and trusting certain individuals to perform specific tasks was eventually extended to the role of the music director. Although the music director's professional credentials are paramount to the overall musical success of the group, LGCW members had a harder time accepting

this concept, probably because they had experience in self-direction, a tradition of self-programming, and an intense passion for the group's work.

Toward the end of Bowman's tenure, the LGCW established a music and
program committee that began to select concert themes, music, and program
order. Bowman characterized his role as music director: "I'll be honest with
you. I actually think that when I was the director, in spite of believing that
things were sort of open, I think I was a benevolent dictator. I took a lot of
input from a lot of people, and actually a lot of music we did was recom-
mended by other people, but until the very last year or two that I was directing, I think I essentially made decisions about what we were going to sing by
myself. It really wasn't done by committee. That was just beginning to form
when I left."[15]

When Bowman left, the music and program committee took on a much
larger role with Regina Carlow, LGCW's third music director. Recently, the
music and program committee has once again examined its statement of
purpose, returning to a self-concept that is closer to what Bowman experienced, the difference being its clear articulation and its acceptance as a
standard procedure of LGCW operations.

Like all LGCW meetings, discussions about music are open to any LGCW
member. Meetings of the music and program committee are a conduit for
music suggestions from the members and the music director, a place to
discuss and choose musical emphases collaboratively, and an educational
forum about choral music and vocal production. The music director takes
the input from the committee meetings and creates a program. The music
director presents the concepts and reasons for the program and its particular
selections to the committee and the LGCW-at-large. This collaborative process draws on the professional skills of the music director and achieves the
investment of members in the music they will be learning and performing.
The overall result has been an improvement in the musicianship and sound
of the ensemble.

The choice of Robert Convery's *Songs of Children* in 1999–2000 (the
LGCW's sixteenth year) illustrates the way the LGCW selects music to reflect
its basic message and improve its musicianship. Following its 15th Anniversary Year celebration, LGCW members discussed turning its programming
perspective externally to sing for people whose voices society ignored. This
desire was eventually expressed as "voices unheard."[16]

In response to this idea, LGCW music director Ray Killian introduced
Songs of Children because he believed in its potential for teaching and building the ensemble's musicianship. The context of the piece was astoundingly

suited to the concept of "voices unheard." *Songs of Children* for choir, violin, viola, cello, and piano is a cantata of nine poems written by children while interned at Terezin concentration camp. The cantata was composed in memory of all children who perished in the Holocaust.[17]

*   *   *

Consensus can only be learned by practicing. In the LGCW, its articulation has been a continuing journey filled with successes, challenges, and failures. An essential concept in practicing consensus is the understanding that *unanimity is not the same as unity.* Consequently, the group can decide to take action with the knowledge that there is not total agreement. What the group relies on in return is the assistance of each member in implementing the action the group agreed to take. This depends on trust and trust only comes with time, practice, patience, and listening.

Consensus is the governance process for the LGCW, in committees, in meetings for business, and in the group-at-large. The group-at-large selected the current music director, C. Paul Heins, and his predecessors, Ray Killian and Regina Carlow. Consensus was obviously in place when the group chose Mark Bowman, although the process for his selection was significantly less organized. In June 2000, LGCW members voted to accept revised bylaws that are based on the actual practice of consensus.[18] This decision aligned the actual consensual practice of the organization with its legal documents, providing a legal grounding for the LGCW's belief that every voice should be equally empowered within its structure.

The choice of consensus governance directly enforces the choice, made in the beginning days of the organization, not to audition potential members. Any interested person can join. Singers are encouraged to assess for themselves whether they want to belong and whether they can meet the basic expectations of rehearsal, performance, dues, tasks, and musical improvement outlined in the LGCW handbook.[19] Singers are asked to study and understand how they personally affect the LGCW's mission and vision. The choice to join is personally significant. Ultimately, the choice is political because it brings voice to the unheard.

Unlike the unsavory experience of "being chosen," the person chooses to join. The act is healing and the opposite of the social experience of many glbt people, who have been invisible in and to mainstream groups. The choice empowers the individual voice on two levels. First, the individual is empowered because his or her voice is recognized. Secondly, this empowerment is reflected in the development of the individual choral voice. The task of music making as a group is nourished by the journey of the individual. A current member stated, "I sing with the LGCW because I can stand in solidarity and proudly claim who I am . . . knowing I/we make a difference."[20]

In the choral setting, each voice matters. The presence or absence of a single voice changes the overall ensemble sound. The essence of the choral message resonates with the consensus message. For glbt people whose voices have not historically counted and who continue to struggle for acceptance, the choral message is particularly powerful. For here, they find self-esteem, pride, and acceptance. Here they can begin to build bridges. "I sing because I find it healing and it is often a bridge between the many communities to which I belong."[21]

Bowman commented, "Part of the nature of the lesbian and gay choruses is about giving voice to the voiceless or about empowering people who had not been empowered. . . . A chorus is about more than just performing music, . . . it's a whole community life together."[22]

In the history of the LGCW, the operational and musical strengths have not always been equal or in alignment. The realization of operational success moved along at a faster pace. The organization discovered more slowly the necessity of vocal training and selecting repertoire to build musicality and musicianship. When the structure and the music became aligned, the organization made the discovery that its message could be delivered more effectively and powerfully. As a choral ensemble and non-profit organization, the LGCW strives to embody a message that gives voice to the unheard, a message at once grounded in excellent musicianship and principles of social justice. In Bowman's words, "Consensus is . . . well, I can think of what consensus is not. Consensus is not unanimity. Consensus is not all being of the same mind. Consensus is not about the loudest voices outspeaking the quieter voices and winning. In order for consensus to work, it really takes a commitment by the whole group to be part of a process."[23]

In receiving the GALA Choruses Legacy Award in July 2000, Catherine Roma stated, "Our own incredibly vibrant lesbian and gay choral movement succeeds because we ride on the shoulders of musical troubadours who have accompanied all movements for social change. And like them, we wade into troubled waters. Coalition building and change may be stormy, but if we want to change lives, we must walk into it. . . . So together we take risks and dare to make a change. This Legacy Award is for all of us and all of our musical forebears on the front lines of transformation for justice with love."[24] The glbt choral movement is a harmonic convergence of music and politics. The common purpose of making music is complemented by the political act of affirming through music the lives and experiences of a people whose voices have not been heard. This political act is formulated differently in the culture of gay men's choruses, women's choruses, and mixed choruses, but is universally recognized in the GALA Choruses vision statement: Our Voices Win Freedom.[25]

Notes

1. Organizations associated with gay and lesbian rights have only recently begun to include "bisexual" and "transgendered" in their names. I chose to refer to the glbt choral movement because it has been my personal experience that the movement includes glbt people.

2. GALA Choruses is often popularly referred to as "GALA," but I have chosen to use the legal name. Generally, the members of GALA Choruses are the individual chorus organizations.

3. Paul Attinello, "Authority and Freedom/Toward a Sociology of the Gay Choruses" in *Queering the Pitch: The New Gay and Lesbian Musicology,* ed. Philip Brett, Elizabeth Wood, and Gary C. Thomas (New York: Routledge, 1994), 315.

4. Dennis Coleman, "Multiculturalism and Diversity: A Brief History of the Gay and Lesbian Choral Movement," in *A How-to Book for Choral Ensembles* (Washington, D. C.: Chorus America, 1999), 105–6.

5. Catherine Roma, "Dr. Catherine Roma: 25 Years of Social Justice Through Song," in *GALAgram* 12, no. 4 (January 2000): 9.

6. Washington, D.C., was home to many lesbian activists in the 1970s and early 1980s. The Furies, separatist by intention, were a successful and powerful lesbian collective established in the 1970s. Activist and writer Charlotte Bunch is perhaps the Furies' best-known member. A monthly publication, *Off Our Backs,* was managed by another collective of women who explored feminist theory in depth. For many lesbians, feminism was the first "coming-out," with sexual identity following.

7. The GMCW vision statement was provided by John Perkins, GMCW's former executive director.

8. The BRFS statement of purpose was provided by member Carol Wheeler. The BRFS statement of purpose grows out of the earlier DCAFC experience. As with so many women's choruses, DCAFC/BRFS members were/are not all lesbian.

9. J. Reilly Lewis, quoted in Robert Sinclair, "Sing, Sing, Sing," *Washingtonian* 32, no. 12 (September 1997): 86.

10. Ibid.

11. Concert program for the First Presbyterian Church of Salem, Ohio, July 2002.

12. Mark Bowman, interview with the author, August 23, 2000. Transcript available.

13. Adopted in 2002, the LGCW mission statement is: Every Voice Matters. The vision statement is: A World That Listens.

14. Bowman, interview.

15. Ibid.

16. "what i want," a composition by Canadian composer Stephen Smith, was the epitome of this concept. Smith set a poem of Pat Lowther (1935–75), a Canadian poet who struggled with domestic abuse and was unable to leave her destructive marriage. She was murdered by her husband. Smith's music and Lowther's words powerfully convey the voice of the unheard.

17. Robert Convery holds degrees from the Curtis Institute of Music, Westminster Choir College, and the Juilliard School, where he received his doctorate. He has written the opera *Clara* (on composer Clara Schumann), four one-act operas, twenty-two cantatas, *Mass* for choir and orchestra, choral works of every description, nine song cycles, and more than 150 songs for voice and piano. The LGCW performed selections from *Songs of Children* at GALA Choruses' Festival 2000. Convery, who is gay, attended the LGCW's performances in Washington, D.C., and San Jose.

18. Under the law of the District of Columbia, a non-profit corporation must have no fewer than three directors, but there is no upper limit. LGCW members created a "board" composed of all its members.

19. The general statement of membership is as follows. "Membership in the Chorus is a serious commitment and the strength of the group lies in the active participation of each member. . . . Your role as a member is to understand how you personally affect the Chorus' mission and vision." LGCW Handbook, November 1999.

20. Salem, Ohio, concert program.

21. Ibid.

22. Bowman, interview.

23. Ibid.

24. From Roma's remarks at the GALA Choruses Legacy Award Dinner on September 29, 2000, in San Jose, California. See www.musechoir.org.

25. The LGCW is not currently a member of GALA Choruses.

PART 5

In the Western Tradition

12

Men and Women of the Chorus: Music, Governance, and Social Models in Nineteenth-Century German-Speaking Europe

KAREN AHLQUIST

Human beings sing, and perhaps nowhere have masses of singing humans been harnessed with more enthusiasm than in nineteenth-century German-speaking Europe. As elsewhere, the chorus offered the amateur a ready path into music, one that became the last opportunity for the *Liebhaber,* the ordinary music lover, to "produce" as well as "consume" Western art music in a public setting. Although its artistic position and organizational forms are widely taken for granted today, in Germany, its nineteenth-century development depended on, and contributed to, important social and musical change.

Unlike its older incarnations in the church or opera house, the nineteenth-century choral society was both a chorus and a *society.* The mixed chorus in particular was set up to foster an idealistic approach to German high culture, artistic taste, conventional religious and moral beliefs, the value of history and a historical repertoire, and the role of the arts in *Bildung,* or individual cultivation. As such, it was serious business. It inspired new works: Even in the choral backwater of Vienna, a collective instrument could be found to sing the premiere of Beethoven's Ninth Symphony in 1824. The first wave of mass choral singing and organization, roughly 1820–1850, also marks the heyday of the dramatic oratorio. While the oratorio is sometimes seen as a bone thrown by composers to an ignorant and philistine bourgeoisie, its broad appeal nevertheless renders it worthy of scrutiny. And indeed, the time, energy, and money put into concerts, festivals, commemorations, and other events speak to the high value placed on choral singing by its many participants.

In addition to its musical role, the chorus also performed, so to speak, the social roles its members could play and a social as well as aesthetic vision for Western art music. Thus it may serve as a window into the relative positions of middle-class men and women in a widespread and leading institution. As the mixed chorus idea grew, women gained access to the activity itself—choral singing—on a more-or-less equal basis with men. Changes in conditions of leadership and other rules, however, show choral societies grappling with the effect of women's necessary role as singers on their role in the organization. These changes ran in tandem with changes in the music itself. The variety of textures and uses of the choral instrument in the first half of the century coincided with a variety of organizational forms in the chorus itself. Both sides of the equation changed after the revolutions of 1848. From the 1850s on, the bourgeois mixed chorus's role became less varied socially and musically even as the chorus became more firmly established as an institution. The choral society and its music presented a view of each individual's position in a larger musical and social order to participants and audiences alike.

The growth of amateur choral singing in secular settings belongs to the massive political and social reconfiguration that resulted from the Enlightenment and the growth of bourgeois culture. The emerging individual—a human being increasingly aware of himself (*sic*) and his place in society—wanted to group himself in new ways. Politically, increased freedom of association allowed people to organize themselves beyond long-standing boundaries and lines of authority such as family, religion, occupation, social position, and town or region. Historians of German voluntary societies argue that as people became increasingly free to choose friends and associates based on mutual interest, individuals banded together with like-minded others in fellowship and in pursuit of common goals. Associations offered independence from traditional social structures and individualism in the form of freedom of choice.[1]

In Germany these groups, often referred to as *Vereine,* or unions, included reading, patriotic, social, religious, gymnastic, student, fraternal, and eventually, choral organizations. Organization leaders of the late eighteenth and nineteenth centuries understood that such structured participation could have political potential. Decision making, rules formulation, programming, elections, financial management, membership controls, and public outreach not only put organizational power into members' hands but also taught them—often in the important general meetings—how to use it. This practice helped political associations of the 1848 revolutions spring up on short notice and make necessary decisions in short order.[2]

One of the clearest examples of this process was the male chorus movement. Beginning in the 1810s, men's choruses appeared in small villages and major cities alike, including areas (such as Bavaria) where mixed choruses were hardly in evidence. Like other *Verein* movements that developed in the wake of the Napoleonic wars, the male chorus movement was imbued with German cultural nationalism. In his writings and travels on behalf of the movement, the Swiss music educator Hans Georg Nägeli (1773–1836) stressed the male chorus as a symbol of the German nation and people. Thus he aimed to foster a burgeoning movement with a highly public profile. Nägeli favored four-part singing and social inclusiveness for their symbolic value—solidarity out of diversity—and as a way to enhance public impact through large numbers. "When a people's voice rings out ennobled by art," he asserted, "one believes one hears the voice of an ennobled people."[3]

A political orientation would have been inappropriate—indeed illegal—for mixed choruses. Yet by the early nineteenth century, women's acceptance as choral singers in many German-speaking areas was no longer seriously questioned, and chorus lists even show male and female singers together on the alto part, especially in festival performances (Figures 12.1–2). Thus singing in a chorus and belonging to an organization were of necessity not the same thing. The variety of terms under which women sang, especially before 1848, reflects an uneven application of new social models common among male associations. Eighteenth-century reading clubs and Masonic lodges had expressly excluded women; other clubs assumed female membership to be "unnatural."[4] After the French Revolution, the tenets of citizenship for men encouraged in turn an ideology of difference that, under the guise of marking women for a romanticized domestic and dependent existence, barred them from public political activity in Germany until 1907.[5] The idea of women in public life and organizations was a complex issue for both sexes. In fields other than music, women were sometimes invited to visit male associations, but they could neither participate nor join. While they did organize into independent societies, their associations, usually oriented toward charity or education, were often church-sponsored and operated away from the public arena.[6] Moreover, membership often included financial responsibility. Decision making belonged by definition to dues payers; in most cases, women lacked the means to pay on their own accounts.

Nevertheless, choral singing on any terms offered women new social, intellectual, and physical opportunities and a performance outlet that solved the
potential problem of unseemly self-display. It allowed them to participate
publicly in an artistic activity without claiming artistic or professional ambition. Eventually it offered many of them solo opportunities in public and
travel to festivals. Sometimes, however, they were offered even more. At a
time when only males sang in church choirs and other public choral performances, the Berlin Singakademie of 1791 included women on more-or-less
equal terms with men. The founding music director, Carl Friedrich Fasch,
appointed a precedent-setting board of directors made up of three men and
three women.[7] By 1821, the Singakademie's constitution mandated that this
board (now four and four) meet regularly to make all non-musical decisions
for the society. The only exception, cases of large financial outlay, required
the board to consult with an all-male committee with no other duties.[8]

By including women (albeit of high social position) as leaders, members,
and singers, the Singakademie not only surpassed society at large, but also
other associations, musical and non-musical, that followed in its wake. Unlike
virtually all votes cast in early-nineteenth-century Germany, the 1832 vote that
denied Felix Mendelssohn the music directorship in favor of Carl Friedrich
Rungenhangen was cast by men and women both.[9]

Equally important for women in the Singakademie was its development of
a public profile. Not originally a concert-giving chorus of the type familiar
today, the Akademie began as a group of musically inclined individuals who
met in the tradition of contemporaneous reading clubs and salons. In 1791
members sang at the Marienkirche, a performance said to be Berlin's first
public church music sung by men and women together.[10] Listeners, restricted
to invited family members and friends, were first admitted to meetings in
1794.[11] The chorus's first performance for a paying public was a charity concert (the Mozart Requiem) in a church in 1800, the beginning of a tradition
of regular concerts that continues today.[12] It was also the beginning of a
movement that produced dozens of other similar organizations, along with
concerts, festivals, and other musical events—achievements taken for many
years as a source of national, local, and artistic pride.

Other mixed choral societies followed the Singakademie's lead, eventually
putting thousands of *Liebhaber* men and women of the chorus on the public
stage. Berlin's precedent-setting organizational role for women was sometimes
followed. In Leipzig, bylaws mandated four men and four women on the
board.[13] In 1818, a leaflet was circulated in Aachen soliciting members for a Singakademie with *"Vorsteher und Vorsteherinnen"* [directors and directoresses]

Fräul. Jansen I. aus Aachen.	Fräul. Veling B. aus Aachen.
,, Ibels ,, ,,	Frau Wergifosse ,, Düren.
Frau Kesselkaul sr. a. Aachen.	Fräul. Zitterland I. ,, Aachen.
,, Küchen aus Aachen.	,, Zitterland II. aus ,,
Fräul. Kühnen aus Krefeld.	Herr Bayer aus Aachen.
,, von Lasaulx aus Aachen.	,, Cohen ,, ,,
,, Lueder II. ,, ,,	,, Cramer ,, ,,
,, Lülsdorff ,, ,,	,, Cremer ,, ,,
,, von der Lundt aus Köln.	,, Dubusc ,, ,,
Frau Mathieu. aus Bonn.	,, Freudenthal II. a. Aachen.
Fräul. Meyer aus Aachen.	,, Guisez III. aus Aachen.
,, Nolten ,, ,,	,, Gründgens ,, ,,
,, Offenbach aus Köln.	,, van Gülpen , II., aus ,,
,, v. Riemsdyck a. Mastricht.	,, Heyse aus Aachen.
,, Ruperti aus ,,	,, Hoffmann a. ,,
Frau Schmahl aus. Aachen.	,, Hund III. aus Aachen.
,, Schmalhausen a. Aachen.	,, Kämpfer ,, ,,
Fräul. Schopen aus Aachen.	,, Laruelle I. ,, ,,
,, Schramm ,, Bonn	,, Lofgnié ,, ,,
,, Schulz aus Krefeld.	,, Lülsdorf ,, ,,
,, Spies aus Aachen.	,, Müller ,, ,,
,, Steenaerts aus Aachen.	,, Nuellens ,, ,,
Frau Stephan ,, & ,, ,,	,, Packenius ,, ,,
Fräul. Stiegler ,, ,,	,, Redlich ,, ,,
,, Sturenburg I. a. Aachen.	,, Rumpen ,, ,,
,, Stürtz aus Aachen.	,, Spies ,, ,,
,, Thyssen II. aus Aachen.	,, Wayaffe, A., a. ,,
,, Veling, L., ,, ,,	===== 73.

TENORI.

Herr Amerahl aus Krefeld.	Herr Barth aus Aachen.

Figure 12.1 Chorus list excerpt, Lower Rhine Music Festival program, Aachen, 1840. The male altos in the right column were probably boys. Twelve of their names appear on the 1846 chorus list under tenor or bass.

Fräul. A. Rheininger.	Fräul. A. von Stark.
„ A. Ritsert.	„ Joh. Thomas.
„ Schaub.	Frau M. Warthorst.
Frau A. Schleiermacher.	Fräul. M. Weber.
Fräul. L. Schleuning.	„ L. Weiß.
„ Schneider II.	„ S. Werner.
Frau M. Schulz.	„ Theod. Wernher.
Fräul. Schwarzkopf.	„ Joh. Wernher.
„ A. Stanger.	„ S. Weygand. = 52.

Altisten aus dem Großherzoglichen Gymnasium.

II. Rothe.	Seyd.
III. Basset.	Thomas.
Schöbler.	Zeller.
von Webekind.	W. Zimmermann.
IV. Adam.	Werner.
Becker.	VI. Böhler.
Brill.	Brill.
Draubt.	von Gehren.
Frohnhäuser.	F. Mann.
von Grolman.	Römer.
Hügel.	Schleuning.
Marx.	VII. Beck II.
Pistor.	Hallwachs.
Reuling I.	Kamm.
Wimmenauer.	Scriba.
V. Heibacker.	Spamer I.
Krömmelbein.	
Pabst.	Privatschüler:
Sartorius.	Arthur Steppes.
Schüßler.	= 37.

2. Damengesangverein von Mainz:

Fräul. Beyer.	Fräul. M. Lorch.
„ von Bubna.	„ Monnard.
„ d'Avis.	„ Bertha Menges.
„ Dreymann.	„ Luise Nittius.
„ Eulenhaupt.	„ A. Piccard.
„ C. Harburger.	Frau Luise Reis, (geb. v. Zabern).
„ Jos. Harth.	„ Betty Schott.
„ Soph. Harth.	Fräul. Th. Schott.
„ M. Keppel.	„ M. Stumpf. = 18.

3. Musikverein von Mannheim:

Fräul. Berth. Amling.	Fräul. Aug. Battlehner.
„ El. Barth.	„ C. Esser.

Figure 12.2 Chorus list excerpt, first Middle Rhine Music Festival program, Darmstadt, 1856. Along with women, the list includes thirty-seven male altos from a local secondary school (*left page*) and two male alto members each from the Mannheim Musikverein and the academic chorus of Giessen (*right page*).

7

Fräul. Hetsch.
" App. Lutz.
" Joh. Quilling.
" Henr. Sammet.

Fräul. E. Schmidt.
" Seuffert.

Altist Kuhn.
" Stiefel.   = 12.

4. Cäcilienverein von Wiesbaden:

Fräul. Jean. Becker.
" Th. Bender.
" El. Esaias.
" Emma Frankenfeld.
" Math. Frankenfeld.
" Th. Franz.
" Joh. Habel.
" Luise Hauth.
" Luise Held.

Fräul. Henr. Hoffmann.
" Alb. Müller.
" L. Schindling.
" Th. Schlichter.
" A. Schmidt.
" C. Weilbacher.   = 15.

5. Akademischer Gesangverein von Gießen:

Fräul. A. Asmus.
" Berth. Bork.
" A. Frech.
" C. Hanstein.
" Jos. Klipstein.
" M. Koch.

Fräul. A. Metzler.
" Henr. Schäffer.
" M. Schlapp.

Altist Conzen.
" Leop. Langen.   = 11.

6. Gesangverein von Offenbach:

Fräul. Math. Camesaska.
" Dor. Deißler.
" Lina Dillenberger.
" Jul. Dillenberger.
" Soph. Engelhardt.
" Emma Faiß.

Fräul. Elis. Hartwig.
" Nan. Hill.
" Dor. Lorenz.
" Dor. Mock.
" Mar. Zimmermann.   = 11.

III. Tenor.

1. Von Darmstadt:
a) Musikverein:

Herr A. Baur.
" Beck.
" Bergmann.
" Dr. Casella.
" Emmerling.
" Ewald.
" Fischer.
" Dr. Fölsing.

Herr Glock.
" C. Grein.
" Grimm.
" Ludw. Hallwachs.
" W. Heim.
" Jul. Heumann.
" F. von Heffert.
" Kapesser.

Figure 12.2 Continued.

in leadership positions.[14] Nevertheless, gender and family determinants played a role in defining the levels of participation open to women. The place of the female bourgeois choral singer was, in practical terms, up for grabs.

Two examples will illustrate. Founded in 1832, the Musikverein of Darmstadt permitted its female members to vote for, or even be, members of the board of directors or the music committee, which ran the chorus. In fact, however, these leadership posts were held by men almost of necessity—of the nearly 300 founding members, only thirteen were women. The female choral singers were, for the most part, not members but were allowed to sing through the membership of male relatives.[15] Similarly, the 1848 bylaws of the mixed Cäcilien-Verein of Bingen show two categories of active (i.e. singing) members: ordinary and extraordinary. The latter consisted of "ladies with their own households"—that is, independent single women (of which there were probably few) and widows. But only ordinary members had the right to vote for the officers and board of directors. And in fact, although they sang, it seems that these dependent females in families (in most choruses the majority of the women singers) were not members at all.[16]

Regardless of the degree of power a particular chorus offered its female singers, however, the musical leadership and, as far as is known, the financial leadership were in the hands of men. But at least sometimes, women played a role in choosing leaders and musical direction or took leadership roles themselves. In no other type of organization in early-nineteenth-century Germany were women offered such an opportunity in conjunction with men.

Women were offered similar opportunities in musical terms as well. Throughout the first half of the century, the choral society offered both women and men participation in an active musical life with a growing repertoire of new compositions and revived older works. Music by local composers, often including the chorus's music director, was locally performed, sometimes later to reach a wider audience, sometimes not. Many genres, including Catholic liturgical music from the sixteenth through the nineteenth centuries, mixed-genre works such as the Mendelssohn *Lobgesang,* cantatas (often composed as occasional pieces), and a range of secular pieces were regularly heard. But as Table 12.1 shows (along with the astonishing success of Felix Mendelssohn), many of the most successful works composed in Germany through 1848 were oratorios.[17]

The oratorio's rapid development coincided with the growth of the mixed choral society itself—a twin expansion that enhanced the chorus's musical, dramatic, and social role. As in operas of the same era, the chorus moved toward the center of the drama, representing groups of people good or bad,

Table 12.1. Successful New Mixed Choral Works with Orchestra, 1815–49, in Rank Order

Composer	Title	Genre	First performance in a German-speaking city	No. through 1849	Rate per year
Mendelssohn	*Paulus*	oratorio	1836	77	5.5
Mendelssohn	*Elijah*	oratorio	1847	16	5.44
Mendelssohn	*Die erste Walpurgisnacht*	cantata	1833, 1843	22	3.14
Friedrich Schneider	*Das Weltgericht*	oratorio	1819	94	3.03
Louis Spohr	*Die letzten Dinge*	oratorio	1826	34	1.42
Mendelssohn	*Lobgesang* (Symphony No. 2)	symphony-cantata	1840	14	1.4
Mendelssohn	*Psalm 42*	cantata	1837	17	1.3
Beethoven	*Symphony No. 9*	symphony	1824	26	1.0
Ferdinand Hiller	*Die Zerstörung Jerusalems*	oratorio	1838	12	1.0
Anton Radziwill	*Faust*	incidental music	1835	14	.94
Spohr	*Des Heilands letzte Stunden*	oratorio	1835	14	.94

Note: All performances found have been counted, including those at festivals and by church or opera choruses. Large partial performances (i.e., a major section of a full-program work) are counted except in the case of Beethoven Symphony no. 9, which is only counted when evidence exists that the last movement was performed. Single movements and short excerpts are not counted. The list is considered comprehensive but makes no claim to being complete. Even small differences in rate per year can determine the order of adjacent works, which is therefore not necessarily significant. Julius Alf, "Geschichte und Bedeutung der Niederrheinischen Musikfeste in der ersten Hälfte des neunzehnten Jahrhunderts" (*Düsseldorfer Jahrbuch* 42 [1940]: 131–245 and 43 [1941]: 1–73); *Allgemeine Musikalische Zeitung* 17–50 (1815–48), *Neue Folge* 1–3 (1863–65), *Dritte Folge* 1–15 (1866–80); *Der Basler Gesangverein. Festschrift zu dessen fünfzigjährigem Jubiläum* (Basel: J. G. Baur, 1874), 30–61; Alfred Dörffel, *Geschichte der Gewandhausconcerte zu Leipzig* (Leipzig: n.p., 1884), 184–92; Reinhold Dusella, *Die Oratorien Carl Loewes* (Bonn: Gudrun Schröder, 1991); Martin Geck, *Deutsche Oratorien 1800 bis 1840. Verzeichnis der Quellen und Aufführungen* (Wilhelmshaven: Heinrichshofen, 1971); Paul Langer, *Chronik der Leipziger Singakademie* (Leipzig: Julius Klinkhardt, 1912); Helmut Lomnitzer, "Das musikalische Werk Friedrich Schneiders (1786–1853) insbesondere die Oratorien" (Ph.D. dissertation, Philipps-Universität zu Marburg, 1961), 375–76; Lower Rhine Music Festival Programs, 1818–85 (library, Heinrich-Heine-Universität, Düsseldorf); Christoph-Hellmut Mahling, "Zum 'Musikbetrieb' Berlins und seinen Institutionen in der ersten Hälfte des 19. Jahrhunderts," in *Studien zur Musikgeschichte Berlins im frühen 19. Jahrhundert*, ed. Carl Dahlhaus (Regensburg: Bosse, 1980), 240–63; Theodor Müller-Reuter, *Festschrift zum Jubiläums-Konzert des Singvereins in Krefeld am 17. Dezember 1910* (Krefeld: Singverein, 1910), 10–25, 36–40; *Neue Berliner Musikzeitung* 1–20 (1847–66), 22–34 (1868–80); Richard von Perger and Robert Hirschfeld, *Geschichte der k. k. Gesellschaft der Musikfreunde in Wien* (Vienna: n.p., 1912), 285–307; Harald Pfeiffer, *Heidelberger Musikleben in der ersten Hälfte des neunzehnten Jahrhunderts* (Heidelberg: Brigitte Guderjahn, 1989), 170; Theodor Seemann, *Geschichte der Dreyssig'schen Singakademie in Dresden* (Dresden: Gilbers, 1882), 33–53; Ludwig Voltz, *Die Konzerte des Musikvereins zu Darmstadt 1832–1907* (Darmstadt: n.p., 1907), 33–59.

"the people" themselves, or, as in the case of a women's chorus in *Paulus* (1836), even God.[18] Divisis, solo parts drawn from the chorus, and male or female divisions of the whole enhanced the chorus's dramatic position. Sometimes a libretto did the same. For example, instead of opening with a choral "overture" that precedes the drama, as in *Paulus,* in *Elijah* (1847) Mendelssohn used the opening chorus to begin the story itself. Directed onto a theme of affirmation, the oratorio's dramatic force created a predictably optimistic, often didactic genre able to present the moral vision of the day in artistic terms. While every point in the libretto is not a happy one, the most distressing moments are usually either minimized or deflected onto what Leon Botstein, referring to Mendelssohn, has called a "'filling' of the soul with precise and deep feeling."[19]

An example from *Paulus* shows how this deflection (or substitution) works. Early in the piece, the Christian martyr Stephen is stoned to death. The soprano storyteller announces, "Godfearing men displayed Stephen and held a great lament over him." But there is no lament. Instead, the chorus (presumably those around Stephen) exclaims, "See, we call blessed the one who has endured" (Example 12.1, CD no. 18). The music's main characteristics are lyricism and clear harmonic motion. A repeated undulating pattern in the violins gives a rippling effect to the texture and a light forward motion to the phrase. The harmonic rhythm moves the phrase precisely: two measures of tonic, a doubling of the harmonic rhythm, then a second doubling followed by a measure of dominant and back to the tonic. The melody uses the harmony: The opening exclamation "*siehe*" [see] attracts attention with its exclamatory accent on the first syllable, while the next measure, which starts the melody proper, offers a slight dissonance (on "*prei-*") above the second measure of tonic. A second choral voice comes in (m. 13) as the harmonic motion speeds up toward the cadence, at which time the whole chorus exclaims "*siehe*" a second time. The amount of musical material is small and it carefully leads the listener to the second, elaborated but easily recognizable statement (m. 17).

This text and texture make up the bulk of the chorus. Eventually a second text enters, however: "For although the body dies, the soul will live," with which the piece ends (Example 12.2). As it does so, it alternates a cappella phrases with the violin figuration that had begun the movement. The chorus presents the new message in as simple a manner as possible—chorale style. While the violins recall the first theme, "We praise the one who has endured," the second theme, eternal life, gets the last and clearest word.

As often in the oratorios of Mendelssohn and others, the most affecting passages are lyrical like these. Rather than make the audience shout for joy, they can make it cry. The structural and affective model of this chorus served Mendelssohn well for the rest of his career.[20] These contemplative moments, sometimes given by soloists but more often by the chorus, function as statements of main ideas. The symbolic value of the chorus as the human community supports this subtle lyricism, which, as Botstein says, imparts affirmation and introspection both.[21] Regardless of the presence or absence of applause (Henry Chorley remarks about an 1839 festival performance

Example 12.1 Felix Mendelssohn, "Siehe, wir preisen selig," from *Paulus,* mm. 10–19. Piano reduction by the composer. Bonn: Simrock, n.d. Music Division, the Library of Congress.

Example 12.2 Felix Mendelssohn, "Siehe, wir preisen selig," from *Paulus,* mm. 68–78.

with Mendelssohn conducting, "Applause, of course, there was none"), the audience needed to understand the work immediately and to feel the sum of the emotional effect in a physical way.[22]

To have this kind of impact, the oratorio needed a large choral instrument and a large, receptive audience. The music festival provided both, and its character as both a music festival and a *Volksfest*, or "people's festival," has been well documented. In 1839, Chorley described pre-dawn preparations in Braunschweig: "By six o'clock, a.m., there was no possibility of further sleep. Not only was the entire 'Blue Angel' [Hotel] stirring and clamorous for its breakfast; the whole town was blithely alive." Everyone attended: "Elegantly dressed girls in the transparent and gay toilettes of an English ball-room, might be seen, sitting side by side with the gipsy-coloured, hard-handed peasant-women of the district. . . . Here, again, was a comely youth, tight-laced in his neat uniform, and every hair of his moustache trimmed and trained to an agony of perfection, squeezed up against a dirty, savage, half-naked student."[23] Travel, eating (Chorley notes that snacks brought into the church were eaten during intermission), parties and balls, lodging of guests, informal performances, and a general holiday atmosphere attracted a broad population, making this festival, like many others, a major event in the social year of a city and its surrounding communities and a source of pride in an artistic and logistical achievement.

It is no surprise, then, that the configuration of chorus, music, and social event would undergo substantial change over time. Like society at large, the choral society and its music responded to the politically volatile 1840s, the revolutions of 1848, and the subsequent reaction of the standing rulers. This process occurred relatively quickly. The increased politicization of German society brought an increase in associations of all kinds and dozens of festivals of both mixed and all-male choral music through 1847.[24] Moreover, although overt political activity was forbidden by law, distinctions between the political and non-political spheres were not always clear.[25] The chorus, especially but not exclusively the male chorus, was widely linked to the revolutionary principles of German unity, nationalism, and constitutionalism, and its festivals and regional associations fostered communication and travel across political boundaries.[26] Harald Pfeiffer argues that the mixed chorus festivals held at Heidelberg castle from 1834 to 1843 substituted for the more overtly political male song festivals a format that would pass muster with government officials and the police.[27] Male choruses in cities such as Aachen and Mainz formed *Damenchöre* [ladies choruses] that performed with the men in non-political settings but never in public alone. The presence of women, who were excluded from political participation, defined an activity as non-political. And yet uniting people from various locales to create a great work (the festival) made up of great works (the performances) could, as a music periodical stressed in 1841, "achieve the awakening of a noble national pride and a true sense of community."[28]

The 1840s are also widely considered a watershed period in German gender relations. Leading the change was a dissident movement that encompassed both Protestant and Catholic Christianity. The movement's platform included greater equality for women and sometimes even female voting rights in local congregations.[29] In addition, the 1849 founding of a feminist newspaper by Louise Otto, herself an occasional writer for the *Neue Zeitschrift für Musik,* brought feminism to the attention of a nationwide public.[30]

The intense political pressures came to a head in the revolutions of 1848. As in other areas of society, the restoration of stability by 1850 brought a quick return to, and fact a great expansion of, musical life. But the reaction of the standing rulers to the revolutions rendered "restoration" of the status quo ante impossible. Beginning in 1849, rulers of the individual German states, supported by government civil service, the military, and the police, rolled back the rights of the press, assembly, and association, and began a campaign of political repression and depoliticization of society that lasted almost a decade.[31]

Thus the 1850s brought an immediate and widespread reshaping of musical life in Germany. Legal restrictions on male choral singing, especially in festivals or other large gatherings, varied geographically, but were evident to some degree in most areas in the first half of the decade.[32] By the mid-1850s, the more explicitly art-oriented institutions had recovered, and musical societies in many cities controlled an eventually flourishing, politically safe, and increasingly professional concert culture, along with the chorus's role in it. Some recent scholars have argued that the bourgeoisie made its peace with the political situation after 1848 because their social and (especially) economic interests were well-served without continued political engagement.[33] And indeed, if the members of the *Bürgertum,* the supporters of the choral society and of formal musical life in general, had replaced the nobility as the embodiment of German society, they would not need to link musical participation with any particular social or political point of view.

The reconfiguration of musical life in turn affected the mixed chorus's position in the musical and social world. Without the force of the 1840s political movement, the chorus settled down to contribute to the status quo. As it became more closely linked with concert-giving organizations or city music directorships, it increasingly served as a branch of professional concert life, providing vocal parts as needed for performances organized from beyond its borders.[34] Ironically perhaps, this narrowing in scope coincided with a great increase in numbers of participants: Choruses were founded in new cities, second and sometimes third choruses in a city competed with their predecessors, and the number of singers in individual choruses and at festivals increased.[35] The energies of the middle-class amateur singers and their organizers began to be channeled toward a more clearly establishment institution. Evidence of a tradeoff—growth for convention—can be found in both the choral organizations and the music they sang.

These changes, along with enhanced political awareness and the expansion of women's educational opportunities and activities in society, altered the terms under which singers, men and women both, participated in choruses. Particularly noticeable, as the number and size of choruses increased, was the change in the gender balance. Evidence exists that before 1848 mixed choruses had been fairly well-balanced and sometimes actually short of women. In 1830, a music periodical attributed a lack of festivals to insufficient numbers of adequate sopranos.[36] In 1844, the Lower Rhine Festival declined to invite an interested male chorus for lack of enough women to balance the voice parts.[37] As late as 1855, organizers of a festival in Munich invited the women only of the Nürnberg Singverein for the same reason.[38]

As Table 12.2 shows, what became more common after mid-century was something new: Women began to join mixed choruses in droves even as men pulled away from them. As earlier in the century, the women remained 90 percent or more single and presumably young, suggesting that married women still gave their responsibilities in the home top priority.[39] But an 1875

Table 12.2. Chorus Membership in Nineteenth-Century Cities

A. Berlin, Singakademie[1]

Date	Women	Men	Total	% Women
1791	12	15	27	44
1814	185	131	316	59
1821	158	124	282	56
1832	207	152	359	58
1848	243	163	406	60
1851	195	118	313	62
1858	248	118	366	68
1863	270	114	384	70
1868	259	98	357	72
1878	341	130	471	73

Table 12.2. Continued

B. Darmstadt, Musikverein[2]

Date	Women	Men	Total	% Women
1832	32	30	60	52
1841	50	50	100	50
1848	65	63	128	51
1858	110	60	170	65
1871	134	44	178	75

C. Leipzig, Singakademie[3]

Date	Women	Men	Total	% Women
1814	30	40	70	43
1823	27	33	60	45
1848	48	30	78	62
1852	73	34	107	69
1854	84	33	117	72
1863	54	28	82[4]	67
1878	45	34	79	57
1881	51	30	81	62

D. Vienna, Singverein of the Gesellschaft der Musikfreunde[5]

Date	Women	Men	Total	% Women
1858	55	88	143	39
1862	143	121	264	54
1868	145	100	245	60
1878	178	60	238	75
1886	211	123	334	63

E. Zurich, Gemischter Chor Zürich[6]

Date	Women	Men	Total	% Women
1863	63	32	95	69
1868	108	80	188	57
1878	154	84	238	65
1886	225	85	310	73

Note: The first date given for the Leipzig chorus is the earliest year for which membership numbers are available. The first date given for each of the other choruses is its founding year.

1. Martin Blumner, *Geschichte der Sing-Akademie zu Berlin. Eine Festgabe zur Säcularfeier am 24. Mai 1891* (Berlin: Horn and Raasch, 1891), 251–56.

2. Friedrich Schmidt, *Hundert Jahre Darmstädter Musikverein. Eine Geschichte seiner Vorläufer, seines Werdens und seiner Entwicklung* (Darmstadt: U. Bergstrassers Verlag W. Kleinschmidt, 1932), 37, 56–57, 80–81.

3. Paul Langer, *Chronik der Leipziger Singakademie* (Leipzig: Julius Klinkhardt, 1902), 7, 17, 22–3, 36–7, 43, 50, 72, 79.

4. The low numbers reflect the Singakademie's organizational and membership difficulties, which reached a low point in 1874 with a membership of thirty-two singers, including eight men. Langer, *Chronik,* 60.

5. Albrecht Claus, *Geschichte des Singvereines der Gesellschaft der Musikfreunde 1858–1933* (Vienna: Stockinger and Morsack, 1933), 154.

6. *Der gemischte Chor Zürich. Festschrift zur Feier seines fünfundzwanzigjährigen Bestehens* (Zurich: Zürcher and Furrer, 1888), 94.

comment from the conductor of the Breslau Singakademie supports the notion that men, too, were putting their energies elsewhere: "So few men who have a secure place in society take an active part in the meetings [i.e., rehearsals] of the Singakademie. Their number stands not at all in comparison with the great number of educated men in our city, of whom such participation would be assumed."[40]

Rules changes and surviving chorus rhetoric also show a continued awareness of gender issues as they affected the role of women in choral society governance. Sometimes the women held their own. In Berlin Singakademie, for example, women continued in the leadership roles they had from the beginning. But in general, a less egalitarian model won the field, and women lost rights previously held and sometimes taken for granted.

In the Leipzig Singakademie, for example, women, eligible for board positions as late as 1852, were no longer eligible by 1854.[41] After a long decline in male relative to female membership (Table 12.2C), the women—by now the large majority—were ejected from their former share of organizational leadership. The situation in Darmstadt was similar. In 1836, the Musikverein had been taken over by the city's main social organization, the Vereinigte Gesellschaft [united society]. In 1840, its chorus committee was limited by statute to the music director and four members of the tenor and bass sections chosen by the male singers. In 1856, the Musikverein split off from the Vereinigte Gesellschaft. At this point, the statutes forbade female members even to attend the annual meeting, much less vote for their leaders. Separate *Damen* and *Herren* committees were, in fact, elected at this time. However, these members were charged only with the admission of new singers.[42]

The situation in other cities was similar. In Krefeld the women kept their places in the leadership but complained in 1858 when an all-male committee ran a music festival in which the Krefeld Singverein performed.[43] The Singakademie of Vienna, founded in 1858, allowed women to vote for, but not be, leaders.[44] The Gemischte Chor of Zürich, founded in 1863, had a ladies' committee that reported concerns of the female members to the all-male board.[45] In Aachen, where in 1818 a mixed board of directors had been proposed, by 1868 women could join members of the male Gesangverein to sing mixed choral music by invitation only.[46] Reintegrated later in the century, they were granted three board positions (out of nine) in 1912. The committee of the whole, however, consisted of these three women and the entire male membership.[47]

Probably the most telling instance of change in chorus governance took place within Vienna's most prominent musical organization, the Gesellschaft der Musikfreunde [Society of the Friends of Music]. Organized choral singing in the Hapsburg city developed late out of governmental fears of political subversion: Austria's Prince Metternich is quoted as calling the male chorus movement "poison from Germany."[48] And in fact, the city's first male chorus, the Männergesangverein, was only established in 1843. Without organized mixed choral societies, Vienna's female choral singers had no membership opportunity as they sometimes did in Germany proper. Although the Gesellschaft had a few female members, as a *music* society, it was male-controlled.[49] For each public choral performance, the leadership recruited singers ad hoc, using available Gesellschaft members liberally supplemented by the professional, mixed Court Opera chorus, conservatory students, the Männergesangverein, or, as late as 1857, church choirboys.[50]

Surviving minutes, annual reports, and histories of the Gesellschaft show its leadership reluctant to organize a Singverein and only doing so in 1858 in response to competition from the newly formed Singakademie. Establishing a mixed chorus on the *Verein* model at such a late date marked a departure from Gesellschaft tradition. With women participating in broader areas of social and economic life, their likely interest brought the potential for large numbers of female members, in turn forcing the Gesellschaft leadership to define women's membership role in both the chorus and the parent society itself.

Not surprisingly, women fared better in the chorus, where they were allowed to vote for members of its all-male governing board.[51] Not long after, however, they lost ground in the Gesellschaft proper. Female Gesellschaft members had been permitted to attend and participate in the society's general meetings. In 1860, however, two changes were made. In response to pressure from the Singverein, chorus members (men and women both) who paid an extra contribution were allowed to join the parent society. This was a new right that created the potential for an influx of women. So at the same time, all women in the Gesellschaft lost the right to attend the general meeting and therefore the right to speak or vote. The debate on the issue of women's participation continued through the 1860s. With references to Adam's rib, Goethe, and Clara Schumann as the exception that proves the rule, among others, in 1868 the men granted women who contributed financially above a certain level to speak and vote in annual meetings by proxy only. All other women were to be organizationally silent.[52]

Despite these limitations, the predicted influx of women into the Singverein took place. The chorus began its first season with fifty-five women and eighty-eight men, the women's ranks supplemented by female voice students from the conservatory.[53] Four years later, female membership exceeded male membership for the first time. As the overall numbers grew, the proportion of women increased, and conservatory "ringers" were naturally no longer needed (Table 12.2D).[54]

As these examples show, after mid-century, choral societies became increasingly conservative in their handling of female members. Welcome as singers, women were more often explicitly denied leadership and decision-making opportunities than earlier in the century, as if to state a preference for established social practice over change. Institutional changes such as these ran parallel with artistic ones. As summarized in Table 12.3, the choral repertoire became increasingly historical. Beethoven's biggest choral works established themselves, the *Ninth Symphony* more strongly than earlier in the century, the *Missa Solemnis* for the first time. The Mendelssohn canon became more clearly ranked as his music faced competition from that of his successors. Robert Schumann's music remained a favorite long after his death and Luigi Cherubini's *Requiem in C Minor,* like the Beethoven *Missa,* held a higher place later in the century than previously.[55]

Equally striking are the growth in the number of performances recorded and the increase in shorter works relative to full-program compositions. Music societies incorporated vocal, chamber, and instrumental music into their programs, so that shorter choral pieces had increasingly greater chances of performance. Thus many of the small works on major composer worklists—Schubert's *Ellens Zweiter Gesang* and Brahms's songs for women's chorus with two horns and harp, Op. 17, for example—found places on the public concert stage.

These changes left less room for the oratorio. Oratorios of dead composers still found considerable favor after mid-century. But despite the continued creation of new oratorios, the most successful works composed after 1850 include only three, only one of them biblical (Friedrich Kiel's *Christus;* see Table 12.3). Meanwhile, formerly successful oratorios by Schneider, Spohr, and Hiller fell largely by the wayside.[56] Many composers, of course, continued to see the chorus itself as worth their effort. Of composers now highly regarded, however, only Liszt took the oratorio seriously. Despite the continued growth in choral singing and composition, as Donald Mintz has put it with regard to Mendelssohn, established genres such as the oratorio "moved to the fringes of progressive musical life as the century moved on."[57]

Mintz's use of the word "progressive" here is telling. The increasing status of dramatic opera on Wagnerian lines and questions about whether the oratorio could or should be truly "dramatic" went hand in glove.[58] Some of

Table 12.3. Successful Mixed Choral Works with Orchestra in Rank Order, Composition 1815–80, Performance 1850–80.

Composer	Title	Genre	First performance in a German-speaking city	No. from 1850	Rate per year
Brahms	*Ein deutsches Requiem*	sui generis	1868	89[a]	7.42
Max Bruch	*Odysseus*	oratorio	1873	45	6.4
Mendelssohn	*Elijah*	oratorio	1847	161	5.37
Mendelssohn	*Paulus*	oratorio	1836	158	5.27
Beethoven	*Symphony No. 9*	symphony	1824	150	5.0
Verdi	*Requiem*	liturgical	1875	25	5.0
Brahms	*Schicksalslied*	cantata	1871	44	4.88
Bruch	*Schön Ellen*	ballad	1867	55	4.23
Mendelssohn	*Die erste Walpurgisnacht*	cantata	1832	126	4.2
Friedrich Kiel	*Christus*	oratorio	1874	22	3.66
Schumann	*Der Rose Pilgerfahrt*	cantata	1852	98	3.5
Schumann	*Das Paradies und die Peri*	oratorio	1843	103	3.33
Liszt	*The Legend of St. Elizabeth*	oratorio	1866	43	2.87
Beethoven	*Missa Solemnis*	liturgical	1824	76	2.53
Cherubini	*Requiem in C*	liturgical	1819	66	2.2

Note: See notes and sources for Table 12.1. Additional sources: Klaus Blum, *Hundert Jahre Ein deutsches Requiem von Johannes Brahms* (Tutzing: Hans Schneider, 1971), 110; August Böhm, *Geschichte des Singvereines der Gesellschaft der Musikfreunde in Wien Beilage* (Vienna: Adolf Holzhausen, 1908), *Beilage*: 38–43; *Deutsche Musik-Zeitung, 1860–62; Der gemischte Chor Zürich* (Zurich: Zürcher and Furrer, 1888), 42–56; *Der Gesangverein Basel in den Jahren 1824–1899. Festschrift beim fünfundsiebzigjährigen Bestand des Gesangvereins* (Basel: Kreis, 1899), 60–63; Albert Göhler, *Der Riedel-Verein zu Leipzig. Eine Denkschrift zur Feier sines fünfzigjährigen Bestehens* (Leipzig: Riedel-Verein, 1904), 3–52; Max Kalbeck, *Johannes Brahms*, 2d ed. rev. (Berlin: Deutsche Brahms-Gesellschaft, 1908), vol. 2, 281–83; *Kölnische Zeitung*, December 1875–February 1876, June 1877; Peter Muck, *Einhundert Jahre Berliner Philharmonisches Orchester. Darstellung in Dokumenten* (Tutzing: Hans Schneider, 1982), vol. 3; *Neue Zeitschrift für Musik* 63 (1867)–76 (1880), no.27; Carl Ferdinand Pohl, *Denkschrift aus Anlass des fünfundzwanzigjährigen Bestehens des Singvereines der Gesellschaft der Musikfreunde in Wien* (Vienna: the Singverein, 1883), 31–52; Pohl, *Die Gesellschaft der Musikfreunde des österreichen Kaiserstaates und ihr Conservatorium* (Vienna: Wilhelm Braumüller, 1871), 72–90; Matthias Schwarzer, *Die Oratorien von Max Bruch. Eine Quellenstudie* (Kassel: Merseburger, 1988).

a. The three-movement premiere in Vienna on December 1, 1867, is not counted. However, otherwise complete performances before Brahms added the fifth movement have been counted.

the newer choral works crossed generic divides by carrying dramatic or narrative uses of the chorus from the oratorio into the secular realm. Popular examples include Bruch's *Schön Ellen* and Robert Schumann's *Rose Pilgerfahrt*. Compared with *Elijah* or *Saint Paul,* these works are shorter, lighter in texture, and more genial in style. The Schumann has been called both a cantata and an oratorio; the first edition score titles it a *Märchen*—a fairy tale.

These compositions notwithstanding, changes in notions of what counted as dramatic meant that by and large the chorus would now send messages of different sorts. In the three liturgical works and two Brahms pieces on Table 12.3, for example, the chorus conveys a broadly human perspective on a text. But the kind of characterization seen in the oratorio—divided parts, choruses representing groups of people or God, for example—has become less common, even as the reversion to a standard four-part choral texture helps mitigate the ill effects of a top-heavy Singverein.

A good example of this approach to the chorus and its message is the Brahms *Schicksalslied* (1871), on a poem by Friedrich Hölderlin. As Table 12.3 shows, it was one of the more successful choral works composed after the death of Mendelssohn. It also exemplifies a new, shorter choral composition easily integrated into concert programs of the time.[59] Following in the wake of the *Requiem,* the smaller *Schicksalslied* offered performers a piece in a similar vocal style without the major effort of the larger one. Further, its contemplative character stands in contrast to the oratorios of Mendelssohn and his contemporaries. Gone are characters such as Elijah or Paul, replaced in the *Requiem* with unnamed soprano and bass soloists and not in the *Schicksalslied* at all. This change, in which distance and reflection replace dramatic immediacy, is echoed in musical structures. Where the oratorios had presented a sequence of genres to push the story forward, in the Brahms works, tempo changes create sections more akin to movements of a symphony.

The chorus's role in the *Schicksalslied* may be its greatest difference from the oratorios of the earlier era. Because there are no soloists, the chorus is the only bearer of the text. The text uses the first and second persons—"you" and "us"—thus giving the singers a human role to play. But it differs significantly from their role in the oratorio. There, the chorus gets key texts at key places. In *Elijah,* for example, after a thunderous show of earthquakes, crashing waves, and fires, God comes as "a still small voice" sung by the chorus first in unison, then in chorale parts. Later in the work, the ultimate didactic message comes as a chorale at the end of a dramatic unit, "He that shall endure to the end shall be saved." In the *Schicksalslied,* on the other hand, a point is made, or, one might argue, left intentionally unclear, by the *absence* of the chorus at an important place in the music.[60]

The piece consists of an adagio introduction, two contrasting choral sections, and a modified return of the adagio at the end [*Nachspiel*]. The first choral section takes the adagio tempo, key of E-flat, quadruple meter, largely homorhythmic texture, and elegiac, contemplative affection from the introduction (mm. 29–103). A triple-meter allegro follows (mm. 104–379). Contrapuntal and tonally ambiguous, it projects an agitated, turbulent mood. The contrast between the two choral sections reflects the text. In the first two verses of the poem, the chorus addresses the "blessed spirits" [*selige Genien*] who wander in bliss, "free of fate like a sleeping baby." The fate of humanity (the choral allegro), on the other hand, is something else entirely: "To us is given no place of rest;" instead, we are "thrown from cliff to cliff, forever down to uncertainty." The last line of the second section seems to end the piece as it does the poem: The allegro finishes with four statements of an "uncertainty" [*Ungewisse*] motive, each softer and thinner in texture than the one before (mm. 317–364). Underpinning the last three statements is a dominant pedal point on C in the cello and, ominously, the tympani. The chorus and the suffering humanity it represents seem to fade away to nothing at all.

Yet the piece is not over. As the music winds down (mm. 364–379), the dominant pedal recasts itself as a tonic and the orchestral adagio returns in C instead of E-flat (mm. 380–409). Emotionally, the music evokes the same light and carefree spirits as at the beginning. This time, however, the chorus is gone, having been left hanging on the dominant in the allegro (m. 364). The beauty of the last section still moves the listener, perhaps even more after the tumultuous middle section than before it. But it leaves the chorus in a different position entirely: Having expressed the eternal hopelessness of suffering humanity, it is left silent—in a live performance mutely facing the audience—as the orchestra completes the heavenly vision alone. Brahms had his doubts about the chorus's silence, calling it possibly a "foolish whim" [*dummer Einfall*].[61] And at one point he even sketched choral parts for the closing adagio.[62] John Daverio suggests that their deletion "may well have been motivated by a desire to avoid too great a sense of finality."[63] Indeed, the deleted vocal parts have a retrospective character reminiscent of the short vocal "tag" phrases at the ends of the first two movements of the German Requiem (mm. 154–58 and 333–37 respectively). Irrespective of Brahms's intent, however, in performance, the silent chorus members no longer "own" the text and its theme the way they would in an oratorio. Rather, they receive the message (and the chance to ponder it) as does the audience. An early reviewer remarked that the orchestra controls the composition, allowing the chorus only a subsidiary role.[64] From that perspective, any optimistic interpretation of the piece draws necessarily on the weighty and heartfelt conclusion for orchestra alone.

This is a long way from the blessed assurance of the oratorio from earlier in the century. While Romantic composers sometimes allowed instrumental music to complete what the voice had started (Robert Schumann's *Dichterliebe* comes to mind), silencing a mass of choral singers to make a point instrumentally was striking. Affirmative by definition, the big works of Mendelssohn, Schumann, Spohr, and Schneider had allowed the chorus and its members to bask in personal, social, political, aesthetic, and moral optimism. On the other hand, while Brahms was capable of overt triumphalism (in fact composing a *Triumphlied* around the time of the *Schicksalslied*), the ambiguity and pessimism of Hölderlin's text would have been beyond the conception of the earlier composers. And although the *Schicksalslied* is an extreme example, it does symbolize visually and audibly the chorus's diminished role in furthering Germany's musical tradition.

The dramatic oratorio rose with the mixed choral society on the Verein model and fell with its establishment as a branch of professional concert culture. That is, "progressive" musical life left the oratorio behind even as the mixed choral society lost its hold on independence and social innovation. In a discussion of the voice in opera, Carolyn Abbate argues that performers complicate authority, allowing them, in ways that vary from one genre to another, to create voices independent of the historical author.[65] On these terms, the German mixed chorus after mid-century had less of its own authority and less independence from the composer's message, while the message itself turned from the idealism previously expected to inspire listeners.

Choral independence was not completely lost, however; the *Liebhaber* tradition of maintaining musical culture voluntarily through participation still obtained as the century progressed. German men, for example, continued as avid choral singers in male-only societies. Thus the change in gender balance in the mixed chorus suggests that in part at least, men no longer considered the vision and purpose it now represented worth their time and energy. New groups of singers, such as publicly performing women's and workers' choruses in the last third of the century, on the other hand, featured the same social innovation that had characterized the earlier mixed societies, along with a marginal social position the older groups had been able to shake. Using their voices as musical instruments and vehicles for verbal texts, the men and women of the chorus still communicated socially in ways that could be understood.[66]

Notes

1. Thomas Nipperdey, "Verein als soziale Struktur in Deutschland im späten 18. und frühen 19. Jahrhundert. Eine Fallstudie zur Modernisierung I," in Nipperdey, *Gesellschaft, Kultur, Theorie. Aufsätze zur neueren Geschichte* (Göttingen: Vandenhoeck and Ruprecht, 1976), 174–205; David Blackbourn and Geoff Eley, *The Peculiarities of German History: Bourgeois Society and Politics in Nineteenth-Century Germany* (Oxford: Oxford University Press, 1984), 195–97; Richard van Dülmen, *The Society of the Enlightenment: The Rise of the Middle Class and Enlightenment Culture in Germany*, trans. Anthony Williams (New York: St. Martin's Press, 1992).

2. Wolfram Siemann, *The German Revolution of 1848–49* (1985), trans. Christiane Banerji (London: Macmillan, 1998), 37–38. On adherence to rules, see David Blackbourn, *The Long Nineteenth Century: A History of Germany, 1780–1918* (New York: Oxford University Press, 1998), 212. On general meetings, see van Dülmen, *Society of the Enlightenment*, 87–88.

3. Dieter Düding, *Organisierter gesellschaftlicher Nationalismus in Deutschland (1808–1847): Bedeutung und Funktion der Turner- und Sängervereine für die deutsche Nationalbewegung* (Munich: Oldenbourg, 1984), 162–65; quotation 165.

4. Van Dülmen, *Society of the Enlightenment*, 57, 89, 97, 123, 129.

5. Geneviève Fraisse and Michelle Perrot, eds., *Emerging Feminism from Revolution to World War*, vol. 4, *A History of Women in the West*, (Cambridge, Mass.: Belknap Press of Harvard University Press, 1993), 4, 48–53; Joan B. Landes, *Women and the Public Sphere in the Age of the French Revolution* (Ithaca, N.Y.: Cornell University Press, 1988), Ch. 6; Geoff Eley, "Nations, Publics, and Political Cultures: Placing Habermas in the Nineteenth Century," in *Habermas and the Public Sphere*, ed. Craig Calhoun (Cambridge, Mass: MIT Press, 1993), 309–11; Ute Frevert, *Women in German History: From Bourgeois Emancipation to Sexual Liberation* (1986), trans. Stuart McKinnon-Evans in assoc. with Terry Bond and Barbara Norton (New York: Berg, 1989), 11–21, 115, 138–39; Blackbourn and Eley, *Peculiarities*, 242–43. See also *Gender Relations in German History: Power, Agency, and Experience from the Sixteenth to the Twentieth Century*, ed. Lynn Abrams and Elizabeth Harvey (London: University College London Press, 1996), 16–27.

6. Thomas Nipperdey, *Germany from Napoleon to Bismarck 1800–1866* (1983), trans. Daniel Nolan (Princeton, N.J.: Princeton University Press, 1996), 106; Sabine Rumpel-Nienstedt, "'Thäterinnen der Liebe'—Frauen in Wohltätigkeitsvereinen," in *"Schimpfende Weiber und patriotische Jungfrauen": Frauen im Vormärz und in der Revolution 1848–49*, ed. Carola Lipp (Moos: Elster, 1986), 206–31.

7. Georg Schünemann, *Die Singakademie zu Berlin 1791–1941* (Regensburg: Bosse, 1941), 16.

8. *Grundverfassung der Sing-Akademie zu Berlin* (Berlin: Gädicke Brothers, [1821]), Arts. 12–15.

9. Ibid., Art. 5. In an 1833 letter, Lea Mendelssohn notes that underage women were not permitted to vote. Quoted in Peter Ranft, *Felix Mendelssohn Bartholdy. Eine Lebenschronik* (Leipzig: VEB Deutscher Verlag für Musik, 1972), 34.

10. Dietrich Sasse, "Berlin," *Die Musik in Geschichte und Gegenwart*, 1st ed. (1949–51), vol. 1, col. 1721; Schünemann, *Singakademie zu Berlin*, 16.

11. Walter Salmen, *Das Konzert: Eine Kulturgeschichte* (Munich: C. H. Beck, 1988), 49.

12. Schünemann, *Singakademie zu Berlin*, 24.

13. *Statuten der Sing-Academie des Musikdirektor's Schulz in Leipzig* (Leipzig: J. B. Hirschfeldt, 1815), 8–9.

14. Alfons Fritz, *Festschrift aus Anlass des hundertjährigen Bestehens des Städischen Gesangvereins Aachen, 27 Januar 1921* (Aachen: Wissenschaftliches Antiquariat und Verlagshandlung Creutzer, 1921), 4.

15. Friedrich Schmidt, *Hundert Jahre Darmstädter Musikverein. Eine Geschichte seiner Vorläufer, seines Werdens und seiner Entwicklung* (Darmstadt: U. Bergsträsser's Verlag W. Kleinschmidt, 1932), 26–31, with quotations from bylaws.

16. *Statuten des Cäcilien-Vereins zu Bingen* (Bingen: A. J. Pennrich, [1848]), 3, 9.

17. For a different approach to evaluating the relative success of choral works in nineteenth-century Germany, see Howard E. Smither, *A History of the Oratorio*, vol. 4: *The Oratorio in the Nineteenth and Twentieth Centuries* (Chapel Hill: University of North Carolina Press, 2000), 4.

18. On opera choruses in this era, see Karen Ahlquist, "Opera, Theatre, and Audience in Antebellum New York" (Ph.D. dissertation, University of Michigan, 1991), 198–202; Philip Gossett, "Becoming a Citizen: The Chorus in *Risorgimento* Opera," *Cambridge Opera Journal* 2, no. 1 (March 1990): 41–64; James Parakilas, "Political Representation and the Chorus in Nineteenth-Century Opera," *19th Century Music* 16, no. 2 (fall 1992): 181–202.

19. Leon Botstein, "The Aesthetics of Assimilation and Affirmation: Reconstructing the Career of Felix Mendelssohn," in *Mendelssohn and His World*, ed. R. Larry Todd (Princeton, N.J.: Princeton University Press, 1991), 6, 33. Howard Smither, who has studied many nineteenth-century German oratorios, says that there may be "a pessimistic oratorio—textually or musically—from that period, . . . but none comes to mind." Personal communication, March 12, 2001.

20. See, for example, "Wohl dem, der den Herrn fürchtet" and "Siehe, der Hüter Israels" from *Elijah*, and "Es wird ein Stern aus Jacob aufgehn" from the oratorio fragment, *Christus*.

21. Botstein, "Aesthetics of Assimilation," 34.

22. Henry F. Chorley, *Music and Manners in France and Germany* (1844), 3 vols. (New York: Da Capo, 1984), vol. 1, 245.

23. Chorley, *Music and Manners,* vol. 1, 230–31, 233–34.

24. In this regard, differences between Germany proper and Austria are clear. Leon Botstein's statement that "political control before 1848 suppressed public cultural life" is best applied to Austria only. "Listening Through Reading: Musical Literacy and the Concert Audience" *19th-Century Music* 16, no. 2 (Fall 1992): 133.

25. Dieter Langewiesche, *Liberalism in Germany,* trans. Christiane Banerji (Princeton, N.J.: Princeton University Press, 2000), 24–25.

26. Hans-Werner Boresch, "Der 'alte Traum vom alten Deutschland': Musikfeste im 19. Jahrhundert als Nationalfeste," *Die Musikforschung* 52, no. 1 (1999): 55–69; Düding, *Organisierter gesellschaftlicher Nationalismus,* 178–204; Düding, "The Nineteenth-Century German Nationalist Movement as a Movement of Societies," *Nation-Building in Central Europe,* ed. Hagen Schulze (Leamington Spa: Berg, 1987), 19–50.

27. Harald Pfeiffer, *Heidelberger Musikleben in der ersten Hälfte des 19. Jahrhunderts* (Heidelberg: Brigitte Guderjahn, 1989), 100–102.

28. *Zeitschrift für Deutschlands Musik-Vereine und Dilettanten* 1 (Karlsruhe, 1841), 229; quoted in Pfeiffer, *Heidelberger Musikleben,* 102. On German national identity at music and song festivals, see Cecelia Hopkins Porter, *The Rhine as Musical Metaphor: Cultural Identity in German Romantic Music* (Boston: Northeastern University Press, 1996), 171–74; Alf, *Geschichte,* 187–88.

29. Dagmar Herzog, "Religious Dissent and the Roots of German Feminism," in Abrams and Harvey, *Gender Relations in German History,* 82.

30. Siemann, *German Revolution,* 187; Jurgen Thym, "Schumann in Brendel's *Neue Zeitschrift,*" in *Mendelssohn and Schumann: Essays on Their Music and its Context,* ed. Jon W. Finson and R. Larry Todd (Durham, N.C.: Duke University Press, 1984), 25.

31. Elaine Glovka Spencer, *Police and the Social Order in German Cities: The Düsseldorf District, 1848–1914* (DeKalb: Northern Illinois University Press, 1992), 30–33, 39–41; Siemann, *German Revolution,* 216–17; Nipperdey, *Germany,* 599–608; James J. Sheehan, *German History, 1770–1866* (Oxford: Clarendon Press, 1989), 716–29; Frevert, *Women in German History,* 324.

32. Otto Elben, *Der volksthümliche deutsche Männergesang. Geschichte und Stellung im Leben der Nation; der deutsche Sängerbund und seine Glieder,* 2nd ed. (1887), reprint ed. by Friedhelm Brusniak and Franz Krautwurst (Wolfenbüttel: Möseler, 1991), 141–42; Düding, "Nineteenth-century German Nationalist Movement," 43–44; Friedhelm Brusniak, "Chor und Chormusik," *Die Musik in Geschichte und Gegenwart,* 2nd ed. (Kassel: Bärenreiter, 1995), *Sachteil* vol. 2, cols. 800–801.

33. Blackbourn and Eley, *Peculiarities,* 190; Blackbourn, *Long Nineteenth Century,* 232.

34. Kurt Gudewill, "Gemischter Chor," *Die Musik in Geschichte und Gegenwart,* 1st ed., vol. 4 (1955): cols. 1700–01.

35. On the Lower Rhine Festival choruses, see Porter, *Rhine as a Musical Metaphor,* 205–7.

36. "Musikfeste," *Musikalischer Hausfreund* (Mainz: Schott, 1829–30), 54–55.

37. Alf, *Geschichte und Bedeutung,* 236.

38. *Erinnerungsblätter für die Mitglieder des Nürnberger Sängertages* 3, whole no. 52 (June 6, 1857): 84. I thank Friedhelm Brusniak for calling this periodical to my attention and furnishing copies.

39. Chorus lists identify each female singer as either *Frau* (Mrs.) or *Fräulein* (Miss).

40. *Allgemeine Musikalische Zeitung,* new series 10, no. 25 (June 23, 1875): 395.

41. Paul Langer, *Chronik der Leipziger Singakademie* (Leipzig: Julius Klinkhardt, 1902), 36, 43.

42. Schmidt, *Hundert Jahre,* 42, 72–73.

43. Theodor Müller-Reuter, *Festschrift zum Jubiläums-Konzert des Singvereins in Krefeld am 17. Dezember 1910* (Krefeld: Singverein, 1910), 31.

44. *Satzungen der Singakademie in Wien* (Vienna: Singakademic, 1869), 4.

45. *Der gemischte Chor Zürich Festschrift zur Feier seines 25–jährigen Bestehens* (Zurich: Zürcher and Furrer, 1888), 19.

46. *Deutsche Musik Zeitung* 2, no. 26 (29 June 1861), 206.

47. Fritz, *Festschrift,* 45.

48. Gottfried Kraus, ed., *Musik in Oesterreich. Eine Chronik in Daten, Dokumenten, Essays und Bildern* (Vienna: Christian Brandstätter, 1989), 262.

49. The distinction here between a music society and a choral society is important. Some music societies included choruses, others orchestras and/or chamber music groups. I have found no evidence of women in leadership roles in any music society in this period.

50. August von Böhm, *Geschichte des Singvereins der Gesellschaft der Musikfreunde in Wien* (Vienna: A. Holzhausen, 1908), 5, 26, 36–37, 51; Pohl, *Denkschrift,* 6.

51. Böhm, *Geschichte des Singvereins,* 64, 134.

52. Böhm, *Geschichte des Singvereins,* 126–33; Albrecht Claus, *Geschichte des Singvereins der Gesellschaft der Musikfreunde 1858–1933* (Vienna: Stockinger and Morsack, 1933), 3–5.

53. Claus, *Geschichte des Singvereines,* 154.

54. Also in Vienna, the Singakademie imposed a moratorium on new female members in hopes of keeping an acceptable gender balance. *Jahres-Bericht der unter dem Allerhöchsten Protectorate Seiner Kaiserlichen Hoheit des durchlauchtigsten Herrn Erzherzogs Carl Ludwig stehenden Wiener Singakademie* 25 (Vienna: Singakademie, 1883), 4.

55. Music of earlier composers also contributed to the growing historicism, including that of Mozart, Haydn, Handel, and especially Bach, whose Matthew Passion increasingly replaced the Graun *Tod Jesu* on Good Friday programs. On historicism at the Lower Rhine Music Festivals, see Porter, *Rhine as Musical Metaphor,* 211–12;

on historicism and the nineteenth-century German oratorio, see Smither, *History of the Oratorio,* vol. 4, 8, 9, 16–20, 63, 110–14.

56. Hiller's music remained in the repertoire until he retired as music director at Cologne in 1884. The Spohr oratorios were occasionally performed after mid-century, the Schneider rarely. For the theoretical underpinnings of the oratorio's decline, see Glenn Stanley, "The Oratorio in Prussia and Protestant Germany: 1812–1848" (Ph.D. dissertation, Columbia University, 1988), Chapter VIII.

57. Donald Mintz, "1848, Anti-Semitism, and the Mendelssohn Reception," in *Mendelssohn Studies,* ed. R. Larry Todd (Cambridge: Cambridge University Press, 1992), 148. On the decline in oratorio composition, see Smither, *History of the Oratorio,* vol. 4, 63.

58. Stanley, "Oratorio," 270–72; Smither, *History of the Oratorio,* vol. 4, 83–86.

59. Other such works include Bruch's *Schön Ellen,* Niels Gade's *Comala* and *Erlkönigs Tochter* (Danish: *Elverskud),* and Brahms's *Nänie, Triumphlied,* and *Gesang der Parzen.*

60. The long *Nachspiel* has been much discussed by Brahms scholars. For a summary of the main lines of argument, see John Daverio, "The *Wechsel der Töne* in Brahms's Schicksalslied," *Journal of the American Musicological Society* 46, no. 1 (spring 1993): 87–90.

61. The comment comes from a letter of about October 24, 1871, to conductor Karl Reinthaler in Bremen. See *Johannes Brahms Briefwechsel,* ed. Wilhelm Altmann (Berlin: Deutsche Brahms-Gesellschaft, 1908), vol. 3, 40. An English translation is found in *Johannes Brahms. Life and Letters,* selected and annotated by Styra Avins, trans. Josef Eisinger and Styra Avins (New York: Oxford University Press, 1997), 428.

62. Mm. 390–95 and 402–06. The autograph score is in the Library of Congress in Washington. For a transcription of the passages with the deleted choral parts, see Daverio, "*Wechsel der Töne,*" 88–89.

63. Daverio, "*Wechsel der Töne,*" 108.

64. August Guckeisen, *Neue Berliner Musikzeitung* 26, no. 47 (November 20, 1872), 371. The reported performance took place in Cologne. For further reception, see Annette Kreutziger-Herr, "Hölderlin, Brahms und das *Schicksalslied,*" in *Johannes Brahms: Quellen—Text—Rezeption—Interpretation. Internationaler Brahms-Kongress Hamburg 1997,* ed. Friedhelm Krummacher and Michael Struck with Constantin Floros and Peter Petersen (Munich: G. Henle, 1999), 363–66. Kreutziger-Herr suggests that "concrete pictures" (i.e., words) would have diminished the peaceful vision at the end of the work (367).

65. Carolyn Abbate, "Opera; or, the Envoicing of Women," in *Musicology and Difference: Gender and Sexuality in Music Scholarship,* ed. Ruth Solie (Berkeley: University of California Press, 1993), 234–36.

66. The title phrase of this essay is borrowed from Rosabeth Moss Kanter, *Men and Women of the Corporation* (New York: Basic Books, 1977).

13

Symphonic Choirs: Understanding the Borders of Professionalism

ROSALYND SMITH

The members of the choir lower their scores as the last notes of Beethoven's *Missa Solemnis* die away. It is an exhausting work and not easy, but they feel confident that the performance in two days' time will be a good one. Opening the city's annual arts festival is not a new experience for them, and as usual, they are working with one of the best orchestras in the country. They feel that the conductor and soloists have all lived up to the glowing international reputations that preceded them, and they know that the performance is eagerly awaited; although the concert hall is a large one, it is sold out for two performances. But as they file offstage, not all of them are talking about the performance; there is other choir business to be done. One of the altos (the choir's librarian) seeks out the manager to check whether a parcel of scores has arrived. A huddle of singers near the greenroom door is organizing an impromptu fund-raising committee. A bass and a soprano are discussing the agenda for next week's board meeting. One of the section leaders is speaking to a new singer about the dress code for the concert.

The contradictions inherent in this scene are obvious: These highly skilled musicians have been working with professional commitment and concentration toward a performance that will take place within the world of professional music at the highest levels, yet the musicians involved are amateurs. But this scene is not unusual. It is repeated in classical music circles throughout the world where professional concert performances call for large-scale choral forces to sing with an orchestra.

This type of choir is referred to here as a "symphonic choir": the kind of choir whose core business is to sing the standard oratorio and large-scale accompanied choral repertoire with a symphony orchestra. Such choirs may be formally associated with an orchestra or independent; they may perform other types of repertoire as well; and they may be part of a larger choral organization that includes, for example, a chamber choir. One thing that most have in common, as well as a repertoire focus, is that the members are not paid.

Professional choirs do exist, but apart from opera choruses, elite chamber choirs, and recording choruses, they are rare. Most professional orchestras could not continue to present the standard choral-orchestral works in their programs if they had to use the services of a large-scale, fully professional choir. Even in the United States, where the more prestigious orchestras usually pay at least a professional core of the chorus, most professional orchestras do not. From the standpoint of the choirs, however, this involvement with professional music making has implications that make them stand apart from other amateur and community choirs.

This essay examines the nature of amateurism in the context of symphonic choirs and considers the way the choirs and their members negotiate this gray area between the amateur and professional music worlds. Data are drawn from a study of one Australian symphonic choir conducted between 1996 and 1999. From the outset of the study, it was clear that singers were aware of their ambiguous status and of the tensions it created. The final stage of the study demonstrated the consequences for the choir when singers and management took differing views of their roles and responsibilities and the delicate balance between professional and amateur elements was not maintained.

What is an "amateur"? Etymology suggests it is one who does something for the love of it. In common parlance, it is one who does something only for the love of it, not for monetary gain. But the word also has negative connotations, as in the epithet "amateurish," applied to work of less than professional standard.

In musical performance, especially, perhaps, in choral singing, the distinction between the amateur and the professional is far from clear-cut. Ruth Finnegan comments that "the concept of 'amateur' musician is a relative, partly arbitrary and sometimes disputed label rather than a settled division."[1] Robert Hutchison and Andrew Feist put it this way: "The amateur and professional arts are intertwined and interdependent; the term amateur is not unambiguously separated from 'professional;' rather than a clear amateur/professional divide, there is a complex amateur/professional continuum or spectrum of ambition, accomplishment and activity."[2] Hutchison and Feist propose the model of a continuum that takes into account this wide spectrum, its two ends representing the extreme cases. At one end is the complete amateur: the self-taught artist who pursues an activity as a spare-time recreation or hobby, with no serious artistic aspirations, lacking experience, originality, status and income from the pursuit. At the other end is the complete professional: creative and talented, fully trained, experienced and businesslike, harboring high artistic aspirations, and enjoying the income appropriate to public recognition as a professional.[3]

This model may be close to the way most of us think about amateurs and professionals, but it gives a misleading picture when applied to choristers. The implication is that singers will gradually progress along this continuum, some stopping near the amateur end, others continuing to achieve more on each of the criteria listed until they can be counted as real professionals. This is not what we find in a good amateur choir. The singers there will typically be at quite different points on the continuum, depending on which criteria are examined. On the criteria of income and usually of time allocated, they will be at the amateur end, but some may rival professionals in experience, artistic aspirations, even in skill or training.

A more appropriate model for amateurism has been put forward by Robert A. Stebbins, who has studied amateurs in a number of fields, including astronomy, baseball, and theater.[4] Amateurs, according to Stebbins, engage in *serious leisure,* defined as "the systematic pursuit of an amateur, hobbyist or volunteer activity that is sufficiently substantial and interesting for the participant to find a career there in the acquisition and expression of its special skills and knowledge."[5] Other indications of the *seriousness* of this kind of activity include significant personal effort and perseverance, the unique ethos that grows up around such pursuits, and the tendency participants have to identify strongly with them. Amateurs reap durable benefits from their pursuits, namely "self-actualization, self-enrichment, self-expression, recreation or renewal of self, feelings of accomplishment, enhancement of self-image, social interaction and belongingness, and lasting physical products of the activity."[6] Casual leisure activities, by contrast, are undertaken with less regularity, commitment, and perseverance.

* * *

This definition of what Stebbins calls "modern amateurism" seems to fit much better the reality not only of symphonic choirs, but of much choral activity, where commitment, accomplishment, and self-enrichment are necessary ingredients of the experience. What sets many of the best symphonic choirs apart is that they function on some levels as purely professional organizations. Some of them perform exclusively with professional orchestras, conductors, and soloists, receiving substantial fees that are shared only indirectly with individual performers. Performances by such choirs will be regularly reviewed in the press, and music critics will rarely make allowances for the amateur status of the singers.

In most pursuits, it is relatively easy to distinguish the amateur because a professional equivalent exists, and most discussions of amateurism assume that this is normally the case. Stebbins states, "The term amateur should be used only with those that constitute for somebody, a *professional* work role."[7] Yet the rarity of large professional choirs other than opera choruses means that for practical purposes, amateur symphonic choirs contain the most professional singers of their kind performing.

How do the singers in these choirs, their directors, and management regard their status? The term "semi-professional" is sometimes heard in an attempt to describe this middle ground and perhaps to depict an organization that is amateur without being amateurish. Can this ambivalence lead to tensions deriving from contradictory goals, or to opposing views between performers and management? Or do the professional milieu and standards merely serve to inspire and challenge the singers?

*   *   *

A study of an amateur symphonic choir in Australia, consisting of a survey of members and later interviews with some retired members, attempted to answer these questions and elicit information about the composition and opinions of membership for the benefit of the choir's committee of management.

The choir in question is based in one of Australia's largest cities and at the time the study began had been in existence for a little more than thirty years. For most of that time, it had been the choir that performed the standard choral literature with the city's best professional orchestra. In the past, sections of the choir had performed a much wider repertoire, including light or popular music and a cappella repertoire (the organization included a separate chamber choir). With the advent of a new music director, the focus of the choir had been narrowed to its core business of singing with the orchestra and presenting its own series of concerts, also with orchestra. There were occasionally engagements by other organizations such as the city's annual arts festival.

The choir was a not-for-profit organization, employing a part-time music director, a manager, and, later in the period of the study, a second administrator. Management was in the hands of a committee of management with broad community representation and limited singer representation, advised by a committee that more directly represented the interests of the singers. The choir had started life as an unincorporated association, but as its budget grew and it began to attract some government funding, it was incorporated. Shortly after this study began, the committee of management was replaced by a two-tier system that allowed less direct input from the singers but enabled the choir to draw on the experience, expertise, and contacts of members of the community. Given the now substantial amount of public funding that was received, the object was to acknowledge accountability to the community and to embrace a management structure considered more in keeping with the professional milieu in which the choir operated.

There were around 250 singing members, not all of whom sang in every concert. The choir prepared eight or nine major programs each year, some of them performed more than once. While the choir received a fee for all performances other than its own concerts, the singers did not, but instead paid an annual fee of around A$100 to participate. The survey followed closely on the appointment of a new director, at a time when there had been a rethinking of goals and priorities, a significant turnover of membership, and the introduction of a more stringent system of re-auditioning.

A survey was given or mailed to all singing members of the choir, and responses were received from 76.49 percent. The questionnaire included both closed- and open-ended questions. Many of the questions were designed to collect demographic and statistical information of value only to the choir itself. Other information, especially the qualitative data describing members' views on a range of issues, is of more general interest in considering the nature of amateur music performance.

Choir members were not asked to comment directly on issues relating to amateurism or professionalism. They wrote about their reasons for joining the choir and the aspects of their involvement they most valued. They were generous in the extended answers they gave to the open-ended questions and seemed eager to express what the choir meant to them. Their descriptions of what they gained from their involvement were often passionate and even moving, as this selection demonstrates:

> A fantastic creative and spiritual outlet that occurs on a regular basis—quite addictive! Adds meaning to life.

> Singing and performing with [the choir] is a very enriching and nurturing aspect to my well-being. The choir has developed enormously during the past three years and is now an organization of which I am immensely proud to be a part of.

I have sung since I could talk and will continue to sing until I die. I enjoy the performance opportunities provided by being in [the choir]. I get a real buzz out of coming to grips with unfamiliar works and "conquering" them.

[The choir] has been for me the most important continuing activity of the last twenty years. It was my lifeline after the accident, at times even my raison d'être [*sic*]. My social life, my continuing musical education and a great privilege to have worked with so many fabulous conductors over that time.

Singing has helped me relearn coordination in both my speech and thought patterns. Apart from the physical improvement, my sense of importance in myself and as a member cannot be measured.

The ground covered by these comments is remarkably similar to the list that Stebbins proposes as the benefits of amateurism: All the points he mentions are here, even "lasting physical products of the activity," which might be less typical for singers.

In their remarks about the daily business of the choir, singers commented slightly more often on rehearsals than on performances, and their rehearsal comments are of particular interest. The favorable comments were mostly about the recent improvement in the organization and conduct of rehearsals and expressed strong appreciation for the new director's skill as a conductor and his ability to make rehearsals both satisfying and enjoyable. The negative comments were minor but numerous and varied; targets included poor lighting, inefficient organization of the coffee break, hard seats, and the undermining effect of the few singers who tapped their feet or talked during rehearsal or whose musical preparation was inadequate.

Both kinds of remarks indicate that rehearsals were not regarded as merely a means to an end—the all-important performance. Singers valued the rehearsal experience in itself. It was clearly seen as the core of their leisure activity, and they wanted it to be enjoyable even though they had to work hard.

Remarks made by a number of singers about the social climate of the choir suggest the same thing. When asked how highly they valued a number of aspects of their participation, few rated socializing with members highly, and it was also evident that this was not an important reason for joining the choir in the first place. However, they made it clear that they wanted a welcoming, collegial atmosphere at rehearsals and they wanted to get to know the other singers better. Some suggested ways in which the choir could foster a better social atmosphere, while others felt that the barriers posed by the size of the choir and the nature of rehearsal were insuperable: "I would like to get to know more people at [the choir] but find the break an almost impossible time. . . . I don't know what can be done about that—as I really appreciate the way we start on time, finish on time and work hard all night."

This emphasis on the experience of rehearsal confirms the findings of a study by Susana Juniu, Ted Tedrick, and Rosangela Boyd into the intrinsic and extrinsic motivations of amateur and professional orchestral musicians.[8] This study found that there was little difference between how the two groups of musicians felt when it came to performances: for both amateurs and professionals the thrill of being onstage, the appreciative audience, and the challenge of performance produced a high level of intrinsic motivation. When it came to rehearsal, however, there was a significant difference between the two groups. Professionals were more influenced by the extrinsic motivation of remuneration, while for amateurs this influence was naturally not present, and their motivation was, as for performance, dependent on satisfactions deriving from the activity itself.

In these respects, singers in the choir demonstrated the reactions that might be expected of serious amateurs. But the choristers were also aware of their situation as singers in a professional choir, and this manifested itself in several ways.

First, whereas all amateurs are likely to strive for high standards of achievement and to see the performance of professionals as the benchmark, the singers in this choir actually saw themselves as obliged to achieve professional standards. They were aware that in the absence of any choir of professionals in the same city, they were themselves responsible for setting the professional standard of choral singing. The angriest and most critical comments made on the questionnaires were reserved for other members whose behavior was felt to have undermined the choir's professionalism. For example: "The most frustrating thing about [the choir] is lack of commitment. . . . People tend to miss too many rehearsals and also don't seem to put in the preparation time. Consequently, conductors are having to spend a lot of rehearsal time repeating details. . . . This becomes *exceedingly* tedious for the people who come regularly and have bothered to look at their music." Second, after a performance, it was the reaction of the orchestra that carried the most weight, certainly more than that of the critics. This was not only because members of the orchestra were regarded as knowledgeable judges, but also because they were the choir's professional colleagues, and their approbation signified acceptance at their level of performance.

A third indication of the choir's desire to feel and be accepted as professionals was the importance they placed on singing in the city's main concert hall. More than 77 percent of members rated performing in this hall (as opposed to several other concert venues in the city suitable for large choir and orchestra) as having a high or very high value for them. The hall is large, prestigious, and very expensive to rent; other local choirs rarely get to sing there. Performing in this hall is pleasant because of the superior facilities, but also because it is a symbol of professional status.

More than 77 percent of the respondents felt that there were costs as well as rewards in singing with the choir, citing the amount of time, time conflicts, time away from the family, financial cost, and fatigue as the most important costs. Most singers recognized the inevitability of this kind of tension, but many still felt strongly enough about it to expand their answers to describe the frustration they felt in trying to reconcile their choir commitment with their other lives: "I sometimes wish there was a tiny acknowledgment of the fact that most of us are people with full-time jobs and that evening rehearsals are often after a trying day with [grade] 7P, an after school meeting, a rush home through traffic to make a meal, a rush to [the rehearsal], etc. Some consideration that we are mostly very weary by the end of the day would be gratefully received."

A large majority of the singers stated that they sometimes found it difficult to fulfill their obligations to the choir, and many expressed their distress as a conflict that they could find no way of resolving. A very small number suggested more lenient rules about rehearsal attendance, but in general singers strongly supported the stricter requirements that had recently been put into place, even when they found them difficult to meet.

These singers were apparently very conscious of the contradictions and tensions that resulted from their ambiguous status as amateurs doing a professional job. Stebbins states that the costs for amateurs consist in unfulfilled hopes or the absence of expected rewards.[9] For these singers, that could mean a disappointing performance or not being chosen to sing in a particular program; but it was not these kinds of disappointments that singers mentioned in their answers. Of far more concern to them were the tensions created by the unresolvable conflict between the professional demands of the choir and the demands of their other lives.

"Professionalism" was a word that had been much used by both singers and management while grappling with the problem of raising standards. The singers' depiction of their choral experience suggests that it is important to understand this term within the context of this particular choir and not to make the mistake of thinking that the members could be treated just like other professional musicians. The choir might be more likely to achieve its goals if it were instead to tap into the most important quality that amateurs bring to their participation: the passion which, because they are shut out from many of the benefits of a fully professional life, is directed solely toward the activity itself.

*   *   *

In spite of the tensions felt by many of the singers, all those who completed the original survey were performing with the choir at the time, and so on balance even the most critical respondents apparently believed the positive aspects outweighed the negative. This was not necessarily the case for those who had retired from the choir, and who might, with a little distance between them and the choral experience, view many aspects of their participation differently. The survey had demonstrated that a typical member had a long choral "career," involving almost lifelong singing, performing with different kinds of choirs, and often other musical involvement or study.[10] After retirement, singers would be able to view their membership in the symphonic choir in the context of a lifetime of singing, and they might evaluate it differently.

In 1999, as a follow-up to the survey, a small group of members (five men and two women) who had retired in the previous two years were interviewed. For two, this had been voluntary. The remainder had failed their auditions in an unexpectedly harsh cull of the membership by a new director. All had invested a great deal of time and commitment in the choir over periods ranging from fifteen to twenty-eight years.

For all of them, their motivation and greatest satisfaction had been to sing in a choir that attained high standards and worked with professional musicians. Retirement brought with it the need for a substitute musical involvement. Three were content to focus more on concertgoing and mentioned the satisfaction of hearing the choral works they knew so well from the other side of the orchestra, although this had not been the reaction they had expected:

> I thought I would miss it desperately, and I thought I would want to go on singing. But I found a tremendous satisfaction in listening to things I might have been involved in at one time or another.

> At first I wondered how I would feel hearing music and works that I had performed with [the choir] on the radio and on CDs, and would I be really upset and so forth. I actually didn't, I enjoyed listening to it and thinking, "Yes, I sang in that, and that was just a wonderful experience." I can sit back and enjoy it and think, "Well, I was part of that for a long time."

The others wanted to continue making music, which posed dilemmas for them, especially for those who wanted to continue singing. The problem was not in finding a choir to sing with, but in adjusting to the lower standards and lesser skills of the available ensembles. Two of them commented:

> [The conductor of a recommended choir] never retires anybody, so they sing until they are falling off the edge of the perch. There are always struggles with not enough men. So I suppose the fact that they do anything worthwhile is meritorious, but I thought, "I could not work with a group like that."

> I expect it to [be] disciplined, and people to obey and cooperate. The trouble with the smaller choirs is that they giggle and talk when the conductor starts to talk and that is what I will probably miss and get very irritated about.

The retirees enjoyed reminiscing about past performances, and their narratives confirmed the findings of the survey that what they most valued was the professional standard of the choir. One anecdote tellingly illustrates this point. The choir was performing Mahler's Symphony No. 2 and had to sit for an hour before the choral finale. The concert management had allocated only 82 seats for 120 singers and refused to move the audience members who had been allocated seats in the side choir stalls. "We said, 'This is no way to treat people,' and [the concert manager] turned around and he said, 'Of course we can do that, who are you, you are amateurs.' Well at that, of course, all these large ladies drew themselves up to their full height and descended on this little man and said, 'If you require a professional standard from us, you treat us like professionals. Now go and sort this out.' So of course the concert hall . . . moved these people up into the boxes, which was finally done about ten minutes before the concert. Needless to say, we didn't get any concert appointments for about 12 months after that." The importance to the choristers of recognition of their status as professional-standard singers had been evident in the choir's reaction to the campaign to improve standards over the previous few years. Singers almost unanimously supported these efforts, even when extra rehearsals, stricter attendance codes, and required workshops made their lives difficult. They had also welcomed the arrival of the orchestra's new and demanding permanent conductor because, although he was strict with the choir, his attitude to the members of the orchestra was the same. In the past, singers had resented some conductors' tolerance of the foibles of orchestral players while treating the choir as amateur interlopers to be tolerated when the repertoire demanded it—an attitude that naturally rubbed off on the orchestra. As performance standards in the choir improved, it had not been the reviews of the critics but the spontaneous praise of players that the singers had really valued.

The survey suggested that the singers nevertheless did not expect to be treated by their own organization as merely professionals. Many stressed this when speaking about the costs of participation. They felt that they gave to the organization and to the musical life of the community as much as they took from the enterprise, and they expected some recognition of this fact from the management. For the most part, they felt they had received it.

The situation seemed to be a little different for the five singers who had failed their auditions. None of them considered the dismissal unfair, and none suggested that the director should not have the absolute right to make this decision. But for most of them (the exception being the singer for whom dismissal solved a problem, his wife having just retired from the choir) the situation brought into high relief the contradiction between what is owed to a professional and to a member of a community organization.

Although none of the singers had taken the audition for granted, most had expected to pass. Four of the five expressed their hurt at dismissal from an organization they had given so much, and they found it difficult not to take their rejection personally. One singer—also an instrumentalist—commented on how much more personally involved he felt in a voice audition, compared with an audition on the instrument he played. He summed up his sense of loss in this way: "I was devastated really. For a long time afterwards I was quite sad about it. I miss the music. I miss being associated with a group of people all working towards the one thing. I miss hearing the piece develop and seeing it polished, and I miss performing."

These four singers were highly critical of the process and timing of their dismissals. This may have been a way of coping with the hurt and disappointment, but they had some pointed comments to make about what they saw as the responsibilities of the choir's administration.

First, they considered the way the decision had been communicated to be impersonal and inappropriate for an organization they had served for many years. One singer contrasted unfavorably the form letter she had received with a rejection letter from another choir that was personal and detailed, pointing out that the particular quality of her voice was unsuitable and mentioning also her strong points as a singer. Another commented, "What was hurtful was the way we were dismissed—off the data base and the whole thing. I think people who manage community choirs should realize they are not just dealing with professional musicians who get paid to do it and can expect summary dismissal. They are dealing with people who put their whole lives into it, and there are better ways of saying to people, 'Look, I am sorry, it is really time you retired. You are not worthless. You have given a tremendous contribution in community choirs; that contribution is important.'"

Second, they were annoyed that they had been notified in the middle of a rehearsal period, and that, having worked hard for the previous six weeks on a difficult piece of contemporary music (which few of them had enjoyed), they were not permitted to take part in the performance. Again, they felt that the choir was prepared to accept their contribution without giving any consideration in return.

Third, they were embarrassed that, having been informed between rehearsals, they had no idea who else had been "culled," and in some cases only found out much later that some singers they assumed would have survived had suffered the same fate. They did not feel like discussing their own failure with all their acquaintances in the choir, but had to do so to find out who had and had not failed. One singer, after finding how many of her friends had failed, held a "grief party" to try to dissipate some of the distress they were feeling.

In general, it was felt that the choir had just wanted to get the nasty business of informing them over and done with without considering its obligations to former singers. The letter of appreciation and free concert ticket that followed did not diminish their outrage. One singer said that she actually felt she had been treated like a wrongdoer: "The next rehearsal should have been on the Wednesday. The letter came on Tuesday: . . . Don't come back tomorrow. . . . Probably it will take [me] a long, long time to get over it. I mean, fourteen years, and you're dismissed within three days. I've paid to be a member until the end of the year. This was sort of instant dismissal, as though you have done something bad. That's what we feel at work: If you have to leave immediately, that means you have done something that wasn't proper."

On the whole, the interviews with the retired singers supported the findings of the original study: Retired singers did not view their experience in any radically different light. Naturally enough, they placed more emphasis on the rewards of singing that had remained with them after retirement, such as the "inside" knowledge of repertoire that enabled them to enjoy choral concerts with a deepened understanding.

Their understanding of their ambiguous status between the amateur and professional music worlds had remained, but for some the crisis of failing an audition had thrown this tension into a different light. While they had been singing, the emphasis was always on the obligations owed by members of the choir. Now the obligations owed to members by the management had become an issue and management had clearly been found wanting. In answers to the survey of members, the phrase "community choir" was only rarely found, while there was much written about "professional" standards. In the later study, singers shifted within the same interview between emphasizing *professional* standards and insisting on what was owed to them as members of a *community* choir. The survey answers had suggested that members felt the choir management recognized the problem, even though it could have gone further to accommodate it. The singers who failed their auditions were outraged at what they took to be evidence that this was not the case: The management treated them as replaceable performers, with no recognition that they were partners in a community organization with obligations on both sides.

*   *   *

This study highlights the problems and misunderstandings that can easily arise from the ambiguous situation in which many "serious amateur" choirs exist. Although the choir in question could have conducted its auditions with more sensitivity, there are tensions inherent in the position of performers who are neither fully amateur nor fully professional. What is clear about their status is that the job they are doing is a professional one, a point that distinguishes them from the other "serious amateurs" considered by Stebbins. The exploitative practice of not paying them is tolerated in part because the history of choral singing is that of an amateur tradition, and there is no shortage of skilled choristers eager to sing for the artistic, social, recreational, and spiritual rewards it brings. Significantly, none of the singers in this choir suggested that they should be paid: It was only when the value of their contribution was not recognized that they felt exploited.

In the long term, the most satisfactory solution would be to treat choristers like orchestral musicians and pay them when they are performing in a professional context, as is already the case with a small number of choirs. But in view of the financial constraints on most professional orchestras it is hard to see such a change becoming widespread. Choirs with an ambiguous status will probably continue to exist, and many of them will prefer it this way, valuing their independence and community links as well as the chance to engage in professional performances. For these choirs to flourish, a precondition would appear to be a recognition of the dual nature of the organization and a mutual understanding on the part of the director, the management, and the membership of obligations owed by and to all the stakeholders.

Notes

1. Ruth Finnegan, *The Hidden Musicians: Music-Making in an English Town* (Cambridge: Cambridge University Press, 1989), 18.

2. Robert Hutchison and Andrew Feist, *Amateur Arts in the UK* (London: Policy Studies Institute, 1991), xiii.

3. Ibid., 10.

4. Robert A. Stebbins, *Amateurs, Professionals, and Serious Leisure* (Montreal: McGill-Queen's University Press, 1992).

5. Ibid., 3.

6. Ibid., 6–7.

7. Ibid., 41.

8. Susana Juniu, Ted Tedrick, and Rosangela Boyd, "Leisure or Work? Amateur and Professional Musicians' Perception of Rehearsal and Performance," *Journal of Leisure Research* 28, no. 1 (1996): 44–56

9. Stebbins, *Amateurs, Professionals, and Serious Leisure*, 100–102.

10. For a discussion of the concept of "career" in the context of amateur music performance, see Dietmar Pickert, "Musikalische Werdegänge von Amateurmusikern im Bereich der klassischen und populären Musik—ein Forschungsproject," in *Musiklernen: Aneigung des Unbekannten*, ed. G. Olias (Essen: Die blaue Eule), 1994, 69–86.

Foreign-Language Pieces on the Compact Disk: Texts and Translations

GIDEON MDEGELLA, "KAA KIMYA USIKILIZE" [KEEP QUIET AND LISTEN]

Kaa kimya, kaa kimya usikilize	Be quiet and listen
Liweke moyoni neon la Bwana	Put the word of the Lord in your heart
Mungu yupo hapa anatungojea	God is with us, waiting for us
Anatukaribisha, Atufundishe	He welcomes us so that He may teach us
Kaa kimya hapa ni patakatifu	Be quiet, this is a holy place
Neno la neema lahubiriwa	The word of grace is being preached
Ni ujumbe wake Bwana wenye uzima	It is the message of life from the Lord
Anatukaribisha, Akatujulishe.	He welcomes us so that He may inform us.

WASHINGTON MUTAYOBA, "TWENDENI KWA YESU" [LET'S GO TO JESUS]

Let's go to Jesus, he welcomes us all.
Chagga of Moshi, what do you say? / "Let's go to Jesus."
Wapare of Pareland, what do you say? / "Let's go to Jesus."
Wameru of Arusha, what do you say? / "Let's go to Jesus."
Masai of Arusha, what do you say? / "Let's go to Jesus."
Wasambaa, what do you say? / "Let's go to Jesus."
Wanyaturu, what do you say? / "Let's go to Jesus."
Wanyiramba, what do you say? / "Let's go to Jesus."
Wagogo of Dodoma, what do you say? / "Let's go to Jesus."
Wazaramo of the coast, what do you say? / "Let's go to Jesus."
Wahele of Iringa, what do you say? / "Let's go to Jesus."
Wanyakyusa of Mbeya, what do you say? / "Let's go to Jesus."
Wahaya of Kagera, what do you say? / "Let's go to Jesus all the tribes."

STABAT MATER ("STABBA")

Stabat Mater dolorosa
juxta crucem lacrymosa,
dum pendebat filius.

The grieving mother
stood weeping by the cross,
where her son was hanging.

Quando corpus morietur
Fac ut animae donetur
Paradisi gloria.

When my body dies,
may my soul be given
the glory of paradise.

ALEKSANDR DAVIDENKO, "KONNITSA BUDENNOGO" [BUDENNYI'S CAVALRY]

Leader:

(1) S neba poludennovo zhara ne podstupi, konnaia Budionnovo raskinulas' v stepi.

From the heavens' mid-day scorching ray, there was no escape, Budyonnyi's cavalry spread out across the steppe.

Chorus:

Konnaia Budionnovo raskinulas' v stepi.

Budynonnyi's cavalry spread out across the steppe.

Leader:

(2) Ne otsovskoi slavoiu nash vyvodit bogat, sami padat' lavoiu uchilis' na vraga.

We are not rich from our fathers' glory, we have been taught how to pour ourselves like lava on the enemy.

Chorus:

Sami padat' lavoiu uchilis' na vraga.

We have been taught how to pour ourselves like lava on the enemy.

Leader:

(5) Budet belym pomnit'sia, kak travy shelestiat, kogda nesotsia konnitsa rabochikh i krestian.

The Whites will be reminded how the grass rustles when the workers' and peasants' cavalry comes.

Chorus:

Kogda nesotsia konnitsa rabochikh i krestian.

When the workers' and peasants' cavalry comes.

Leader:

(9) Nikto puti proidonnovo u nas ne otberyot, konnaia Budyonnovo, diviziia vperyod.

No one can deny the path we've gone down, Budyonnyi's cavalry, the division goes forth.

Chorus:
Konnaia Budyonnovo diviziia vperyod.
Budyonnyi's cavalry, the division goes forth.

DMITRII VASIL'EV-BUGLAI, "UROZHAINAIA PLIASOVAIA" [HARVEST DANCE]

(1) Leader: Bogatie ezhatsia:
Chorus: Net mezhi, net mezhi.
Leader: Nynche ne umnozhatsia
Chorus: Baryshi, baryshi.

The rich are shrinking down:
No more strips, no more strips.
No more speculation
The profits, the profits.

(2) Leader: Starushonki okhali,
Chorus: Kruglyi god, kruglyi god.
Leader: Rasprostilsia s sokhami
Chorus: Ves' narod, ves' narod.

The old peasant women groaned
All year round, all year round.
Tilling with a wooden plow
All the people, all the people.

(3) Leader: Armiia kolkhoznaia
Chorus: velika, velika
Leader: Ne strashny ugrozy nam
Choir: kulaka, kulaka.

The collective farm army
Is great, is great.
We don't fear threats from
The kulaks, the kulaks.

(4) Leader: Nov'iu kto napugannyi,
Chorus: Storonis', storonis.
Leader: Ne na vek i plugi nam
Chorus: Zadalis', zadalis'.

Those who fear new times,
Step aside, step aside.
Not for a century our plows
There's better, there's better.

(5) Leader: Tselinnoiu, traktami,
Chorus: Tut i tam, tut i tam.
Leader: Zaguliali traktory
Chorus: Po poliam, po poliam.

Soil upturned by tractors,
Here and there, here and there.
The tractors drove up and down
Across the fields, across the fields.

DAVID EDELSTADT, "IN KAMF" [IN STRUGGLE]

Mir vern gehast un getribn,
Mir vern geplogt un farfolgt;
Un alts nor derfar vayl mir libn
Dos oreme shmakhtnde folk.

We've been driven and despised,
We've been tortured and persecuted
Because we love the poor
And the weak.

Mir vern dershosn, gehangen,
Men roybt undz dos lebn un rekht;

We've been shot and hanged,
We've been robbed of our lives and our
rights

Derfar vayl mir emes farlangen
Un frayhayt far oreme knekht.

Because we demand truth
And freedom for poor slaves.

Shmidt undz in ayzerne keytn,
Vi blutike khayes undz rayst;

Cast us into iron chains,
Rip us apart like savage beasts.

Ir kent undzer kerper nor teytn	You can only kill our bodies,
Nor keyn mol undzer heylikn gayst.	You will never destroy our sacred spirit.

Ir kent undz dermordn, tiranen,	You can murder us, tyrants,
Naye kemfer vet brengen di tsayt;	But new fighters will take our places.
Un mir kemfn, mir kemfn biz vanen	And we will fight on and on
Di gantse velt vet vern bafrayt.	Until the whole world is freed.

Felix Mendelssohn, "Siehe, wir preisen selig," from *Paulus*

Siehe, wir preisen selig die erduldet. Denn ob der Leib gleich stirbt, doch wird die Seele leben. (Adapted from James 1:12)

Behold, we call blessed the one who endures. For although the body dies, the soul will live.

Contributors

KAREN AHLQUIST is an associate professor and chair of the music department at the George Washington University and a former conductor of choral music. She is the author of *Democracy at the Opera: Music, Theater, and Culture in New York City, 1815–60,* as well as essays and reviews in the *Journal of the American Musicological Society,* the *Journal of American History, Women and Music,* and other publications. Her interests include nineteenth-century vocal music, music institutions, immigration, and music historiography.

GREGORY BARZ is an associate professor of ethnomusicology at the Blair School of Music, the Department of Anthropology, and in the Divinity School at Vanderbilt University. He teaches African music, world music, music and religion, Afropop, blues, and jazz. He is a former member of Kwaya ya Upendo in Dar es Salaam and a former faculty member at the University of Dar es Salaam, Tanzania. His current research focuses on music, dance, and drama as medical intervention among women's village groups in rural Uganda to promote, communicate, and support HIV/AIDS awareness.

Ethnomusicologist **MARC BENAMOU** is an associate professor of music at Earlham College in Richmond, Indiana. His research on Javanese music is centered on music and language, emotion, and gender, as well as cross-cultural aesthetics. Among other degrees, he holds a Diplôme d'études approfondies in philosophy and ethnomusicology from the University of Paris X and has worked as a translator and interpreter from French and Indonesian. His book *Rasa: Language, Affect, and Meaning in Javanese Musical Aesthetics* will be published in 2006.

WESLEY BERG is a professor emeritus at the University of Alberta, where he taught music theory and Canadian music history. He has published a book and numerous articles on the music of the Mennonites in Canada and Russia and on the music history of the Canadian prairies. Recently he has been studying the singing styles of the Germans from Russia and similar traditions in the Scandinavian countries.

MARVA GRIFFIN CARTER is an associate professor of music history and literature at Georgia State University and has served for a decade as organist at the historic Ebenezer Baptist Church in Atlanta. She has published more than a dozen articles in scholarly publications and is completing a musical biography of Will Marion Cook. She has received an award for her professional and humanitarian achievements from Soka Women's College in Tokyo.

MARION S. JACOBSON is an assistant professor of music and humanities at the Albany College of Pharmacy. She has worked as a music critic for the *Washington Post* and a public sector folk-arts consultant for the Smithsonian Folklife Center, Citylore, Inc., the Brooklyn Council on the Arts, and the Westchester Arts Council. Yiddish was spoken and sung in her family and she has performed with three Yiddish choruses. She holds a Ph.D. in musicology from New York University with a dissertation on the history and ethnography of the Yiddish folk-chorus tradition.

BERNARD LORTAT-JACOB, director of research at the Centre National de la Recherche Scientifique, was head of the ethnomusicology laboratory at the Musée de l'Homme in Paris from 1990 to 2003. His research focuses on musics of the Mediterranean, in particular Morocco, Sardinia, and the Balkans. He has published numerous articles and books, including *Sardinian Chronicles.*

CHARLES EDWARD McGUIRE is an associate professor of musicology at the Oberlin College Conservatory of Music and an expert on British music of the nineteenth and twentieth centuries. His research topics include the British music festival, sight-singing techniques, choral singing and moral reform movements, and the music of Edward Elgar and Ralph Vaughan Williams. He is the author of *Elgar's Oratorios: The Creation of an Epic Narrative* (Ashgate, 2002), as well as essays in *19th-Century Music, The New Grove Dictionary of Music and Musicians, The Elgar Society Journal,* and other publications.

Musicologist and flutist **HELEN METZELAAR** was co-founder and for many years was a staff member at the Dutch Women and Music Foundation in Amsterdam. She is currently affiliated with the University of Amsterdam as a researcher. Her publications include *From Private to Public Spheres: Exploring Women's Role in Dutch Musical Life from c. 1700 to c. 1880* and a biography (in Dutch) of composer and pianist Henriëtte Bosmans. She has also written essays in *Women Composers: Music Through the Ages, The New Grove Dictionary of Music and Musicians, Die Musik in Geschichte und Gegenwart,* and other publications, and is preparing a modern edition of concert arias by Josina van Boetzelaer (1733–95).

AMY NELSON is an associate professor of history at Virginia Polytechnic Institute and State University. Her book *Music for the Revolution: Musicians and Power in Early Soviet Russia* was awarded the Heldt Prize for the best book by a woman in any area of Slavic Studies in 2005. Before pursuing a Ph.D. in history, she earned a Bachelor of Music degree in piano at the University of California, Santa Barbara. Her current research projects include a study of animal protection in Imperial Russia and a collective biography of Soviet space dogs.

MELINDA RUSSELL is an associate professor of music at Carleton College. She is associate editor with Bruno Nettl of *In the Course of Performance: Studies in the World of Musical Improvisation.* She has also contributed essays to *From Tejano to Tango: Essays on Latin American Popular Music; Community of Music: An*

Ethnographic Seminar in Champaign-Urbana: and *Schladminger Gespräche zum Thema Musik und Tourismus.*

ROSALYND SMITH is a senior lecturer in the Faculty of Education at Australia's Monash University. Trained as an ethnomusicologist, she studies music education, teaching world musics, ethnography of performance organizations, music curriculum, and children's choirs. Her research is published in conference proceedings and other journals internationally.

JILL STRACHAN is a consultant to nonprofit organizations and was general manager of the Lesbian and Gay Chorus of Washington, D.C. (LGCW) for seventeen years. She served for six years on the board of the international Gay and Lesbian Association Choruses, including two years as president and six months as interim executive director. She is a founding member of the LGCW and its a cappella ensemble Not What You Think. She was a finalist for the Shayne Leadership Award of the Washington Council of Agencies in 2001. She holds a Ph.D. in history of religions from Syracuse University.

KENNETH C. WOLENSKY is a historian with the Pennsylvania Historical and Museum Commission in Harrisburg who studies the history of labor, industry, public policy, working class culture, and workers' education. He is coauthor of *Fighting for the Union Label: The Women's Garment Industry and the ILGWU in Pennsylvania* and *The Knox Mine Disaster.* He is on the American Studies faculty at Pennsylvania State University Harrisburg, is a Commonwealth Speaker for the Pennsylvania Humanities Council, and is a Distinguished Lecturer for the Organization of American Historians.

Index

Aachen: choruses in, 268, 281

Abbate, Carolyn, 287

Abrams, Jo, 213

accord, 88, 109n3

Adama van Scheltema, C. S., 167, 169, 172, 180, 182n12, 184n54

aesthetics: of choral sound, 9, 14n18, 78, 123, 189, 192–93, 202, 215; of performance, 76, 128; political reform and, 141–57 passim; religion and, 4–5, 63–64, 120–23; of singing (*see also* singing). *See also* amateur chorus; art music; bourgeois culture; mass singing, mass song; New Negro; popular music

Africa: heritage of, 178, 187; identification with, 185; music of, 25; religions of, 22–23; suffering of, 174, 180. *See also* community: in Africa; *kwaya;* Tanzania

agitational music (*agitki*), 143, 146, 148, 149, 154. *See also* ORK

Ahlquist, Karen, 6

amateur: as culture-bearer, 265–66; defined, 294–96; music-making of, 1–2. *See also* amateur chorus; Germany/German-speaking Europe: voluntary societies in; leisure; Stebbins, Robert A.

amateur chorus: distinguished from professional ensemble, 140, 143–44, 303–4; management of, 296–97; professional elements in, 65–66, 294, 295–96; rehears-als of, 299; standards of, 79–80, 237, 294, 299–300, 302; treatment of, 7, 294, 300–304. *See also* choral singing; community chorus; membership; orchestra; professionalism

"America the Beautiful," 50

Anabaptists, 71

Anglican Church, 112, 137n54

Anna Crusis Women's Choir, 249

anthropology. *See* chorus: study of; ethnography

art music: distinguished from folk music, 178–80; history of, 2, 47; legacy of, 145, 146, 265; objections to, 254; preference for, 5, 54–55, 134, 145, 178, 219n4. *See also* aesthetics; symphonic choir

Attinello, Paul, 249

audience. *See* chorus: audience for

Australia: chorus in, 294, 296–97. *See also* amateur chorus; symphonic choir

Averill, Gage, 14n14

Azania Front Lutheran Cathedral (Dar es Salaam), 34–35, 37; temporary communities at, 36, 44n29. *See also kwaya*

Band of Hope movement, 113–14, 121, 123

Banfield, Stephen, 1

Baptists. *See* Christianity: representations of

barbershop chorus, 14n14, 54, 55

Barnwell, Ysaye M., 253

Vienna Männergesangverein, 282
Vienna Singakademie, 281, 282, 291n54
voce lunghe, 92, 108

Wagner, Roger, 9
Waring, Fred, 9
Washington, D.C.: activists in, 260n6; choral
traditions in, 253; glbt musical groups in,
253. *See also* Lesbian and Gay Chorus of
Washington; Zemer Chai
Washington National Cathedral, 9
"Was kann es schönres geben" (arr. Wiebe),
78
"We are" (Barnwell), 253
"We Shall Not Be Moved," 55–56, 235
"We want the vote!" (Barnwell), 253
Wessels, George, 47, 48
Western art tradition. *See* art music
White, George L., 165, 186
Wilcox, Diana, 252
Williams, Raymond, 7
Williamson, John Finley, 9
wimbo (song), 21
Wolensky, Kenneth, 6
women: choral opportunities for, 6, 266,
268, 272; in garment industry, 6, 227;
229–30; in public life, 267. *See also* chorus:
gender and, governance of; Germany/
German-speaking Europe: female singers
in; Lesbian and Gay Chorus of Washing-
ton; mixed chorus; "women's music"

"women's music," 250
workers' clubs: activities of, 142–43, 156;
adult education in, 140–41; political education in, 144, 145. *See also* choral circle
working class: reform of, 112–13, 116–18,
127, 139, 176–77, 215; representations of,
229–31, 232; women in, 227. *See also* garment industry; ILGWU; Tonic Sol-fa,
workers' clubs
Workmen's Circle, 202, 208, 213
Wyoming Valley, Pennsylvania. *See* garment
industry; ILGWU; ILGWU chorus

Yiddish choruses, 202–10 passim, 219n17.
See also Jewish People's Philharmonic
Chorus
Yiddishkeyt (Yiddish culture), *Yiddishvelt*,
203, 204, 206, 212–14, 218
"You Gotta Know the Score," 234–35, 239,
246n20
Young, Percy, 9
Young Park Singers (Decatur), 53, 60
youth choir: in the United States, 9. *See
also* Band of Hope movement; Decatur:
school music in; *kwaya ya vijana;* Pripetshik Choir

Zamir Chorale, 206, 215
Zemer Chai chorus, 216
Ziffern, 72, 73
Zuckerman, Mark, 208, 210, 218

Contents of the Compact Disk

1. "Ajabu" ["I Depend"], *pambio* (call-and-response chorus); Kwaya ya Upendo, Gideon Mdegella, *mwalimu* (2:33)
2. "Kaa Kimya Usikilize" ["Keep Quiet and Listen"], *wimbo;* Kwaya ya Upendo, Gideon Mdegella, composer and *mwalimu* (1:46)
3. "Twendeni kwa Yesu" ["Let's Go to Jesus"], *wimbo;* Kwaya ya Usharika Kanisa la Kulutheri Kijitonyama, Dar es Salaam, Washington Mutayoba, composer, Joachim Kisasa, *mwalimu* (4:20)
4. "America, the Beautiful," words by Katharine Lee Bates, music by Samuel A. Ward, arranged by David Alderman; Decatur Park Singers, 1994, David Alderman, music director (3:04)
5. "Was kann es schönres geben," arr. Esther Wiebe, Festival Chorus, Henry Engbrecht, conductor; Faith and Life Choral Festival, Winnipeg, 1994. Used by permission of Faith and Life Communications of the Mennonite Church Manitoba (2:36)
6. "Stabat mater," members of the brotherhood of Santa Croce ("Oratory," Antonello Sanna, Giovannino Cimino, Giovanni Pintus, Nicola Brozzu), Castelsardo, Sardinia, 1993 (7:29)
7. "Drink Water," words by C. M. Cady, music by William B. Bradbury; West Singers, Cherry Hill High School West, New Jersey; Christine Bass, conductor (1:23)
8. "O come and sign the pledge," words and music anonymous; West Singers (1:00)
9. "Truth Shall Be Victorious," words by A. Sargant, music adapted from Franz Joseph Haydn; West Singers (1:26)
10. "Konnaia Budennogo" ["Budennyi's Cavalry"], Aleksandr Davidenko; Maya Rozenblat, Stephanie Engelbrecht, Zachary Borichevsky, and Jeffrey Consoletti, soloists; Dobrovol'tsy [The Volunteers] (2:29)

11. "Urozhainaia" ["Harvest Dance"], Dmitrii Vasil'ev-Buglai; Maya Rozenblat, soprano; Alice Mikolajewski, accordion, Dobrovol'tsy (2:48)

12. "Elijah Rock!" spiritual arranged by Hall Johnson; Heritage Signature Chorale, Stanley Thurston, conductor. Recorded in concert at the National City Christian Church, Washington, D.C. by Steven Campbell Hilmy, Icarus Sound, and by permission of G. Schirmer, Inc. (2:15)

13. "In Kamf," David Edelshtat, arranged by Mark Zuckerman; Jewish People's Philharmonic Chorus, New York, Binyumen Schaechter, conductor. Used with permission of Ione Press (2:00)

14. "This Is a Strike!" words and music by James Corbett and Michael Johnson; chorus of the Northeast Department, International Ladies Garment Workers Union (ILGWU), James Corbett, production supervisor. *The Northeast Sings,* live LP recording from the 32nd convention of the ILGWU, May 17, 1965. Used by permission of the Union of Needletrades, Industrial & Textile Employees (UNITE!), AFL-CIO, CLC (2:06)

15. Medley: "Northeast Department" and "Solidarity Forever" (melody: "The Battle Hymn of the Republic," attributed to William Steffe); chorus of the Northeast Department, ILGWU. Used by permission of UNITE! (2:28)

16. "We Are," words and music by Ysaye M. Barnwell; Lesbian and Gay Chorus of Washington, Ray Killian, conductor, Jane Hoffman, soloist. © 1993 Barnwell's Notes Publishing (BMI/Harry Fox Agency). Used by permission (2:24)

17. "We Want the Vote!" words and music by Ysaye M. Barnwell; Lesbian and Gay Chorus of Washington. © 2002 Barnwell's Notes Publishing (BMI/Harry Fox Agency). Used by permission (1:17)

18. "Siehe! Wir preisen selig" (*Paulus*), Felix Mendelssohn; The George Washington University Singers, Matthew Mehaffey, conductor, Alice Mikolajewski, organist (3:29)

The University of Illinois Press
is a founding member of the
Association of American University Presses.

Composed in 10.5/13 Adobe Minion
with Meta display
by Jim Proefrock
at the University of Illinois Press
Manufactured by Thomson-Shore, Inc.

University of Illinois Press
1325 South Oak Street
Champaign, IL 61820-6903
www.press.uillinois.edu